THE
MANCHURIAN
PRESIDENT

THE MANCHURIAN PRESIDENT

BY AARON KLEIN

WITH BRENDA J. ELLIOTT

WND Books

THE MANCHURIAN PRESIDENT
WND Books

Published by WorldNetDaily
Washington, D.C.

Copyright © 2010
WND Books

WRITTEN BY AARON KLEIN AND BRENDA J. ELLIOTT
BOOK EDITED BY BENYAMIN KORN
JACKET DESIGN BY MARK KARIS
INTERIOR DESIGN BY NEUWIRTH & ASSOCIATES

WND Books are distributed to the trade by:
Midpoint Trade Books
27 West 20th Street, Suite 1102
New York, NY 10011

WND Books are available at special discounts for bulk purchases.
WND Books, Inc. also publishes books in electronic formats.
For more information call (541-474-1776) or visit www.wndbooks.com.

First Edition

ISBN 13 Digit: 978-1-935071-87-7

Library of Congress information available

Printed in the United States of America

10 9 8 7 6 5 4 3 2 1

CONTENTS

Introduction   vii

1:   Obama Tied to Bill Ayers...at Age 11!   1

2:   Unmasking the Mysterious College Years   18

3:   "Obama Was Quite Religious in Islam"   39

4:   Obama's Radical Alinsky Trainers   51

5:   Issues of Eligibility   65

6:   Obama Participated in Socialist Party   80

7:   Obama's Ties to Nation of Islam and Black Radicals   89

8:   The ACORN President   105

9:   Obama's Socialist-Led Union Army   124

10: Obama's Top Guns Exposed   152

11: The White House and "Media Justice"   187

12: Coalition of Extremists Pushing Obama Agenda   205

13: Anti-American Radicals Drafting Obama Legislation   221

14: Extremists behind Health Care for America Now   239

     Notes   273
     Index   329

INTRODUCTION

I N EARLY 2008, the Democratic presidential primary campaign was getting into full swing. Increasingly it was becoming clear that a little-
known contender, Illinois' junior senator Barack Obama, was positioned
to upset the well-financed and popular candidacy of Hillary Clinton for
the nomination. Major questions immediately loomed large about this
young senator. What were his background and personal history? What
were his politics, and who and what had shaped his views? What was his
record as a politician? And what was he promising to do as president?

All of these critical issues are usually raised as a matter of course when
anyone—particularly someone "new" and virtually unknown—runs for a
major political office, especially the presidency of the United States, the
most powerful of all political offices.

And yet, astonishingly, none of our "watchdogs" in the news media
seemed to care. In any other election, such questions would have been
investigated, debated, and dissected ad nauseam, for such is the nature
of campaign coverage in modern, robust democracies.

Instead, I watched, incredulously, from my position as an American reporter stationed in Jerusalem, as most of the establishment news
media failed to conduct any real inquiry into Barack Obama's politics or
personal history, with the exception of Fox News Channel, talk radio,

and some industrious blogs and online news venues. Given his complex and unusual personal background, this was just amazing.

Rather than investigate the eloquent but remarkably unknown Barack Obama, the establishment news media seemed to publish more exposés on those few individuals who *did* investigate Obama than on the presidential candidate himself. Later they focused their intense and relentless journalistic spotlights on Alaska governor Sarah Palin, once Senator John McCain selected her as his running mate in late August.

Much of Obama's already known past, as well as that of some of his closest associates, was remarkably radical for so prominent a politician. Still, the news media remained mysteriously uninterested. Future historians will have to grapple with the fantastic phenomenon of the U.S. news media's having, as a class, almost completely abdicated their traditional responsibility when it came to investigating the background of the "unknown" politician running for the country's highest office.

And now, despite an astonishingly radical first year in office, which has awakened unprecedented voter outrage and caused Obama's popularity to plunge, the news media largely continue to ignore the reality of who Obama is, what he really stands for, and who influences him. I hope this book helps to rectify such obvious journalistic malpractice.

Five thousand eight hundred miles from Washington, at the start of the presidential campaign season, while most of the Washington press corps released one Obama puff piece after another, I began independently to investigate this intriguing politician. I was startled by what I found. On February 24, 2008, I first reported at *WorldNetDaily.com* on Obama's extensive association with Weatherman terrorist Bill Ayers. In the same article, I documented Obama's personal and professional ties to pro-PLO, anti-Israel professor Rashid Khalidi.

Immediately I was slammed by *The Nation* magazine for leading a "smear campaign" against Obama, with the pro-Obama publication lamenting at *CBSNews.com*: "Klein's stories gained an audience beyond the narrow confines of WorldNetDaily . . . mainstream reporters now call the Obama campaign to ask about Klein's articles." The Bill Ayers story would eventually become a prominent election theme. And as I would later discover, the Ayers connection barely scratched the surface of Obama's extensive, but as yet largely uncovered, nearly lifetime ties to anti-American extremists—radicals who are still playing a role in the president's political career and White House policy.

In April 2008, in a now-notorious WABC Radio interview with myself and host John Batchelor, the Palestinian terrorist organization Hamas "endorsed" Obama for president. Our interview made world headlines and became yet another prominent theme of the campaign, with Obama and McCain repeatedly trading barbs over Hamas' "endorsement."

To be fair, an outside terrorist group's positive sentiments toward Obama may have merely reflected the presidential contender's advocacy of engagement with America's foes. Far more troubling to me, however, was what I began uncovering about Obama's relationships with our country's domestic foes. I continued reporting on his relationships with troubling individuals and organizations, including his ties to communists, socialists, Marxists, Nation of Islam leaders, and former 1960s radicals, as well as to the Association of Community Organizations for Reform Now, or ACORN.

In one investigation in April 2009, I reported that President Obama's "green jobs" adviser, Van Jones, had founded a communist organization and that he called for "resistance" against the United States, among other extremist statements. Fox News Channel's Glenn Beck crucially used his television platform to report on Jones's radicalism, prompting the Obama "czar's" resignation.

In the course of my investigations, I befriended Brenda J. Elliott. She is a prodigious researcher, historian, and author of hundreds of articles. At the time, Brenda was running a blog that carefully and thoroughly documented Obama's ties to Chicago "bundler" Antoin "Tony" Rezko, as well as to a host of other problematic characters. Elliott would eventually morph her blog into a larger, more encompassing database, as we both began to realize the scope of Obama's radical associates and mentors— most of whom traveled together in the same far-left circles. We realized we were piecing together an intricate puzzle that revealed a man with an agenda far more radical and dangerous than he portrays—a politician backed by groups and individuals who seek to drastically alter the U.S. system or destroy it altogether. I am grateful to Brenda for her co-authorship of this book.

Barack Obama's radical associates have an explicit, though publicly concealed, agenda of "boring from within" America's democratic and capitalist free-enterprise system, in order to weaken or destroy it. Their radical duplicity is the reason for the title of this book. These radicals have learned well the tactics of concealing their true agenda, cloaking their policies in democratic and populist rhetoric, while admitting among themselves their profound hostility to the American system.

The book title is taken from *The Manchurian Candidate*, a 1959 spy thriller by Richard Condon, who depicted the son of a prominent political family in America who has been brainwashed into becoming an unwitting assassin for the Communist Party. The book was adapted into two movies. The first, in 1962, starred Frank Sinatra, Angela Lansbury, Laurence Harvey, and Janet Leigh, and followed the book's original theme of an international communist conspiracy. In the second screen version, released in 2004, with Denzel Washington, Liev Schreiber, Jon Voight, and Meryl Streep, an American presidential candidate is a brainwashed sleeper agent for the international weapons manufacturer Manchurian Global.

The authors are by no means arguing herein that President Obama has been brainwashed by anyone or is a sleeper agent for any international party or weapons conglomerate. However, the main theme of *The Manchurian Candidate*'s various incarnations—that of a powerful politician whose true past has been intentionally obscured, and who has become the vehicle for implementing a hidden radical agenda—absolutely fits with the theme of this work and with the facts that are carefully documented in these pages.

In particular, Barack Obama is backed by and deeply tied to an anti-American fringe nexus that, as this book will show, was instrumental not only in mentoring Obama and helping him to build his political career, but essentially in overthrowing the moderate wing of the Democratic Party and in securing and powerfully influencing Obama's presidency. As will be seen, these radical associates not only continue to influence Obama and White House strategy, but some are directly involved in creating the very policies intended to undermine or radically transform the United States of America.

This book uncovers, among many other things, Obama's early years, including his previously overlooked early childhood education in a radical church with ties to Bill Ayers' organization; his boyhood years in Indonesia, the world's most populous Muslim nation; and important aspects of Obama's mysterious college years, tying him to extremist groups while he was a student at Occidental College, and later at Columbia University.

Obama's associations with the Nation of Islam, radical anti-American Black Liberation Theology, and to black extremists are also revealed, with extensive new information on those subjects.

Also uncovered here are Obama's deep ties to ACORN—much more extensive than previously documented elsewhere—including information on how Ayers and Obama funded ACORN together, with an additional chapter on how a socialist-led, ACORN-affiliated union helped facilitate Obama's political career and now exerts major influence in the White House.

Alarmingly, this book also exposes an extremist coalition of communists, socialists, and other radicals working both without and within the administration to draft and advance White House policy goals. In just one shocking example, a founder of Ayers' Weatherman anti-American terrorist group serves on an organization, the Apollo Alliance, which helped to craft Obama's $787 billion "stimulus" bill. An entire chapter is dedicated to exposing the president's ties to the radicals at Apollo.

In another chapter, we unmask the extremists among Obama's "czars" and other top advisers, including communist-linked Valerie Jarrett and David Axelrod, who, it turns out, was himself mentored by a communist activist.

The many issues pertaining to Obama's eligibility to be president—the raising of which are not only utterly ignored but routinely ridiculed in the establishment press—are carefully examined here, including questions about Obama's birth documentation and whether or not he actually qualities as a "natural-born citizen" according to the U.S. Constitution.

We also expose how Obama's healthcare policy, masked by moderate, populist rhetoric, was pushed along and partially crafted by extremists, whose principal aim is to achieve corporate socialist goals and a vast increase in government powers.

We believe our work is crucial to Americans from across the political spectrum, including mainstream Democrats who should be alarmed that their party has been hijacked by an extreme-left fringe bent on permanently changing the party to fit its radical agenda. Indeed, this book will document, with new information, Obama's own involvement with a socialist party whose explicit goal was to infiltrate and eventually take over the Democratic Party and mold it into a socialist organization.

What you hold in your hands is the product of nearly two years of exhaustive research. It is not a work of opinion, but rather a thoroughly documented and footnoted study based on original source materials, including socialist newspaper archives, church newsletters, the writings of radical Obama associates, court documents, and an unpublished doctoral thesis.

Naturally, it is our hope that other investigative journalists will pick up the trails where we have left off. The Internet, digital search engines, and electronic mail have all opened new vistas for research and publishing, even if the traditional news media have abandoned their role as the "watchdogs of government."

Finally, a word of reply to those who assert that in critiquing President Obama, we should all focus on his policies, and not on the man. Respectfully, we disagree. We do not believe in "guilt by association" nor in "the politics of personal destruction." In other words, a political figure should not be judged by his casual political relationships, nor by personal vulnerabilities—and certainly not by his race. We have instead labored to uncover the actual political history, beliefs, mentors, associates, appointments, and motivations of the 44th president of the United States. Many of these he and others have tried hard to conceal behind the façade of soothing rhetoric and personal charisma.

But as Abraham Lincoln, whom President Obama so likes to invoke, reputedly said: "You may fool all the people some of the time, you can even fool some of the people all of the time, but you cannot fool all of the people all of the time."

Aaron Klein

1

OBAMA TIED TO BILL AYERS...
AT AGE 11!

This is a guy who lives in my neighborhood.
—President Obama characterizing his relationship to unrepentant Pentagon bomber Bill Ayers.[1]

O F ALL PRESIDENT Obama's radical associates from the past, few received more attention or were as shocking as his connection to Pentagon bomber-conspirator and Weather Underground terrorist Bill Ayers. However, despite the eventual news media spotlight placed on the Obama-Ayers relationship, most Americans are still unaware of just how extensive are the president's ties to the man who proudly proclaimed, "Everything was absolutely ideal on the day I bombed the Pentagon."[2]

The Obama camp's success, in the heat of the 2008 presidential primary, in concealing and mischaracterizing this relationship as a casual coincidence in which the Obama and Ayers families "happen to know each other" because they are neighbors in Chicago, was astonishingly successful in fending off normally inquisitive reporters and political operatives, including the seasoned attack forces of the Clinton camp.

Even those who followed the few news reports that bothered to probe the depths and significance of Obama's ties to Ayers may still be in the dark as to the extent of that relationship. Indeed, we here present new information that links Obama to Ayers much earlier than previously thought and that astoundingly connects the president's little-scrutinized boyhood years to Ayers' radical ideology.

By April, 2008, it was clear that candidate Obama was a serious contender to defeat Hillary Clinton in the Democratic presidential primary. During this period, the Clinton camp—who are normally world-class experts at the politics of personal destruction (i.e., ad hominem attacks on their political foes)—were struggling to find ways to damage her opponent's standing in the primaries and polls.

Less than a month before the primary, on April 16, 2008, to be precise, was to be the first time candidate Obama would be asked a direct question in a public forum about his relationship with Ayers. The setting was an ABC News presidential debate with fellow candidate Senator Hillary Clinton in Philadelphia, prior to the Pennsylvania primary.

Moderator George Stephanopoulos asked Obama:

A gentleman named William Ayers. He was part of the Weather Underground in the 1970s. They bombed the Pentagon, the Capitol, and other buildings. He's never apologized for that.

And, in fact, on 9/11, he was quoted in the *New York Times* saying, "I don't regret setting bombs. I feel we didn't do enough." An early organizing meeting for your State Senate campaign was held at his house, and your campaign has said you are "friendly."

Can you explain that relationship for the voters and explain to Democrats why it won't be a problem? [3]

Obama's now classic reply was:

This is a guy who lives in my neighborhood, who's a professor of English in Chicago, who I know and who I have not received some official endorsement from. He's not somebody who I exchange ideas from on a regular basis.

And the notion that somehow as a consequence of me knowing somebody who engaged in detestable acts 40 years ago, when I was 8 years old, somehow reflects on me and my values doesn't make much sense. . . . [4]

Stephanopoulos' reference to Obama having been "friendly" with Ayers comes from a February 26, 2008, article on the news and public affairs website Politico. Journalist and blogger Ben Smith reported there about a similar query regarding the Obama-Ayers relationship to Obama's chief political strategist, David Axelrod. But by that time the campaign had apparently already synchronized its message about Obama and Ayers, and Axelrod launched the campaign's "guy in his neighborhood" bandwagon.

> "Bill Ayers lives in his neighborhood. Their kids attend the same school," he said. "They're certainly friendly, they know each other, as anyone whose kids go to school together."[5]

(Obama resided for many years in the same Chicago Hyde Park neighborhood; what is not even remotely true is that the Ayers-Dohrn children and the Obama children could have attended the same school. In fact, at the time of the Philadelphia debate, the three Ayers-Dohrn children were all in their mid-to-late 20s, while Obama's daughters, Sasha, six, and Malia, nine, attended elementary school.)[6]

The present authors are quite familiar with Obama's relationship with Ayers, as it was Aaron Klein who broke the first story on the subject. On February 24, 2008, Klein's article on WorldNetDaily, "Obama worked with terrorist," was the first news article to expose that Obama had been a paid director of Chicago nonprofit Woods Fund, where he worked alongside Ayers.[7]

The Bill Ayers story would eventually become a prominent election issue. And it would soon emerge, as we shall see, that Obama and Ayers worked closely together on a hundred-million-dollar education foundation, the Chicago Annenberg Challenge. It also turns out that Obama had a more extensive relationship with Ayers than has previously been disclosed, and that the future president worked with Ayers as early as 1988.

OBAMA'S RADICAL SUNDAY SCHOOL

Obama's earliest exposure to Ayers' ideology, astonishingly enough, traces back to Obama's childhood and the Hawaiian church at which the future U.S. president attended Sunday school as a boy. While a firestorm ignited during the campaign over Obama's 20-year membership, as an adult, in the church of radical Rev. Jeremiah Wright, almost nothing has been reported about his Sunday school attendance at First Unitarian Church of Honolulu, a radical activist church that may have influenced the future president's early outlook.

First Unitarian of Honolulu, a member of the Unitarian-Universalist denomination, served as a sanctuary for draft dodgers during the 1960s and 1970s and was strongly linked to the Students for a Democratic Society, or SDS, during the time Weatherman radical Bill Ayers was a leader in that organization.[8] Ayers' Weatherman domestic terrorist group was an offshoot of the SDS.

The SDS had been established in late 1959 as an extremist student activist organization that went on to spearhead the 1960s anti–Vietnam War movement. A *Discover the Networks* profile notes that SDS aspired to overthrow U.S. democratic institutions, remake the American government in a Marxist image, and help our enemies be victorious on the battlefield in Vietnam. Many key SDS members were "red-diaper babies," children of parents who were Communist Party members or Communist activists in the 1930s.

After President Lyndon Johnson abolished student draft deferments in 1966, more than 300 new SDS chapters were formed nationwide with the goal of disrupting ROTC classes, staging draft card burnings, and harassing campus recruiters for the CIA and for firms that conducted research tied in some way to national defense. The SDS also notoriously staged college demonstrations in protest of the Vietnam War and occupied buildings at universities such as Columbia.

But it was at the 1968 Democratic Convention in Chicago that the SDS would make its play for national power, as SDS protestors fomented a riot with the intention of sinking the nomination of pro-war liberal candidate Hubert Humphrey. Despite the ensuing mayhem, replete with extensive television coverage of Chicago cops violently suppressing SDS-instigated protests, Humphrey won the convention's nomination, though not without inflicting significant damage on the Democratic Party.

The Chicago riots also led to major infighting within SDS about the future direction of the group, causing it to fragment into factions led by various radical personalities, many of whom, as we document in this book, are intimately associated with President Obama and his administration.

One of the SDS splinter groups, the Weatherman, led in part by Ayers, sought the downfall of the U.S. government while proclaiming the launch of resistance and a race war on behalf of the Third World and against America. *Discover the Networks* notes that the new Weatherman entity dissolved SDS and formed a terrorist collective in its place, which was given the name Weather Underground.

The Weather Underground would go on to bomb the New York City police headquarters in 1970, the United States Capitol in 1971, and the Pentagon in 1972. The group was responsible for some 30 bombings aimed at terrorizing the defense and security establishments of the United States.

In its glory days, the SDS used Obama's boyhood church as a political staging ground and a sanctuary for draft dodgers. "The Sunday school has always been and to this day still is involved in political activism," Rev. Mike Young, current pastor of First Unitarian Church of Honolulu, told Klein in a June 2009 interview. "We are involved in community organizing, helping churches in foreign countries, social justice issues, like making sure inmates get dinner," said Young, speaking from Hawaii.[9]

After moving at age seven with his mother and stepfather to Indonesia, where he was enrolled as a Muslim in public schools (to be detailed in Chapter 3), Obama was sent back to Hawaii at age 11 in 1971 to reside with his grandmother. His mother moved back to Hawaii in 1972 and stayed there until 1977, when she relocated again to Indonesia, the world's most populous Muslim nation. In his autobiography, *Dreams from My Father*, Obama recounts on page 17 moving to Hawaii and being enrolled in the Unitarian church.

When Obama's maternal grandmother died in November 2008, the memorial service, attended by the then-presidential candidate, was held in the same Honolulu Unitarian Church. According to an account in the *Tampa Tribune*, when Pastor Young reminded Obama at his grandmother's memorial service that he attended the church's Sunday school as a kid, Obama's eyes lit up, and he turned to his wife, Michelle, and said, "Hey, that's right. This is where I went to Sunday school."

Young recounted to Klein how the bathrooms for the main sanctuary were fully occupied after the service for Obama's grandmother. Obama said he had to use the restroom, so Young directed the presidential contender and his secret service detail to instead utilize the upper-floor facilities, located at the church's Sunday school operations. "When he returned," Young recalled, "I asked Obama if the Sunday school looked familiar. He said it didn't, but I explained to him we recently remodeled."

Obama was a student at First Unitarian just after it served as a hotbed of antiwar activism. The church notoriously granted sanctuary to U.S. military deserters recruited by the SDS. The deserters' exploits at the church were front-page news for months in 1969, including multiple articles in the *New York Times*. Eventually, police raided the church as well as another nearby Honolulu house of worship, known as Crossroads, which was also providing sanctuary to draft dodgers.

Andrew Walden, publisher and editor of the *Hawaii Free Press*, dug up Hawaii newspaper clippings from the period of Obama's attendance at First Unitarian. He also found print editions of *The Roach*, an SDS publication describing the group's draft-dodging activism, including at the Unitarian church.

In its January 15, 1969, edition, *The Roach* refers to a draft-dodger, Young C. Gray, receiving two years in prison after being found guilty of "'attempting to possess' mescaline and marijuana." *The Roach* reports: "Gray had also written some disparaging remarks about [non-commissioned officers] and lifers concerning their intellects and temperaments. These statements appeared in 'A Call to Join Us,' a piece read to the congregation assembled at the Unitarian Church."

The secretary of Honolulu Unitarian's board, Martha D. McDaniel, published a letter in the August 26, 1969, *Honolulu Star-Bulletin*, calling the church a "symbolic sanctuary to those who in conscience oppose the machinery of war by nonviolent means." McDaniel announces, "the Board of the Church, at its regular August meeting, offers its commendation on behalf of the Unitarian Church of Honolulu to the Church of the Crossroads for its courageous support of the men now in sanctuary."

Reverend Young explained that the church was always activist, including during the years Obama attended. He confirmed his church was instrumental, for example, in activating a local branch of the American Civil Liberties Union.

The church is still active in liberal politics. It helped to launch the Save Our Constitution effort to fight the constitutional amendment against same-sex marriages. In 2003, the church sponsored a Death with Dignity poll that collected a 72 percent response in favor of end-of-life legislation. In February 2003, the Unitarian church celebrated its 50th anniversary at a ceremony replete with "Liberal Religion for 50 Years" T-shirts. The *Honolulu Star-Bulletin* reported that bumper stickers on cars outside the church gave insight into its members' beliefs: "No War." "If you want peace, work for justice." "An eye for an eye makes the whole world blind."

While the Unitarian church may have helped provide Obama with a liberal activist education in the early 1970s, it has up to now generally been believed that Obama did not associate personally with Ayers until 20-some years later, in 1995, when Obama was picked by a committee that included Ayers to serve as the first chairman of the Chicago Annenberg Challenge, or CAC, which bills itself as a school reform organization.

It turns out, however, that Obama worked closely on a project with Ayers earlier than the mid-1990s—earlier than was in general previously believed—to be exact, starting in June 1988.

AYERS RESURFACES, WORKS WITH OBAMA

Ayers founded the Weatherman with his wife Bernardine Dohrn, who was also one of the main leaders of the domestic terrorist group. Characterizing the Weatherman as "an American Red Army," Ayers summed up the organization's ideology: "Kill all the rich people. Break up their cars and apartments. Bring the revolution home. Kill your parents."[10]

"Everything was absolutely ideal on the day I bombed the Pentagon," Ayers recalled in his 2001 memoir, *Fugitive Days*. "The sky was blue. The birds were singing. And the bastards were finally going to get what was coming to them." He continued with a disclaimer that he did not personally plant the bombs, but his group set the explosives and planned the attack.[11]

Ayers brandished his unrepentant radicalism for years to come, as for example in his now notorious 2001 interview with the *New York Times*—published one day after the 9/11 attacks—in which Ayers stated, "I don't regret setting bombs. I feel we didn't do enough." Ayers also posed for a photograph accompanying the *New York Times* piece that showed him stepping on an American flag. The *Times* quoted him as saying of the United States: "What a country. It makes me want to puke."[12]

Ayers' 2001 statements to the *Times* directly contradict what Obama would tell talk radio host Michael Smerconish in an interview on October 9, 2008. Barely a month before the general presidential election, candidate Obama told Smerconish and his listeners of Ayers: "I assumed that he had been rehabilitated."[13]

In 1980, after nearly eleven years living "underground," Ayers and Dohrn surfaced together. Criminal charges pressed against the radical duo were later dropped due to prosecutorial misconduct. This was big news in major U.S. newspapers. As a student at the time at Occidental College, Obama might have read about it. Obama attended Occidental in Los Angeles for two years before transferring to Columbia in 1981. (We will detail Obama's mysterious college years in the next chapter.)[14]

Then on October 20, 1981, a group of "heavily armed" American terrorists, including Weather Underground members David Gilbert and Katherine Boudin, gunned down Sgt. Edward O'Grady, Patrolman Waverly Brown, and Brinks guard Peter Paige in a Rockland County, New York armed robbery. Although not proven to have been involved, Dohrn served eight months in federal prison after refusing to talk to the grand jury investigating the Brinks robbery. Her release, in December 1982, was also big news. Columbia College transfer student Obama might have heard about this, too.[15]

More than three years before his arrival in Chicago, in 1985, Obama might have been acquainted through the news media with the criminal political past of his future Hyde Park neighbors, Ayers and Dohrn, who had married in 1982. Regardless of what he knew and when he knew it, Obama was about to begin working directly with Ayers.

After nearly two years in New York City following graduation from Columbia University, Obama took a job in Chicago in 1985, working for the Developing Communities Project, or DCP, an institutionally based community organization on Chicago's far south side. At the DCP, former antiwar and civil rights organizer Gerald "Jerry" Kellman "recruited, trained and supervised" Obama as a community organizer. Obama eventually became DCP Director.[16]

Chicago Sun-Times columnist Lynn Sweet wrote an August 2004 article about Obama's memoir, *Dreams from My Father*, in which he talked about his first job in Chicago as a community organizer and about his boss at DCP, "Marty Kaufman."[17]

It is instructive to reference Sweet's report here—though it has been related elsewhere numerous times—because it illustrates the unreliability of things Obama has said or put into print about his past. Sweet subsequently learned from Obama that "Marty Kaufmann" was actually Kellman. Sweet learned her lesson the hard way—when she failed to locate "Kaufmann." She wrote:

> I was dismayed, however, at what I found when I read *Dreams from My Father*. Composite characters. Changed names. And reams of dialogue between Obama and other people that moves the narrative along but is an approximation of the actual conversation.
>
> Except for public figures and his family, it is impossible to know who in Obama's memoir is real and who is not.

Kellman is real. For 40 years, writer Stephanie Block has followed the Catholic Campaign for Human Development's "funding of radical, left-wing political organizations, many of them carrying the brand of [radical organizer] Saul Alinsky." Block wrote on September 28, 2008 at CatholicCitizens.org, that Kellman was trained by the late community organizer Saul Alinsky.[18]

Block also writes that when Obama was the lead organizer for DCP, "it received a $40,000 Catholic Campaign for Human Development grant in 1985 and a $33,000 grant in 1986."

For what was that money used? Block explains:

> Relatively little money from the Catholic Campaign for Human Development collection goes to "help the poor. Alinskyian networks

are political. They work closely with politicians—such as Obama—and other organizations that are fighting for abortion and homosexual rights." Strange bedfellows for a Catholic charity!

Meanwhile, the same year—1985—that Obama joined the DCP, a separate group, Chicagoans United to Reform Education, or CURE, was established. By April 1987, CURE had convened a citywide conference at Loyola University, which "called for local school councils with authority to hire (and fire) the principal and teachers, establish curriculum, control lump-sum budgeting, and develop a school improvement plan."[19]

Ayers' father, Thomas Ayers, former chairman and CEO of Commonwealth Edison, was one of the main movers behind Chicago United, as it came to be called. According to education professor Dorothy Shipps, in her unpublished 1995 doctoral dissertation, Thomas Ayers "co-authored a report of a joint public-private task force on school reform and was later nominated [by Chicago Mayor Jane Byrne] to head up Chicago United, a business-backed school reform group that [Thomas] Ayers helped found."[20]

On November 7, 1987, Chicago's school reform planning got a kick in the pants when Secretary of Education William Bennett named Chicago schools as the "worst in nation." The political furor that ensued would also bring Obama and Ayers together for the first time.[21]

According to Dorothy Shipps, in her unpublished Sanford University doctoral dissertation, "one of the key events that lead to the 1988 Chicago School Reform Act was the formation of a coalition between business and community groups concerned with the sad state of Chicago schools. This alliance was forged, in large measure, through the effort of Chicago's first black mayor, Harold Washington." At the time, Washington convened a summit to change Chicago's education system. Shipps recounts how "Mayor Washington revived the summit process, but died shortly afterward. By the middle of 1988 it became clear to Chicago business that Washington's summit was not going to produce the kind of changes that they felt needed to be made. Three summit subgroups were preparing legislation to be considered in Springfield."[22]

Shipps documents how Thomas Ayers' Chicago United responded to the summit "by forming a business/community advocacy coalition called the Alliance for Better Chicago Schools (ABCs Coalition). The goal of this coalition was to draft a consensus school reform bill."[23]

In creating his ABCs Coalition in June 1988, Ayers included Obama as director of the DCP, as well as other "respected black and Hispanic leaders" who were part of the People's Coalition for Educational Reform (PCER), a coalition of frustrated African American and Latino parents who marched in major protests. The contact for the ABCs Coalition was none other than Bill Ayers himself, who at the time was at University of Illinois at Chicago.[24]

Journalist Ben Joravsky wrote in the November 1990 *Chicago Reader* that it was community activist and PCER leader Coretta McFerren "and others" who invited Ayers to attend ABCs Coalition meetings. Ayers started attending the group's monthly meetings, held over breakfasts of eggs, sausage, rolls, fruit, and coffee in a conference room on the 57th floor of First National Bank's downtown headquarters.[25]

In many ways, Ayers' philosophy was ideal for ABCs'. The targets of his criticism—both central office bureaucrats and supposedly ineffective classroom teachers—were not among his constituents. For ABCs' frustrated minority groups, he had almost nothing but praise. Within a few weeks, the group named Ayers as convener, which means he ran their meetings.

There can be no doubt, then, that Obama and Ayers were well-acquainted by 1988, brought together through an acolyte of Alinsky, Kellman, who in turn was a major influence for radical Obama mentor Frank Marshall Davis. Perhaps this period serves as the missing link, providing background to understand how Ayers was so comfortable with Obama's capabilities that he later would hire the future politician to head the Chicago Annenberg Challenge, or CAC, a job Obama would in turn claim had qualified him to run for public office.[26]

OBAMA-AYERS DUO FUND ACORN

The CAC was formed in 1995 as another Chicago public school reform project with the stated purpose of revamping the public schools in the city. The organization was funded by an original $49.2 million, 2-to-1 matching challenge grant over five years from the Annenberg Foundation, the philanthropic organization of billionaire newspaper publisher Walter Annenberg, who was also ambassador to the United Kingdom under President Richard Nixon. The Annenberg grant was contingent on being matched by $49.2 million in private donations and $49.2 million in public money.

Bill Ayers was involved in the CAC from the very beginning. He was one of three co-authors of the grant proposal to the Annenberg Foundation.[27]

Obama was appointed as the CAC's first chairman in 1995, a key year for the Obama-Ayers relationship. In that same year the first organizing meeting for Obama's state senatorial campaign reportedly was held in Ayers' apartment.

During the presidential campaign, Obama's team worked carefully to distance the politician from domestic terrorist Bill Ayers' involvement in the CAC. In response to a query by *National Review Online* writer Stanley Kurtz, the Obama campaign issued a statement claiming Ayers was not involved with Obama's "recruitment" to the CAC board. The statement claimed Deborah Leff and Patricia Albjerg Graham, who served as presidents of other foundations, had recruited Obama.

But Kurtz diligently reviewed the CAC archives at the Richard J. Daley Library at the University of Illinois at Chicago, which houses CAC board meeting minutes and other documentation from the education foundation. Kurtz found that along with Leff and Graham, Ayers was one of a working group of five who assembled the initial board of the CAC, which hired Obama. The records also show that Obama's and Ayers' CAC foundation granted money to radical leftist activist causes, including the Association of Community Organizations for Reform Now, or ACORN, which, as we will document in Chapter 8 of this book, has an extensive history with Obama and his associates.[28]

"Ayers founded CAC and was its guiding spirit. No one would have been appointed the CAC chairman without his approval," Kurtz wrote in a *Wall Street Journal* opinion piece.[29]

Indeed, several articles in 1994 and 1995 in the *Chicago Tribune* detail Ayers' extensive work to secure the original grant for the CAC from Annenberg's foundation, as well as Ayers' molding of the CAC guidelines.

It is highly unlikely that Ayers would not have been involved in the selection of Obama.

Kurtz also reported that the CAC archives document how Obama and Ayers worked as a team to further the foundation's agenda. Obama was in charge of fiscal matters, while Ayers' position was more concerned with shaping educational policy.

The documents show Ayers served as an ex-officio member of the board that Obama chaired through the CAC's first year. Ayers also served on the board's governance committee with Obama and worked with him to craft CAC bylaws. According to the documents, Ayers made presentations to board meetings chaired by Obama. Ayers also spoke for the Chicago School Reform Collaborative before Obama's board, while Obama periodically spoke for the board at meetings of the collaborative, the CAC documents reviewed by Kurtz show.

The CAC also granted money to far-leftist causes other than ACORN, according to the CAC archives. Klein reported at *WorldNetDaily* that while Obama chaired the CAC board, more than $600,000 was granted to an organization founded by Ayers and run by Mike Klonsky, a former top communist activist who, we will show later in this book, is part of a coalition still supporting Obama's presidential efforts. Klonsky had been leader of the Marxist-Leninist Communist Party, which was effectively recognized by China as the all-but-official U.S. Maoist party.[30]

Of the money going to ACORN, Kurtz wrote: "Instead of funding schools directly, [the CAC] required schools to affiliate with 'external partners,' which actually got the money. Proposals from groups focused on math/science achievement were turned down. Instead CAC disbursed money through various far-left community organizers, such as ACORN."[31]

To underscore Ayers' radical mentality in 1995, while he worked closely with Obama, the unrepentant terrorist gave an interview in that year for author Ron Chepesiuk's book *Sixties Radicals*, in which Ayers stated, "I'm a radical, leftist, small 'c' communist."[32]

Obama, meanwhile, held his Ayers-associated CAC experience to be of such high import that the politician cited his CAC chairmanship as evidence of his qualification for public office while he was running for his failed Congressional bid in 2000.[33]

At the time, a Chicago television host posed the following question to candidate Obama: "One of the criticisms that arises in connection with your candidacy is that you haven't been in the Senate very long, the state Senate. You have a limited track record in terms of time. What is your argument, based on the one term that you served in the Senate so far, that makes you prepared for the Congress?"[34]

Obama replied: "Well, I'm in my second term, but it's true that certainly both Senator Trotter and Congressman Rush have been in elected office longer than I have. I can't deny that."

"I would argue, though, that my experience previous to elected office equips me for the job. You know, I have a background as an attorney. I've represented affordable housing organizations to build affordable housing, something that is a major issue in the district. I've chaired major philanthropic efforts in the city, like the Chicago Annenberg Challenge that gave $50 million to prop school reform efforts throughout the city."

DID AYERS GHOSTWRITE OBAMA'S "BEST-WRITTEN" MEMOIR?

The year 1995 was busy for Obama. Not only was he hired by Bill Ayers to chair the CAC, not only did he launch a state senatorial campaign, but Obama also released *Dreams from My Father*, which *Time* magazine regarded as possibly "the best-written memoir ever produced by an American politician."[35]

With everything else he had going on, Obama was also reportedly under deadline pressure from the Time Books division of Random House to submit his manuscript, after already having failed to deliver on a contract with Simon & Schuster. Confronted with the threat of a second canceled contract, there has been much evidence produced to support the contention that Obama turned to Ayers for help in writing his book. Indeed, Ayers may have ghostwritten most of the work.[36]

Author Jack Cashill, writing at *WorldNetDaily*, first developed this theory after reviewing samples of Obama's writings unearthed before 1995, finding them to be "pedestrian and uninspired" as compared to the lyrical masterwork of *Dreams*. Cashill proceeded to compare *Dreams* to Ayers' known writings, particularly Ayers' 2001 memoir, *Fugitive Days*, finding a high degree of unusual stylistic similarities which Cashill argues should be apparent to any serious writer or editor.[37]

Cashill was able to document a large number of specific similarities in phraseology, story-line development, themes, even use of particular metaphors, such as sections of both books that use a many similar nautical metaphors, like the use of the word "ship" or descriptions of the sea, to denote feelings. In fact, after dropping out of college, Ayers took up the life of a merchant seaman, whereas Obama has no known sailing history.

Cashill also noted Obama's memoir was written with a post-1960s consciousness. In *Dreams*, Obama relates an experience at Columbia— while he was 20 years old—with "the kind of insight and regret that only someone like Ayers could have felt and expressed."

Cashill's literary detective work received major verification when author Christopher Andersen, in his 2009 book, *Barack and Michelle: Portrait of a Marriage*, quoted Obama insiders stating that Ayers was brought in to help Obama finish his memoir. Obama had taped interviews with relatives to flesh out his family history, and those "oral histories, along with a partial manuscript and a truckload of notes, were given to Ayers," writes Andersen.[38]

The author quotes a neighbor in the Hyde Park area of Chicago where Obama and Ayers lived, who says of the two, "Everyone knew they were friends and that they worked on various projects together.

"It was no secret. Why would it be? People liked them both," the neighbor told Andersen.

Andersen writes:

> In the end, Ayers' contribution to Barack's *Dreams from My Father* would be significant—so much so that the book's language, oddly specific references, literary devices, and themes would bear a jarring similarity to Ayers' own writing.

Andersen concludes, "Thanks to help from the veteran writer Ayers, Barack would be able to submit a manuscript to his editors at Times Books."

Andersen also has penned "marriage portraits" of George and Laura Bush, Bill and Hillary Clinton, and John and Jackie Kennedy. Cashill wrote in a column that he believes Andersen relied on inside sources, quite possibly Michelle Obama, in writing his book. Andersen cited Cashill as a source, but Cashill pointed out that Andersen "clearly has access to inside information that I did not have."

Added Cashill: "Only in America could an America-hating terrorist conspire with an unskilled writer of uncertain origins on an untruthful memoir and succeed in getting the man elected president. This plot is so absolutely rich, so thoroughly cinematic, that the literary gatekeepers refuse to believe it is true."[39]

MICHELLE ORGANIZED AYERS EVENT

Obama, meanwhile, worked with Ayers on other projects. Klein reported that Obama served alongside Ayers on the board of the Woods Fund, a Chicago-based nonprofit that describes itself as a group helping the disadvantaged. Obama was a director on the Woods Fund board from 1999 to Dec. 11, 2002, according to the Fund's website.[40] According to tax filings, Obama received compensation of $6,000 per year for his service in 1999 and 2000.

In 2001, the Woods Fund provided a $40,000 grant to the Arab American Action Network, or AAAN, which was an anti-Israel group run by Mona Khalidi, wife of Columbia University professor Rashid Khalidi. The Fund provided a second grant to the AAAN of $35,000 in 2002.[41]

Rashid Khalidi, who was a close associate of Obama, is a harsh critic of Israel and public apologist for Palestinian terror. Khalidi reportedly did freelance work on behalf of the press agency associated with the Palestine Liberation Organization (PLO) during the years before the 1993 Oslo Accords, when the PLO was involved in anti-Western terrorism and officially designated by the State Department as a terrorist group. Khalidi was quoted in several press accounts speaking on behalf of the PLO. (More will be said of Obama's ties to Khalidi in Chapter 3.)

Unsurprisingly, speakers at Khalidi's AAAN dinners and events routinely take the standard rejectionist anti-Israel line. A 2005 AAAN co-sponsored art exhibit titled "The Subject of Palestine," featured works related to what some Palestinians call the "Nakba" or "catastrophe" of Israel's founding in 1948.

According to the widely discredited Nakba narrative, Jews in 1948 forcibly expelled hundreds of thousands—some Palestinians claim over one million—Arabs from their homes and then took over the territory. Historically, it is true about 600,000 Arabs fled Israel after surrounding Arab countries threatened to destroy the Jewish state in 1948, warning local Arabs to get out of the way. Some Arabs also were driven out by Jewish forces while they were trying to push back invading Arab armies. At the same time, over 800,000 Jews were expelled or left Arab countries under threat after Israel was founded.

The theme of AAAN's Nakba art exhibit, held at DePaul University in 2005, was "the compelling and continuing tragedy of Palestinian life . . . under [Israeli] occupation . . . home demolition . . . statelessness . . . bereavement . . . martyrdom, and . . . the heroic struggle for life, for safety, and for freedom."

Another AAAN initiative, titled "Al Nakba 1948 as experienced by Chicago Palestinians," seeks documents related to the "catastrophe" of Israel's founding. A post on the AAAN website asked users: "Do you have photos, letters or other memories you could share about Al-Nakba-1948?" But that posting was removed after Klein's article appeared.

Barack is not the only Obama with ties to Bill Ayers. Michelle Obama, on November 20, 1997, directed a university event for which she had invited her husband, then a state senator, to serve on a panel discussion with Ayers about whether child murderers should be tried as adults. Both Barack Obama and Ayers argued the side that opposed treating offending minors as adults. Michelle Obama at the time was the University of Chicago's associate dean of Student Services and director of the college's Community Service Center, which sponsored the juvenile detention discussion. Obama and Ayers spoke together at numerous other events.[43]

2

UNMASKING THE MYSTERIOUS
COLLEGE YEARS

I N ONE OF the many strange features of Barack Obama's presidential candidacy, his campaign went to great lengths to conceal normally routine
information about the candidate's college years. These include his first
two undergraduate years at Occidental College in Los Angeles, followed
by his final two years and graduation from Columbia University in New
York City. No official or unofficial records were ever made available. No
college transcripts, published records, or even contemporary newspaper
announcements about his education have ever been released.

Such withholding of a presidential candidate's educational record is
unusual in American politics, and it speaks volumes about the irresponsi-
bility of the mainstream news media when it comes to covering Obama,
that a serious investigation has never been launched until now, nor a
major furor raised in response to Obama's continuing refusal to provide
standard biographical data.

What was the Obama team trying to hide?

Former classmates and teachers have also revealed little about Obama
as a college student. Of those who have been interviewed, few have been
forthcoming with any details.

One can only conclude that this information blackout is by design and
not accidental. The authors were at first reduced to reliance upon the

few breadcrumbs Obama left behind in his 1995 book, *Dreams from My Father*, appended by a few bits and pieces and quotes gleaned from interviews granted by those who knew Obama during his days at Occidental College, fondly known as Oxy.

Fortunately, by using those "breadcrumbs" as a point of departure, the authors were able to piece together a clearer picture of Barack Obama's college years, though many questions remain. This chapter includes many revelations on those covered-up college years—including tracing Obama's first political speech, while an undergraduate student, to an organization chaired by an associate of Bill Ayers—as well as clues to further research.

It is well known that Oxy was the undergraduate school of choice for Obama after his 1979 graduation from the Punahou School in Hawaii. In his 2007 biography, *Obama: From Promise to Power*, David Mendell relates that Obama had been awarded a full scholarship at Oxy. He studied there until fall 1981, when he transferred to Columbia University.[1]

Remarkably, Obama tells us in *Dreams* that, beginning at Oxy, he surrounded himself with an assortment of radicals, socialists, Marxist-Leninists, Maoists, and Communists of both the large "C" and small "c" varieties. What little Obama does reveal in *Dreams* of himself at Oxy is certainly suggestive of what he might be concealing:

> To avoid being mistaken for a sellout, I chose my friends carefully. The more politically active black students. The foreign students. The Chicanos. The Marxist professors and structural feminists and punk-rock performance poets. We smoked cigarettes and wore leather jackets. At night, in the dorms, we discussed neocolonialism, Frantz Fanon, Eurocentrism and patriarchy. [2]

(Frantz Fanon, author of *Wretched of the Earth*, famously advocated "revolutionary violence.")[3]

And who are these "Marxist professors and structural feminists" toward whom Barack Obama gravitated at Oxy? The politician provides us with neither names nor clues. We do know, however, that Oxy is where Barack Obama first engaged in community activism, delivering what has been described as the first political speech of his career. On February 18, 1981, Obama addressed students gathered outside Coons Hall administration building, exhorting Oxy's trustees to divest from South Africa.[4]

Whether U.S. corporations should have divested themselves of ties with South Africa's apartheid regime was described as "one of the most complex and difficult ethical issues faced by many U.S. and multinational corporations in the 1980s." The movement pushing divestment, however, which reached its height in 1986, became a mainstay of the American left.[5]

[Should corporations continue operations in South Africa under pressure from] individuals and organizations who believed that the mere presence of U.S. corporations in South Africa supported that country's government and its unjust apartheid policies? . . .

Influential, well-meaning people such as religious leaders, university presidents, and politicians disagreed over what was the most moral and effective means of exerting pressure on the South African government to end its apartheid policies. Should U.S. corporations be asked or even forced to pull out of South Africa thus isolating the government by denying it essential goods and services? Or should corporations continue to operate in South Africa and work against apartheid by hiring black African employees, training them to become technicians and managers, providing them with better housing and educational opportunities—in short, undercutting apartheid by creating growing enclaves of economic and personal equality within that repressive system? Should the United States government take a more active role in its opposition to apartheid by imposing economic and political sanctions?

Obama writes in *Dreams* about the rally in which he took part, reportedly led by the Black Student Alliance and Students for Economic Democracy:

But entering sophomore year I could feel it growing stronger, sturdier, that constant, honest portion of myself, a bridge between my future and my past.

It was around that time that I got involved in the divestment campaign. It had started as something of a lark, I suppose, part of the radical pose my friends and I sought to maintain, a subconscious end run around issues closer to home. But as the months passed and I found myself drawn into a larger role—contacting representatives of the African National Congress to speak on campus, drafting letters to the faculty, printing up flyers, arguing strategy—I noticed that people had begun to listen to my opinions.[6]

Obama agreed to deliver the opening remarks for the rally, for which "the agenda had been carefully arranged beforehand." In the middle of his speech "a couple of white students" were to come onstage, "dressed in their paramilitary uniforms," to drag him away. "A bit of street theater, a way to dramatize the situation for activists in South Africa," Obama writes. His anticipated "two-minute speech" was cheered on by the crowd when, as planned, he was grabbed from behind and yanked from the stage with "so much left to say."[7]

Serge F. Kovalkeski reported blandly in the February 9, 2008, New York Times: "Mr. Obama was involved in the Black Students' Association and in the divestment campaign to pressure the college to pull its money out of companies doing business in South Africa. To make a point, students camped out in makeshift shantytowns on campus."[8]

But reporter Roy H. Campbell, who was closer in time and place to the original event, provided more detail, in a story filed June 5, 1986, for the Los Angeles Times. For the past fifteen years, Campbell wrote, South African divestment protests at Oxy had been "relatively small affairs, such as candlelight vigils and rallies involving only about 40 students." Student organizations had tried "to apply pressure through meetings with trustees, administrators and President Richard C. Gilman." Campbell also wrote that Phillip Terry, co-chairman of the Anti-Apartheid Coalition at Oxy, said, "We took a peaceful strategy. We wanted to try to resolve the issue of divestment through governmental channels."[9]

Note that "the past fifteen years" would have encompassed the period 1971 to 1986, during which time Campbell reported there were no "students camped out in makeshift shantytowns on campus." The first instance of such activity, as Campbell reports, was on May 12, 1986, when "12 students rose at dawn and, dragging wood, nails and other materials, converged at the center of the 120-acre Eagle Rock campus. For six hours, the students hammered. . . . By noon, they had built a four-shack shantytown to symbolize their opposition to the school's financial investments in corporations that do business in South Africa."

Campbell writes that the effort was named "'Biko Commons' in honor of Steven Biko, a black South African leader who died in police custody in 1977, it stands in the rose garden in front of the administration build-ing. The wood and cardboard structures are covered with spray-painted messages such as 'Freedom for All' and 'Divest Now.'"

Campbell cited the *1986–87 Insider Guide to Colleges*, which called Occidental "an exclusive school with a student body that is generally con-servative. Tuition is about $14,000 a year, and about 25% of the student body is made up of minorities." The controversial shantytown, Campbell reports, was "the likes of which the campus has not seen for a decade, administrators and faculty members say." In fact, Brigada Knauer, dean of students, remarked: "I don't think this campus has experienced anything like this since the Vietnam War protests."

So, between 1971, the era of Vietnam War protests, and May 12, 1986, Oxy had never seen the likes of a "four-shack shantytown" on its campus. And Barack Obama, beginning with his 1981 speech and the agit-prop theater accompanying it, was in the center of the movement that turned the quiet, conservative campus into a scene of protest.

An official account of the "early phase of the anti-apartheid movement" on the campus—which would have been before the shantytowns—comes from Jane Jaquette, Emerita Professor of Politics and DWA at Oxy, who served as chair of the Humanitarian Task Force from 1990 to 1993:[10]

> [In June 1978, the Oxy Board] voted not to divest on grounds of the estimated cost to the College and a preference for using proxy votes to support the Sullivan Principles (a set of rules [developed by black activ-ist minister Rev. Leon Sullivan] on how corporations should operate to improve conditions for workers and press for change in South Africa). In addition, the Board expressed its opposition to the College's acting "as an agent of social change." The Student Committee Against Apartheid,

founded in 1978 by Gary Chapman, with Professor [Roger] Boesche and [Eric] Newhall taking a leadership role on the faculty side, organized teach-ins, and continued to press for a new vote, to no avail. It was during this period that future President "Barry" Obama was active in the movement, as he records in his autobiography.[11]

EXTREMIST MENTORS

This brings us to another issue. Who were Barack Obama's political mentors at Oxy?

According to a 2007 report by Larry Gordon of the *Los Angeles Times*, one was Roger Boesche, who has taught at Oxy since 1976. Boesche is the Arthur G. Coons Distinguished Professor of the History of Ideas, and teaches the history of European and American thought. He told Gordon: "the young man from Honolulu was 'a very thoughtful student and a very curious student.'" [12]

"Obama enrolled in two of Boesche's courses," Gordon wrote, "a survey of American government and political thought from the Revolution through the civil rights movement and an advanced look at modern European political thought, which tackled such philosophers as Friedrich Nietzsche and Max Weber."

But Oliver Haydock, writing in 2008 for the UK *Observer*, was not so sure. He asserts that Boesche's "media credentials may have been artificially enhanced when former *Chicago Tribune* reporter David Mendell referred to him as an important influence in Obama's life in his 2007 Obama biography *From Promise to Power*."[13] Haydock writes that Boesche himself "disputes this characterization, and it raises the question of just how much a professor is able to remember about a student three decades after their last classroom meeting."[14]

So Boesche does not appear to have been Barack Obama's Oxy political mentor. However, Professor Jaquette mentions two other names, Gary Chapman and Eric Newhall.

A story in *The Occidental Week* from November 2008 quotes Newhall, English and Comparative Literary Studies Professor at Oxy, saying, "South African apartheid was the major issue of the 1980s." Newhall said: "It was the issue that galvanized a lot of student activism."[15]

The third and most likely prospective Obama mentor is Gary Chapman, whose background includes "military service, academic research and organizational experience." A former U.S. Army Green Beret, Chapman was an Oxy alumnus with a degree in political science, who earned his doctoral degree at Stanford University.[16] But Chapman's political organization and campaign experience also includes "peace issues" with the New American Movement.[17]

The lineage of the New American Movement is associated with that of the Democratic Socialists of America. The DSA website includes the undated "A Brief History of the American Left" by Communist Party USA "revisionist" historian Maurice Isserman.[18]

Isserman writes:[19]

> The Democratic Socialist Organizing Committee (DSOC) had been founded [in February 1973] by Michael Harrington out of some fragments of the old Socialist Party. DSOC continued to operate, in the old Socialist or Communist manner, as the left-wing of the New Deal coalition, clearly now not as a separate political party but as an explicitly socialist force within the Democratic Party and the labor movement. . . .
>
> The New American Movement (NAM) emerged at about the same time, more from the new left than from the old, though it counted in its number some former Communists who had left their party after 1956. NAM, true to these new left origins, was more skeptical about the long-term future of the New Deal coalition, and accordingly devoted its energies more than did DSOC to the new movements of the 1960s, especially feminism, gay and lesbian liberation, and local community organizing.[20]

NAM is also identified as a "splinter group" of Students for a Democratic Society (SDS).[21] And in an April 1998 list-serv, liberal economist Max B. Sawicky remarked, "how many leaders in the non-profit world started out in one or another of the many Marxist sects of the 1970s," including "many community activists" in the Saul Alinsky "tradition," such as Harry C. Boyte, who came out of DSOC or NAM or "organizations to their more militant Marxist left."[22]

The Harry C. Boyte to whom Sawicky refers is now a Senior Fellow at the Herbert H. Humphrey Institute of Public Affairs, at the University of Minnesota, and is a founder and co-director of the Center for Democracy and Citizenship. Boyte wrote regularly for the New American Movement and "other socialist publications on socialist theory and organization." He also served as co-chair of the Civic Engagement Group for Barack Obama's presidential campaign.[23]

Gary Chapman's background with the New American Movement dates from about the same time that Barack Obama was a student at Oxy. Obama's involvement with the anti-apartheid movement there coincides with the Student Committee Against Apartheid, founded by Chapman in 1978.

In a 2004 interview with Oxy's magazine, Barack Obama said it was his "involvement in the South African divestment movement at Occidental that first set him on his current path. 'I got into politics at Occidental . . . I made a conscious decision to go into public policy.'"[24]

One other professor at Oxy might have been an Obama political mentor, though with no evident leftist connections. Larry T. Caldwell joined the Oxy faculty in 1967, becoming a full professor of Politics in 1980. Caldwell currently teaches U.S. National Security at Oxy, has served at The National War College, and was a scholar in residence at the Office of Soviet Analysis at the CIA, at RAND, and at the International Institute of Strategic Studies in London. However, no direct connections between Caldwell and Obama have been found.[25]

AYERS ASSOCIATE

Another unknown is whether Barack Obama became an actual member in either the Black Student Alliance or Students for Economic Democracy, which had both organized that first rally at which he spoke at Oxy.[26] We do know that Students for Economic Democracy was a national student advocacy group established by soon-to-be California State Representative Tom Hayden, now a professor at Oxy, and his former wife, Hollywood actress Jane Fonda.[27] If Obama were indeed a member of SED, it would link him during his college years to one of America's most prominent leftists. And even if not actually a member of SED, Obama certainly collaborated with them on at least the divestment movement, principal leftist activity on Oxy's campus.

SED-founder Hayden was a seminal figure of the American New Left, who—à la Alinsky's methodology—eventually entered mainstream politics. Hayden authored the 1962 "Port Huron Statement," the first official document of Students for a Democratic Society. He helped organize antiwar riots at the 1968 Chicago Democratic Convention, for which he was arrested and stood trial as one of the original Chicago Seven.[28] Hayden was a principal organizer of Students for a Democratic Society, from which Bill Ayers' Weatherman terrorist organization splintered. Hayden authored the SDS's political manifesto.

His wife, "Hanoi Jane" Fonda, is remembered for posing, "on location," atop a North Vietnamese tank, before she made millions "deflabbing" the "overweight women of America with her 'Work-Out' books, records, and video cassettes"—all the while "subsidizing" Hayden's political career, writes Myra MacPherson in *Vietnam and the Haunted Generation*. "At her fitness studio there was a sign declaring: 'Profits from the Workout support the Campaign for Economic Democracy.'"[29] Students for Economic Democracy, described in 1981 as the "campus arm" of Hayden's CED, operated as a "direct outgrowth" of Hayden's unsuccessful 1976 California campaign versus John Tunney for the United States Senate.[30]

"[T]his is the same Tom Hayden who has been quoted as saying that 'Communism is one of the options that can improve people's lives,' and . . . Jane Fonda's public utterances have included her statement that 'we should strive toward a socialist society—all the way to communism,' it was noted in 1980."[31]

Another example of Hayden's brash rhetoric dates to a decade prior to Obama's arrival at Oxy. During Hayden's December 1968 testimony before the House Committee on Un-American Activities on the Chicago "anti-war protests," the following was read from an instructional flyer he had co-authored with fellow SDSer and protest leader, Rennie Davis:

> disobey your parents: burn your money: you know life is a dream and all
> of our institutions are man-made illusions effective because YOU take

the dream for reality. . . . Break down the family, church, nation, city, economy; turn life into an art form, a theatre of the soul and a theatre of the future; the revolutionary is the only artist. . . . What's needed is a generation of people who are freaky, crazy, irrational, sexy, angry, irreligious, childish and mad: people who burn draft cards, burn high school and college degrees; people who say: "To hell with your goals!"; people who lure the youth with music, pot and acid; people who re-define the normal; people who break with the status-role-title-consumer game; people who have nothing material to lose but their flesh. . . .

The white youth of America have more in common with Indians plundered, than they do with their own parents. Burn their houses down, and you will be free.[32]

When asked if this was "the way to have a better America," Hayden called them "beautiful sentiments."[33]

That Tom Hayden continues to this day spreading his radical ways is without question. He serves on the advisory board of Progressive Democrats of America, which was established in 2004 to "redirect the resources of our government from destruction to creation, from war to peace, from military spending to social spending, from sickness to health, from selfish desires to universal needs."[34] He is a member of Movement for a Democratic Society, formed in 2006 by original, older SDS members and "sympathizers" as a support group for a new, younger SDS. This re-founded SDS is the "muscle behind the new protest movement"; its might was prominent in the violence at the 2008 Republican National Convention at St. Paul, Minnesota, according to New Zealand researcher Trevor Loudon, writing in September 2008. "MDS is the brains behind the SDS brawn," Loudon stated.[35]

Hayden is also a founding member of Progressives for Obama. Loudon describes Progressives for Obama as an "activist matrix" of SDS sixties radicals and supporters of Democratic Socialists of America, the Communist Party USA, and the Committees of Correspondence for Democracy and Socialism.[36] Speaking on his own behalf, in June 2008, Hayden penned a now famous piece, "Bobby and Barack," which was published at *The Huffington Post* and elsewhere on the Internet:

I didn't see him coming. When I heard of the young state senator with a background in community organizing who wanted to be president, I was at least sentient enough to be interested. When I read *Dreams of My Father*, I was taken aback by its depth. This young man apparently gave his first public speech, against South African apartheid, at an Occidental College rally organized by Students for Economic Democracy, the student branch of the Campaign for Economic Democracy, which I chaired in 1979–82. [37]

Among Campaign for Economic Democracy's "principal activists" were veterans of Hayden's campaign and SDS.[38]

Campaign for Economic Democracy founding members included former U.S. Representative for California's Ninth District, Ronald V. Dellums, and the late United Farm Workers leader, César Chávez. Longtime political activist Michael Dieden, who "organized against the Vietnam War and for the United Farm workers in the 1960–70s," served as Campaign for Economic Democracy's political director. Black Panther founding member and former chief of staff, David Hilliard, moved to Los Angeles after the party disbanded and worked for Campaign for Economic Democracy lobbying for divestiture of "U.S. involvement in South Africa."[39]

In the December 2008 issue of *Socialist Review*, Hilliard writes that Obama as president "symbolizes change." Hilliard adds that all the sacrifices made by the Black Panther Party—"giving up more than 20 of our lives for the struggle. Some 40 of our members are still in prison, others are in exile, and lives were lost in the civil rights struggle in this country"—paved the way for Obama.[40]

The *LA Weekly*'s Bill Bradley was coordinator for Campaign for Economic Democracy's political action team, a "network of campaign operatives." One other CED member, Derek Shearer, "re-branded democratic socialism." In 1980 he co-authored *Economic Democracy* with Martin Carney and later worked "on the program" for Hayden's Senate race.[41] Shearer, an economist, has served since 1981 as Chevalier Professor of Diplomacy and World Affairs at Oxy. He served in the Clinton administration as ambassador to Finland and was a foreign policy advisor to Al Gore during the 2000 presidential campaign and to Senator Hillary Clinton during the

2008 presidential primary.[42] Former New Jersey Senator and 2000 presidential candidate, Bill Bradley, waited until after the Iowa primary and endorsed Obama on January 5, 2008. Bradley traveled to New Hampshire to campaign on Obama's behalf with independent voters.[43]

To understand the goals of Hayden's Campaign for Economic Democracy, one need look no further than CED's declared statement of purpose: "Economic democracy means that ownership and control will be spread among a wide variety of public bodies: city, state and Federal governments, churches, trade unions, cooperatives and community groups, small business people, workers and consumers,"[44] as Jon Weiner wrote approvingly in a 1986 article in *The Nation* magazine, "Tom Hayden's New Workout."

"The organization attacked corporations for endangering the environment with toxic emissions; it organized renters to fight landlords, argued that research and development of solar energy were being thwarted by the energy multinationals, and made pro-choice politics a top priority," Wiener wrote.

While Barack Obama was at Oxy, in February 1980, Students for Economic Democracy lead antiregistration demonstrations, in California, as 18-year-olds were again required to register for the draft beginning in 1981. Obama makes no mention of the demonstrations, and we do not know whether he participated.[45]

Nor, perhaps, did Obama know that his undergraduate encounter with Campaign for Economic Democracy/Students for Economic Democracy would reconnect decades later on his political path to the White House. This was a path described presciently by William T. Poole in a September 1980 study for the Heritage Foundation:

> In the 1960s and early 1970s, radicals of varying hues coalesced, largely under Communist influence, in mass demonstrations, which frequently had as rallying cries a variety of slogans about the need to bring down the "system." Now, as the nation moves into the 1980s, many of these Vietnam-era radicals have elected to become a part of the same system, their aim being to use the nation's political machinery to effect their goals from [a] base of political power on the inside of the very system they were

challenging in the streets just a few short years ago. It is this development that gives CED a significance it might not otherwise enjoy.[46]

A more contemporary summation comes from Richard Flacks, a collaborator with Hayden and Robert "Al" Haber on the "Port Huron Statement." In his June 2008 review of *Writings for a Democratic Society: The Tom Hayden Reader*, Flacks writes of Hayden's failed U.S. Senate bid:

> An internal premise of key organizers was that the campaign, when it was over, would be the foundation for a permanent progressive electoral organization in California, and within a few weeks after the June [1976] primary race, the "Campaign for Economic Democracy" came into being. The CED became a significant electoral force in several cities and counties over about five years. It came to an end as Tom focused on his own political career, getting elected from Santa Monica to the California State Assembly, while many other CED activists found niches in government, party politics and mass media.[47]

In other words, those former radicals and revolutionaries have been preparing and waiting for more than three decades. As *American Thinker's* Kyle-Anne Shiver pointed out in October 2008, with Hayden's endorsement of the "Obama movement last year on the *Huffington Post*, he signaled to the vast array of socialist political activists, not only in America, but around the world," that Barack Obama is the "one" they've been waiting for.[48]

MOVING UP TO COLUMBIA

By his sophomore year at Oxy, Obama was reportedly finding the college "too small and inconsequential a stage." He applied for a transfer to Columbia University in New York City. Obama said he "wanted to find a community of blacks where he could 'put down stakes and test my commitments.'"[49] In a 2004 interview with Oxy's Jim Tranquada, Obama said that when transferring to Columbia he had already made the "conscious decision to go into public policy."[50]

Obama has shared almost nothing about his last two years as an undergraduate at Columbia University's Columbia College. Nor has much been uncovered about his time there as a student from fall 1981 until his spring 1983 graduation. We find little about Obama's Columbia years in his autobiographical *Dreams,* and "not much" in David Mendell's 2007 biography.[51]

Lysandra Ohrstrom claimed in September 2008, at the *New York Observer,* that Obama had "left a light footprint," reportedly spending most of his time in the library. Janny Scott wrote in October 2007, in the *New York Times,* that Obama called his time at Columbia "an intense period of study," adding that he was "like a monk."[52] And yet, "no one from the library in the School of International Public Affairs, the building he would have had most of his classes in as a political science major, remembered him," Ohrstrom wrote.[53]

In September 2008 Wayne Allyn Root, the Libertarian Party's vice president, told Aaron Klein he and Obama graduated from Columbia the same day with the same major. However, Root told Klein he "never spoke to a single former Columbia student or faculty member who remembered Obama."[54] Since, as with those from Oxy, Obama's transcripts from Columbia have never been made available, Root "speculates Obama is keeping his Columbia transcript under wraps so as not to reveal a less-than-stellar record, which would raise questions as to how he was accepted to Harvard," Klein wrote.

In September 2008, Root publicly challenged candidate Obama to reveal his Columbia grades. Reported Matt Welch at *Reason.com*: "[Root] was willing to bet a million dollars that he earned a better grade point average at Columbia than his old classmate, and that the only reason Obama went on to Harvard Law School was the color of his skin."[55] Root also told Welch: "I think the most dangerous thing you should know about Barack Obama is that I don't know a single person at Columbia that knows him, and they all know me. I don't have a classmate who ever knew Barack Obama at Columbia. Ever!"[56]

Obama did say that he had been involved with the Black Students Organization, which emerged in the sixties in response to a growing black student population at Columbia. Undergraduates formed SAAS (Student

Afro-American Society), "which was concerned with the affairs of black students and issues of the greater black community." By the early 1970s SAAS had faded and SOBU (the Student Organization of Black Unity) was created. It too "had a fleeting organizational stint, then dwindled away," and was replaced in 1976 by the Black Students' Organization.[57]

Mark Attiah, a Black Students' Organization former vice president, told Ohrstrom he was "shocked to learn that Obama was even a member." Scott writes that Obama said "he was somewhat involved with the Black Student Organization and anti-apartheid activities, though, in recent interviews, several prominent student leaders said they did not remember his playing a role."[58] Ohrstrom and others have remarked that "there is not a single picture of Senator Obama in any of the yearbooks from the period when he was a student." When the Black Students' Organization photo was taken in 1983, Obama "is not even listed as absent."[59]

Obama's involvement with the anti-apartheid movement at Columbia is similarly unclear, even though the university itself was known in the 1980s as "the site of large anti-apartheid protests, and was one of the first universities in the U.S. to divest from apartheid South Africa."[60]

The Coalition for a Free South Africa began as a Black Students' Organization committee to "promote Columbia University's divestment in stock in companies doing business in South Africa." CFSA, which split from the Black Students' Organization in 1981, was a "loosely structured group with a predominantly black steering committee of about a dozen individuals who made decisions by consensus, and a less active circle of about 50 students who attended meetings and the group's protests and educational events."[61] Early CFSA leaders were Danny Armstrong, a Columbia College student who played forward for Columbia's basketball team, and Barbara Ransby, a student from the School of General Studies.[62]

AYERS SUPPORTER

As CFSA spokeswoman, Barbara Ransby famously convinced Columbia's student senate "to support full divestment." The following year she was instrumental in getting a "unanimous endorsement from the far more conservative faculty, student and administration representatives of the university senate."[63] According to Eric L. Hirsch, in his recently published case study on Columbia's divestment campaign:

> [CFSA] tried to convince Columbia and Barnard students that blacks faced injustice under apartheid, that U.S. corporations with investments in South Africa profited from the low wages paid to blacks, that Columbia was an accomplice in apartheid because it invested in the stock of these companies, and that divestment would advance the anti-apartheid movement by putting economic and political pressure on the white regime of South Africa.[64]

In a fall 1998 retrospective on the April 1984 Hamilton Hall divestment blockade—for which neither Obama nor Ransby were present, as both had graduated—Columbia students quoted Ransby as saying:

> One of the most glaring weaknesses of the Sullivan Principles is that they do not even attempt to address some of the most outrageous features of the apartheid system. Apartheid is a system of rule which denies the majority of the country's population the most basic political freedoms. Against this grim reality it matters very little whether a company has integrated restrooms or pays its black workers 50 cents more an hour.[65]

None of this jibes with another report, claiming Obama's involvement with on-campus protest shantytowns. "While at Columbia, Obama camped out in makeshift shantytowns with other members of Black Students' Association to pressure the university to cut ties with companies doing business with apartheid South Africa," reported Samantha Sharf on November 3, the day before election day 2008, in the *Daily Pennsylvanian*.[66] But how credible is this claim?

First of all, the name of the organization, as stated earlier from the Black Students' Organization history, was never the Black Students' Association. Second, the BSO breakaway committee involved with the anti-apartheid movement on campus was the Coalition for a Free South Africa. Lastly, Obama's account cannot be substantiated. In fact, all indications are, like Obama's account of 1981 shantytowns on the Oxy campus, that this never happened.

According to Sarah A. Soule, in a 1997 article on the "Student Divestment Movement in the United States and Tactical Diffusion: the Shantytown Protest," the "new tactic of protest, the shantytown, spread rapidly among U.S. campuses between 1985 and 1990." In fact, Soule wrote that 1985–1986 "was the year of the shanties, makeshift structures disrupting the campus landscape of tidy quadrangles and plazas, symbolizing the viciousness of apartheid and the oppression of South Africa's blacks." Soule mentioned Columbia University by name, but for the school year 1985–1986, and not for 1981, 1982, or 1983, when Obama was there.[67]

In their April 1985 account of anti-apartheid campus activity at Columbia, Kim Parks and Sandra V. Williams make no mention of shantytowns in the SUNY-Stonybrook school paper, *Blackworld*. What they do mention is the Coalition for a Free South Africa, coordination with campus authorities, as well as efforts for education and attempts to mobilize opposition to apartheid on campus.[68]

Barbara Ransby, now an associate professor of African American studies and history at the University of Illinois–Chicago, and the executive director of Public Square, was in the class of 1984 at Columbia, only one year behind Obama.[69] It is unknown whether the two knew each other very well back then. However, it is known that in April 2002 Ransby appeared at a University of Illinois–Chicago forum, and sat on the same panel—"Intellectuals in Times of Crisis: Experiences and applications of intellectual work in urgent situations"—with both Obama and former Weather terrorist leader Bill Ayers.[70]

Ayers had graduated in 1984 from Bank Street College, a school located less than a quarter mile from Columbia. Again, it is unknown whether Ransby and Ayers knew each other in New York. However, in February 2008, Ransby was one of three authors of a letter supporting "our colleague, Bill Ayers, who was the target yesterday of Jonah Goldberg's mean-spirited muckraking journalism. Goldberg asks why Bill Ayers is allowed to have a job as a college professor, despite his leftist views and political activities from some forty years ago?"[71]

Ransby was one of approximately 70 who met in Chicago to form the

Black Radical Congress. Trevor Loudon cited the following from a June 1998 BRC document:

> It seemed to us the idea of bringing together the varied sections of the Black radical tradition—Socialists and Communists, revolutionary nationalists, and radical Black feminists and womanists—was long overdue. We began talking with others about the idea and possibilities for such a gathering. . . .
>
> Those who gathered reflected a broad spectrum of the radical tradition. Participants came as individuals but represented connections to groups ranging from New Afrikan People's Organization, Black Workers for Justice, The Labor Party, The Communist Party, The Malcolm X Grassroots Movement, African American Agenda 2000, The Chicago Ida B. Wells Forum and the Committees of Correspondence.[72]

MORE EXTREMISTS

Others in attendance at the 1998 Black Radical Caucus meeting included now-DSA President Manning Marable, Bill Fletcher, Jr., and Cornel West, who were all leaders of the socialist New Party.[73] In 1995 Obama sought out the New Party's endorsement, and he was considered one of the party's success stories when he first won his Illinois State Senate seat, which the authors discuss in Chapter 6. All three men have continued to be Obama supporters, with West having served as a liaison to the black community for Obama's presidential campaign.[74]

Another name that emerges from Obama's involvement with the Black Students' Organization and Coalition for a Free South Africa is that of Julius Genachowski.[75]

In October 2008, Genachowski, co-founder of the venture capital firm LaunchBox Digital, was described as "an advisor to Democratic presidential nominee Barack Obama." At a meeting of the Potomac Officers Club in Virginia, Genachowski discussed the "role of technology in the campaign." He also shared the Obama Campaign's "vision for a newly created Chief Technology Officer," a position for which Genachowski was already on the short list.[76]

Obama and Genakowski were later Harvard Law School classmates. In August 2008 it was reported in the *New York Times* that Genachowski, who led the Obama campaign's technology working group, was also a big fundraiser. Genachowski raised at least $500,000 as an Obama "bundler."[77] In March 2009, Genachowski's investment paid off. President Obama nominated him to chair the Federal Communications Commission and he was sworn in June 29, 2009.[78]

Also unreported by Obama is his Columbia University association with "influential Palestinian activist and intellectual," Professor Edward Said. Andrew McCarthy writes at the *National Review Online* that Obama took a class at Columbia with Said, who was then a professor there; Obama and Said were photographed sitting together in 1998 at an Arab-American dinner at which Said gave the keynote speech, "showing they must have continued their friendship"; and, in 2001, Said "wrote a blurb" for Bill Ayers' Weather Underground memoir, *Fugitive Days*. McCarthy wonders why Obama has said nothing about Said.[79]

Another BSO/CFSA contact, Danny Armstrong, won Columbia College's Van Am Award for his work with the CFSA. Armstrong connects Barack Obama to life after he graduated in 1983 from Columbia.[80]

In fact, Armstrong's account is nearly the opposite of an endorsement. Steve Gilbert wrote on September 14, 2008, at *Sweetness & Light*, that there seems "an especially conspicuous absence of witnesses to the years after [Obama] graduated from Columbia and before he moved to Chicago to work as a community organizer."[81] Gilbert wrote that Armstrong, one of Obama's co-workers, "has written about Mr. Obama during those days. And while he is an admitted fan of Obama's, he claims that he has inflated his resume considerably."

(Charles Krauthammer observed in September 2008 in the *Washington Post* that Obama's "talents have been largely devoted to crafting, and chronicling, his own life. Not things. Not ideas. Not institutions. But himself." Krauthammer notes: "Eerily missing at the Democratic convention this year were people of stature who were seriously involved at some point in Obama's life standing up to say: I know Barack Obama. I've been with Barack Obama. We've toiled/endured together. You can trust him. I do.")[82]

Janny Scott talked with Armstrong for her January 2007 article about the time Obama spent in New York City. It seems that following graduation, in 1984, Armstrong worked with Obama at Business International Corporation. Armstrong "has deconstructed Mr. Obama's account of the job on his blog, *analyzethis.net*," Janny writes. "All of Barack's embellishment serves a larger narrative purpose: to retell the story of the Christ's temptation. The young, idealistic, would-be community organizer gets a nice suit, joins a consulting house, starts hanging out with investment bankers, and barely escapes moving into the big mansion with the white folks."[83]

Armstrong told Janny: "There may be some truth to that. But in order to make it a good story, it required a bit of exaggeration." Janny writes: "Contrary to Obama's more glowing account, Armstrong described BIC thusly: small newsletter-publishing and research firm, with about 250 employees worldwide, that helped companies with foreign operations (they could be called multinationals) understand overseas markets, they said. Far from a bastion of corporate conformity, they said, it was informal and staffed by young people making modest wages. Employees called it 'high school with ashtrays.'"[84]

Obama was "a researcher and writer for a reference service called Financing Foreign Operations. He also wrote for a newsletter, Business International Money Report," in Janny's account.[85]

It is also from Janny's article that we learn what followed—prior to Obama making his way to Chicago in 1985. Obama was hired after about a year by the New York Public Interest Research Group, "a nonprofit organization that promotes consumer, environmental and government reform. He became a full-time organizer at City College in Harlem, paid slightly less than $10,000 a year to mobilize student volunteers."[86]

In what may have been Barack Obama's first contact with a future new green economy, Janny wrote that Obama "spent three months 'trying to convince minority students at City College about the importance of recycling'—a description that surprised some former colleagues. They said that more 'bread-and-butter issues' like mass transit, higher education, tuition and financial aid were more likely the emphasis at City College."

Obama's NYPIRG supervisor, Eileen Hershenov, told Janny: "You needed somebody—and here was where Barack was a star—who could make the case to students across the political spectrum." Unsurprisingly, Janny writes, the "job required winning over students on the political left, who would normally disdain a group inspired by Ralph Nader as insufficiently radical, as well as students on the right and those who were not active at all." The New York Public Interest Research Group's website, which offers congratulations to President Obama, states that his first job was as Project Coordinator, a full-time organizer on NYPIRG's staff for three months, beginning in February 1985 until the end of the academic year. Obama ran NYPIRG's office at the City College of New York.[87]

Obama "spent hours with students in the trailer that served as the group's office just below 140th Street and Convent Avenue, giving lessons on how to organize rallies and letter-writing campaigns, how to speak to legislators and lobby for change in public policy," Jason Fink reported November 2008, in the *New York Daily News*.[88] Obama also continued his anti-apartheid activism at CUNY. Alison Kelley, then a sophomore at CCNY, and later NYPIRG chairwoman, claimed to Fink that Obama "was among the early leaders in the successful push to get CUNY to divest itself of holdings in apartheid South Africa."[89]

On the other hand, as Eric L. Hirsch writes, few at Columbia—and perhaps elsewhere in New York City—were involved in the anti-apartheid "movement" until 1985, at such time as Obama was leaving the city and was headed for Chicago.[90]

And thus, the more we try to learn about Obama's Columbia years, the less we actually know. From 1981 to 1983, the president of the United States was essentially an Invisible Man.

3

"OBAMA WAS QUITE RELIGIOUS IN ISLAM"

Whatever we once were, we are no longer just a Christian nation; we are also a Jewish nation, a Muslim nation, a Buddhist nation, a Hindu nation, and a nation of nonbelievers.

—Barack Obama, Call to Renewal Conference, June 28, 2006.[1]

FOR MORE THAN two years before he was elected president, Barack Obama had been portraying America as "no longer a Christian nation." But his statements on the subject went largely unreported until in 2008, when bloggers started circulating a YouTube video depicting the president making the above-quoted speech.

Obama also took aim at the "Christian Right," in his speech to the Call to Renewal Conference, for "hijacking" religion and using it to divide the nation: "Somehow, somewhere along the way, faith stopped being used to bring us together and started being used to drive us apart. It got hijacked. Part of it's because of the so-called leaders of the Christian Right, who've been all too eager to exploit what divides us," the president said.[2]

Asked by the Christian Broadcast Network a year later to clarify his remarks, Obama literally repeated them: "I think that the right might worry a bit more about the dangers of sectarianism. Whatever we once were, we're no longer just a Christian nation; we are also a Jewish nation, a Muslim nation, a Buddhist nation, a Hindu nation, and a nation of nonbelievers," Obama wrote in an e-mail to CBN News senior national correspondent David Brody.[3]

"We should acknowledge this and realize that when we're formulating policies from the state house to the Senate floor to the White House, we've got to work to translate our reasoning into values that are accessible to every one of our citizens, not just members of our own faith community," wrote Obama.

In his January 20, 2009, Inaugural Address to the nation, Obama echoed his earlier remarks, declaring America to be a nation of many faiths that includes Muslims and "nonbelievers."[4]

Obama's outspoken emphasis on religious pluralism is at the very least debatable, coming as it has from a U.S. senator and now from the U.S. president, of a country of more than 300 million people, who are on the whole quite religiously observant by Western standards, and of whom about 76 percent are Christians. One could legitimately argue over the need for, the appropriateness of, or the public policy implications of, Obama's "post-Christian" rhetoric. And one could say it is the president whose notions of America are "divisive," rather than those of conservative Christians.

But such "post-Christian" rhetoric, coupled as it is with the distorted view by the president of the size of America's Muslim population—as detailed by him in an interview for French television five months after his inauguration, and in his much-ballyhooed address to the Muslim world in Cairo a month later—is not debatable. It is simply wrong.

In the French television interview, Obama claimed the number of American Muslims would make America "one of the largest Muslim countries in the world."[5] That assertion, however, is demonstrably false. Even if it were true that the number of America's Muslims were anywhere near the politically inflated figure of seven or eight million, this would barely place the U.S. in the top 50 of countries having significant Muslim populations.[6] In his major speech on Islam delivered on June 4th in Cairo, Obama cited the figure of "seven million American Muslims." But most scientific, or at least de-politicized, estimates put the U.S. Muslim population at well under four million, or well under half of the president's number.[7]

Obama, meanwhile, has talked at length about his Christian faith and his journey to Christianity. He was baptized in 1988 at Chicago's Trinity United Church of Christ, his church of about 20 years, a mostly black congregation led by the Reverend Jeremiah Wright, Jr., whose inflammatory statements on race, America, and Israel stirred a major controversy for Obama during the presidential campaign.[8] Yet rumors persisted that Obama is a closet Muslim. A July 2008 poll by *Newsweek* taken in the heat of the presidential campaign found that 12 percent of Americans at the time believed Obama was a Muslim.[9]

The authors of this book found no evidence whatsoever indicating that Obama is today a Muslim. His professed Christianity and long association with churches (however radical) must be taken at face value. In this chapter we will review the brand of Christianity practiced for many years by Obama, as well as his Islamic roots, his ongoing ties to Islam and Kenyan tribalism—as well as to radical Middle Eastern associates, individuals whom the politician has acknowledged helped to color his world views.

"OBAMA WAS QUITE RELIGIOUS IN ISLAM"

Widely distributed reports have noted that in January 1968, Obama was registered as a Muslim at Jakarta's Roman Catholic Franciscus Assisi Primary School under the name Barry Soetoro. He was recorded as an Indonesian citizen whose stepfather, listed on school documents as "L Soetoro Ma," worked for the topography department of the Indonesian Army. As we note in Chapter 5, a 2007 Associated Press photograph emerged of Obama's school registration papers at Assisi showing the future politician listed as a "Muslim" with "Indonesian" citizenship.[10] Indonesia is the world's largest Muslim nation, with a population nearing 240 million.

Catholic schools in Indonesia routinely accept non-Catholic students, but exempt them from studying religion. After attending the Assisi Primary School, Obama was enrolled—also as a Muslim, according to documents— in the Besuki Primary School, a public school in the capital of Jakarta.[11]

The *Loatze* blog, run by an American expatriate in Southeast Asia who visited the Besuki school, noted, "All Indonesian students are required to study religion at school and a young 'Barry Soetoro' being a Muslim would have been required to study Islam daily in school. He would have been taught to read and write Arabic, to recite his prayers properly, to read and recite from the *Quran* and to study the laws of Islam."[12] Indeed, in Obama's autobiography, *Dreams from My Father*, he acknowledges studying the *Quran* and describes the public school as "a Muslim school." "In the Muslim school, the teacher wrote to tell mother I made faces during *Quranic* studies," Obama wrote.[13]

The Indonesian media have been flooded with accounts of Obama's childhood Islamic studies, some describing him as a religious Muslim. The principal of Obama's school while he was enrolled there, Tine Hahiyary, said she recalls Obama then going by the name Barry Soetoro, studying the *Quran* in Arabic, in an interview with the country's *Kaltim Post*. "At that time, I was not Barry's teacher but he is still in my memory," claimed Tine, now 80 years old. The *Kaltim Post* says Obama's teacher, named Hendri, died. "I remember that he studied *mengaji* ([recitation of the *Quran*])," Tine said. *Mengaji*—the act of reading the *Quran* with its correct Arabic punctuation—is usually taught to more religious pupils and is not known as a secular study.[14]

The Indonesian daily *Banjarmasin Post* caught up with Rony Amir, an Obama classmate and Muslim, who described Obama as "previously quite religious in Islam."[15]

"We previously often asked him to the prayer room close to the house. If he was wearing a sarong ([waist fabric worn for religious or casual occasions]) he looked funny," Amir said.

The *Los Angeles Times* sent a reporter to Jakarta, who spoke with Zulfin Adi, self-identified as among Obama's closest childhood friends. Adi stated the future U.S. president prayed in a mosque, something Obama's presidential campaign was quick to deny.[16] "We prayed but not really seriously, just following actions done by older people in the mosque. But as kids, we loved to meet our friends and went to the mosque together and played," Adi said.

At one point, the Obama '08 campaign site had a page titled "Obama has never been a Muslim, and is a committed Christian." The page stated, "Obama never prayed in a mosque. He has never been a Muslim, was not raised a Muslim, and is a committed Christian who attends the United Church of Christ." But the campaign changed its tune when it issued a slightly different statement to the *Los Angeles Times*, stating Obama "has never been a practicing Muslim."[17]

An article in the *Chicago Tribune* seems to contradict Adi's portrayal of Obama's Muslim childhood to the *Los Angeles Times*. The *Tribune* catches up with Obama's declared childhood friend, who then described himself as only knowing Obama for a few months in 1970 when his family moved to the neighborhood. Adi told the *Tribune* he was unsure about his recollections of Obama.[18] But the *Tribune* did find Obama to have attended a mosque. On the one hand, "interviews with dozens of former classmates, teachers, neighbors and friends show that Obama was not a regular practicing Muslim when he was in Indonesia," stated the *Tribune* article. However, it quoted the presidential candidate's former neighbors and third grade teacher recalling Obama "occasionally followed his stepfather to the mosque for Friday prayers."

Islamic scholar Daniel Pipes, director of the Middle East Forum, noted that the *Tribune* article—cited by pro-Obama blogs to refute claims that Obama was Muslim—in fact implies Obama was an irregularly practicing Muslim and twice confirms that Obama attended mosque prayer services.[19]

KENYAN TRIBAL ROOTS

Some attention has also been paid to the paternal side of Obama's family, who are members of Kenya's Luo tribe. Obama's father, described in various accounts as an atheist, polygamist, and alcoholic, was buried in Kenya as a Muslim. Obama Sr. had three sons with another woman, who all reportedly are Muslims.

Obama's brother, Roy, is described as a practicing Muslim and a Luo activist. Obama's paternal grandmother, Sarah Obama, reportedly traveled to Saudi Arabia to perform the Muslim *haj* pilgrimage.[20] Writing in a chapter of his book, *Dreams from My Father*, describing his 1992 wedding, Obama related: "The person who made me proudest of all was Roy. Actually, now we call him Abongo, his Luo name, for two years ago he decided to reassert his African heritage. He converted to Islam, and has sworn off pork and tobacco and alcohol."[21]

Obama's Muslim family roots may have played a role in his apparent involvement in Kenyan politics since at least 2006, when, as a U.S. senator, he clearly backed the country's controversial opposition leader

Raila Amollo Odinga, who was running in his country's 2007 elections. Odinga later became prime minister in a power-sharing government, following a post-electoral crisis in which about 1,500 Kenyans were killed, in violence largely originally triggered by Odinga's supporters.

Odinga comes from the same Luo tribe as the paternal side of Obama's family. He has been described as Obama's cousin, but it was thought the family relationship was distant. Then, in a January 2008 interview with the BBC, Odinga stated that Obama's father was his maternal uncle.[22]

Odinga today is a social democrat who once served as a leader of the underground Kenyan Revolutionary Movement. He was accused of collaborating in a failed, bloody 1982 coup attempt against Kenyan President Daniel Arap Moi, and was later charged with treason and detained without trial for six years. Odinga's son is named after Cuban leader Fidel Castro.[23]

Odinga's bid for his country's 2007 elections received a boost when his putative cousin, then-Senator Obama, seemed to campaign for him. At the time, Odinga was running against President Mwai Kibaki, who was seeking a second term. Though Obama visited Kenya for six days in 2006, he later denied his trip was meant to campaign for Odinga. According to the *Washington Times*:

> Mr. Odinga and Mr. Obama were nearly inseparable throughout Mr. Obama's six-day stay. The two traveled together throughout Kenya and Mr. Obama spoke on behalf of Mr. Odinga at numerous rallies. In contrast, Mr. Obama had only criticism for Kibaki. He lashed out against the Kenyan government shortly after meeting with the president on Aug. 25. "The [Kenyan] people have to suffer over corruption perpetrated by government officials," Mr. Obama announced.[24]
>
> "Kenyans are now yearning for change," Obama declared.[25]

"The intent of Mr. Obama's remarks and actions was transparent to Kenyans—he was firmly behind Mr. Odinga," the *Washington Times* concluded.

Lynn Sweet of the *Chicago Sun-Times* accompanied Obama on his Kenya trip. She reported that Obama appeared at campaign stops with Odinga. If there had been any question as to Obama's intentions, that doubt was removed when the Kenyan government called Obama a "stooge" for Odinga.[26]

Odinga and Obama reportedly had met several times before Obama's 2006 trip and were in touch several times since. On January 8, 2008, *Newser* reported Obama "wades into Kenyan fray," noting that Obama "called Kenyan opposition leader Raila Odinga in an effort to help defuse the bloody post-election standoff in the African nation."[27]

If Joe Klein at *Time* was correct in his January 7, 2008, article, "Obama's Other Life," in 2008 Obama was having "near-daily conversations with the U.S. Ambassador in Kenya or with opposition leader Raila Odinga." This was at the time of postelectoral violence in which supporters of Odinga alleged the 2007 elections had been manipulated, a contention later confirmed by international observers.[28] Targeted ethnic violence was directed at first mainly against the Kikuyu tribe—the community of which Kibaki, the claimed winner, is a member. The violence led to a UN-brokered power-sharing agreement, installing a cabinet headed by Odinga as prime minister.

BLACK LIBERATION THEOLOGY

While Obama professes Christianity, an issue which received a significant amount of coverage in spring 2008, what's often overlooked has been the brand of Christianity preached in Obama's Chicago church of 20 years, the Trinity United Church of Christ. Its pastor during Obama's tenure at the church, Rev. Jeremiah Wright, Jr., closely follows the ideology of James Cone, considered the founder of black-liberation theology. Cone's main thesis is that true Christianity is specific to the black liberation experience, and that traditional Christianity as commonly practiced in the United States is racist and against "true" Christianity.[29]

"The black theologian must reject any conception of God which stifles black self-determination by picturing God as a God of all peoples. Either God is identified with the oppressed to the point that their experience becomes God's experience, or God is a God of racism," writes Cone in his defining book, *A Black Theology of Liberation*.[30]

"The blackness of God means that God has made the oppressed condition God's own condition. This is the essence of the biblical revelation,"

Cone argues. Cone's brand of Christianity strongly condemns any Christian practice that does not take a specific political approach that is largely very liberal and liberation-focused.

We document in Chapter 7 that Wright's publication, *Trumpet* magazine, evidenced close links between the pastor and the Nation of Islam. Additionally, however, the magazine was filled with Cone-style views on Christianity, as noted by Stanley Kurtz, a *National Review Online* contributor who reviewed two years of *Trumpet* editions.[31]

The April 2007 *Trumpet*, for example, featured an article by black-liberation theologian Obery M. Hendricks, Jr., who attacks conservative Christians as "emulating those who killed Jesus, rather than following the practice of Jesus himself."[32] "Many good church-going folk have been deluded into behaving like modern-day Pharisees and Sadducees when they think they're really being good Christians," contends Hendricks, who writes in *Trumpet* that these believers have become "like the false prophets of Baal."

"George Bush and his unwitting prophets of Baal may well prove to be the foremost distorters of the true practice of Jesus' Gospel of peace, liberation, and love ever seen in modern times," Hendricks writes.

In an August 2007 issue of *Trumpet*, Wright argues that Jesus is "African," and he attacks "white" Christianity as "make-pretend": "How do I tell my children about the African Jesus who is not the guy they see in the picture of the blond-haired, blue-eyed guy in their Bible or the figment of white supremacists [sic] imagination that they see in Mel Gibson's movies?"[33] Authentic, liberation Christianity, says Wright, "is far more than the litmus test given by some Gospel music singers and much more than the cosmetic facade of make-pretend white Christianity." Wright denounces "colored preachers" who do not subscribe to black liberation theology as people who "hate themselves, who hate Black people, who desperately want to be white and who write and say stupid things in public to make 'Masa' feel safer."

Separately, Aaron Klein reviewed years of back issues of Obama's church newsletter during the 20 years the politician attended Trinity. Klein found that, aside from preaching black liberation theology, the publications were virulently anti-Israel.[34]

In the July 22, 2007, church newsletter, for example, Wright features a reprinted article on his "pastor's page" by Mousa Abu Marzook, identified in the publication as a "deputy of the political bureau of Hamas." In the article, Marzook defends terrorism as legitimate resistance, refuses to recognize the right of Israel to exist, and compares his terror group's official charter—which calls for the murder of Jews and Israel's destruction—to America's Declaration of Independence.[35] A church newsletter from June 10, 2007, first discovered by the *Sweetness & Light* blog, features an open letter from a Palestinian activist that labels Israel an "apartheid" regime, and claims the Jewish state worked on an "ethnic bomb" manufactured to kill "blacks and Arabs."[36]

TERROR-SUPPORTING FRIEND

Obama's ties to Palestinian radicalism extend far beyond his church. Perhaps one of Obama's closest Palestinian associates is Columbia University professor Rashid Khalidi, a harsh critic of Israel who not only makes statements supportive of Palestinian terror, but reportedly worked on behalf of the press agency associated with the Palestine Liberation Organization while it was involved in anti-Western terrorism and was labeled as a terror group by the State Department.[37]

Khalidi is said to have been an officer of the official PLO press agency WAFA in Beirut from 1976 to 1982.[38] At times Khalidi has denied working directly for the PLO, although he was also quoted numerous times by U.S. news organizations as seemingly speaking on behalf of the PLO. Khalidi's relationship with the PLO can be seen in his involvement, closely probed by Klein, with the Institute for Palestine Studies, a think tank established in Beirut in 1963 that stresses on its website it is an "independent, non-profit Arab institute unaffiliated with any political organization or government."[39] Khalidi started writing articles in the late 1970s for the institute's *Journal of Palestine Studies*. He currently serves as the general secretary of the institute and is considered one of its main leaders.

Although it claims to be independent, the Institute functioned as the clear intellectual arm of the PLO from its foundation until the early 1990s. Many of its board members and featured authors were early pioneers of

PLO ideology.[40] During documented speeches and public events, Khalidi has called Israel an "apartheid system in creation" and a destructive, "racist" state. He has multiple times expressed support for Palestinian terror, calling suicide bombings a response to "Israeli aggression."[41] He dedicated his 1986 book, *Under Siege*, to "those who gave their lives . . . in defense of the cause of Palestine and independence of Lebanon." Critics assailed the book as excusing Palestinian terrorism.[42]

According to a professor at the University of Chicago who told Aaron Klein he has known Obama for 12 years, the president first befriended Khalidi when the two worked together at the university. The professor spoke on condition of anonymity. Khalidi lectured at the University of Chicago until 2003 while Obama taught law there from 1993 until his election to the Senate in 2004. Khalidi in 2000 held what was described as a successful fundraiser for Obama's failed bid for a seat in the U.S. House of Representatives, a fact not denied by Khalidi. Speaking in a joint interview with Klein and the national *John Batchelor Show*, Khalidi was asked about his 2000 fundraiser for Obama.

"I was just doing my duties as a Chicago resident to help my local politician," Khalidi stated. Khalidi told Klein that he supports Obama for president "because he is the only candidate who has expressed sympathy for the Palestinian cause." Khalidi also lauded Obama for "saying he supports talks with Iran. If the U.S. can talk with the Soviet Union during the Cold War, there is no reason it can't talk with the Iranians." Khalidi terminated the call when petitioned further about his links with Obama.

In 2001, the Woods Fund, a Chicago-based nonprofit describing itself as a group helping the disadvantaged, bestowed a $40,000 grant upon the Arab American Action Network, or AAAN, for which Khalidi's wife, Mona, serves as president. The Fund provided a second grant to the AAAN for $35,000 in 2002. Obama served on the Woods Fund board at the same time as former Weatherman Bill Ayers.[43]

When Khalidi departed from the University of Chicago for a new teaching position at Columbia University, Obama delivered an in-person testimonial at Khalidi's farewell dinner. In a piece in April 2008, *Los Angeles Times* reporter Peter Wallsten claimed that he obtained video of Obama's 2003 testimonial, in which the politician praised Khalidi.

Obama reportedly reminisced about conversations over meals prepared by the professor's wife, Mona. The *Los Angeles Times*—at the height of the Democratic presidential primary campaign—refused to release the video.[44]

According to Wallsten's account of the farewell dinner, Obama said his talks with the Khalidis served as "consistent reminders to me of my own blind spots and my own biases. . . . It's for that reason that I'm hoping that, for many years to come, we continue that conversation—a conversation that is necessary not just around Mona and Rashid's dinner table," but around "this entire world."

Khalidi's farewell dinner was replete with anti-Israel speakers. One, a young Palestinian American, recited a poem in Obama's presence that accused the Israeli government of terrorism in its treatment of Palestinians and sharply criticized U.S. support of Israel, the *Times* reported. Another speaker, who reportedly talked while Obama was present, compared "Zionist settlers on the West Bank" to Osama bin Laden.[45]

Earlier, in the 1990s, Obama was involved in Palestinian activism in the sizable Palestinian immigrant community of Chicago. Obama spoke at Chicago fundraisers for Palestinians living in what the United Nations terms Middle East refugee camps.[46]

Ali Abunimah recalls introducing Obama as a speaker at one such event, a 1999 fundraiser for the Deheisha Palestinian "camp" in the West Bank. Abunimah is a Chicago-based Palestinian American activist and co-founder of *Electronic Intifada*, a pro-Palestinian online publication. Abunimah is also a harsh critic of Israel and has protested outside pro-Israel events in the Chicago area.

"I knew Barack Obama for many years as my state senator—when he used to attend events in the Palestinian community in Chicago all the time," stated Abunimah during a January 2008 interview with "Democracy Now!" a nationally syndicated radio and television political program.[47]

"I remember personally introducing [Obama] onstage in 1999, when we had a major community fundraiser for the community center in [the] Deheisha refugee camp in the occupied West Bank. And that's just one example of how Barack Obama used to be very comfortable speaking up for and being associated with Palestinian rights and opposing the Israeli occupation," Abunimah said.

Abunimah was also quoted as saying that until a few years ago, Obama was "quite frank that the U.S. needed to be more evenhanded, that it leaned too much toward Israel."[48] Abunimah noted Obama's unusual stance toward Israel, commenting, "these were the kind of statements I'd never heard from a U.S. politician who seemed like he was going somewhere, rather than at the end of his career."

Abunimah previously described meeting with Obama at a fundraiser at the home of Columbia University professor Rashid Khalidi. "[Obama] came with his wife. That's where I had a chance to really talk to him," Abunimah recalled. "It was an intimate setting. He convinced me he was very aware of the issues [and] critical of U.S. bias toward Israel and lack of sensitivity to Arabs. . . . He was very supportive of U.S. pressure on Israel."[49]

Abunimah recalled a 2004 meeting in a Chicago neighborhood while Obama was running for his Senate seat. Abunimah quoted Obama telling him "warmly" he was sorry that "I haven't said more about Palestine right now, but we are in a tough primary race."[50]

"I'm hoping when things calm down, I can be more up-front," Abunimah quoted the senator as saying. Abunimah said Obama urged him to "keep up the good work" at the *Chicago Tribune*, where Abunimah contributed guest columns that were highly critical of Israel.[51]

Perhaps it was Obama's reputed fondness for the Palestinian cause that was, at least in part, behind remarks by a top Hamas official to Aaron Klein and radio host John Batchelor during the presidential campaign. Hamas' chief political adviser in the Gaza Strip, Ahmed Yousef, notoriously told Klein and Batchelor during an April 2008 broadcast interview that he hoped Obama would win the presidential elections and "change" America's foreign policy.[52]

"We like Mr. Obama, and we hope that he will win the elections," Yousef said, speaking from Gaza. "I hope Mr. Obama and the Democrats will change the political discourse. . . . I do believe [Obama] is like John Kennedy, a great man with a great principle. And he has a vision to change America."

4

OBAMA'S RADICAL
ALINSKY TRAINERS

I N AN AUGUST 31, 2008, letter to the editor of the *Boston Globe*, radical organizer Saul Alinsky's son praised presidential candidate Barack Obama for having stirred up the masses at the Democratic National Convention, "Saul Alinsky style."

"Obama learned his lesson well," said the letter, signed L. David Alinsky. He closed by saying, "I am proud to see that my father's model for organizing is being applied successfully."[1]

There are those who point out that Barack Obama neither met, nor was trained by, radical community organizer and theorist Saul Alinsky. And this is almost certainly true, given that Alinsky passed away in 1972, before Obama was even a teen.

But the question of whether the two ever met is irrelevant, because, as we shall see, Obama was carefully educated and trained by Alinsky's personal disciples. And an understanding of Alinsky and his methods is absolutely fundamental to understanding the whole Obama phenomenon, including the defeat of Hillary Clinton and the overthrow of the moderate wing of the Democratic Party.

By far the most important analyst to date of the Alinsky/Obama phenomenon is sixties "radical-turned-conservative" author David Horowitz.

A self-described "red diaper baby," Horowitz edited the influential leftist monthly *Ramparts* magazine in the sixties and early seventies, and was a Students for a Democratic Society protester. But Horowitz became increasingly alienated from "the movement" in part after witnessing the impact of the U.S. abandonment of South Vietnam on the people of Indochina, as he later related in his political memoir, *Radical Son.*

Horowitz describes Alinsky as the "Communist/Marxist fellow-traveler who helped establish the dual political tactics of confrontation and infiltration that characterized the 1960s and have remained central to all subsequent revolutionary movements in the United States."[2] Although he never was a Communist Party member, Alinsky "became an avatar of the post-modern left," Horowitz says. Alinsky is generally considered the founder of the modern American movement of "community organizing." Though he was not trained directly by Alinsky, Barack Obama was trained by those who had been "immersed" for decades in Alinsky's "stratagems."[3]

Horowitz writes about his own career in the 1960s as an author of leftist books and editor of the "influential left wing rag" (pro-Hanoi, pro-Castro) *Ramparts* magazine. There Horowitz worked with fellow SDSers Todd Gitlin, now professor of journalism at Columbia University, and Robert Scheer, who started his own online magazine, *TruthDig*, after being fired from the *Los Angeles Times* in 2005. Horowitz recalls that some time after the men departed from *Ramparts*, in the early seventies, he encountered Scheer, "all decked out in establishment clothing," and questioned his "new look."[4] Scheer's response to Horowitz should be framed in gold leaf as the motto for Alinskyist "progressives" in America: He replied that he was working at the *LA Times* and said, "I'm going to bore from within."[5]

In the fall of 2009, Horowitz published a pamphlet analyzing Barack Obama and the influence Alinsky's thought and methods exercise over him. In "Barack Obama's Rules for Revolution": *The Alinsky Model*, Horowitz writes:

> The strategy of working within the system until you can accumulate
> enough power to destroy it was what sixties radicals called "boring from

within." It was a strategy that the New Left despised even as Alinsky and his followers practiced it. Alinsky and his followers infiltrated the War on Poverty, made alliances with the Kennedys and the Democratic Party, and secured funds from the federal government. Like termites, they set about to eat away at the foundations of the building in expectation that one day they could cause it to collapse.

As Horowitz points out, there was originally considerable hostility among New Left leadership over Alinskyist tactics, which departed from the Marxist-Leninist template of violent overthrow of the state. But as author Gary Starr points out, "Scheer crystallized the New Left's strategy . . . an ongoing effort since the 1970's to undermine the media, academia and the cities and become part of the process by joining the establishment they railed against as young 60's radicals."[6]

"ACCUMULATION OF POWER TO MAKE THE REVOLUTION"

One man who trained Barack Obama in Alinskyian techniques, when he first arrived in Chicago, was Gregory Galluzzo, a veteran community organizer. In a 2009 interview, Galluzzo described how he taught Obama "to embrace the organizing theories of Chicago radical Saul Alinksy, putting his pre-convictions on hold and conducting scores of interviews—'one-on-ones'—with local residents and community leaders in an attempt to find areas in which their self-interests converged and could be harnessed to create power and to drive communal action."[7]

Saul Alinsky was no orthodox communist. Alinsky was "too independent to join the Communist Party but instead became a forerunner of the left that emerged in the wake of the Communist fall," as David Horowitz writes.[8] For Alinsky, Horowitz writes, Communism was inflexible and dogmatic. Instead, Alinsky "proposed as a solution that radicals should be 'political relativists,' that they should take an agnostic view of means and ends." In Alinsky's view, the "revolutionary's purpose is to undermine the system and then see what happens. The Alinsky radical has a single principle—to take power from the Haves and give it to the Have-nots." This, Horowitz writes, is the "classic revolutionary formula in which the goal is power for the political vanguard, who get to feel good about themselves in the process."[9]

"At the height of his campaign," Horowitz relates, Barack Obama declared: "We are the ones we've been waiting for." This was the culmination of the movement Alinsky helped set in motion. Horowitz credits Alinsky with "[weaving] the inchoate relativism of the post-Communist left into a coherent whole, and [helping] to form the coalition of communists, anarchists, liberals, Democrats, black racialists, and social justice activists who spearheaded the anti-globalization movement just before 9/11, and then [created] the anti-Iraq War movement." This "coherent whole," as Horowitz calls it, in the end, "finally positioned one of their own to enter the White House."[10]

Contrary to Obama's claims in his 1995 book, *Dreams from My Father*, Obama "didn't quite find himself reliving the civil rights era," wrote Ryan Lizza on March 9, 2007, in *The New Republic*. Instead, Obama "soon found himself succumbing to the appeal of Alinsky's organizing methodology."[11] In Horowitz's words, "Infiltrating the institutions of American society and government—something the 'counter-cultural' radicals of the 1960s were reluctant to do—was Alinsky's *modus operandi*."[12] Lizza notes that, in his book, Obama devoted "some 150 pages on his four years in Chicago working as an organizer, but there's little discussion of the theory that undergirded his work and informed that of his teachers. Alinsky is the missing layer of his account."[13]

We know that Alinsky founded the Industrial Areas Foundation in 1940, saying his "idea was to train people to reorganize and rehabilitate their own neighborhoods." Alinsky used the IAF to infiltrate "faith-based organizations (such as churches)." After Alinksy's death in 1972, other "IAF-like organizing networks" emerged, such as the Association of Community Organizations for Reform Now (ACORN), Citizen Action, National People's Action, PICO, DART, and the Chicago-based Gamaliel Foundation.[14]

The Gamaliel Foundation is especially important in Obama's political development. Gamaliel blandly states that it believes in "shared abundance for all." Gamaliel "evolved from the Contract Buyers League, an African American Group founded in 1968 to fight discrimination in housing." The

foundation has its own "network with affiliates in nearly every major metropolitan area of the Midwest, as well as California, New York, and Pennsylvania." It has "launched more than forty-five congregation-based federations, a national clergy caucus of more than one thousand members,
and a women's leadership program."[15]

It was into the Gamaliel network that Barack Obama stepped when he
left New York at the end of the academic year, around June 1985, after
working for only three months as a community organizer for the New
York Public Interest Research Group. He applied for and was hired to
work as a community organizer in Chicago for the Developing Communities Project (DCP), a "group of about 10 poor and small black churches"
that "spanned communities in Northwest Indiana, the South Suburbs
and parts of the City of Chicago,"—all part of the Calumet Community
Religious Conference (CCRC).[16]

Describing it as an "organizing institute working throughout the
Midwest," Obama termed the Gamaliel Foundation a "cooperative think
tank."[17] The young Obama's work with Gamaliel was funded, in turn,
by the Woods Foundation. Later, from 1993 to 2002, Obama served on
the Woods Foundation board with former Weather terrorist leader and
"socialism advocate" William Ayers.[18]

Over the decades, Alinsky's vision went through various adaptations,
especially by Edward T. Chambers, the Alinsky acolyte who succeeded
the master himself in running the Industrial Areas Foundation, after
Alinsky died in 1972. The IAF "focuses on drawing people into active participation in the political and economic decisions that affect their lives
through the vehicle of their religious congregations," writes Danny Duncan Collum, in the April 2008 issue of *Sojourners* magazine, a left-leaning
Christian publication. "This brand of community organizing is congregation-based and faith-based," with the aim to "build metropolitan-area
networks of community leaders able to mobilize large numbers of their
parishioners and neighbors to change public policy and hold public officials accountable," Collum explains.[19]

The operative phrase in the above description is "through the vehicle
of their religious congregations." As David Horowitz emphasizes, citing
an SDS radical who once wrote, "'The issue is never the issue. The issue

is always the revolution.' In other words, the cause—whether inner city blacks or women—is never the real cause, but only an occasion to advance the real cause which is the accumulation of *power* to make the revolution. *That* was the all consuming focus of Alinsky and his radicals."[20]

OBAMA'S ALINSKY MENTORS

Gregory Galluzzo, Obama's first trainer in Chicago, described himself as an Alinsky "true believer" in a 2007 interview with Ryan Lizza of the *New Republic*. As had Obama's other teachers at the Gamaliel Foundation, Michael Kruglik and Gerald Kellman—who had hired Obama—Galluzzo said he had studied all of Alinsky's Industrial Areas Foundation "teachings."[21]

Galluzzo is an ex-Jesuit, a lead Gamaliel Foundation organizer, and an Obama mentor. He writes that at the same time the Foundation was being created, he met with Barack Obama "on a regular basis as he incorporated the Developing Communities Project." He writes that Obama was moving DCP into action and developing its "leadership structure." Obama, Galluzzo writes, "would write beautiful and brilliant weekly reports about his work and the people he was engaging."[22] In July 1988 Obama told *Illinois Issues* that, while working for the Developing Communities Project, he had also been a "consultant and instructor" for the Gamaliel Foundation, the "congregation-based Alinsky-style" organization.[23]

In reality, Barack Obama was not only working for the Gamaliel Foundation as a "consultant and instructor," but he was also helping to create Gamaliel itself, "Alinsky-style." Obama's fourth Gamaliel Foundation teacher is John L. McKnight, a "student of Alinsky's radical tactics." Referred to as Obama's principal community organizing mentor, McKnight is a former ACLU director and currently a Professor of Education and Social Policy at Northwestern University. He is also co-director of Northwestern University's Asset-Based Community Development Institute, where he "directs research projects focused on asset-based neighborhood development and methods of community building by incorporating marginalized people." McKnight also sits on the board of National People's Action, "an organization that employs the aggressive street tactics of Alinskyite organizing."[24]

Investor's Business Daily reported in September 2008 that McKnight "schooled" Obama in "the gospel according to Alinsky" because he "apparently saw much promise in the budding politician, [and] a way to advance Alinsky's radical socialist agenda into the highest levels of government." Prior to entering Harvard, Obama "praised McKnight and his organizing principles in an article titled "After Alinsky: Community Organizing in Illinois." While campaigning for the Presidential primary in Iowa, Obama called his community organizing years "the best education I ever had, better than anything I got at Harvard Law School."[25]

Galluzzo said Obama decided sometime in spring or early summer 1988 to leave the Developing Communities Project and the Gamaliel Foundation to attend Harvard Law. Obama approached McKnight for a letter of recommendation. Galluzzo said, upon his departure, that Obama "made sure that Gamaliel was the formal consultant" to the Developing Communities Project, the "organization he had created and to the staff that he had hired." Galluzzo added: "Barack has acknowledged publicly that he had been the director of a Gamaliel affiliate. He has supported Gamaliel throughout the years by conducting training both at the National Leadership Training events and at the African American Leadership Commission. He has also attended our public meetings."[26]

OBAMA AND "ALINSKY UNIVERSITY"

Investor's Business Daily commented in an August 28, 2008, editorial that, for three years, Obama had agitated "with marginal success for more welfare programs in South Side Chicago" and left to "study law to 'bring about real change'—on a large scale."[27]

"While at Harvard Law School," *IBD* added, Obama "still found time to hone his organizing skills. For example, he spent eight days in Los Angeles taking a national training course taught by Alinsky's Industrial Areas Foundation. With his newly minted law degree, he returned to Chicago to reapply—as well as teach—Alinsky's 'agitation' tactics."[28]

Here we have a minor, though not crucial, discrepancy as to when it was that Barack Obama attended the Industrial Areas Foundation training.

IBD indicates it was while he was still a law student at Harvard. Ryan Lizza agrees. In his March 2007 article, Lizza writes: "Even at Harvard, Obama kept a foot in the world of organizing. He spent eight days in Los Angeles taking a national training course taught by the IAF, a station of the cross for Alinsky acolytes."[29]

But Charlotte Allen of *The Weekly Standard* places the timing for Obama's training prior to his enrollment at Harvard. In the magazine's November 3, 2008, issue, Allen writes: "Not long before enrolling at Harvard Law School in 1988, Obama underwent IAF's standard eight-day training session for organizers. 'I was very impressed by him,' [IAF's Ed] Chambers told me. 'I told him that once he finished his schooling, to get back in touch with us. But he never did get back to us.'"[30]

Chambers dates Obama's IAF training in Los Angeles as sometime near the end of his Harvard education. Chambers "trained Barack Obama in street organizing when he moved from the *Harvard Law Review* to Chicago's South Side; and in the difference between what is, and what should be!" according to his 2008 and 2009 speaker profile for the American Monetary Institute's annual Reform Conference.[31]

That Obama trained under Chambers is without question, including in Alinsky's pragmatic radicalism. In an October 2008 *Rocky Mountain News* item, Zack Saidman writes: Obama "quotes a past IAF supervisor, Ed Chambers, who taught us all about the importance of 'understanding the world as is, as opposed to as we like it to be.'"[32] In fact, a chapter on "The World As It Is and the World As It Should Be" is included in Chambers' 2003 Alinskian book, *Roots for Radicals: Organizing for Power, Action, and Justice*.[33]

Alinsky's worldview found its way into an April 2009 talk to a London girls' school by First Lady Michelle Obama, who explained that, on her first date with Barack Obama, he took her to a "community meeting":

> As he talked to the residents in that community center, he talked about two concepts. He talked about "the world as it is" and "the world as it should be." And I talked about this throughout the entire campaign. What he said, all too often, is that we accept the distance between those two ideas. And sometimes we settle for the world as it is, even when it

doesn't reflect our values and aspirations. But Barack reminded us on that day, all of us in that room, that we all know what our world should look like. We know what fairness and justice and opportunity look like. We all know. And he urged the people in that meeting, in that community, to devote themselves to closing the gap between those two ideas, to work together to try to make the world as it is and the world as it should be, one and the same.[34]

It is obvious that Michelle and Barack Obama's words did not originate with the Obamas. Although they appear to have been taken straight from the teachings of his Industrial Areas Foundation mentor, Ed Chambers, we can also trace them directly to the writings of Chambers' mentor, Saul Alinsky himself. On page xix of Alinsky's *Rules for Radicals*, we find:

> As an organizer I start from the world as it is, as it is, not as I would like it to be. That we accept the world as it is does not in any sense weaken our desire to change it into what we believe it should be—it is necessary to begin where the world is if we are going to change it to what we think it should be. That means working in the system.[35]

Obama tied himself directly to Alinsky's tenets in a 1990 article, perhaps inspired by his Industrial Areas Foundation training, when Obama penned "Why Organize? Problems and Promise in the Inner City," published both in *Illinois Issues* and as Chapter 4 in *After Alinsky: Community Organizing in Illinois*.[36]

UNKNOWNS

It appears that following his graduation from Harvard Law School, Obama was not yet clear on what direction his career would take.

According to Lew Finfer, director of the Massachusetts Community Action Network and Organizing and Leadership Training Center, in 1991 a "former intern recommended that [I] recruit a Harvard Law School classmate who had been a community organizer in Chicago. The classmate's name was Barack Obama." According to Finfer, Obama "came for an interview" but said he was "interested in going back to Chicago and getting into politics."[37]

It is also unknown as to where in Los Angeles, whether while he was yet a student or following graduation, and with what host organization, Obama took his Industrial Areas Foundation training.

One likely host to Obama in that period is the United Neighborhoods Organization, "another broad-based, church-sponsored community in East Los Angeles." UNO was founded by Ernesto Cortés, Jr. UNO and IAF were "officially" affiliated in June 1972 after Cortés attended IAF's leadership training institute in Chicago and worked with IAF "leaders in Wisconsin and Indiana for a year developing his skills as a community organizer."[38]

Before departing Boston, it is also quite possible that Obama made two other contacts, which served him well after returning to Chicago, as well as on the presidential campaign trail. Both men served as his campaign advisers.[39]

The first is Marshall Ganz, a lecturer in public policy at the Hauser Center for Nonprofit Organizations at Harvard's John F. Kennedy School of Government. Ganz is a former civil rights activist and staff member for the Student Nonviolent Coordinating Committee who worked with César Chávez and the United Farm Workers beginning in 1965. In 1980 Ganz became UFW's Director of Organizing. In 1991 Ganz returned to Harvard to complete his undergraduate degree in history and government; in 1993 he earned an MPA from the Kennedy School; and Ganz completed his Ph.D. in sociology in 2000.[40]

In California, Ganz was "mentored by figures from Saul Alinksy's community organizing movement," skills which he put to good use during the Obama campaign in training organizers. According to one account, Ganz may have cut his teeth in 2004 when he was a "key advisor" for a "special organizing program" in New Hampshire for presidential candidate Howard Dean.[41]

The second Obama advisor possibly from his Boston/Cambridge years is Peter Dreier, who is currently E.P. Clapp Distinguished Professor of Politics, and director of the Urban & Environmental Policy Program, at Occidental College in Los Angeles.[42] While Obama was a student at Harvard Law, Dreier served for nine years, 1984–1992, as director of housing for the Boston Redevelopment Authority and senior policy adviser to Boston Mayor Ray Flynn. He was also on the board of the National Housing Institute, publisher of *Shelterforce* magazine.[43]

Dreier is often referred to as an urban policy expert or a federal housing expert; his name is associated with "housing justice" and "social justice." His Oxy curriculum vitae states that he worked with both of the Alinskyist groups, ACORN and IAF, and that he "wrote a report for the Ford Foundation and Demos (a public policy think tank) evaluating current federal housing programs and recommend[ed] a variety of reforms to strengthen housing policy's effectiveness and political constituency." In 1999 Obama was one of those tapped to help develop Demos.[44]

Dreier has been active with Democratic Socialists of America since the 1980s in New Jersey. At the 2005 DSA convention, it was former Boston DSA Executive Board Member Dreier who gave a "moving speech eulogizing DSA Founding Chair Michael Harrington." Dreier is also a signatory for the radical support group formed during Obama's presidential campaign, Progressives for Obama.[45]

Both Dreier and Obama left Boston in 1992. Having graduated from Harvard, Obama returned to Chicago to lead Project VOTE! in conjunction with ACORN. The leadership of a "little-known" African American lawyer and community organizer, Barack Obama, resulted in the "most effective minority voter registration drive in memory," wrote Gretchen Reynolds in the January 1993 issue of *Chicago Magazine*. "More than 150,000 new African-American voters were added to the city's rolls" for the November 1992 election. It was "an all-time high," Reynolds wrote.[46]

ALINSKYITE-LED GROUP

But by January 1993, Project VOTE! operations in Chicago had "officially closed down." And so, as he had told MCAN director Lew Finfer in Boston, Obama was returning to Chicago to seek political office. When asked the same question in Chicago, Obama had coyly responded: "My sincere answer is, I'll run if I feel I can accomplish more that way than agitating from the outside."[47]

Also in 1992, Obama served on the founding board of the nonprofit Public Allies, an organization dedicated to training a cadre of community organizers. The story goes that, when co-founders Vanessa Kirsch and Katrina Browne started putting together a "new organization to train young people for public service," Kirsch kept hearing about "this guy in Chicago; you've got to meet with him," wrote Suzanne Perry in April 14, 2008, issue of *The Chronicle of Philanthropy*.[48]

Obama "ended up playing a critical role" in Public Allies, which was funded from the beginning with federal money from the Commission on National and Community Service.Perry wrote that Obama attended a "conference that laid the groundwork" for Public Allies. When Public Allies decided to open a Chicago office, Barack Obama "suggested the group interview his wife, Michelle."[49-50]

But there is a slightly different version of the story. Obama's Gamaliel Foundation Alinsky mentor, John L. McKnight, and Jody Kretzmann headed the Asset-Based Community Development Institute at Northwestern University. Public Allies CEO, Paul Schmitz, was also an original faculty member at ABCDI. A fourth ABCDI original faculty member was Michelle Obama.[51]

It just so happens that ABCDI has a "strategic alliance" with Public Allies' consulting group, The Leadership Practice, "through which [it] provide[s] training and consulting services on how to better identify and mobilize local community assets and participation to strengthen communities." Little imagination is needed to understand how Michelle Obama became the founding Executive Director of Public Allies Chicago from spring 1993 until fall 1996. As well, she served on Public Allies national board of directors from 1997 until 2001. Barack Obama left the Public Allies national board when Michelle Obama was hired.Public Allies reports that Barack Obama continued with Public Allies as "an active volunteer and supporter." Obama "trained several classes of Allies in community organizing" and spoke at Public Allies Chicago events.[52-54]

Even while seeking a political office, Obama continued his ties with both the Developing Communities Project and the Gamaliel Foundation, as Greg Galluzzo wrote. And the DCP was rapidly growing in power. As Steven Malanga wrote on September 8, 2008, in the *New York Post*, the

Developing Communities Project, which had started out as a "faith-based grass-roots organization organizing and advocating for social change . . . evolved into a government contractor."[55]

Obama adopted the big-government ethos that prevails among neighborhood organizers, who view attempts to reform poverty programs as attacks on the poor. . . . He also derided the "old individualistic bootstrap myth" of achievement that conservatives were touting and called self-help strategies for the poor "thinly veiled excuses for cutting back on social programs."

Obama stuck by those ideas as a state senator. His supporters count among his biggest victories his work to expand subsidized health care in Illinois with social-justice groups like United Power for Action and Justice (an offshoot of Alinsky's Industrial Areas Foundation).

"Alinsky Comes Home to Chicago," reported the November/December 1997 issue of *New Ground*, the Chicago Democratic Socialists of America's online newsletter. The occasion was the launch of the new leftist organization, "an offshoot of Alinsky's Industrial Areas Foundation"—United Power for Action and Justice.[56]

New Ground reported that nearly 10,000 people gathered for UPAJ's first conference at the University of Illinois Pavilion on October 19, 1997. Described as a "fulfillment of the late Cardinal Joseph Bernardin's vision for a broad based community organization, to which the Archdiocese offered to match funds from other groups," the "purpose was to demonstrate a unity already existing" with Jewish, Catholic, and Muslim groups. The report also touted that the "ability to bring out people by the thousands indicates a significant power base." Most of that "power base" came from four unions: SEIU Local 73, IBEW Local 134, Illinois Education Association, and Chicago Federation of Labor, a small number of unions compared with the large number of religious bodies. Although at the time the Chicago Democratic Socialists of America "expressed interest in the group, no response [had] yet been received."[57-58]

Alinsky protégé Ed Chambers, and "his small band of organizers— never more than three—expanded United Power's sponsoring list to include unions," according to David Moberg, senior editor at *In These Times*, writing in 2006 in *The New Chicago: A Social and Cultural Analysis*. Besides those previously mentioned, the sponsoring unions included the American Federation of State, County and Municipal Employees (AFSCME), as well as the Muslim community and the Jewish community "(although official Jewish community sponsorship lapsed, and only a few congregations [had] remained active)."[59]

Moberg called United Power for Action and Justice an "organization of organizations." In Saul Alinsky's IAF "parlance," Moberg wrote, a "broad-based organization." Although Moberg refers to community organizations "and other institutions, such as community health centers," who became UPAJ members, he does not name them.[60]

UPAJ "adopted FamilyCare as a major campaign" and worked on it with "key legislators," Moberg writes. In particular, UPAJ collaborated with State Senator Barack Obama to "expand children's health insurance in Illinois."[61]

United for Power and Justice "gave Obama a prominent platform to address its multiracial, metropolitan membership during his 2004 bid for the U.S. Senate," Moberg wrote at the National Housing Institute's website in spring 2007. Ever the community organizer, "Barack was not just willing to meet with community-based groups, not only to be a good vote for us, but he also strategized with us to help move our position forward,"said William McNary, co-director of Citizen Action/Illinois.[62]

Not much has changed since then. The Industrial Areas Foundation, and all "its progeny," were instrumental in promoting Barack Obama's presidential candidacy."[63] The same ties formed with United for Power and Justice and Citizen/Action since he was an Illinois State Senator have now put Barack Obama in the White House. And these ties continue into his presidency.

"The activist community knows he's one of them. As an organ of the National Housing Institute, a social-justice group, has observed: 'Barack Obama carries lessons he learned as a community organizer to the political arena. Both organizers and politicians would be wise to study them closely,'" Steven Malanga writes.[64]

5

ISSUES OF ELIGIBILITY

Like much of President Obama's life, the facts surrounding the politician's birth and childhood years are clouded in mystery. None of the issues, known or unknown, that might raise legal questions about his Constitutional eligibility to serve as president have been explored in any depth by the U.S. government or the mainstream news media. Naturally, if a sitting president were subsequently found to have been ineligible to hold that office, it would precipitate a profound political crisis.

According to Hawaiian documentation, Barack Obama was born on August 4, 1961, to Stanley Ann Dunham and Barack Obama, Sr. Dunham was a white American of predominantly English descent from Wichita, Kansas, and was 18 years old at the time of Obama's birth. Obama Sr. was a member of the Luo tribe from Nyang'oma Kogelo, Nyanza Province, Kenya, which at the time was still a British colony. While Obama Sr. was a foreign student on scholarship at the University of Hawaii at MÐnoa, he met Anna Dunham.

The official story claims Dunham and Obama Sr. were married on February 2, 1961. The pair separated two years later, and they divorced in 1964. Obama's father returned to Kenya and saw his son only once more before being killed in an automobile accident in 1982.

It is not clear whether Obama's parents were ever legally married. No official records have ever been produced showing that a legal ceremony took place. No wedding certificate or photograph of a ceremony for Dunham and Obama Sr. have ever been found or published. In his book, *Barack and Michelle: Portrait of an American Marriage*, former *Time* magazine contributing editor Christopher Andersen elaborates: "There were certainly no witnesses ([to the alleged civil marriage ceremony])—no family members were present, and none of their friends at the university had the slightest inkling that they were even engaged." Andersen further quoted Representative Neil Abercrombie (D-HI), a self-described friend of Barack Obama Sr. and Anna Dunham in 1961, as saying that "nobody" was invited to the wedding ceremony.

Obama himself, on page 22 of his autobiographical *Dreams from My Father*, wrote of his parents' wedding: "In fact, how and when the marriage occurred remains a bit murky, a bill of particulars that I've never quite had the courage to explore. There's no record of a real wedding, a cake, a ring, a giving away of the bride. No families were in attendance; it's not even clear that people back in Kansas were fully informed. Just a small civil ceremony, a justice of the peace. The whole thing seems so fragile in retrospect, so haphazard."

Obama's birth status is further complicated by the fact that when Obama Sr. arrived in Hawaii at the age of 23, in September 1959, he was already married. His wife, since age 18, was a Kenyan woman named Kezia Aoko, who was allegedly pregnant with Obama Sr.'s first child when he abandoned her in Africa in 1957. Obama Sr. later returned to Kenya and ultimately had four children with Aoko. There is no evidence to suggest Obama Sr. was divorced from Aoko either in Kenya, before he left for Hawaii, or in Hawaii prior to the purported marriage with Dunham.[1]

On page 126 of *Dreams from My Father*, Barack Obama, Jr. described his father's marriage with Aoko by quoting his mother Ann: "And then there was a problem with your father's first wife . . . he had told me they were separated, but it was a village wedding, so there was no legal documentation that could show a divorce." The suggestion seems to be that bigamy was not at issue in Obama Sr.'s purported marriage with Dunham since Obama Sr.'s marriage to Aoko was a "village wedding" that possibly would not have been recognized under Hawaiian civil law. Obama Sr.

was reportedly a polygamist who had at least four wives, including Ruth Nidesand, an American whom Obama Sr. later met while at Harvard. Nidesand followed Obama Sr. back to Kenya.

There are further questions about the exact period in which Dunham became pregnant and whether she and Obama Sr. ever truly lived together as man and wife, but those issues are tangential to this discussion. Other questions, regarding Obama's birth certificate, will be raised later in this investigation.

What is immediately clear, however, is that, if Obama's parents are indeed Dunham and Obama Sr., then Obama was the son of an American mother and a father who was a citizen of Kenya, and thus a British subject, in 1961. It is undisputed that Obama's father was not a U.S. citizen, a fact that should have led to congressional debate about whether Obama is eligible under the United States Constitution to serve as president.

NATURAL BORN CITIZEN?

Article 2, Section 1, Clause 5 of the U.S. Constitution stipulates presidential eligibility, requiring the nation's elected chief to be a "natural born citizen." Specifically, the clause states: "No person except a natural born Citizen, or a Citizen of the United States, at the time of the Adoption of this Constitution, shall be eligible to the Office of President; neither shall any Person be eligible to that Office who shall not have attained to the Age of thirty-five Years, and been fourteen Years a Resident within the United States."

The Fourteenth Amendment to the Constitution specifically defines "citizen": "All persons born or naturalized in the United States, and subject to the jurisdiction thereof, are Citizens of the United States and of the State wherein they reside." However, no definition of "natural born citizen" was provided anywhere in the Constitution, and to this day the precise meaning of the term is still being debated. There are no records of any definitive discussion on the matter during the Constitutional Convention. That—coupled with the absence of definitive Supreme Court rulings and a wide array of opinions throughout the centuries—has only further confused the question of what "natural born" actually means.

The first United States Congress actually passed a law that began to define "natural born." The Naturalization Act of 1790 rejected the condition of being born on U.S. soil, and referred only to parentage: "The children of citizens of the United States, that may be born beyond sea, or out of the limits of the United States," the Act states, "shall be considered as natural born citizens: Provided, that the right of citizenship shall not descend to persons whose fathers have never been resident in the United States."[2] Five years later, however, Congress repealed the Act.

Still, it was clear that the intention of the Constitution's "natural born citizen" qualification was to ensure the country would not be led by an individual with dual loyalties. On July 25, 1787, Founding Father John Jay, one of the three authors of the *Federalist Papers*, wrote to George Washington, who was at the time presiding over the Constitutional Convention in Philadelphia. Jay discussed the dual loyalty concern, writing: "Permit me to hint, whether it would be wise and seasonable to provide a strong check to the admission of Foreigners into the administration of our national Government; and to declare expressly that the Commander in Chief of the American army shall not be given to nor devolve on, any but a natural born Citizen." Jay, however, also did not define "natural born."[3]

In trying to understand what the Founding Fathers meant by "natural born," some have turned to prominent legal tomes of the day. *The Law of Nations*, a 1758 work by Swiss legal philosopher Emmerich de Vattel, was read by many of the American Founders and informed their understanding of the principles of law, which became established in the Constitution of 1787. De Vattel writes in Book 1, Chapter 19, of his treatise, "The natives, or natural-born citizens, are those born in the country, of parents who are citizens. As the society cannot exist and perpetuate itself otherwise than by the children of the citizens, those children naturally follow the condition of their fathers, and succeed to all their rights. . . . In order to be of the country, it is necessary that a person be born of a father who is a citizen; for, if he is born there of a foreigner, it will be only the place of his birth, and not his country."[4]

So by de Vattel's standards, Obama arguably would not be eligible to serve as president.

Representative John Bingham of Ohio, a principal framer of the

Fourteenth Amendment, offered some definition for presidential quali-fications in a discussion in the House on March 9, 1866: "[I] find no fault with the introductory clause [S 61 Bill], which is simply declaratory of what is written in the Constitution, that every human being born within the jurisdiction of the United States of parents not owing allegiance to any foreign sovereignty is, in the language of your Constitution itself, a natural born citizen."[5]

So according to Bingham, as well, Obama would not be eligible to serve as president.

Numerous Supreme Court decisions have yielded conflicting views of citizenship and what it means to be a "natural born citizen." In *Dred Scott v. Sandford* (1857), for example, the Court ruled that citizenship is acquired by place of birth, not through blood or lineage.[6] But much of that case's decision—which had notoriously excluded slaves, and their descendants, from possessing Constitutional rights—was overturned in 1868.

Another case, *Minor v. Happersett*, in 1874, mentions the "natural born" issue:

> At common law, with the nomenclature of which the framers of the constitution were familiar, it was never doubted that all children born in a country, of parents [plural] who were its citizens [plural], became themselves, upon their birth, citizens also. These were natives or nat-ural-born citizens, as distinguished from aliens or foreigners. Some authorities go further, and include as citizens children born within the jurisdiction, without reference to the citizenship of their parents. As to this class there have been doubts, but never as to the first. For the purposes of this case, it is not necessary to solve these doubts. It is suf-ficient, for everything we have now to consider, that all children, born of citizen parents within the jurisdiction, are themselves citizens.[7]

According to this definition, and scores of other Supreme Court rul-ings, Obama may not be eligible to serve as president.

The authors of this book are not constitutional lawyers (though Presi-dent Obama is), and while we did consult with some, we do not purport to be experts in constitutional law. Yet a layman's reading of readily available legal resources regarding the definition of "natural born citizen" clearly indicates a series of legitimate questions about Barack Obama's eligibility for the presidency, given that Obama's father was not an American citizen. The resources warrant further debate. Still, the legislative and judicial bodies of the U.S. government have held no formal discussions, nor did they conduct a single formal investigation into whether Obama is eligible to serve under the Fourteenth Amendment.

Congress did, however, question the "natural born" qualifications of Obama's 2008 presidential opponent, Senator John McCain. The scion of distinguished U.S. naval officers, McCain was born to two American parents in the Panama Canal Zone. On April 30, 2008, the U.S. Senate sought to answer the question by passing a nonbinding resolution, which states, "Whereas John Sidney McCain, III, was born to American citizens on an American military base in the Panama Canal Zone in 1936: Now, therefore, be it resolved, that John Sidney McCain, III, is a 'natural born citizen' under Article II, Section 1, of the Constitution of the United States."[8] For some reason, the Senate did not address Obama's "natural born" status.

KENYA OR HAWAII?

Aside from the "natural born" debate, there is the question of whether Barack Obama has ever provided documentation that proves he was born in the United States. Understandably, given the unusual and complex story of his origin, there is ample speculation that he may have been born in Kenya. However, as of this writing, the authors find no convincing evidence that Obama was born in Kenya, nor that his birthplace was any place other than Hawaii, his declared state of birth.

The problem is that an extensive investigation by the authors also finds that the documentation President Obama has publicly released to date does not definitively prove his birthplace. Indeed, the released documents and information, and even statements from Hawaiian officials, raise crucial questions, largely ignored or ridiculed in the mainstream news media, which remain to this day unanswered.

Speculation that Obama was born in Kenya was stirred by a taped telephone conversation with Obama's Kenyan grandmother, Sarah Obama, on October 16, 2008, in which she purportedly claims that Barack Obama, Jr., was born in the Kenyan coastal city of Mombasa. The Sarah Obama interview was conducted by American Christian minister Ron McRae, who describes himself in an affidavit for an Obama eligibility lawsuit as an overseer of the Anabaptist Churches in North America and a "Presiding Elder on the African Presbytery."[9]

McRae called Sarah Obama in Kenya from Detroit, and says grandmother Sarah was in a public setting at the time, with several hundred people listening to the telephone call on a speakerphone. Unfortunately, the talk's audio content is quite difficult to decipher, and was conducted through an interpreter, identified by McRae as Vitalis Akech Ogombe, the community chairman of Sarah Obama's village of Nyang'oma Kogelo in Western Kenya, 30 miles west of the Lake Victoria city of Kisumu. As McRae testified in his sworn statement:

> In the ensuing public conversation, I asked Ms. Obama specifically, "Were you present when your grandson was born in Kenya?" This was asked to her in translation twice, and both times she replied, "Yes! Yes she was! She was present when Obama was born."[10]

During that conversation, however, Sarah Obama immediately clarifies that her illustrious grandson was born in Hawaii, not Kenya, and that she was not present for Obama's birth.

So the entire ensuing controversy involves a brief few seconds of the conversation in which President Obama's proud grandmother appears to have said she was present in Kenya for Barack's birth. Critics point out many reasons to be skeptical of the claim, including the possibility that something was lost in the translation between an American minister who presupposed Obama was born in Kenya and an elderly African woman who reportedly knows no English. Amid cross-talk in a combination of English, Swahili, and the local Luo tribal dialect, could she have understood McRae simply to be asking where she was when Barack Obama Jr. was born?

Many versions of the tape posted by bloggers, who contend it is proof that Obama was born in Kenya, are cut off immediately after the point where the grandmother apparently affirms her presence at the birth. The truncated versions leave out the section—fully available on YouTube—in which the interpreter insists she actually meant the birth took place in the United States.

A story by Tim Jones of the Tribune News Service, filed March 27, 2007, is based on interviews with childhood acquaintances of Obama and of his mother, Stanley Ann Dunham. The Tribune article reports their accounts of how grandmother Sarah Obama received a letter from her son, Barack Obama Sr., telling of his plan to marry Stanley Ann Dunham. Sarah's husband, Hussein Onyango Obama, was said to be angered by the news. Six months later, Jones reported, the Kenyan family received a letter announcing the August 4, 1961, birth of Barack Jr. The Tribune reporter noted an interview with Sarah Obama in which she said she was "so happy to have a grandchild in the U.S."[11]

Aside from the inference that the grandmother first learned of the birth through a letter, the Kenyan patriarch's anger over the marriage makes it even more unlikely that Ann Dunham would have traveled to Kenya during her pregnancy.

Other skeptics have pointed to comments by the Kenyan ambassador to the United States, Peter N.R.O. Ogego, who implied in a November 6, 2008, radio interview—two days after Obama's presidential victory—that Obama was born in Kenya. Ogego was asked by Detroit radio talk-show hosts Mike Clark, Trudi Daniels, and Marc Fellhauer, on WRIF's "Mike in the Morning" program: "One more quick question: President-elect Obama's birthplace over in Kenya, is that going to be a national spot to go visit, where he was born?" The ambassador replied, "It's already an attraction. His paternal grandmother is still alive." But Ambassador Ogego's assistant later insisted the diplomat was speaking about Barack Obama, Sr., and not President Obama.[12]

Even had Sarah Obama insisted to this day that the U.S. president was born in Kenya, and had Ambassador Ogego indeed meant that the U.S. leader was birthed in his home country, such claims would not be sufficient evidence to prove Obama's birthplace. One would require Kenyan birth documentation—documents never produced despite numerous unsubstantiated claims, including debunked documents claiming to be Obama's Kenyan birth certificate that were put up for sale on eBay.

THE BIRTH CERTIFICATE ISSUE

On the other hand, neither does the sole document produced by the Obama camp, ostensibly to prove his U.S. birth, in fact definitively establish the politician's origin.

After the release of a "Certification of Live Birth," or COLB, made available online during the 2008 presidential campaign, Obama and his team then claimed, and continue to claim, that the politician had released his birth certificate. However, there are major, important differences between the COLB Obama has produced and a regular, long-form birth certificate. And so the question remains: where is his normal birth certificate, if one exists, and what does it say? And why has the Obama team never produced it?

An official long-form birth certificate is an exact photocopy of the original birth record prepared by the hospital or attending physician at the time of a child's birth. Such a document usually includes parents' information (address of residence, race, birthplace, date of birth, etc.), additional information on the child's birthplace, and information on the doctors who assisted in the birth. The long form also usually includes the signature of the doctor involved and of at least one of the parents.

The short form COLB which Obama has made public is a computer-generated certification that lists the child's name, date of birth, gender, place of birth and time, and the names of Obama's parents. No birth hospital or doctor is listed.

Some might be inclined to accept Obama's COLB as proof of his birthplace since it is a state-generated document specifying the president's place of birth as Hawaii. The fact is, however, that in 1961, the year of Obama's birth, there were multiple ways to obtain a Hawaiian COLB that would leave open the possibility of the child being born outside the state.

An investigation published on the website of the Western Journalism Center claimed to have found four ways to obtain a COLB in 1961. Also, the State of Hawaii's Department of Health still lists on its website at least one method, described below, of obtaining a COLB without providing the state with conclusive proof of a Hawaiian birth.[13]

Among the methods of obtaining a Hawaiian COLB in 1961, according to the Center's report:

- If the birth was attended by a physician or midwife, the attending medical professional was required to certify to the Department of Health the facts of the birth date, location, parents' identities, and other information.
- If a person was born in Hawaii but not attended by a physician or midwife, then one parent must provide the state with proof of residence in Hawaii as well as a pre-natal and post-natal certification by a physician. The pre-natal report would certify the mother was pregnant. The post-natal report would certify an examination of a newborn baby. This leaves open the possibility of a child being born outside of Hawaii but still receiving a state COLB.
- If a person was born in Hawaii but not attended by a physician or midwife, then, up to the first birthday of the child, a "Delayed Certificate" could be filed, which required that "a summary statement of the evidence submitted in support of the acceptance for delayed filing or the alteration [of a file] shall be endorsed on the certificates," which "evidence shall be kept in a special permanent file." The statute provided that "the probative value of a 'delayed' or 'altered' certificate shall be determined by the judicial or administrative body or official before whom the certificate is offered as evidence."[14]
- If a child is born in Hawaii for whom no physician or midwife filed a certificate of live birth, and for whom no Delayed Certificate was filed before the first birthday, then a Certificate of Hawaiian Birth could be issued upon testimony of an adult if the Office of the Lieutenant Governor was satisfied that the person was born in Hawaii, provided that the person had attained the age of one year.[15]

In 1955, the "secretary of the Territory" was in charge of this procedure. In 1960 it was transferred to the Office of the Lieutenant Governor.

This provision left open the possibility of a child being born outside of Hawaii but still receiving a state COLB.

Amazingly, to this day Hawaiian procedures leave open the possibility of obtaining a short-form COLB for children or even adults born elsewhere. As of this publication, the Hawaiian government's official website lists in S338-17.8 of its state law on official forms, what it titles "rules to obtain Certificates for children born out of State."

That law states:

(a) Upon application of an adult or the legal parents of a minor child, the director of health shall issue a birth certificate for such adult or minor, provided that proof has been submitted to the director of health that the legal parents of such individual while living without the Territory or State of Hawaii had declared the Territory or State of Hawaii as their legal residence for at least one year immediately preceding the birth or adoption of such child.

(b) Proof of legal residency shall be submitted to the director of health in any manner that the director shall deem appropriate. The director of health may also adopt any rules pursuant to chapter 91 that he or she may deem necessary or proper to prevent fraudulent applications for birth certificates and to require any further information or proof of events necessary for completion of a birth certificate.

(c) The fee for each application for registration shall be established by rule adopted pursuant to chapter 91. [16]

In other words, the form released by Obama could still today seemingly be legally obtained by a mother who gave birth to a child outside Hawaii, although such a certificate would not list "Hawaii" as the birthplace, as Obama's does. However, the methods previously described as being in force in 1961 allow several possibilities of obtaining a short-form COLB that lists Hawaii as the place of birth, even were a child not born in the state.

. . .

NEWSPAPER PROOF? STATEMENTS FROM HAWAIIAN OFFICIAL?

Two Hawaiian newspaper announcements from 1961 support the assertion of Obama's Hawaiian birth. However, both the newspapers in
question, the *Honolulu Star-Bulletin* and the *Honolulu Advertiser*, simply
reprint birth information they receive from Hawaii's Department of
Health, meaning Obama's parents did not have to place the announcements in the papers. The only legitimate conclusion that can be gleaned
from those newspaper announcements is that the State of Hawaii issued
a COLB documenting Obama's birth. This we already know. Regardless,
newspaper announcements, even if they had been placed at the time by
Obama's parents, are hardly official proof of birth.

Others claim the entire birth certificate matter was put to rest on July 22,
2009, when Hawaii's health director, Chiyome Fukino, released a statement
that she saw "original vital records" that prove "Barrack [sic] Hussein Obama
was born in Hawaii and is a natural-born American citizen":

> I, Dr. Chiyome Fukino, director of the Hawai'i State Department of
> Health, have seen the original vital records maintained on file by the
> Hawai'i State Department of Health verifying Barrack Hussein Obama
> was born in Hawai'i and is a natural-born American citizen. I have noth-
> ing further to add to this statement or my original statement issued in
> October 2008 over eight months ago.[17]

Thus read the entire statement, in which the president's first name was
misspelled and no detail given of the specific "vital records" reviewed.

Fukino's extremely careful statement actually raises more questions
than it answers. Which documents did she review? Was she referring
only to Obama's short-form COLB? Perhaps she was referring to pre-
natal and post-natal certifications that could technically allow for a parent to obtain a COLB for a child not born in Hawaii.

Also, it is inappropriate for Fukino to assert that Obama "is a natural-
born American citizen," since it is not within the authority of a Department of Health director to declare an individual "natural born," when
even the greatest legal minds of the last 235 years could not agree on

exactly what that term means. Indeed, as we saw earlier, according to the stated views of our Founding Fathers and multiple Supreme Court decisions, Obama may not be constitutionally qualified as "natural born," even if he were proved to have been birthed in Hawaii, given that his father was never a U.S. citizen.

In July 2009, Fukino referenced her October 2008 statement, in which she first announced she had "personally seen and verified that the Hawaii State Department of Health has Senator Obama's original birth certificate on record in accordance with state policies and procedures." That statement told us nothing new, unless there is a long-form birth certificate in the files. Otherwise, anyone with an Internet connection could see Obama's COLB, as posted on his campaign website.[18]

Despite the many questions left unanswered, no official government body has ever investigated these issues. Amazingly, one Republican lawmaker, Senator Jon Kyl of Arizona, when questioned by constituents about birth certificate issues, cited a website, *Snopes.com*, as conclusively laying these issues to rest.

Snopes.com is a "rumor-checking" website run by husband and wife team David and Barbara Mikkelson. The *Snopes* explanation to which Kyl referred directed readers back to another website, *FactCheck*, which in turn cites as documentation the COLB that the Obama campaign posted online, which, as we have shown, may not conclusively prove Obama's place of birth.[19]

YOUNG OBAMA WAS "INDONESIAN CITIZEN"

Another glaring eligibility issue—largely ignored by U.S. lawmakers as well as mainstream news media—centers around Obama's boyhood years in Indonesia, the world's most populous Muslim nation, where an investigation into Indonesian citizenship law and a review of Obama's biography and travels suggest the politician may have at one point been a citizen.

During the 2008 presidential campaign, Aaron Klein first broached the subject at *WorldNetDaily* after a little-noticed 2007 Associated Press photograph emerged of Obama's school registration papers as a child in Indonesia, showing the politician listed as a "Muslim" with "Indonesian"

citizenship. Jack Stokes, manager of media relations for the AP, confirmed to Klein the picture is indeed an AP photo.[20]

The photograph in question was taken by Tatan Syuflana, an Indonesian AP reporter and photographer. It shows an image of Obama's
registration card at Indonesia's Fransiskus Assisi School, a Catholic
institution. In the picture of the registration card, Obama is registered
under the name Barry Soetoro by his stepfather, Lolo Soetoro. The
school card lists Barry Soetoro as an Indonesian citizen born Aug. 4,
1961, in Honolulu, Hawaii. His religion is listed as Muslim. Following
his attendance at the Assisi Primary School, Obama was enrolled at
SDN Menteng 1, an Indonesian public school.

Obama's mother, Anna Dunham, was separated from Obama Sr. in
1963. She then married Lolo Soetoro, an Indonesian citizen, and moved
to Indonesia sometime between 1966 and 1967. It is not clear whether
Soetoro had legally adopted Obama, either in Hawaii or in Indonesia, but
there is strong circumstantial evidence that he did so in Indonesia, as far
as Indonesian law was concerned.

In Indonesia, which was under tight government rule in 1967, Obama
clearly took on the last name of his stepfather in school registration documents. All Indonesian students were required to carry government identity cards, or *Karty Tanda Pendudaks*, which needed to bear the student's
legal name, and which should be matched in public school registration
filings.[21]

Obama attended an Indonesian public school, following his enrollment
at the private Assisi School, until he returned to Hawaii at age ten. According to Indonesian legal experts contacted by Klein, it would have been
difficult to enroll a non-Indonesian citizen in public schooling. According to most accounts, Obama arrived in Indonesia at about the age of five,
although a few sources put his arrival there at age six. The age difference
matters, because if Lolo Soetoro adopted Obama at age five or younger,
then Obama would automatically have become an Indonesian citizen
according to the country's laws in the 1960s, which stipulated any child
aged five or younger adopted by an Indonesian father was immediately
granted Indonesian citizenship upon completion of the adoption process.[22]

Lolo Soetoro could also have adopted Obama in Hawaii, although such an adoption would not necessarily have been recognized by Indonesia.

Indonesian law at the time also did not recognize dual citizenship, meaning if Obama became Indonesian, then as far as that country was concerned, his U.S. citizenship was no longer recognized by Indonesia. But U.S. law would still recognize Obama as an American citizen.

One revelation by Obama raised a few eyebrows. In April 2008 the candidate disclosed he had traveled as a college student to Pakistan in 1981. "I traveled to Pakistan when I was in college—I knew what Sunni and Shia was before I joined the Senate Foreign Relations Committee," Obama reportedly stated at a fundraising event. The senator had never previously disclosed any trip to Pakistan, either in his books or in scores of policy talks regarding the country.[23] ABC News the next day contacted the presidential candidate's campaign, which affirmed that in 1981—the year Obama transferred from Occidental College to Columbia University—Obama visited his mother and sister Maya in Indonesia, and then went on to Pakistan with a friend from college whose family was from that country. Obama was in Pakistan for about three weeks, said the campaign, staying with his friend's family in Karachi and also visiting Hyderabad in southern India.[24]

Pakistan in 1981 was under military rule, and it was difficult for U.S. citizens to obtain a visa to enter the country. At that time it would have been easier for someone to enter Pakistan on an Indonesian passport.

If Obama indeed possessed Indonesian citizenship as a child, it is unlikely he retains such citizenship. The country's bylaws require any Indonesian citizen living abroad for more than five years to formally declare his intention to return, or otherwise risk losing his citizenship status.[25] The law does not necessarily mean Indonesian citizenship would be immediately lost. The law can be overruled by ministerial order.

Obama's registration in Indonesia under the name "Barry Soetoro" also raises questions as to whether he adopted that name in the United States at any time. According to Illinois state filings, when Obama registered as an attorney in 1991, under the name Barack Obama, he stated he did not have any former names.[26]

6

OBAMA PARTICIPATED IN SOCIALIST PARTY

I N HIS MEMOIR, *Dreams from My Father,* Barack Obama mentions in passing a recollection of attending socialist conferences during college:

> Political discussions, the kind that at Occidental had once seemed so intense and purposeful, came to take on the flavor of the socialist conferences that I sometimes attended at Cooper Union or the African cultural fairs that took place in Harlem or Brooklyn during the summers—a few of the many diversions that New York had to offer, like going to a foreign film or ice-skating at the Rockefeller Center.[1]

This account does not even scratch the surface of Obama's real involvement with socialism and socialist organizations. One largely untold but crucial story involves Obama's participation with a U.S. socialist party—a radical organization active as a party from 1992 to 1998—whose founders and members were instrumental in helping to facilitate Obama's political career, and some of whose key members are still associated with Obama and with the development of White House policy.

The New Party was established in 1992, seeking to elect members to public office with the aim of moving the Democratic Party far leftward to ultimately form a third major U.S. political party with a socialist agenda.

USA Today reported on the founding of the New Party on November 16, 1992. The paper reported the New Party was "self-described [as] 'socialist democratic.'"[2]

The New Party was a creation of union activist Sandy Pope and University of Wisconsin professor Joel Rogers. Rogers later was a founder of the Apollo Alliance, which was involved in drafting Obama's 2009 Stimulus Bill and the Cap and Trade Bill (discussed in Chapter 13). Roger's wife, Sarah Siskind, worked at the same law firm that employed Obama.[3]

Comprised largely of members of the Democratic Socialists for America, or DSA, the party was an electoral alliance that worked alongside ACORN—the Association of Community Organizations for Reform Now. The New Party's aim was to help elect politicians who espouse its agenda to office.

The New Party was created to take strategic advantage of what was known as electoral "fusion," which enabled candidates to run on two tickets simultaneously, attracting voters from both parties. One year after the fusion loophole was halted by the U.S. Supreme Court, in 1997, the New Party essentially became defunct, although it still maintains a website and a membership seeking to lobby for the reinstitution of fusion.[4]

COMMUNISTS, SOCIALISTS, ACORN

The New Party's founding members included such DSA luminaries as radical professor Noam Chomsky, Marxist activist Carl Davidson, Harvard Labor studies lecturer Elaine Bernard, black activist and academic Cornel West, sociologist Frances Fox Piven (acknowledged as the theoretician behind ACORN), former Maoist Bill Fletcher, feminist Barbara Ehrenreich, and Chicago physician and "single payer" health activist Quentin Young. As we document later in this chapter, many of these characters still are involved with Obama.

DSA literature extensively reviewed by the authors describes the group's long-term role in the New Party. For example, the January–February issue of the Chicago DSA's *New Ground* newsletter reports, "On Saturday, January 14, the New Party in Chicago took another step in its effort to establish itself as a political force by holding a major outreach meeting directed at Chicago's Left. About 100 people, with sizable delegations from DSA and Committees of Correspondence among others, heard Bruce Colburn and Elaine Bernard preach the gospel of the New Party."[5]

The DSA, which describes itself as the "principal U.S. affiliate of the Socialist International," is perhaps the largest socialist organization in the United States. "We are socialists," reads the organization's agenda, "because we reject an international economic order sustained by private profit, alienated labor, race and gender discrimination, environmental destruction, and brutality and violence in defense of the status quo." The DSA's official website states that to "achieve a more just society many structures of our government and economy must be radically trans-formed."[6] The above-mentioned Committees of Correspondence is a breakaway of the Communist Party USA.

The New Party's own official agenda outlined its goals of radically changing the U.S. system. "The New Party believes that the social, eco-nomic, and political progress of the United States requires a democratic revolution in America—the return of power to the people. Democracy in America does not work today," reads the party's literature. The New Party's clearly socialist guiding principles, to which each new member was required to agree, included:

- The establishment, defense, and facilitation of worker, con-sumer, shareholder, and taxpayer rights to democratic self-organization.
- The creation of a sustainable economy based on the responsible and reverent use of our earth's resources—taking no more than we need, replacing and reusing all that we can.
- A society in which we all take seriously our responsibilities as parents, workers, and citizens.
- The democratization of our banking and financial system—includ-ing popular election of those charged with public stewardship of our banking system, worker-owner control over their pension assets, community-controlled alternative financial institutions.

- A Bill of Rights for America's Children, guaranteeing true equality of opportunity, providing equal education for all students, and achieving an adequate standard of health care, nutrition, housing, and safety.
- Community-control and equitable funding of our schools, within which we seek true excellence in public education along with equal opportunity to achieve it.
- Full employment, a shorter work week, and a guaranteed minimum income for all adults; a universal "social wage" to include such basic benefits as health care, child care, vacation time, and lifelong access to education and training; a systematic phase-in of comparable worth and like programs to ensure gender equity.
- A progressive tax system based on the ability to pay.
- A reduction of national military spending to that necessary to the defense of the United States and an end to unilateral military interventions.
- Trade among nations consistent with mutual improvement in living standards, reduced cross-national inequalities, and sustainable development.
- In all aspects of our economy and social life, an absolute bar to discrimination based on race, gender, age, country of origin, and sexual orientation, and absolute security in reproductive rights, fundamental liberties, and privacy. [7-8]

The New Party worked extensively with ACORN and its low-income affiliates, especially the ACORN-allied Service Employees International Union, which formed the main bases of support for the New Party. The DSA's newsletters documented ACORN's extensive ties to the New Party. The group's September/October 1995 newsletter calls ACORN and its SEIU affiliate "the harbingers of the New Party."[9]

A local ACORN newsletter in Little Rock documented how the city "is just one city in which the New Party is building grassroots political power around an affordable housing and living wage agenda. In Chicago, the Illinois New Party participates actively in the ACORN-led Chicago

Jobs & Living Wage Campaign that this summer won Living Wage ordinances in both the City of Chicago and Cook County after an intense three-year community/labor campaign."[10]

OBAMA WAS A SOCIALIST PARTY MEMBER?

Barack Obama's exact involvement with the New Party has not been fully discovered, but what is known is that he sought and received the party's endorsement when he successfully ran for the Illinois State Senate in 1996 and that New Party members were part of his voter registration drive. The New Party's own literature, as well as an interview conducted by Aaron Klein with party founder Carl Davidson, strongly suggest Obama was an actual member of the party.[11]

The *New Zeal* blog dug up print copies of the *New Party News*, the party's official newspaper, which show Obama posing with New Party leaders, list him as a New Party member, and include quotes from him.[12] The party's Spring 1996 newspaper boasted: "New Party members won three other primaries this Spring in Chicago: Barack Obama (State Senate), Michael Chandler (Democratic Party Committee), and Patricia Martin (Cook County Judiciary). The paper quoted Obama saying: "these victories prove that small 'd' democracy can work." The newspaper lists other politicians it endorsed who were not members, but it specifies Obama as a New Party member.

The DSA's *New Ground* newsletter reported in its July/August 1996 edition that Obama attended a New Party membership meeting April 11, 1996, in which he expressed his gratitude for the group's support and "encouraged NPers ([New Party members]) to join in his task forces on Voter Education and Voter Registration."[13]

Becoming a New Party member required some effort on behalf of the politician. Candidates needed to be approved by the party's political committee and, once approved, signed a contract stipulating they would have a "visible and active relationship" with the party.

In an August 23, 2009, e-mail interview with Aaron Klein, New Party founder Carl Davidson recalled: "A subcommittee met with [Obama] to interview him to see if his stand on the living wage and similar reforms was the same as ours. We determined that our views on these overlapped, and we could endorse his campaign in the Democratic Party."[14]

Beside his involvement with the DSA and the New Party, Davidson had also served as national secretary for the Students for a Democratic Society antiwar group, from which the Weatherman domestic terrorist organization later splintered.[15]

Davidson remembers Obama attending one New Party meeting to thank attendees for voting for him. Asked whether Obama signed the New Party contract, Davidson replied to Klein that there was "no need for him to do so. At the end of our session with him, we simply affirmed there was no need to do so, because on all the key points, the stand of his campaign and the New Party reform planks were practically the same."

Obama not only participated with the New Party, but he also attended several DSA events and meetings, including a DSA-sponsored town hall meeting February 25, 1996, entitled "Employment and Survival in Urban America." He sought and received an endorsement from the DSA for his 1996 campaign.[16]

Asked by Klein whether he thinks Obama has socialist leanings, Davidson stated, "The truth is that Obama was and is a liberal Democrat and an Alinskyist community organizer—which if you know much about Alinsky, is just militant liberalism.

"Obama was never a man of the left, either in his views or in being a member of an actual socialist organization," added Davidson.

NEW PARTY MEMBERS INSTRUMENTAL IN OBAMA'S CAREER

Obama worked closely with Chicago Congressman Daniel K. Davis, a New Party member, forming a strong relationship that has endured to this day. The pair worked on several projects in Illinois while Davis played a significant role in Obama's Senate and presidential campaigns. Indeed, Davis was a "super delegate" pledged to Obama. In a 2004 speech to the Chicago Teamsters Union, Obama described Davis as "one of our best congressmen" because "he shares our values." And what are Davis' values? Aside from being an active New Party member, he was also a DSA member.[17]

Additionally, Davis attended the 1990 fundraising dinner of *People's Daily World*, the official newspaper of the Communist Party USA. (The newspaper later changed its name and publication schedule to *People's Weekly World*.) The communist newspaper's July 28, 1990, edition, reported Davis, "applauded those at the banquet, who, he said, are always in the midst of struggle." *PDW* readers, he said, are "steadfast in the fight for justice." The fundraiser netted $2,500, the communist newspaper reported.[18]

Meanwhile, New Party founder and "single payer" health activist Quentin Young became a longtime Obama friend and adviser, particularly in 1996, when he reportedly advised Obama on issues of health care. Young was reportedly present at the 1995 meeting at the home of former Weatherman terrorist Bill Ayers that was said to have helped launch Obama's political career.[19]

In a January 2008 interview, Young said his opinion of Obama changed in 2005 after the politician voted to confirm Condoleezza Rice as secretary of state and waffled on supporting single-payer health care. "I knew him before he was political," Young said of Obama. "I supported him when he ran for state senate. When he was a state senator he did say that he supported single payer. Now, he hedges. Now he says, if we were starting from scratch, he would support single payer."[20]

The *New Zeal* blog documents how Young has been active in Chicago socialist circles and was previously accused of membership in a communist group. In 1992, Chicago's branch of the DSA awarded Young with its highest honor—the Debs Award.[21]

Another key New Party founder is Manning Marable, an openly socialist Columbia University professor with strong ties to Obama's radical associates, including Weatherman terrorist Bill Ayers. Marable, a long time DSA activist, now is also a member of the New York Working Families Party, which is an ideological descendant of the New Party. In 1998, Marable helped found the Black Radical Congress, which is a coalition of black radical socialists.[22]

In a December 2008 piece published in the *Socialist Review*, Marable divulged: "A lot of the people working with him [Obama] are, indeed, socialists with backgrounds in the Communist Party or as independent

Marxists. What makes Obama different is that he has also been a community organizer. He has read left literature, including my works, and he understands what socialism is."[23]

The radical professor contended: "Obama is not a Marxist or a socialist—he is a progressive liberal."

Continued Marable: "Obama represents a generation of what might be called post-racial black politicians—by which I mean they espouse a politics that minimizes matters of race. They do not like to talk about race and subsume it under the rubric of poverty and class."

Speaking in a telephone interview with Aaron Klein, Marable refused to identify the individuals working with Obama that he claimed were socialists with Communist Party backgrounds. He said, however, those individuals strongly believe Obama would change the "tenor of politics within the Democratic party."[24]

"I think the point I was making is that there are a number of people with left histories who were early participants in Obama's mobilization. They have a strong belief in Obama as a candidate with the possibility of changing the tenor of politics within the Democratic Party," Marable told Klein.

In 2007, Marable was elected chair of Movement for a Democratic Society, or MDS, an arm of the radical Students for a Democratic Society from which the Weatherman terrorist organization later splintered. Some Weatherman terrorists, including Ayers, now participate in Marable's MDS. In November 2007, for example, Ayers participated in an MDS panel entitled "Resisting endless war." Ayers' wife, and fellow former terrorist and felon, Bernardine Dohrn was an MDS board member.[25]

Another New Party member, controversial race scholar Cornel West, aided Obama's political career. As we will detail extensively in the next chapter, West is an Obama friend who introduced the politician at his first presidential campaign stop in Harlem in 2007. During that 2007 introduction, West first railed on stage against the "racist" U.S. criminal justice system of the "American empire." Obama then took the stage hailing West.

West, who is currently a professor at Princeton University, served as an adviser on Louis Farrakhan's Million Man March and is a personal friend of the Nation of Islam leader. West authored two books on race with the more moderate Harvard professor, and chairman of African American studies, Henry Louis Gates, Jr, who was at the center of a 2009 controversy, in which Obama remarked on Gates' being handcuffed by police outside his home after a report of a burglary.

OBAMA FIRM FOUGHT FOR SOCIALIST PARTY

Perhaps unsurprisingly, the law firm at which Obama served as counsel led a legal charge to overturn state bans on allowing politicians to run as members of more than one party. The New Party was a primary bene-factor of the case—which the firm, Davis, Miner, Barnhill & Galland, took to the Supreme Court. Obama was employed at Davis, Miner until 2004.

In 1997, Davis, Miner's Madison, Wisconsin–based partner Sarah Siskind went to the Supreme Court to lead the main fight to allow electoral "fusion," which, as we noted, enabled candidates to run on two tickets simultaneously. Siskind lost the Supreme Court case, and the New Party, which had been created to take advantage of this electoral loophole, went defunct in 1998, a year later.[26]

Siskind worked with Obama at Davis, Miner and later donated to Obama's presidential campaign. She has also been one of the key attorneys representing ACORN, and is the wife of Joel Rogers, the socialist activist who co-founded and was national chair of the New Party.

Like other episodes in Barack Obama's past, his involvement with the New Party seems to evidence a goal of moving the Democratic Party far leftward, using and working with groups who specialize in manipulating the democratic process to achieve this goal.

7

OBAMA'S TIES TO NATION OF ISLAM AND BLACK RADICALS

This young man is the hope of the entire world that America will change and be made better.

—Nation of Islam Minister Louis Farrakhan praises candidate Obama, to an estimated crowd of 20,000 people, in a February 25, 2008, speech marking Farrakhan's first major public address since a cancer crisis.[1]

ISPLAYING HIS TRADEMARK ultraracialist mindset, Farrakhan goes on to compare Obama to the Nation of Islam's founder, Fard Muhammad, who also had a white mother and black father. "A black man with a white mother became a savior to us. A black man with a white mother could turn out to be one who can lift America from her fall."

Two days later, however, Candidate Obama declines to return Farrakhan's praise. In a Democratic presidential debate in Cleveland, Ohio, broadcast on MSNBC, Obama denounces Farrakhan and calls the minister's incendiary comments on Judaism "unacceptable and reprehensible."[2]

"I did not solicit this support. He expressed pride in an African American who seems to be bringing the country together," Obama says.

In renouncing Farrakhan during his campaign, candidate Obama resorted to the same tactics he used in minimizing and distorting his relationship with domestic terrorist Bill Ayers as "just someone who lives in my neighborhood." During the debate, Obama says of his ties to Farrakhan: "This is something that—I live in Chicago. He lives in Chicago. I've been very clear, in terms of me believing that what he has said is reprehensible and inappropriate." Obama clearly wanted to conceal his extensive and—until now—largely undisclosed relationship to Farrakhan and his radical ideology.

The Nation of Islam is essentially a cultic variation of orthodox Islam, founded in Detroit in 1930 by Wallace Dodd Fard, who also went by several other names, including Wallace Fard Muhammad. Upon Fard's mysterious disappearance in 1934, the movement was taken over by grad-school dropout and alcoholic Elijah Poole, also known as Elijah Muhammad, one of Fard's earlier converts.

A *Discover the Networks* profile notes Elijah Muhammad advocated the creation of a separate black nation on the U.S. mainland, distinct from white society in every way—economically, politically, and spiritually. Muhammad also claimed that Fard was, variously, Allah, the reincarnation of Jesus, the prophet the world had been awaiting for the last 2,000 years, and the Son of Man.[3]

In 1965 Muhammad published a 300-page book titled *Message to the Blackman in America*, claiming that Allah had originally created the black race before all others and that whites had been created some 6,000 years ago by a renegade black scientist named Yakub. Muhammad wrote, "The whole Caucasian race is a race of devils . . . the evil and murderous race."

Muhammad essentially controlled the NOI for more than four decades, but in the 1960s the fiery Malcolm X became by far the movement's most visible spokesman. When Malcolm later moved toward orthodox Sunni Islam, and rejected the notion that all whites were evil, he was sidelined from NOI leadership. Malcolm also accused Muhammad of impregnating teenage girls. The accusations, plus his earlier change of attitude, got him suspended from his position as the leader of the Harlem Mosque. In this he was replaced by Louis Farrakhan, who denounced Malcolm in the NOI newspaper as "worthy of death," ten weeks before Malcolm's assassination.

In the early 1970s, four NOI activists, leaders of a faction called the "Death Angels," were convicted of murdering 71 white people in the San Francisco Bay area. *Discover the Networks* notes that it became apparent the group were systematically stalking and killing whites simply because of the color of their skin. Death Angels believed they could earn "points" toward going to heaven if they killed whites. The NOI paid for the legal representation of each of the killers except one, who had already admitted to the murders.

After Elijah Muhammad's death in 1975, his son Wallace Deen Muhammad attempted to integrate the NOI into mainstream Islam, leading to a schism with Farrakhan's group. But today the faction headed by Farrakhan and headquartered in Chicago is considered the main NOI base that dictates the organization's ideology.

The *Discover the Networks* profile noted that Farrakhan "regards the United States as an irredeemably racist, oppressive nation; he has consistently condemned American policies, both foreign and domestic. He opposes U.S. aid to Israel; opposes the war in Iraq; has been critical of the war on Islamist terror; and urges young men to resist any proposed military draft. He insists, however, that his anti-white, anti-American positions are overstated by a hostile, Jewish-dominated press."

Farrakhan has given speeches referencing "white devils" and Jewish "bloodsuckers," referring to Judaism as "a gutter religion." His NOI website posted a list of demands on the United States government, including the right of descendents of slaves to "establish a separate state or territory of their own—either on this continent or elsewhere. We believe that our former slave masters are obligated to provide such land."

OBAMA'S PRO-FARRAKHAN CHURCH

To trace Obama's ties to the Nation of Islam, we must begin with president's controversial pastor for about 20 years, the Reverend Jeremiah Wright, who in 1984 accompanied Farrakhan on a solidarity trip to Libya to visit the anti-American dictator Moammar Kadafi. One year later, Obama, then a Chicago community activist, reportedly first browsed Wright's church, the Trinity United Church of Christ. In Wright, Obama reportedly "had found both a spiritual mentor and a role model."[4]

Obama joined TUCC in 1991 and "walked down the aisle in a formal commitment of faith." Ten years after first stepping foot in Wright's Trinity church, in October 1995, Obama accompanied Wright to Farrakhan's "Million Man March."[5]

Wright closely follows the black-liberation theology of James Cone, who is considered the founder of the movement. Cone's main thesis is that true Christianity is specific to the black liberation experience, and that traditional Christianity as commonly practiced in the United States is racist and against "true" Christianity.

"The black theologian must reject any conception of God which stifles black self-determination by picturing God as a God of all peoples. Either God is identified with the oppressed to the point that their experience becomes God's experience, or God is a God of racism," opined Cone in his defining book, A Black Theology of Liberation.

"The blackness of God means that God has made the oppressed condition God's own condition. This is the essence of the biblical revelation," Cone argued. Cone's brand of Christianity strongly denounces Christian practice that does not take a specific political approach that is largely very liberal and liberation-focused. Trinity church's official website stresses in its mission section that the church was "called by God" to be a congregation that is "not ashamed of the gospel of Jesus Christ and that does not apologize for its African roots!"[6]

In a 2006 speech addressing so-called religious progressives at a Call to Renewal Conference, Obama explained he joined Trinity because of its central focus on black theology: "But as the months passed in Chicago, I found myself drawn to the church," said Obama.

For one thing, I believed and still believe in the power of African-American religious tradition to spur social change. . . . [T]he black church understands in an intimate way the biblical call to feed the hungry and clothe the naked and challenge the powers and principalities. . . . I was able to see faith as more than just a comfort to the weary or a hedge against death; it is an active, palpable agent in the world. It is a source of hope.[7]

"It was because of these newfound understandings," Obama said, "that I was finally able to walk down the aisle of Trinity United Church of Christ one day and affirm my Christian faith."

Jeremiah Wright's church is closely associated with Farrakhan and the Nation of Islam. Obama's pastor founded *Trumpet* magazine, a black-centrist glossy publication, and serves as the publication's CEO, with his daughter, Jeri, in the position of publisher/editor-in-chief. *Trumpet* went national in 2006 and claims a readership of more than 100,000.

Obama has appeared at least three times on the cover of *Trumpet* magazine, which in 2007 gave Farrakhan its Empowerment Award. The business-oriented blog *BizzyBlog* found three *Trumpet* samples in which Obama graces the cover. One featured the Illinois senator and Wright shaking hands. Another was a montage of faces—black leaders, past and present, with the title "The legacy lives on"—that included Wright, Farrakhan, Nation of Islam founder Elijah Muhammad, Rosa Parks, and even O.J. Simpson attorney Johnny Cochran.[8]

After perusing a year's worth of *Trumpet* issues, Stanley Kurtz, an adjunct fellow of the Hudson Institute and a Senior Fellow at the Ethics and Public Policy Center, wrote a lengthy piece for the *Weekly Standard* on his discoveries. He found in the 2006 archives that the incendiary views expressed by Wright in sound bites from the pastor's sermons were reinforced in detail throughout the magazine's text, which was full of pro-Farrakhan material.[9]

Wright, of course, became a dangerous issue for Obama during the 2008 presidential campaign, when samplings of his pastor's anti-American, anti-white, and anti-Semitic statements were aired in loops by the news media, particularly Fox News.

Among Wrights memorable gems are:

- The government lied about inventing the HIV virus as a means of genocide against people of color. The government lied.
- God damn America for threatening citizens as less than humans. God damn America as long as she tries to act like she is God and supreme.
- The government gives them the drugs, builds bigger prisons, passes three-strike laws and wants them to sing God Bless America. No! No! No! God damn America . . . for killing innocent people. God damn America for threatening citizens as less than humans. God damn America as long as she tries to act like she is God and supreme.
- And of the 9/11 attacks: We have supported state terrorism against the Palestinians and black South Africans, and now we are indignant because of stuff we have done overseas is now brought back

into our own backyard. America's chickens is coming home to roost.[10]

At first Obama denounced Wright's publicized statements. And after critics continued to press the issue of his relationship with Wright, Obama, on March 18, 2008, gave a speech titled "A More Perfect Union," in which the candidate denounced Wright's remarks but attempted to place his pastor's comments in a historical and sociological context.[11]

The title of Obama's speech, curiously, was also the main theme of Farrakhan's keynote address at the 1995 Million Man March, attended by both Obama and Wright.[12]

As Farrakhan declared at the march: "And so our brief subject today is taken from the American Constitution and these words, 'Toward a more perfect union.' Toward a more perfect union. Now, when you use the word 'more' with 'perfect,' that which is perfect is that which has been brought to completion. So when you use 'more perfect,' you're either saying that what you call perfect is perfect for that stage of its development, but not yet complete."

For a few weeks after Obama's speech on Wright, the controversy over Obama's ties to the outspoken minister began to fade, but it was renewed in late April after Wright himself made a series of media appearances, prompting Obama to speak more forcefully against his pastor, saying he was "outraged" and "saddened" by Wright's behavior. By the end of May 2008, Obama had officially resigned his membership from Wright's Trinity church.[13]

Many of Wright's defenders, at first including Obama, had claimed some of the pastor's anti-American, anti-Israel, black supremacist statements were taken out of context. Obama stated a number of times he was not aware of some of Wright's ideology during his two decades as a member of Trinity United Church of Christ.[14] However, Kurtz argued, "Obama must have long been aware of his pastor's political radicalism. A careful reading of nearly a year's worth of *Trumpet Newsmagazine* makes it next to impossible to conclude otherwise." Kurtz pointed to Obama's expressed outrage after an April 2008 National Press Club address, when Wright defended Farrakhan and praised him as "one of the most important voices in the 20th and 21st century . . . that's what I think about him."[15]

Aside from appearing alongside Obama on a cover of Wright's magazine, Farrakhan's face was also on the cover of a special November/December 2007 double issue of *Trumpet* announcing Wright's Empowerment Award, which had been given that year to the outspoken Nation of Islam chief. The magazine also praised Farrakhan as a 20th- and 21st-Century "giant."

"It seems inconceivable that, in 20 years, Obama would never have picked up a copy of *Trumpet*," wrote Kurtz. "Obama himself graced the cover. . . . There can be no mistaking it. What did Barack Obama know and when did he know it? Everything. Always." Kurtz noted that *Trumpet* preaches a black liberation theology, typically referring to American blacks as "Africans living in the Western Diaspora." The magazine in which Obama was repeatedly featured abhors American patriotism.

"Columbus Day is a day of rage for Wright. Calling Columbus a racist slave trader, Wright excoriates the holiday as 'a national act of amnesia and denial,' part of the 'sick and myopic arrogance called Western History,'" notes Kurtz.

Trumpet featured an article by Wright claiming that America was actually discovered by Africans, citing as evidence a book that has been widely discredited. The July 2006 issue of *Trumpet* slams Independence Day as "the national holiday of the dominant culture." Kurtz noted that issue featured an article by a Reverend Reginald Williams, Jr., calling July 4th "nothing more than a day off work and a time for some good barbeque to the millions of African Americans who suffer and have suffered under the policies of this government and this country."

One issue of *Trumpet* defended former Congresswoman Cynthia Mc-Kinney's claim that the Bush administration was aware of the 9/11 plot before it was carried out. That column stated the "crimes of 9/11" are "not only unsolved, but covered up by both Democrats and Republicans."

NATION OF ISLAM ACTIVISTS ON OBAMA'S PAYROLL

Obama's ties to Farrakhan go far beyond references in *Trumpet Magazine* and ideology at Wright's church. A former key Obama insider told author Aaron Klein in an interview that Obama's early political team included a disproportionate number of Nation of Islam staffers, and that the presidential candidate had some "worrying" ties to Farrakhan's group. The former Obama insider, who spoke on condition of anonymity, expressed particular concern that Obama employed at least two Nation members in his early days as a state senator, when his office was staffed by only a handful of workers. The same former insider previously also talked with columnist and blogger Debbie Schlussel, who first wrote at her blog about the Nation of Islam employees on Obama's staff.[16] Aaron Klein verified that the former insider had held a key position with the presidential candidate. The former insider said he quit, in part, because of Obama's ties to the Nation of Islam and the senator's positions on Israel.

When Obama was elected to the Illinois state Senate in 1996, he served the 13th district, which then spanned Chicago's South Side neighborhoods, including areas where Farrakhan was highly influential. "When you're a state senator, you have little money given to you to hire staff. It is ironic that two of Obama's employees in those days were known Nation of Islam activists when Obama employed perhaps a total of maybe three or four staffers," said the former insider. "A key constituency for Obama was Hyde Park, where Farrakhan lives. To be successful politically in that area, you need to be involved with Farrakhan, since he's a strong power in the district," the former insider said.

Early employees of Obama's were identified by the former insider as Nation of Islam members—including Jennifer Mason, who, until Obama entered the White House, still worked in his Chicago U.S. Senate office as director of constituency services, a key community liaison position. An employee of Obama's from his early state Senate days, and later the treasurer for his U.S. senatorial campaign, Cynthia K. Miller, was also identified by the former insider as a Nation of Islam activist. According to financial documents, Miller was also a paid consultant in 2003 and 2004. She currently runs a Chicago real estate firm. Neither Mason nor Miller returned numerous phone calls seeking comment.

The former insider said Obama had asked a favor of indicted Chicago businessman and Obama financier Tony Rezko, to get his treasurer—Miller—a state government job with former Illinois Governor Rod Blagojevich. "She got an offer but turned it down," the ex-insider said. "She ended up doing real estate."

DAVID AXELROD TIED TO FARRAKHAN

Another key Obama staffer tied to supporters of Farrakhan is David Axelrod, Obama's top adviser, who served as his chief political strategist during the presidential campaign. Klein discovered that Axelrod sat on the finance committee of St. Sabina, the Chicago Catholic parish led by controversial priest Michael Pfleger. Like Jeremiah Wright, Pfleger is an outspoken Farrakhan supporter who hosted the Nation of Islam chief at his parish several times. Like Wright, Pfleger espouses black liberation theology.[17]

The Archdiocese of Chicago removed Pfleger from his duties at St. Sabina for an unspecified time following a well-publicized May 2008 sermon at Wright's Trinity church—first exposed by Klein—in which Pfleger claimed Hillary Clinton cried in public because she thought being white entitled her to the Democratic Presidential nomination. Pfleger told reporters he felt free to speak about Clinton because he believed his sermon was not being recorded. He said he thought the live Internet link that normally broadcasts Trinity sermons was not running.[18] "They told me it was down," Pfleger said of the Internet link. "Their live streaming had been down all day, and they didn't know whether it was back up. . . . I regret the dramatization that I was naïve enough to believe was just going to be kept among that church."

Pfleger hosted Farrakhan at his church as late as May 2008, one of Farrakhan's first public appearances since he announced in 2006 he had been suffering from prostate cancer and was seriously ill. According to reports, Pfleger spent hours with the Nation of Islam chief during his illness. Pfleger previously enlisted Farrakhan's support for several of his initiatives, including an antigun protest in 2007.

As late as June 2008, Axelrod sat on the finance board of Pfleger's church. St. Sabina had been seeking to raise $1 million to offset the costs of reconstructing sections of the cathedral found to have structural problems. Axelrod was listed on the church's official website alongside an open letter from Pfleger asking for contributions. "St. Sabina needs your help to bring one of the most beautiful sanctuaries in the Archdiocese back to the community. It is estimated that the additional costs will be $1 million, which will fall squarely on the shoulders of St. Sabina, a community not made up of vast wealth but of tremendous faith," wrote Pfleger.

Pfleger regularly served as a guest lecturer at Jeremiah Wright's Trinity church and has been featured a number of times in Wright's *Trumpet* magazine. The June/July 2007 issue of *Trumpet*, for example, described Pfleger as "Afrocentric to the core."

FARRAKHAN FRIEND, "HILLARY I'M WHITE" PASTOR AIDING OBAMA

After Pfleger's caustic remarks about Clinton, and Pfleger's suspension from his job, Obama's campaign removed a testimonial by Pfleger from the "Faith" section of its official website. Pfleger's official testimonial read: "Obama is calling back those who have given up and lost hope in the political system both young and old in the belief that we can fix it. He has the intellect for the job, and I haven't heard anyone since Robert F. Kennedy who is causing such an emotional and spiritual awakening to the political possibilities."[19]

USA Today reported that Obama's relationship with Pfleger spanned decades. In September 2008, the Illinois senator's campaign flew Pfleger to Iowa to host one of several interfaith forums for the campaign. The *Chicago Tribune* reported that Pfleger had given money to Obama's campaigns and that as a state legislator Obama directed at least $225,000 toward social programs at Pfleger's church.[20]

Obama, meanwhile, also reached out to Dr. Conrad W. Worrill, a close associate of Farrakhan who is a leader in the slavery reparations movement. Worill, director of the Carruthers Center for Inner City Studies at Northeastern Illinois University, served as a co-chair for the August 17, 2002, Millions for Reparations rally and preceding mobilization efforts held in Washington, D.C. The rally was closely coordinated with the Nation of Islam.[21]

Worrill served as "Minister of the Interior" for a group calling itself the Provisional Government/Republic of New Afrika, a radical movement that seeks the creation of a black nation in the United States in the states of Louisiana, Mississippi, Alabama, Georgia, and South Carolina. Worrill is also a longtime friend of Wright and has a decades-long friendship and association with Farrakhan. He has written about reparations in Farrakhan's *Final Call* newsletter. In October 2006, Worrill accompanied Farrakhan to Havana, Cuba, where they attended a conference of U.S. and Cuban leaders, including Cuban President Fidel Castro, "to discuss disaster relief and the U.S. government's poor response to Hurricane Katrina."[22]

As Obama prepared for his 2004 campaign for the U.S. Senate, the candidate reportedly visited Worrill and asked for his support. "He wanted me as a representative of the pan-African thinking in Chicago," Worrill told the *Los Angeles Times*. "And he wanted me to support him publicly, which I did on the radio. And he knew I came from a different school of thought" than Obama had.[23] The *Times* noted that during the campaign, Obama "rejected one of Worrill's key causes—seeking monetary reparations for black Americans whose ancestors were slaves. Worrill took to the local airwaves to criticize Obama, but the activist says he now understands his motives. . . . 'He has to appeal to everybody.'"

OBAMA'S BLACK EXTREMIST ASSOCIATES

A high-profile episode involving Obama and a close friend, who is a leading professor of African American studies, would in an ordinary presidency at least have raised eyebrows, involving as it did the association of a U.S. president with black radicals and reparation activists. But as with all the other of Obama's radical ties, he is given a pass by normally voracious newsgathering organizations.

On the afternoon of July 16, 2009, Henry Louis Gates, Jr., who is Director of the W. E. B. Du Bois Institute for African and African American Research at Harvard University, was arrested while apparently trying to break into his own home in Cambridge, Massachusetts. Gates was returning from a trip to China, and attempted to enter his house on tree-lined Ware St., only to find the door to his house jammed. His black driver attempted to help Gates gain entrance. A neighbor, concerned she may have been witnessing a possible break-in, called 911, prompting the dispatch of a Cambridge police officer to the scene. The resulting confrontation, of which Gates and the officer gave conflicting stories, resulted in Gates being arrested and charged with disorderly conduct.

What would have been a local incident turned into a national race scandal, after Obama used a press conference mostly devoted to health care to accuse the police of dealing "stupidly" with Gates. Obama's comments sparked a furor over whether the police had racially profiled the Harvard professor who was also the president's friend.

The facts surrounding Gates' arrest and the ensuing controversy are largely tangential to our discussion. What is crucial—but until now largely ignored—is that the episode should have highlighted the milieu of black radicals in which Obama has traveled.

Since 1991, Gates has been teaching African American studies at Harvard, where he serves as the director of the W. E. B. Du Bois Institute. Du Bois was one of the greatest American civil rights activists, as well as a sociologist, historian, and author, but he was also a card-carrying communist and a socialist sympathizer. Gates himself is, of course, a strong supporter of affirmative action, but more significantly he is a key activist in the movement for massive U.S. government monetary reparations to the descendants of African slaves. He joined an effort to bring a class action lawsuit for reparations and reportedly has been working privately to urge political and business leaders to keep the issue of slavery at the forefront of social-justice discussions and to support his campaign for reparations.

One of Gates' major sources of intellectual inspiration is Herbert Aptheker, a seminal scholar of African American history who was a radical American leftist. Aptheker was for decades a leading theorist of the Communist Party U.S.A. before resigning in 1991.[24]

In a 2008 interview with *Martha's Vineyard Magazine*, Gates described a fundraiser he held at a vacation house in the town of Harthaven for Obama during his race for the Senate.[25] Gates said he talked to Obama numerous times and that he donated the maximum allowable contribution to Obama's presidential campaign.

Gates was quoted as stating Obama's election last year rivaled the day in 1863 when President Abraham Lincoln issued the Emancipation Proclamation, and the day 101 years later when the Rev. Martin Luther King, Jr. delivered his "I Have a Dream" speech.

"There's never been a moment like this in our lifetime, ever," Gates said.

Serving as director for the Harvard institute immortalizing Du Bois, Gates cultivated black radicals within his African American studies department, most prominently bringing in Cornel West, a controversial adviser on Louis Farrakhan's Million Man March with close ties to socialist and black extremist groups. West is a declared personal friend of Farrakhan and is a close and important Obama associate.

Gates authored two books with West, a longtime member and honorary chair of the Democrat Socialists of America. From a young age, West proclaimed he admired "the sincere black militancy of Malcolm X, the defiant rage of the Black Panther Party . . . and the livid black [liberation] theology of James Cone." West left Harvard for Princeton in 2002 after a public spat with Harvard's then-president, Lawrence Summers.

Obama named West to the Black Advisory Council of his presidential campaign. It was West who first introduced Obama on stage at a 2007 Harlem fundraiser, hosting about 1,500 people, which served as Obama's first foray into Harlem since announcing his Democratic presidential candidacy.[26] The authors of this book found a YouTube video of that fundraiser. In West's introductory speech just before Obama takes stage, the Princeton professor claims the "American empire is in such a deep crisis" and slams what he calls the "racist criminal justice system" and "disgraceful schools in our city."[27]

"He is my brother and my companion and comrade," said West of Obama.

The authors also found a video of Obama, upon taking the stage just after West's introduction, expressing his gratitude to West, calling him "not only a genius, a public intellectual, a preacher, an oracle . . . he's also a loving person." Obama asks the audience for a round of applause for West.[28]

Another key radical in the Obama-Gates-West axis is Charles Ogletree, Jr., also a Harvard University professor, who represented Gates during the police scandal. Ogletree is closely linked to the Black Panthers and to radical black ideology. He is a key member of the reparations movement and, like Gates, pursued the possibility of bringing a class action lawsuit to win reparations for descendants of African slaves.[29]

Ogletree was a mentor to both Barack and Michelle Obama, and served on the black advisory council of Obama's presidential campaign. During Obama's senatorial career, Ogletree advised the politician on reforming the criminal-justice system as well on constitutional issues.[30]

"I met Barack when he arrived at Harvard Law School in fall of 1988. He was quiet and unassuming, but had an incredibly sharp mind and a thirst for knowledge," Ogletree said in a 2008 interview with *Essence* magazine. "Even then I saw his ability to quickly grasp the most complicated legal issues and sort them out in a clear, concise fashion," said Ogletree.[31]

Ogletree related that Obama was a regular participant in an after-class activity the Harvard professor created called the Saturday School Program—a series of workshops and meetings held Saturday mornings designed to expose minority students to issues in the study of law. Ogletree also told *Essence* that he mentored Michelle Obama when she enrolled at Harvard three years before her future husband. Ogletree said he gave Michelle career advice.

"I met Michelle when she started her legal career here at Harvard in the fall of 1985, and I was able to watch her develop into a very strong and powerful student leader. She was an active member of the Harvard Legal Aid Bureau, where she served as a student attorney for indigent clients who had civil cases and needed legal help" Ogletree related.

"I routinely gave career advice, and often personal advice, to students who would come in with questions about where they should work, how they should use their legal skills and talent, and was it possible to do well and do good," Ogletree said. "My advice to people like Barack and Michelle was that they could easily navigate the challenges of a corporate career and find a variety of ways to serve their community," he said.

Ogletree is closely linked to radical black activism. As a student in 1970 at Stanford University near San Francisco, a center of black radicalism at the time, Ogletree organized an Afrocentric dormitory. He edited a campus Black Panther newspaper called *The Real News* and traveled to Africa and Cuba as part of student activist groups. Ogletree attended nearly every day of the trial of Black Power activist and communist Angela Davis.[32]

He moved on to Harvard Law School, where he continued his political activism, becoming national president of the Black Law Students Association.

In 1991 Ogletree gained national prominence when he represented Anita Hill during the controversial Senate confirmation hearings of Clarence Thomas, at which she accused the Supreme Court nominee of sexual harassment.

In 2000, Ogletree joined the Reparations Coordinating Committee, serving as the group's co-chair. The committee pursued a lawsuit to win reparations for descendants of African slaves. The committee was convened by Randall Robinson's TransAfrica Forum, a partner organization of the leftist Institute for Policy Studies.

NEW BLACK PANTHER PARTY ENDORSES OBAMA ON HIS WEBSITE

During the presidential campaign, some black radicals and Farrakhan associates stated they had found a supporter in Obama. One even maintained blogs on the politician's official website.[33]

The New Black Panther Party, which inherited its name from the Black Panther Party of the 1960s, is a extremist party whose leaders are notorious for their racist statements and anti-white provocations. The deceased chairman of the NBPP, Khallid Abdul Muhammad, was formerly a Nation of Islam leader who was at one time considered Louis Farrakhan's most trusted adviser. Muhammad gave numerous speeches referring to the "white man" as the "devil" and claiming that "there is a little bit of Hitler in all white people."

The group now is led by Malik Zulu Shabazz, who has led racially divisive protests and conferences, such as the 1998 Million Youth March, in which a few thousand Harlem youths reportedly were called upon to scuffle with police officers, and speakers demanded the extermination of whites in South Africa. Shabaz has given scores of speeches condemning "white men" and Jews.

During the 2008 campaign, Shabazz and his group endorsed Obama on the candidate's website, which allowed users to generate their own blog entries. "Obama is capable of stirring the 'melting pot' into a better 'molten America,'" states the NBPP endorsement posted on Obama's site. After Klein reported on the endorsement, Obama's campaign removed it from the website, a move that Shabazz told Klein was carried out for "understandable political reasons."

"It's the game of politics," Shabazz told Klein in a March 19, 2008, interview. "The Obama camp's move to remove our blog doesn't mean much because I understand politics. We still completely support Obama as the best candidate."

Shabazz boasted that he met Obama in March 2007 when the politician attended the 42nd anniversary of the voting rights marches in Selma, Ala. "I have nothing but respect for Obama," said Shabazz.

8

THE ACORN PRESIDENT

Sen. McCain: We need to know the full extent of Senator Obama's relationship with ACORN.

Sen. Obama: The only involvement I've had with ACORN was I represented them alongside the U.S. Justice Department in making Illinois implement a motor voter law that helped people get registered at DMVs.[1]

— Exchange by the candidates during the third presidential election debate, Hofstra University, Hempstead, New York, October 15, 2008.

B Y THE TIME of the third, and final, election debate between John Mc-Cain and Barack Obama, the interest level of viewers and of the political chattering classes was on the wane. Obama's lead in the polls over McCain had grown steadily since the collapse of financial brokers Lehmann Brothers on September 15th, and the global economic crisis had threatened to precipitate. Less than three weeks away, Obama's victory in the general election seemed more and more a done deal.

Even had political interest been high, few of those viewing the debate would have had any idea whatsoever about an organization bearing the innocuous name ACORN—The Association of Community Organizations for Reform Now. It is unlikely viewers even understood what McCain's question was about. Likewise, it is a sure bet that the majority had not a clue as to the significance of Obama's untruthful answer above and how the politician's deep ties to ACORN are part of a larger trend of his relationships with anti-American extremists.

The founding of ACORN dates back to 1970, when former Students for a Democratic Society radical, Wade Rathke—a colleague of Weatherman terrorist Bill Ayers—was sent to Little Rock, Arkansas. Rathke was dispatched by National Welfare Reform Organization (NWRO) deputy director George Alvin Wiley, an African American militant, with the mission of organizing a statewide welfare rights organization. NWRO, in turn, had been founded in 1966 by Columbia University political scientists, Richard A. Cloward and Frances Fox Piven.[2]

Riley sent Rathke to Arkansas because of its demographics: "a median income below $6,000, a large welfare-eligible population that was 35 percent African-American, and a capital city that was centrally located in the state."[3]

ACORN was originally founded as the Arkansas Community Organization for Reform Now. But it soon "established itself over the 1970s as a national grassroots organization, forged alliances with the International Ladies Garment Workers Union (now merged into UNITE) and other labor organizations and community groups, and began to involve itself in Democratic Party politics," including running candidates for municipal and county offices.[4]

The organization renamed itself in 1976 as the Association of Community Organizations for Reform Now, when it "became a national, multi-state organization." That same year ACORN held its first national convention and "agreed to march on the Democratic Party's National Convention in Memphis, Tennessee, with its 'People's Platform,' which included 'planks on issues ranging from energy to health care to taxes to housing.'[5]

Barely two degrees separated the radical sixties group SDS and the NWRO, Jarol B. Manheim wrote in his 2001 book, *The Death of a Thousand Cuts: Corporate Campaigns and the Attack on the Corporation*. One of SDS's "experimental projects" was the Economic Research and Action Project, which "provided a model for community organizing." It was this SDS plan which the NWRO adopted.[6]

Manheim explained the Rathke plan:

> Rathke hoped to keep what he perceived to be good in his welfare rights experience (the membership base, the use of a replicable model, and the strategic manipulation of the press), while incorporating some parts of the old [Saul] Alinsky model (strong ties to such existing organizations as unions and churches) and experimenting with electoral politics as a way to consolidate organizational victories.[7]

ACORN's 1979 "People's Platform" (updated in 1990) provided a more "comprehensive statement" of the group's radical reformist objectives: "free medical care, a public defender system, the elimination of the state income tax for low-income people, and higher welfare benefits." The 1979 preamble states:

> In our freedom, only the people shall rule. Corporations shall have their role: producing jobs, providing products, paying taxes. No more, no less. They shall obey our wishes, respond to our needs, serve our communities. . . .
>
> Government shall have its role: public servant to our good, fast follower to our sure steps. No more, no less. Our government shall shout with the public voice and no longer to a private whisper. In our government, the common concerns shall be the collective cause.[8]

Manheim points out that ACORN's agenda "meshes closely at some points with that of organized labor, even as it differs at others." In general ACORN and labor "found themselves on the same side and working as allies. Indeed, by 1986, ACORN had forged institutional ties with AFL-CIO Central Labor Councils in at least 30 cities," Manheim writes.[9] (The American Federation of Labor and Congress of Industrial Organizations, commonly AFL-CIO, is the largest federation of unions in the United States and Canada.)

ACORN continued its coalition building in 1989 when it co-hosted a National Living Wage Campaign Training Conference "that brought together organizers from labor, community, and church organizations in 35 cities across the country." According to Manheim, "Organizers from the [major labor unions], as well as from ACORN, discussed the strategic use of living wage campaigns to promote union and community organizing." One ACORN spokesperson said: "The big picture isn't the individual workers being covered by living-wage laws. It's the organizing; . . . it's the new coalitions being built."[10]

ACORN was joined in this effort, Manheim writes, by a "coalition of church-based groups affiliated with" the Industrial Areas Foundation. "Recall," Manheim writes, IAF is "a precursor of the corporate campaign founded by Saul Alinsky."[11]

Manheim also concluded that ACORN "operates at two degrees of separation from organized labor." While ACORN "independently traces its origins to the SDS—in this instance, to ERAP . . . with a bow, too, toward Saul Alinsky," ACORN has "its own agenda and independent leadership." (The SDS-sponsored Economic Research and Action Project was founded in 1963 in an attempt to send white unemployed youths to lead protests for black civil rights.) An "essential component" of that agenda is "labor issues"; to advance its own interests, ACORN had "formed long-term alliances with organized labor to advance those issues."[12]

"WORKING TO TAKE DOWN CAPITALISM"

There is a second aspect to the SDS-ACORN story that involves a previous question asked by Senator McCain in the October 15, 2008, presidential debate. Evidently rushed to pose a question, McCain said: "Yes, real quick. Mr. Ayers, I don't care about an old washed-up terrorist. But as Senator Clinton said in her debates with you, we need to know the full extent of that relationship."[13]

It was a question Sen. Obama was unlikely to answer truthfully on national television.

Bill Ayers and Wade Rathke had both been members of SDS, the same sixties radical antiwar group, which broke up during summer of 1969.

Rathke left the antidraft movement and ended up working for Wiley's National Welfare Reform Organization doing counseling and welfare rights organizing and, like many others, took the path of urban-based community activism. In the seventies Rathke was busy organizing "welfare rights organizers, civil rights activists and an assorted array of lefties," mobilizing welfare recipients and low- and moderate-income people, forming nationwide alliances with organized labor, and working to take down corporate power and capitalism through peaceful and deceptive means.[14]

According to Sol Stern's report in the Spring 2003 edition of *City Journal*—"ACORN's Nutty Regime for Cities":

ACORN departs from the old New Left's playbook. Instead of trying to overturn "the system"—to blow it up, as George Wiley wanted to do—ACORN burrows deep within the system, taking over its power and using its institutions for its own purposes, like a political *Invasion of the Body Snatchers*.[15]

Obama's Hyde Park Chicago neighbors, Ayers and his wife, Bernardine Dohrn, on the other hand, chose the role of domestic terrorist leaders of the SDS separatist group, Weather Underground. In the seventies Ayers and Dohrn occupied themselves with bombings and other acts of violence to take down capitalism "by any means necessary"; by 1970 Weather, which had formed an underground terrorist faction, and many of its supporters, were wanted by the FBI.

As the authors have endeavored to show, Obama became the Manchurian candidate product of both groups. Even though one group was working within the system, while the other was bombing buildings and heisting Brinks trucks, their anticapitalist agenda is very similar to Obama's agenda.

By its own account, ACORN was well aware of Obama when he first came to Chicago. He was noticed by ACORN as a "very good organizer" at the Developing Communities Project, which he directed from 1985 to 1988.[16]

OBAMA RUNS ACORN "AFFILIATE"

Obama's direct contacts with ACORN began in 1992. Since then he has been an ACORN "organizer, trainer, lawyer, funder and political beneficiary."[17]

After graduating from Harvard Law School in May 1991, Obama returned to Chicago to "work on a book about race relations." He had turned down a Supreme Court clerkship—"almost a given" for the *Harvard Law Review's* "top editor"—as well as an offer to clerk for Abner Mikva, the chief judge on the Washington, D.C., Circuit Court. He said he was returning to Chicago to enter politics.[18]

Obama got involved with ACORN to "promote registration among low-income and minority voters." He ran the Cook County Illinois Project VOTE! Campaign from April to November 1992. Project VOTE!, also known as Voting for America, Inc., was a front group spun out of ACORN in 1982 by "partisans" of what became known as the Cloward-Piven strategy, which sought the downfall of U.S. capitalism.

Richard Cloward and Frances Fox Piven were advocating a "crisis strategy," which is based on "forcing political change through orchestrated crisis." The strategy "seeks to hasten the fall of capitalism by overloading the government bureaucracy with a flood of impossible demands, thus pushing society into crisis and economic collapse."[19] The duo's strategy originally appeared as an article in the May 1966 issue of *The Nation* called "The Weight of the Poor: A Strategy to End Poverty" (originally titled "Mobilizing the Poor: How It Can Be Done"), which described it as an "analysis and opinion piece in response to the 1965 Watts riots."

Instructive in the article's title is the phrase "weight of the poor." Originally penned by Bolshevik theorist Leon Trotsky, he complained in Chapter 8 of his 1927 *Platform of the Joint Opposition* that: "The relative weight of the poor is systematically falling everywhere—in the general composition of the rural branches, in the active membership, in the nucleus composed of party members."[20]

The co-founders of Project VOTE!—which Obama ran in Cook County in 1992—were Sandy Newman, a Washington, D.C., lawyer and civil rights activist, and Zach Polett, an ACORN co-founder who came from the National Welfare Reform Organization. Polett left Project VOTE! in June 2008 but continues as political director for ACORN. Polett is also a board member of America Votes, a coalition of organizations that includes ACORN, Project VOTE!, MoveOn.org, and a number of others.[21]

Please note that members of SDS, Project VOTE!, and all the other radical/socialist organizations with which Obama and his supporters have been affiliated are not comprised of "the poor"—they are, for the most part, professionals and college students. SDS alumni such as Ayers, Dohrn, Rathke, and an endless list of aging sixties radicals who either participated in Weather violence, hence going underground to escape arrest, or continued along the radical activist path, were then and are now anything but poor.

The Coward-Piven strategy—which *American Thinker*'s James Simpson calls the "manufactured crisis"—was fully tested in 1968 when the National Welfare Reform Organization implemented a "strategy to end poverty" in the streets.[22]

George Y. Steiner described the scenario in his 1971 book, *The State of Welfare*:

> Interest groups ranging from over two thousand part-time, unpaid, local housing authorities to tens of thousands of banks and retail stores participating in food stamp projects, to the American Legion and a dozen other veterans' service organizations, to name only some of the most obvious, are committed to and involved in public housing, food stamps, and veterans' pensions, respectively. In public assistance the clients themselves are being organized into a National Welfare Rights Organization. Whether the benefits are tangible or psychic, each of these groups is likely to know its program and to have a stake in the program's visible, independent existence. . . .
>
> NWRO did its worst in New York City in 1968, organizing clients to demand special grants authorized under law but rarely paid, it was costly for the city and rewarding for recipients. Later, when NWRO undertook to pressure department stores to provide charge accounts for welfare clients, its tactics made things inconvenient for some uninvolved, middle class persons not touched by an encampment on park land. And it was all legal.[23]

By 1975 the National Welfare Reform Organization's activities had caused a welfare crisis that nearly bankrupted New York City.[24]

NWRO veterans went on to "found the Living Wage Movement and the Voting Rights Movement, both of which rely on the Cloward-Piven strategy and both of which are spear-headed by the radical cult ACORN." The Living Wage Movement is "supported by the majority of the left and today is bankrolled extensively" by George Soros' Open Society Institute.[25]

Richard Poe further explained Cloward-Piven's success in a 2005 article for *Discover the Networks*:

> During the 1960s, the Welfare Rights Movement which Richard Cloward and Frances Fox Piven created succeeded beyond their wildest dreams. Exactly as they predicted, mobilizing masses of poor people to storm welfare offices—both literally and figuratively—demanding

every penny to which the system entitled them by law caused a whole-sale collapse not only of the social services bureaucracy, but of the larger economy which supported it. New York City, where NWRO's legions hit hardest, actually went bankrupt in 1975 as a direct result of the hemor-rhage of city funds into welfare payments.

From the radical perspective of Cloward and Piven, this was success. It demonstrated for all to see that welfare did not and could not elimi-nate poverty. The ruling classes would never allocate enough money to make a difference. If the poor wished to better their lives, they would have to demand fundamental change—a new social compact guarantee-ing a living wage for all Americans, whether or not they worked.[26]

But left-wing professors Cloward and Piven, the conceptualizers of "social control theory," also recognized the limits of welfare activism. In their 1971 book, *Regulating the Poor*, they note that "officials should expand welfare during periods of civil disorder and then roll back ben-efits after political stability is restored." They concluded that "a placid poor hardly constitute a political constituency whose interests must be taken seriously."[27]

Change, therefore, must be pushed along through other means. "Plainly, Cloward and Piven had pushed the welfare gambit as far as it would go," wrote Richard Poe in 2005. "But they had not yet run out of tricks. They still had their 'crisis strategy.' And they knew it worked. The only question was where to apply it next?" The answer is that they released ACORN and Project VOTE! to "put the 'crisis strategy' to work at the polls."[28]

Project VOTE! pioneered in registering low-income and minority vot-ers in "selected areas across the country" in "all the places where the poor are made to wait to receive 'services.'" According to Cloward and Piven, writing in November 1985 in *The Nation*, Project VOTE! "became the first group to register people waiting in lines for food stamps and unemployment benefits—a technique that was adopted by other groups as the campaign grew."[29]

We catch a contemporary glimpse of Project VOTE! from an August 1992 article in the *Chicago Sun-Times*. The author is African American journalist Vernon Jarrett, late father-in-law of Valerie Jarrett, who is a close friend to both Barack and Michelle Obama and now serves as a top White House advisor to the president.[30]

Vernon Jarrett described Project VOTE! as "10 church-based community organizations dedicated to black voter registration." Rolls were increasing at a "7,000-per-week clip." However, according to the program's then-executive director Barack Obama, in order for it to reach "its goal of registering 150,000 out of an estimated 400,000 unregistered blacks statewide, 'it must average 10,000 rather than 7,000 every week.'" Obama said the biggest problem was "the young, the 18 to 35 group. . . . There's a lot of talk about 'black power' among the young but so little action."[31]

A second contemporary report comes from Gretchen Reynolds, who wrote in the January 1993 issue of *Chicago Magazine* that a "saturation media campaign" was helped by "black-owned Brainstorm Communications," whose president, Terri Gardner, was the "sister of Gary Gardner, president of Soft Sheen Products, Inc., which donated thousands of dollars to Project Voters' efforts." Reynolds reported:

> The group's slogan—"It's a Power Thing"—was ubiquitous in African-American neighborhoods. Posters were put up. Black-oriented radio stations aired the group's ads and announced where people could go to register. Minority owners of McDonald's restaurants allowed registrars on site and donated paid radio time to Project VOTE! Labor unions provided funding, as, in late fall, did the Clinton/Gore campaign, whose national voter-registration drive was being directed by Chicago alderman Bobby Rush.[32]

Keith Kelleher, head organizer for the Service Employees International Union 880, wrote in Spring 2008 that the union had been involved in "political action" since its founding in 1983. One example, he states, was working in 1992 with ACORN and Project VOTE!

> Local 880 and Illinois ACORN joined forces with a newly invigorated voter registration group, Project VOTE!, run by former community organizer (and current Democratic presidential candidate and U.S. Senator) Barack Obama, to bring other community groups under the Project

VOTE! umbrella and move a large-scale voter registration program for U.S. Senator Carol Moseley Braun.[33]

ACORN says the voter registration program "made it possible" in 1992 for Carol Moseley Braun to win her U.S. Senate seat that year. Braun is known for her strong ties to the Communist Party and Democratic Socialists of America.[34]

James Simpson, however, writes that, although Project VOTE!'s stated purpose is "to work within the system, using conventional voter mobilization drives and litigation to secure the rights of minority and low-income voters under the U.S. Constitution," in reality, "the organization's actions indicate that its true agenda is to overwhelm, paralyze, and discredit the voting system through fraud, protests, propaganda and vexatious litigation."[35]

None other than Barack Obama himself described the tight relationship between ACORN and Project VOTE! when he addressed ACORN leaders in November 2007. Sam Graham-Felsen, a paid blogger for the Obama for America campaign, wrote:

> [Obama] reminded them of his history with ACORN and his beginnings in Illinois as a Project VOTE! organizer, a nonprofit focused on voter rights and education. Senator Obama said, "I come out of a grassroots organizing background. That's what I did for three and half years before I went to law school. That's the reason I moved to Chicago was to organize. So this is something that I know personally, the work you do, the importance of it. I've been fighting alongside ACORN on issues you care about my entire career. Even before I was an elected official, when I ran Project VOTE! voter registration drive in Illinois, ACORN was smack dab in the middle of it, and we appreciate your work.[36]

In a trifecta of now-obvious lies, Obama's presidential campaign website, *Fight the Smears*, in October 2008, claimed Obama was "never an ACORN community organizer"; "ACORN never hired Obama as a trainer, organizer, or any type of employee"; and "ACORN was not part of Project VOTE!, the successful voter registration drive Barack ran in 1992."[37]

Aaron Klein added on October 12, 2008, at *WorldNetDaily*: "Obama's campaign claims ACORN was 'not part of' Project VOTE!, but the organization's incorporation papers, obtained by WorldNetDaily, show Project VOTE! is a trademark name whose parent company is registered at the same New Orleans address in which ACORN and multiple ACORN affiliates are housed."[38]

Perhaps this is a good time to mention that ACORN and SEIU Local 880 have operated in lockstep in Illinois since at least 1995—the year Barack Obama first ran for the Illinois State Senate. That year Chicago ACORN and Local 880 "built a 60-member coalition that mounted the Chicago Jobs and Living Wage Campaign."[39]

A final example of just how intertwined ACORN and Project VOTE! are surfaced in January 2009 by way of ACORN whistleblower Anita MonCrief, who blogged that a complaint for civil RICO charges against ACORN had recently been filed with details contained in a report prepared by ACORN's "own lawyer," Elizabeth Kingsley,[40] who worried that Project VOTE! had violated federal laws.

Kingsley's "concerns about the way Acorn affiliates work together could fuel the controversy over ACORN's voter registration efforts, which are largely underwritten by an affiliated charity, Project VOTE!," wrote Stephanie Strom in the October 21, 2008, *New York Times*: "Project VOTE! hires ACORN to do voter registration work on its behalf, and the two groups say they have registered 1.3 million voters this year."[41]

As a federally tax-exempt charity, Project VOTE! is "subject to prohibitions on partisan political activity," Strom wrote. But ACORN, a "nonprofit membership corporation under Louisiana law, though subject to federal taxation, is not bound by the same restrictions."

Kingsley "found that the tight relationship between Project VOTE! and ACORN made it impossible to document that Project VOTE!'s money had been used in a strictly nonpartisan manner," Strom wrote. Additionally, prior to an ACORN embezzlement scandal involving Wade Rathke's brother, Dale Rathke, which broke in the summer of 2007, Project VOTE!'s board "was made up entirely of ACORN staff members and ACORN members."

One was indistinguishable from the other. No wonder Sen. Obama had a difficult time explaining his relationship with ACORN during the October 15, 2008, presidential debate.

"OLD FRIEND" OBAMA REPRESENTED, TRAINED ACORN

Truth be told, however, Obama has been well acquainted with ACORN for many years.

Not long after he joined the Davis Miner Barnhill and Galland P.C. (Davis Miner) law firm in 1993, Obama was a junior member of the firm in lawsuits brought on behalf of ACORN. In the first, *Barnett v. Daley*, Obama was part of the legal team that "challenged the racial apportionment of Chicago voting districts as shortchanging blacks, despite the fact that their district power was very close to the black percentage of Chicago's population. Created were 19 black super-majority districts. Obama's team wanted 24."[42]

In the 1994 lawsuit, *Buycks-Roberson v. Citibank Federal Savings Bank*, ACORN alleged racial discrimination in the bank's lending practices. The case summary states the class action lawsuit was filed July 6, 1994, "alleging that Citibank had engaged in redlining practices in the Chicago metropolitan area." Plaintiffs "alleged that the Defendant-bank rejected loan applications of minority applicants while approving loan applications filed by white applicants with similar financial characteristics and credit histories." The case was voluntarily dismissed on May 12, 1998, "pursuant to a settlement agreement."[43]

In 1995, then-governor James Edgar (Republican) "refused to implement the federal 'Motor Voter' law." Edgar argued: "Allowing voters to register using only a postcard and blocking the state from culling voter rolls, could invite fraud," John Fund wrote April 29, 2008, in the *Wall Street Journal*.[44]

The Davis Miner legal team, again including Obama, represented ACORN in three separate lawsuits involving voter registration issues. The first two were filed in 1995 versus Governor Edgar to challenge the state's "refusal to abide by the National Voting Rights Act, also known as motor voter". The third suit was brought against the Illinois State Board of Elections.[45]

· · ·

OBAMA A "FELLOW ORGANIZER"

Obama's acquaintance with ACORN went well beyond involvement in the organization's legal affairs, since he conducted training sessions for ACORN beginning in 1992. Frank De Zutter reported in the December 1995 *Chicago Reader* that Obama was giving classes on community organizing at the Centers for New Horizons south side center for "future leaders identified" by ACORN.[46]

"I can't repeat what most ACORN members think and say about politicians. But Barack has proven himself among our members," De Zutter was told by Madeline Talbott, a lead organizer for Chicago ACORN. "He is committed to organizing, to building a democracy. Above all else, he is a good listener, and we accept and respect him as a kindred spirit, a fellow organizer."[47]

In fact, Talbott was reportedly "so impressed by Obama's organizing skills that she invited him to help train her own staff," wrote Stanley Kurtz, a senior fellow at the Ethics and Public Policy Center, on May 29, 2008, at *National Review Online*. In an appearance on Fox News Channel's *Fox & Friends* on September 30, 2008, Kurtz said Obama had "very close ties" to ACORN, and with Talbott "in particular."[48]

Talbott was an "absolute pioneer" of "intimidation tactics" against banks, such as staging "in-your-face protests in bank lobbies" and filing "complaints meant to hold up mergers sought by targeted banking firms," according to Kurtz. The goal was to force the banks to agree to ACORN's terms—easing down-payment requirements and ignoring weak credit histories—which many banks "understandably" did.[49]

Kurtz said Talbott selected Obama "when he was just sort of a wet behind the ears organizer." Talbott was just beginning her campaign against the banks about the time when Obama returned to Chicago from law school.[50]

These ACORN staffers were the same "people who would later descend on Chicago's banks as CRA [Community Reinvestment Act of 1977] shakedown artists," Mona Charen observed on September 30, 2008, at *NationalReviewOnline*.[51]

ACORN itself stated in 2003, "we have invited Obama to our leadership training sessions to run the session on power every year." New ACORN leaders got to know Obama and turned out as "active volunteers" for his first Illinois State Senate campaign and his failed run for the U.S. Congress in 2000. In 2003, by the time Obama ran for the U.S. Senate, ACORN stated, "we were old friends." ACORN pitched in, including using crews of "paid and supervised canvases" and knocking on doors two weeks in advance of the March 2004 primary to increase the turnout in Chicago's "Little Village and the suburbs," the African American and Latino neighborhoods which were deemed "ACORN communities."[52]

The day after the third Obama-McCain presidential debate, on October 16, 2008, ACORN came out swinging in a conference call with reporters. Carla Marinucci reported in the *San Francisco Chronicle:*

> ACORN organizers this morning said that Sen. Barack Obama, as a local elected official in Chicago, participated in two training sessions for 50 volunteer leaders.
>
> In addition, he and his law firm represented a group of plaintiffs, including ACORN, regarding motor voter registration issues. They said his campaign has also provided about $80,000 in funding to an independent consulting group, which in turn provided some funding to ACORN to get out the vote.[53]

OBAMA FUNDED ACORN

ACORN's passing reference to Obama having procured funding for the organization was a gross understatement.

While serving on the board of directors for the Woods Fund during the decade 1993–2002, Obama directed nonprofit foundation funds to ACORN. Also serving on the board were Bill Ayers and Palestinian activist Rashid Khalidi, who is now a professor at Columbia University. ACORN received five grants from the Woods Fund while Obama was there: $45,000 (2000), $30,000 (2001), $45,000 (2001), $30,000 (2002), and $40,000 (2002).[54]

Beyond repeated grants from the Woods Fund, reporter Stanley Kurtz also discovered—while combing through Chicago Annenberg Challenge files in the Richard J. Daley Library at the University of Illinois in September 2008—that Obama and Bill Ayers had awarded substantial CAC funds to ACORN.[55] Obama was CAC's first executive director in 1995, stepping down in 1999 and remaining on the board until he left the CAC in 2002.

Kurtz discovered that the Grassroots School Improvement Campaign received $75,000 in 1997 from the Chicago Annenberg Challenge "to help develop leadership among parents and community members at several schools." The GSIC, a "partnership" between Chicago ACORN, the Small Schools Workshop, Cross City Campaign for Urban School Reform, and "eight Chicago schools, for parent and community participation in school improvement," received $135,000 in 1998 for "leadership development." It also received $50,000 in 2001 for unspecified programs. Fred Lucas reported in October 2008 at *CNSNews.com* that, based on IRS filings, the GSIC had received a total of $350,000 from the Challenge between 1998 and 2002.[56]

Let us for a moment take a closer look at the GSIC "partners" receiving repeated grants from the fund directed by Obama, along with Ayers.

The Small Schools Workshop, created in the nineties, is co-directed by Ayers and Mike Klonsky. In 1968 Klonsky was Students for a Democratic Society national chairman and a "demonstration organizer." In his post-SDS days Klonsky formed "the October League (Marxist-Leninist) and Communist Party (Marxist-Leninist), part of the new communist movement that emerged in the 1970s." Ayers and Klonsky, both communists, were consultants for Mayor Richard M. Daley's "agenda for public schools."[57]

The Cross City Campaign for Urban School Reform director was Diana Nelson. Klonsky wrote on his *Small Talk* blog that the Campaign was "one of a number of Chicago's first-wave reform groups that led the struggle for school decentralization back in the late '80s."[58]

Nelson later inserted herself into Obama campaign affairs when, on October 13, 2008, she wrote an apologetic letter, published in the *Chicago Tribune*, defending the Obama-Ayers relationship.[59]

Nelson's ties to both Ayers and Obama were also social in nature. She was a member of a 1999 Community Renewal Society 10th Anniversary Prom coordinated by a planning committee that included Michelle

Obama, John Ayers (brother to Bill Ayers), Susan Klonsky (wife of Mike Klonsky), and Linda Lenz, the founder and publisher of Community Renewal Society organ *Catalyst Chicago*. It is Lenz's publication that reported on Chicago schools and the Chicago Annenberg Challenge and Woods Fund annual grants.[60]

Note that Community Renewal Society's executive director, Rev. Calvin S. Morris, was the Democratic Socialists of America honoree in April 2006 at the annual Eugene V. Debs–Norman Thomas–Michael Harrington Dinner. The Society identifies itself with racial and economic justice.[61]

Linda Lenz dutifully penned her own apologetic letter on the Ayers-Obama relationship, published August 30, 2008, in the *Chicago Sun-Times*. Lenz dismissed any connection between Ayers' years with the Weather Underground and his more recent school reform enterprise, the Chicago Annenberg Challenge, and the shared relationship with Barack Obama. Lenz writes: "In other words, Obama does, indeed, know Bill Ayers as more than just a guy from the neighborhood. So do a host of civic leaders in Chicago."[62]

In addition to grant funds, Obama directed his own presidential campaign funds to ACORN. Kurtz references Stanley M. Brown's *Pittsburgh Tribune-Review* report that, between the last week of February and mid-May 2008, Obama's presidential campaign paid $832,598.29 during the Ohio primary to Citizens Services Inc., an ACORN "offshoot." Citizen Services is headquartered at the same New Orleans address as ACORN. The campaign told the Federal Election Commission that Citizen Services worked in "get-out-the-vote" projects, when, in fact, it engaged in such activities as "polling, advance work and staging major events." The Obama campaign agreed to submit an amendment to the FEC, stating the erroneous report was a mistake.[63]

Jim Terry, spokesman for the Consumers Rights League, a Washington, D.C., "advocacy outfit with a libertarian outlook . . . that tracks ACORN," said Citizen Services' "involvement in the Obama campaign raises bigger questions." "All of this just seems like an awful lot of money and time spent on political campaigning for an organization that purports to exist to help low-income consumers," Terry said.[64]

Unsurprisingly, on February 22, 2008, ACORN's political action committee endorsed Barack Obama for president. Katrina vanden Heuvel, editor of *The Nation*, commented: "This is an important nod from a group that understands the urgent needs of Americans most hurt by this economy and how to organize for social and economic justice. . . . The endorsement reflects a belief that Obama—who worked as a community organizer on the South Side of Chicago—understands that change must come from the ground up, as part of a working coalition, rather than from position papers."[65]

Vanden Heuvel quoted ACORN's national president, Maude Hurd: "What it came down to was that Senator Obama is the candidate who best understands and can affect change on the issues ACORN cares about like stopping foreclosures, enacting fair and comprehensive immigration reform, and building stronger and safer communities across America."[66]

In a February 21, 2008, ACORN PAC press release, Alicia Russell of Arizona, the western representative for ACORN Vote, said Obama was "on the same level as we are, and sees our issues as we do."[67]

But far more noteworthy than the bland ACORN endorsements are the constant reports of ACORN fraud, illegality, and corruption. In the words of David M. Brown:

> Accusations of voter fraud have followed ACORN's canvassing projects in about a dozen states. ACORN has dismissed the charges as politically motivated allegations from conservative groups, yet cases are pending and, in other cases, ACORN workers have entered guilty pleas. . . .
>
> ACORN has a long and sordid history of employing convoluted Enron-style accounting to illegally use taxpayer funds for their own political gain. . . . Now it looks like ACORN is using the same type of convoluted accounting scheme for Obama's political gain.[68]

Or as Jim Terry from the Civil Rights League put it:

> Money flows back and forth between ACORN, Citizens Services Inc., Project Vote and Communities Voting Together. ACORN posts job ads for Citizens Services and Project Vote. Communities Voting Together

contributed $60,000 to Citizens Services Inc., for example, in November 2005, according to a posting on CampaignMoney.com. Project Vote has hired ACORN and CSI as its highest paid contractors, paying ACORN $4,649,037 in 2006 and CSI $779,016 in 2006. . . .[69]

Edward T. Chambers, the Saul Alinsky protégé who heads the Industrial Areas Foundation, and who trained Barack Obama in Alinsky tactics in the early nineties, used the words "shakedowns" and "blackmail" when asked about ACORN and "its activities" by Charlotte Allen of the *Weekly Standard*.[70]

OBAMA'S CAMPAIGN USED ACORN-ALINSKY TECHNIQUES

Obama's presidential campaign appears to have taken pages right out of the Saul Alinsky playbook in organizing his successful 2008 presidential campaign.

Obama followed directly in the footsteps of Alinsky and ACORN by organizing house parties to propel his campaign. For starters, Governor Howard Dean, the 2004 Democratic presidential hopeful who picked Barack Obama as one of his original "Dean Dozen," had made wide use of a program connecting his followers on the Internet with meet-up groups in their local area. The Obama campaign, which inherited much of the Dean Internet team, expanded on the concept, mobilizing followers using the campaign's website, *MyBarackObama.com*, FaceBook, and MySpace, as well as sending out emails and text messages.

Both Dean and Obama owe a debt of thanks to earlier organizers, including ACORN's Wade Rathke, who took Saul Alinsky's community organizing methodology to the next level. Obama adviser Harry C. Boyte writes in his 1980 seminal book on citizen organizing, *The Backyard Revolution*, that Rathke "elaborated and refined approaches that stemmed from a related tradition of organizing."[71]

The "roots of Rathke's method," Boyte says, "lie in the organizing efforts of Fred Ross, an Alinsky co-worker who helped organize the Community Service Organization in the Mexican-American community of the southwest in the late 1940's." Ross disagreed with Alinsky, who maintained that the community building block was the churches. Ross said in order to build "an organization throughout the entire region . . . required a new kind of approach that would win the sympathy of local churches but would not rest upon them."[72]

Ross' solution was a "method of holding house meetings around issues of general concerns to the Mexican-American population." Boyte writes that Ross "developed the house meeting approach to a highly polished procedure." Ross and César Chávez put the house meeting concept, "issue-organizing approach" to work in organizing farm workers.[73]

Rathke, Boyte writes, combined Alinsky's "direct action" approach with Ross's house-meeting, "issue-organizing approach" with Wiley's National Welfare Reform Organization "welfare rights organizing efforts."[74]

After receiving "his first experiences" at NWRO's Syracuse, New York, training center, Rathke first tried out his new "majority strategy" method—building the power of the majority—with a "fledging welfare group" in Boston. In 1970 Rathke moved south to Arkansas, where he established ACORN.[75]

Speaking clearly to Rathke's ACORN and other community organizing groups on December 1, 2007, at the Heartland Democratic Presidential Forum in Iowa, Obama confirmed his long-term involvement for all to hear: "I've been fighting alongside ACORN on issues you care about my entire career."[76]

Contrary to his claim during the presidential debate, Obama's involvement has not been confined to representing the organization in an Illinois case on the "motor voter law that helped people get registered at DMVs."[77]

Rather, Obama has been deeply involved with ACORN for many years and is deeply sympathetic to ACORN's agenda. *National Review* writer Mona Charen rightly identified Obama as an "ACORN fellow traveler," and Deroy Murdock nailed it:

> While shocking revelations about this group pile up, as if they had fallen from trees, Barack Obama understandably will treat ACORN like something only a squirrel could love. But don't be fooled. They're old friends.[78]

9

OBAMA'S SOCIALIST-LED UNION ARMY

I T COMES AS no surprise that Barack Obama receives consistent campaign support from unions, and has since he first ran for the Illinois State Senate in 1995. What is surprising, however, is the depth of his relationship with one particular union, the ACORN-affiliated, socialist-led Service Employees International Union. Obama and the SEIU are very old friends.[1]

With almost two million members, SEIU is the second-largest labor union in the United States, after the National Education Association (teachers union).[2]

It is also the largest union within the American Federation of Labor and Congress of Industrial Organizations, or AFL-CIO, the largest federation of unions in the United States. Most of SEIU's members are health care, government, or building services employees.

Barack Obama first received support and political campaign contributions from SEIU in connection with his 1995 socialist New Party candidacy for the Illinois State Senate, which the authors discuss in Chapter 6.[3] But such contributions were paltry compared to the pot of gold SEIU staked on Obama's presidential campaign 13 years later.

From November 1995 through 2000, Illinois State Board of Elections files for the Friends of Barack Obama political action committee show comparatively insignificant contributions from the SEIU, most in the $250 to $1,000 range.

Contrast this with the whopping $60 million SEIU reportedly spent in 2008 "to help elect Obama to the White House." SEIU also deployed "some 100,000 pro-Obama volunteers during the campaign (including 3,000 who worked on the election full time)"—all of which may actually be an understatement of SEIU's support for the Obama campaign.[4]

However, nothing demonstrates Barack Obama's strong ties to SEIU more than words spoken by Obama himself.

"During his presidential campaign, President Obama boasted of his track record of working with the Illinois-based Service Employees International Union, helping it 'build more and more power'—and he promised to 'paint the nation purple with SEIU,'" reporter Chelsea Schilling wrote October 13, 2009, at *WorldNetDaily*.[5]

Proof comes from a January 15, 2008, video that surfaced in October 2009 and was posted online by Andrew Breitbart. Schilling wrote: Obama "told a group of SEIU workers that all presidential, gubernatorial and congressional candidates claim they are pro-union when they are looking for endorsements."

> They'll all say, "We love SEIU." But the question you've got to ask yourself is, do they have it in their gut? Do they have a track record of standing alongside you on picket lines? Do they have a track record of going after the companies that aren't letting you organize? Do they have a track record of voting the right way but also helping you organize to build more and more power? . . .
>
> I've been working with SEIU before I was elected to anything. When I was a community organizer, SEIU local 880 and myself, we organized people to make sure that home-care workers had the basic right to organize. We organized voting registration drives. That's how we built political power on the south side of Chicago. . . .
>
> And now the time has come for us to do it all across this country. We are going to paint the nation purple with SEIU. . . .
>
> I would not be a United States senator had it not been for the support

of your brothers and sisters in Illinois. They supported me early. They supported me often. I've got my purple windbreaker from my campaign in 2004.[6]

At the end of his speech, Schilling wrote, "Obama raised his fist and chanted, 'SEIU! SEIU! SEIU!'"

SEIU's allegiance to Barack Obama was evidenced just prior to the general election, on October 30, 2008, when SEIU claimed that, in its Get Out the Vote efforts, the union had:

- knocked on 1,878,421 doors;
- made 4,405,136 phone calls;
- sent 2,562,689 pieces of mail;
- registered 85,914 voters;
- helped more than 10,982 people vote early;
- distributed 52,005 workplace flyers;
- "made workers' voices heard by investing $13 million in independent expenditure ads that have run more than 10,000 times";
- carried out "election protection work in Ohio; Lake County, Indiana; Florida; Colorado; Virginia and other places and made sure that the voices of working people were not silenced and that every vote would count and be counted in this election";
- "held more than 600 events across the country to ensure voters knew which candidates stood on the side of Americans who wake up and earn a paycheck every day";
- and "another 2,500 members from mid-Atlantic locales [traveled] across the country to join their Change to Win brothers and sisters for rallies calling on candidates to rebuild the middle class in Pennsylvania while another 800 travel to Ohio and more than 260 will be in Virginia."[7]

No wonder SEIU is sometimes described as a "unionized version" of ACORN.

In June 2009, Andrew Stern told Peter Nicholas of the *Los Angeles Times* that "SEIU's political loyalties are solid, reaching back to the 2004

Illinois Senate race, when Obama was a long shot but earned the union's endorsement."[8]

It was no exaggeration, then, when Stern announced the 1.9-million member union's endorsement of Obama's presidential candidacy on February 15, 2008, saying: "There has never been a fight in Illinois or a fight in the nation where our members have not asked Barack Obama for assistance and he has not done everything he could to help us."[9]

Stern's testimony also places in context some heavy post-election maneuvering over cabinet appointments. Less than a week after the general election, "ACORN favorite" Andrew Stern was touted as Obama's favorite to be named secretary of labor. Stern's name also turned up on a list of possible labor secretary nominations compiled by *Politico*.[10]

But given all the attention being paid to numerous allegations of voter-registration fraud committed by ACORN on behalf of the Obama campaign, Michael Gaynor commented in *The Post Chronicle* less than a week after the general election that Stern's "would not be a wise nomination"—even though Stern's platform was pretty much the Obama platform. Likewise, the investigations into ACORN could lead to an investigation of SEIU fraud.[11]

Given the problems preventing him from being appointed Obama's secretary of labor, what did Stern and SEIU expect in return for $60 million and countless man-hours of campaign support?

The answer is, a lot. As Peter Nicholas reported June 18, 2009, in the *Los Angeles Times*:

> They led the most powerful forces in healthcare—the trade groups representing doctors, insurance companies, hospitals and drug makers. Any one of them could stall, if not derail, President Obama's hopes of overhauling the U.S. healthcare system.
>
> Instead, they stood with Obama before TV cameras at the White House and pledged their cooperation. For Obama, the show of unity gave momentum to perhaps his most ambitious domestic goal.[12]

That media moment in May was a victory as well for another man— unnamed in the *Los Angeles Times* report. Andy Stern heads the SEIU, the union that helped corral the industry groups in support of Obama's healthcare "reform," and Stern's presence at the White House photo-op was a fresh sign of his formidable clout with Obama. In a fractious labor movement fraught with rivalries and mutual suspicion, Stern's close association with Obama gives him cachet that can only help in the fierce competition to lure new members.

But when the president met privately with the health industry leaders that day, a second Service Employees International Union official was present with Stern in the room. In fact, he and Stern were the only representatives invited from organized labor. The identity of the second SIEU official was only to emerge later.

"INFILTRATE LABOR MOVEMENT"

Stern's background, and those of the political operatives with whom he has been and continues to be connected, are pedigrees of the American left. Stern was "instructed in the techniques of radical union organizing by the Midwest Academy," according to *Discover the Networks*, which also reports that MWA was co-founded by the husband and wife team of Paul and Heather Booth, both former members of Students for a Democratic Society. MWA's mission is to "train community organizers and infiltrate the labor movement."[13]

"The Midwest Academy is one of those organizations funded via the Woods Fund, upon whose board Obama sat 1999–December 2002 as a paid director, and his neighborhood pal since 1993, unrepentant Communist terrorist Billy Ayers," *Discover the Networks* informs.

Stern, a "New Leftist protégé of avowed socialist Michael Harrington, studied union organization under former members of the radical Students for a Democratic Society."[14]

Harrington is the late "prominent activist who founded the Democratic Socialist Organizing Committee and the Democratic Socialists of America" in the seventies and eighties. Harrington's 1962 book about poverty in the United States, *The Other America*, is said to have "influenced the policies of the Kennedy and Johnson administrations' War on Poverty."[15]

It has not been clearly spelled out is that Andrew Stern had himself been a member of SDS in the sixties, while attending the University of Pennsylvania's Wharton School of Business.[16]

Stern was also active in the Pittsburgh chapter of the New American Movement, "which focused on building support for socialism in unions and feminist groups." NAM merged with Harrington's Democratic Socialist Organizing Committee in 1983 to create the Democratic Socialists of America.[17]

Stern began his rise to SEIU president in 1973. He started out as a "welfare case officer and a member of the SEIU" and "rapidly rose through the ranks and was eventually elected president of his Pennsylvania local. In 1980, he was elected to the union's executive board, and in 1984 the union's then-president John Sweeney put him in charge of its organizing efforts." Stern became SEIU president in 1996 when Democratic Socialists of America member Sweeney became president of the AFL-CIO.[18]

ALINSKY PLAYBOOK, CORRUPT POLITICS

Stern's "organizing efforts," described in July 2004 by Lowell Ponte at *FrontPageMagazine.com*, are straight out of the SDS sixties–Midwest Academy–Saul Alinsky playbook and closely resemble SEIU "organizing" tactics observed during Obama's presidential campaign.

SEIU began as a Chicago-based janitors' union. It was Stern, using New Left tactics of the 1960s with Sweeney's approval, who shut down parts of Los Angeles with a "Justice for Janitors" strike that blocked not just one company but city streets as well. These workers, at Stern's direction, wore red shirts and carried signs depicting brooms held in the clenched fist that symbolizes Marxism.

"We're going to build the strongest grassroots political voice in North America," Stern told more than 3,000 SEIU delegates in his convention address last month.

But Stern's ideological aim has nothing to do with empowering workers. On the contrary, he has pursued a policy of consolidating small SEIU-affiliated unions into larger unions, and of giving the national union total control over its locals, which are now to be prohibited from even having their own logo and symbols. All power and image is to be subsumed under the purple and gold logo of national SEIU and its supreme boss Andy Stern. Stern's current organizing approach, in fact, is to bypass workers altogether.

SEIU and its political, media and leftwing activist allies conspire to attack a company directly with what they call "Corporate Campaigns" or the "death of a thousand cuts." Like the Furies of Greek mythology, this cabal of attackers harasses and disrupts company activities, sends vicious emails and letters to stockholders, intimidates customers, stalks and frightens employees, files baseless lawsuits, plants false stories with media allies to smear the company's reputation, and uses hundreds of other tactics to injure the targeted company in every way they can imagine.

The aim of this concerted swarming attack is to bully and pressure a targeted company into signing an agreement making SEIU the representative of its employees. When this happens, employees who might have voted NO to SEIU representation in an election will get no vote at all. The union yoke is simply locked around each worker's neck—and paycheck. SEIU prefers this because, in a large percentage of past cases, workers who were given a choice voted against joining this thug union.

Bear in mind, when Ponte wrote the following conclusion to his July 2004 article, it was another Democratic presidential candidate, and future Obama supporter, Massachusetts Senator John Kerry, whom the SEIU was underwriting in hopes of achieving its goals.

Stern's ballyhooed vision for "New Labor" is really a century old, akin to the goal of the International Workers of the World (IWW) "Wobblies" to create "One Big Union" for all workers so powerful that it could impose socialist-anarchist government, confiscate all private companies, redistribute all private wealth, and end war by having the world's workers refuse to fight. The IWW refused to forgo strikes during World War I, opposed the war, came to be widely perceived as unpatriotic and anti-American, and this led to the extinction of this early dinosaur version of the labor movement.

These are the same old leftward reptilian footprints, right down to last month's SEIU withdraw-the-troops resolution, that Stern today is following. Because of their stranglehold on the Democratic Party, this is an ominous portent of politics to come.

Also note that the $65 million in financial support provided by SEIU to Kerry's campaign was comparable to the reported mega funds—$60 million—provided to the Obama campaign.[19]

At the time, the failure of the unions to get Kerry elected was attributed to a lack of union membership and "not due to deficiencies in its political program but in good part because there simply aren't enough union members anymore to turn an election." Stern argued the problem was that the AFL-CIO "must overcome its declining membership problem in order to hand over more votes" to the Democratic "big business" party.[20] Of even greater concern to Stern following the 2004 election was the "virtual collapse of the Democratic Party," which posed "very real threats to the income base of the AFL-CIO bureaucracy," and of which SEIU is an important part.

Jerry White wrote on the Socialist Workers website in February 2005:

> The AFL-CIO has always delivered votes to the Democratic Party, so that the Democratic Party would deliver public-sector jobs and dues income to the labor bureaucracy. The threat that this would dry up [became] a matter of life and death for the AFL-CIO bureaucracy, particularly since so few private-sector workers are union members.[21]

Herein we gain an understanding of the incestuous union–Democratic Party relationship. It also spells out why the AFL-CIO bureaucracy and the Democratic Party leadership have thrown so much weight behind the Employee Free Choice Act ("Card Check"), the scheme to control union members' votes in elections, not to mention enlarging union membership rolls and income from dues.[22]

Stern's sphere of influence extends to other power schemes, as well. He is an Executive Committee member of the Democratic Party auxiliary, America Coming Together (ACT), funded by George Soros. Blogger Old Marine writes:

ACT organized the Democratic Party's Government Union wing, which is represented by such leftist labor unions as the Service Employees International Union (SEIU) and AFSCME. ACT was one of the 33 "progressive" member organizations constituting the America Votes coalition. Not being satisfied with the radical activities of his other organizations, Stern, along with George Soros, helped organize Working for Us (WFU), a political action committee that seeks to "elect lawmakers who support a progressive political agenda." This was aimed at moving the Democratic Party ever further to the political left. Stern and WFU work to prevent conservative and moderate Democrats from gaining too much influence in government.[23]

Discover the Networks adds:

Stern is a leading figure in the so-called Shadow Party, a nationwide network of more than five-dozen unions, non-profit activist groups, and think tanks whose agendas are ideologically to the Left, and who are engaged in campaigning for the Democrats. In July 2003, Stern—along with fellow Shadow Party leaders Harold Ickes, Steve Rosenthal, Ellen Malcolm, and Jim Jordan—formed America Votes, a national coalition of grassroots, get-out-the-vote organizations.[24]

U.S. Attorney Patrick Fitzgerald's office identified Stern as the "SEIU Official" named on page 69 of the federal political criminal corruption complaint against Illinois Governor Rod Blagojevich and his chief of staff, John Harris, released December 9, 2008.[25]

In his column that day, *Chicago Tribune* veteran John Kass wrote: "One of those charges was for allegedly trying to sell a seat in the U.S. Senate by the pound, and there were candidates willing to pay the price. [Blagojevich's] alleged co-schemer was his chief of staff, John Harris, who once worked closely with Chicago Mayor Richard Daley."[26]

The U.S. Senate seat up for sale, of course, was that of newly elected president-to-be Barack Obama.

A "Democratic source confirms that SEIU President Andy Stern is the 'SEIU official' referred to in the federal complaint against Rod

Blagojevich," wrote Ben Smith at *The Politico*, also on December 9. "Another Democratic source tells me that Stern [took part] . . . in [the] Chicago November 3 meeting with Blagojevich, a discussion thought to have included talk about the Senate seat—though that meeting isn't mentioned in the complaint."[27]

Commenting on the mention of Andrew Stern, "head of the SEIU, and one of the more powerful figures in Big Labor," in the Blagojevich complaint, Jennifer Rubin wrote in *Commentary Magazine*:

> So the first order of business should be to check the flagpoles and see who in the transition team, if anyone, talked to Stern about the Senate seat. Did Stern carry the message? Was he merely stringing the Governor along? It might be wise, as Big Labor ramps up its push for everything from protectionist legislation to card check to national health care, to make sure one of its principal leaders isn't implicated in the worst political scandal in a generation. At the very least, it is an eye-opener that apparently there was nothing odd for the head of a union to help pick a U.S. Senator. Imagine if it were the head of a major corporation.[28]

But other sources, including an "internal union communication" reviewed by the *Wall Street Journal*, in December 2008, named Tom Balanoff, president of SEIU's Illinois Council, as the "SEIU Official" named in the complaint.[29]

Balanoff is also vice president of SEIU's International Executive Board and president of SEIU Local 1, which "represents 50,000 property service workers throughout the central United States, including 10,000 janitors who recently organized in Texas, Ohio and Indiana." He is also president of the Property Service Section of Union Network International, "which includes more than 50 building service unions in 40 countries."[30]

Commented labor law blogger Stephen Diamond, in December 2008: "Clearly figures within SEIU were attempting to steer interest away from Andy Stern and towards Tom Balanoff."[31]

It was Balanoff's SEIU Illinois Council that was "an early supporter of Barack Obama, and Balanoff led the international union to endorse Obama in the Presidential Primary."[32]

(Balanoff was a member in 1998 of the renamed and reorganized Citizen Action Illinois board of directors following the corruption troubles surrounding Robert Creamer, to be discussed by the authors in the final chapter. Balanoff served on the board with former Obama supporter, Alice Palmer, who lost her Illinois State Senate seat to Obama in the 1995 election.)[33]

Diamond writes:

> A review of what is known about Tom Balanoff indicates that he is, in fact, very close to Andy Stern. . . . Over the past decade he has worked hand in glove with Andy Stern to implement Stern's peculiar agenda for building SEIU power. Stern's top down bureaucratic strategy has engendered widespread criticism and more recently militant opposition from rank and file union members. . . .
>
> Particularly controversial has been Stern's, and Balanoff's, strategy of "organizing politicians first, workers second." This has meant funneling tens of millions of dollars into the campaigns of politicians who can then be called upon to make legal changes that mandate that thousands of previously non-union workers become dues paying union members, sometimes without the clumsy unpredictable practice of actually holding a genuine union election. . . .
>
> Now, it turns out, labor is trying the Stern strategy on a much larger scale. They hope to use the leverage they have created with the Obama victory to put in place something called the Employee Free Choice Act, which would allow unions to be organized once again without bothering about a democratic union election.

Diamond adds: "And to get the necessary legislative change in Congress it helps to have a relationship with the new President."

Thus, all evidence indicates it was Balanoff who was the other SIEU official invited by Obama to be at hand in May 2009, when the grand coalition in support of the president's healthcare "reform" posed for national television audiences.

The Balanoff-Obama acquaintance, Diamond writes, dates back to 1993, "when Obama was just out of Harvard Law School."

Diamond refers to an August 2008 *Progress Illinois* interview with Balanoff, who said his "cousins on the south side of Chicago introduced Obama to Balanoff. Balanoff says they met while Obama was a community organizer there in the mid-1980s."[34]

Diamond adds:

The Balanoff family—including now a judge, politicians, and lawyers—was deeply immersed in the anti-machine wing of Democratic party politics. The Balanoffs would have been critical allies for a young Obama, who was thinking of attempting to duplicate the successful mayoral campaign of his late hero, Harold Washington.

The Balanoffs had close ties to independent black activists, likely a result of their long association with the Communist Party that had such an important presence in black south side Chicago. They were one of the few prominent ethnic families to back Harold Washington, himself once a labor lawyer in Chicago with links to the CP [Communist Party U.S.A.].[35]

Also note that Tom Balanoff has "democratic socialist" ties of his own. On May 10, 2002, at the Democratic Socialists of America's 44th Annual Debs–Thomas–Harrington Dinner, Tom Balanoff, of SEIU Local 1, was the honoree.[36]

Diamond continues: "This introduction led to a close relationship between Balanoff and Obama as Obama began his rise to political prominence. Balanoff spoke on Obama's behalf at the 2008 Democratic National Convention and was instrumental in securing SEIU's endorsement over the more clearly pro-union John Edwards during the campaign itself.

"When Obama was trailing in Nevada during the [January 2008 primary caucus], Balanoff and other Illinois unionists rode in to help, holding a conference call to sing Obama's praises to the locals," Diamond writes. Balanoff, addressing the news media in Nevada, declared:

"He comes from us," said Balanoff on Obama. "He understands our problems. We could count on Barack on all issues important to working families. Healthcare, general economic justice, jobs. . . . Barack was there, not only there but oftentimes leading."[37]

As mentioned above, Balanoff is president of the Property Service Section of Union Network International.

Andrew Stern himself explained that Balanoff, in the late nineties, was SEIU's "top leader in the Midwest," and was "elected chair of one of UNI's sectors, property services, a sector consisting of cleaning and security workers," according to Stern's 2006 book, *A Country That Works: Getting America Back on Track*.[38]

Nowadays, SEIU, and Andrew Stern in particular, want the union to go global.

Although not actually "new" news, this ambition was illuminated by Fox News radio talk show host, Glenn Beck, on his November 13, 2009, program.[39] Beck played a clip from the November 6, 2009, interview with Stern by CNBC.com's Maria Bartiromo, in which Stern declared that we need "global unions"—"unions will have to go global as well."[40]

A partial transcript of the interview, which begins to place Stern's sound bytes into context, was published by Meredith Jessup at *Townhall.com*:

Bartiromo: So I've got this article here; it's says that yourself and other labor union leaders reportedly gave Democrats some $400 million last year. Do you feel that that money has been well-spent? Let me ask you about your number one goal, which of course is card check. A lot of people feel that's dead.

Stern: Well I think what we now know is American workers need a raise; that is pretty clear. And there isn't a lot of money in the government to do it. So the question is how is everyone going to share in the wealth? And I think that after we get through this health care situation and finally solve this problem of 223 years, you know, we are going to see a change in our labor laws that allow people to negotiate their future. . . .

Bartiromo: How does the labor movement survive in an increasingly globalized and technology-advanced world? Obviously jobs are going abroad, technology is taking a lot of our jobs. What do you need to do?

Stern: Well I got in trouble for saying this with Glenn Beck, but I said "workers of the world unite" is not just a slogan anymore, it's a way we need to do our work. And we're involved with unions all over the world, trying to figure how do we raise workers' wages everywhere, 'cause we don't want corporations competing in who can pay the least. And that means company went global, finance went global, capital went global, unions are going to have to go global as well.[41]

Jessup comments:

Soooo basically Obama's friend Andy Stern is saying the best way to bring about the redistribution of wealth is to use unions on a global scale. And apparently the pesky system of capitalism which put America on the map is just a 223-year-old "problem" that needs to be dealt with . . . after we pass government-run health care that is.

Stern has made similar statements several times since at least September 2005, when he said in an interview with *Policy Today*:

We have global conditions and global employers, therefore we need global unions. "Workers of the world unite," which used to be a slogan, is really going to have to be a way of life, because national unions can't deal with global employers successfully.[42]

In his book, Stern wrote that a "mandate" emerged from SEIU's 2004 Convention, when "delegates [began] to build a global union followed by UNI's adoption of global unionism, SEIU assigned staff to Australia, Poland, England, India, France, Switzerland, Germany, the Netherlands, South America, and soon, Africa."[43]

Stern wrote that SEIU was "ramping up to operate on a global stage" by sending "teams of leaders around the world to discuss new forms of alliances and relationships in many sectors, and we invested several million dollars in organizing campaigns that targeted international food-service, cleaning and security employers."

In the October 2008 edition of his book, Stern wrote that, at its August 2008, every-five-year meeting, which was held in Chicago, UNI said it was "time for unions to adapt to a world without borders."

WHITE HOUSE INFLUENCE, OUTSIDE AND INSIDE

More recently, in September 2009, in a move some liken to putting foxes in charge of the hen house, Stern, as well as Obama supporter and presidential transition coordinator John Podesta, president of the Center for American Progress, served on an ACORN Advisory Board tasked with investigating ACORN's alleged corruption. Unsurprisingly, on December 7, 2009, the internal Board announced it had found no wrong doing.[44]

Stern is also a signatory to the support group, Progressives for Obama, which includes a number of former SDSers and assorted socialists, Marxists, and radicals.[45]

At the time of this writing, it was reported that Stern had made an unknown number of visits to the White House since the Obama inauguration. Stern told the *Los Angeles Times*' Peter Nicholas at the end of June 2009 that he visits the White House about once a week.[46]

But that is not the only exhibit of White House clout that Nicholas reported:

> Now in the White House, Obama has continued to derive political benefits from the union. It was the SEIU's health chief, Dennis Rivera, who helped bring industry to the table to start talks on a healthcare overhaul.
>
> With nearly 2 million members, the SEIU says it has people in 13 states whose senators are considered important targets in the lobbying effort behind the emerging Democratic healthcare bill. The union wants to coax those senators into voting for the bill.
>
> Stern can boast that union officials are scattered throughout the Obama administration. White House political director Patrick Gaspard is a former executive at an SEIU local based in New York. No other union has placed anyone at such a high level in the White House.
>
> Anna Burger, SEIU secretary-treasurer, was appointed to Obama's economic recovery board. And union associate counsel John Sullivan was named to the six-member Federal Election Commission.
>
> Moreover, Stern has enjoyed considerable entree to the new administration—starting on Inauguration Day, when he joined Obama and the

new president's family on the reviewing stand outside the White House to watch the inaugural parade.

Stern estimates he visits the White House once a week. SEIU officials talk to senior Obama advisor Nancy-Ann DeParle about healthcare—a top priority for Stern—and to Obama aide Cecilia Munoz about immigration, Stern said.

"We get heard," Stern said.

In 2006, when Stern decided to create a "new national health care workers union that would simultaneously reach out to the unorganized and campaign for universal, national health insurance, he turned to 1199 president Dennis Rivera—and the 1199 [SEIU] political model—to lead the effort."[47]

Long before his appointment as SEIU Healthcare Chair, Rivera was the main supporter for the 1992 political campaign of New York Representative Nydia Velázquez, now chair of the House Small Business Committee. She is Congressional Hispanic Caucus Chair for the 111th Congress, as well as chair of the CHC Institute for the 2009–2010 term. Rivera, now president of Local 1199 of the Drug, Hospital and Health Care Workers Union, participated in the White House's March 5, 2009 Forum on Health Reform.[48]

Following the March 2009 White House gathering, Kate Thomas at the SEIU blog wrote:

> This week Politico dubbed SEIU Healthcare Chair Dennis Rivera "The Organizer" on their list of five people who could play a prime time role in affecting the course of health care reform. Using SEIU's war room operation as an example, Politico highlights how Rivera has "helped SEIU become the most aggressive and ubiquitous player in the healthcare debate;" describing him as a man "with a reputation for getting the job done."

In February 2008, however, the *New York Daily News* described Rivera as a union buster—in Puerto Rico. Critics claimed that Rivera, in collusion with P.R. Governor Anibal Acevedo Vilá, helped get the Puerto Rico

Federation of Teachers, which represented 40,000 teachers, "ousted so he could hijack members."[49] The following month, in March 2008, Governor Acevedo Vilá, an Obama super-delegate, and 12 associates, were indicted on 19 counts of campaign finance violations in Puerto Rico.[50]

One Rivera associate, Patrick Gaspard, is now Obama's White House Political Affairs Director. Glenn Beck aired a segment including Gaspard on July 1, 2009, called "SEIU in a Nutshell," on the Fox News Channel.[51]

Officially, Gaspard's White House duties are "to provide the president with an 'accurate assessment of the political dynamics affecting the work of his administration' and to 'work with powerbrokers around the country to help push the president's agenda,'" wrote New Zealand blogger, Trevor Loudon, October 1, 2009.[52]

But it was not until the end of September 2009 that some right-wing bloggers and *Newsmax.com* rediscovered Gaspard's longtime ties to both SEIU and ACORN.[53]

Loudon made an interesting comparison of Gaspard's background and career to that of Barack Obama. Both Obama and Gaspard's fathers were born in Africa; both "grew up admiring third world leftists and revolutionaries"; both got their start in politics by organizing within the socialist machine (Gaspard in New York City organizing demonstrations for "social justice"; Obama in Chicago organizing voters); both were involved with SEIU (Gaspard as a union organizer and Obama politically supported by the union); and both are involved with the New Party (Gaspard as an organizer in New Jersey and Obama as a member in Illinois when he ran for the State Senate).[54]

Anna Burger, mentioned by the *L.A. Times*' Peter Nicholas above, not only serves as SEIU international secretary-treasurer, but she is also chairwoman of Change to Win. Burger was "hailed by *Gannett* as arguably 'the most influential woman in the U.S. labor movement.'"[55]

Stern precipitated a split in the AFL-CIO empire in 2005. Stern, as head of the SEIU, was "pushing his boss, John Sweeney, president of the AFL-CIO to make reforms or he would lead a walkout from the union federation." When Sweeney "balked," Stern "made good on his threat," and, within a year "formed" Change to Win, "getting the powerful Teamsters and five other unions to join forces with the SEIU. It was the first new labor federation in America in 50 years."[56]

A somewhat dated speaker's profile, perhaps from around 2006, posted on the Center for American Progress website, states that Burger, an activist in the eighties who played a major role in the 1998 SEIU merger with District 1199 in New York, "directs SEIU's political and field operations, including its unprecedented 2004 election program—the largest mobilization by any single organization in the history of U.S. politics. During this cycle, SEIU raised more member dollars than any other union, making SEIU's PAC [political action committee] the largest in the labor movement."[57]

The same profile informs that Burger "began her career in 1972 as a Pennsylvania state caseworker and union activist in SEIU Local 668," rising "through the ranks to become its first female full-time president before moving on to run the state's political field operations and to become SEIU's national director of field operations." Additionally, Anna Burger "has been an active delegate to the Democratic National Convention since 1984 and has worked on the party's platform."

Burger is listed as a Pennsylvania Delegate-at-Large for the 2008 Democratic National Convention.[58]

As long ago as March 2008, Change to Win, headed by Burger, participated in a coalition calling itself Accountability Now.[59] The Accountability Now homepage stated in February 2009 that SEIU, the George Soros–funded MoveOn.org, and the left-wing blog *DailyKos.org* would be joined by communist Van Jones's ColorOfChange.org, Howard Dean's Democracy for America, 21st Century Democrats, and BlogPAC.[60]

The *New York Times'* Jim Rutenberg reported on February 26, 2009:

> A group of liberal bloggers said it was teaming up with organized labor and MoveOn.org to form a political action committee that would seek to push the Democratic Party further to the left.
>
> Soliciting donations from their readers, the bloggers said they were planning to recruit liberal candidates to challenge more centrist Democrats currently in Congress.[61]

DailyKos diarist Barbara Morrill, aka BarbinMD, and numerous left-leaning blogs, re-announced the Accountability NOW PAC on February

26, 2009, allegedly the date of Accountability Now's official launch. She opened with:

> Congressional Democrats who vote out of line with their more liberal constituencies will face some tough times in the next election cycle.[62]

At the time, Accountability Now, calling itself a "grassroots effort," was already running a 2012 campaign—to replace Senator Joe Lieberman, D-Conn. Petition signers were asked to support "whoever runs against Joe Lieberman."[63]

Change to Win, with Anna Burger as union contact, was announced in July 2008 as a member of the Health Care for America Now coalition. (The authors write about HCAN in the final chapter.)[64]

Seeing no apparent conflicts of interest, in February 2009, President Obama named Burger to be a member of his Economic Recovery Advisory Board, formed to provide "advice on reviving the dormant U.S. economy, independent ideas aimed at avoiding the Washington 'echo chamber.'"[65] Note that another labor leader, AFL-CIO secretary-treasurer Richard L. Trumka, was also named to the Economic Recovery Advisory Board.[66]

Burger is also a signatory to the radical group Progressives for Obama. As mentioned above, Andrew Stern is also a signatory.[67]

In his June 2009 *Los Angeles Times* article, Nicholas does not name two other key SEIU players, both SEIU international vice presidents.

SEIU international vice president Eliseo Medina, in 2001, delivered the keynote address at the Democratic Socialists of America annual convention.[68] In August 2004 DSA elected Medina as an honorary chair. Medina's DSA profile says he is "widely credited with playing a key role in the AFL-CIO's decision to adopt a new policy on immigration a few years ago," as well as having been "one of the organizers of the Immigrant Workers Freedom Bus Rides" in 2003. In 2004 Medina received Chicago DSA's Debs-Thomas-Harrington Award.[69]

New Zealand blogger Trevor Loudon writes:

> A former colleague of Cesar Chávez and a supporter of the Communist Party newspaper Peoples Weekly World, Medina also has close ties

to Chicago DSA—the same people who endorsed Barack Obama during his successful bid for Illinois State Senate in 1996. DSA has supported Barack Obama through his entire political career.[70]

On his September 15, 2009, Fox News television show, Glenn Beck played a video clip of President Obama telling union members:

Your agenda has been my agenda in the United States Senate. Before debating health care, I talked to Andy Stern and SEIU members. Before immigration debates took place in Washington, I talked with Eliseo Medina and SEIU members. Before the EFCA [Employees Freedom of Choice Act/Card Check], I talked to SEIU. So, we've worked together over these last few years and I am proud of what we've done. I'm just not satisfied.[71]

The exact dates of the talks Obama had with Eliseo Medina are unknown. However, Medina was a member of Obama's Latino campaign advisory committee and was appointed in November 2008 to serve on Obama's "transition team committee on immigration."[72]

Perhaps the talks were as casual as the one that occurred on August 20, 2009, when Medina convened "a diverse group of labor, advocacy, faith and business leaders," who met with Homeland Security Janet Napolitano to "discuss immigration reform." President Obama "made an unscheduled visit to the meeting and reiterated his support of pushing a comprehensive immigration package through this Congress."[73]

SEIU's other international vice president, Gerland "Gerry" Hudson, is also connected with Democratic Socialists of America. He has served as a member of the board of directors for the Apollo Alliance (which helped craft Obama's stimulus bill) since at least 2006. (The authors expose the Apollo Alliance in Chapter 13.)[74]

As did both Dennis Rivera and Patrick Gaspard, Hudson spent considerable time in New York with SEIU 1199. Hudson's blogger profile at *Talking Union*, a Democratic Socialists of America project, informs:

[Hudson] heads the union's Long Term Care Division, representing nearly 500,000 nursing home and home care workers nationwide. He came to SEIU in 1978 from the Hebrew Home for the Aged in Riverdale, N.Y., where he was a member of SEIU Local 144. Hudson coordinated the merger of Local 144 into SEIU/1199 and was elected as executive vice president for the former–District 1199 in 1989. He is a long time activist on the democratic socialist left and in African-American progressive politics.[75]

Hudson provided information on his DSA background in that blog posting:

I came to DSA (it was DSOC back then) in the 1970s as a young labor activist working in an 1199 nursing home. I joined DSA precisely because of Mike Harrington's vision of a non-sectarian, majoritarian left, with the labor movement at its core. And I joined because, as Michael used to say, good is not the enemy of perfect. He believed—as I do— that incremental change is vital if we are ever going to achieve power for working people. As democratic socialists we don't believe in the big bang of revolution, but rather in the gradual struggle that is sustained over generations and that has real impact on people's daily lives.

Returning for a moment to SEIU president Andrew Stern, although no longer a member, in November 2008 he was listed as a director at the Center for Community Change.[76]

"CCC bases its training programs on techniques expounded by the famed radical organizer Saul Alinsky. Following Alinsky's blueprint for establishing 'grassroots' organizations to agitate for social change, the Center claims it has 'nurtured thousands of local groups and leaders' across the United States," writes Matthew Vadum at *NewsRealBlog*.[77]

CCC's executive director, Deepak Bhargava, is the former legislative director for ACORN. Bhargava arranged the December 1, 2007, gathering at the Heartland Democratic Presidential Forum at which Barack Obama "promised to implement ACORN's agenda as president":

When asked if Obama would sit down with community organizers in the first 100 days of his presidency, Obama said, "Yes, but let me even say before I even get inaugurated, during the transition we'll be calling all of you (community organizers) in to help us shape the agenda."

Obama pledged before leaders of community organizing groups including Gamaliel [Foundation] and ACORN: "We're gonna be having meetings all across the country with community organizations so that you have input into the agenda for the next presidency of the United States of America."[78]

"TRANSFORMING AMERICA"

Trevor Loudon writes that Deepak Bhargava—Indian-born, New York–raised, Harvard-educated—"may have seldom crossed paths with Barack Obama, but he is a key player in [the] 44th president's movement to transform America."

Deepak Bhargava is connected to almost every aspect of the Obama movement—from George Soros to ACORN, to Democratic Socialists of America, to *The Nation*, to the communist-dominated United for Peace and Justice, to a whole raft of "progressive" non profits.[79]

Bhargava joined the CCC in 1994 and became its executive director in 2002.[80]

"Helping Bhargava change America is CCC board member Heather Booth, the former Students for a Democratic Society radical, turned Democratic Party power player," Loudon writes.

In a speech delivered at the September 20–22, 2002, "Confronting the Low-Wage Economy" at the First Congregational Church, Washington, D.C., organized by Democratic Socialists of America, Loudon writes, keynote speaker Bhargava "referred favorably to the work of DSA founder [Michael] Harrington and his book 'The Other America'—which is widely credited with sparking the massive growth of US welfarism" in the sixties under Presidents Kennedy and Johnson.[81]

Bhargava is a member of the National Advisory Board of George Soros' Open Society Institute and is a member of *The Nation* editorial board.[82]

In July 2007 Bhargava was affiliated with United for Peace and Justice, the U.S. "peace movement umbrella group . . . initiated to oppose the Iraq war by the Institute for Policy Studies." UFPJ, Loudon writes, is "completely dominated by communists and radicals, which doesn't seem to bother Bhargava."[83]

United for Peace and Justice is "led by Leslie Cagan, a longtime committed socialist who aligns her politics with those of Fidel Castro's Communist Cuba," Vadum writes.[84]

Andrew Stern and Deepak Bhargava also serve on the board of directors of the Organizer's Forum.[85]

Another Forum board member is Mary Gonzales, associate director of the Gamaliel Foundation and Regional Lead Organizer for Metropolitan Alliance of Congregations. Gonzales, who co-founded the Gamaliel Foundation in 1982 with Gregory A. Galluzzo, worked with Obama beginning in 1985 when he was hired by Jerry Kellman to work as a community activist for the Developing Communities Project.

Two other members of the Forum's board of directors are Drummond Pike and Wade Rathke, who co-founded the Tides Foundation.

It should come as no surprise that Democratic Socialists of America endorsed Barack Obama's 2008 presidential campaign.[86]

DSA also "helped to organize" the House Progressive Caucus, which was founded in 1992 by Representatives Bernard Sanders (I-Vt.), Peter DeFazio (D-Ore.), Lane Evans (D-Ill.), Maxine Waters (D-Cal.), and Ron Dellums, (D-Cal., former). Now known as the Congressional Progressive Caucus, the DSA even supported the HPC on its website until some time in 1999.[87]

DSA is supported by three major entities: the Institute for Policy Studies, *The Nation* magazine, and Progressive Democrats of America.

SOCIALIST AGENDA

The agendas for DSA, the Congressional Progressive Caucus, the Institute for Policy Studies, and Progressive Democrats of America are easy to sort out, as they are nearly identical. In fact, their socialist agenda for America is nearly identical to the platform upon which presidential candidate Barack Obama ran—although theirs is perhaps less shrouded in flowery language: redistribution of wealth; increased income tax on wealthy; tax cuts for the poor (note: 40 percent of Americans pay zero income tax now); more progressive tax system; crackdown on corporate welfare; increased social welfare spending; "cradle-to-grave" health care; complete pullout from Iraq; and cuts in military budget.[88]

Of equal simplicity is the fact that all of these organizations supported Barack Obama's candidacy.

Even more interesting are some of the individuals who have not been named elsewhere by the authors in this book.

For instance, there is Institute for Policy Studies trustee, Jodie Evans, the wealthy radical CODEPINK co-founder and Obama bundler, who raised in the neighborhood of $100,000 for Obama's campaign. Evans is the Sarah Palin protester who met in late September 2008 with Iranian President Mahmoud Ahmadinejad at the Grand Hyatt Hotel in New York City. Evans and CODEPINK co-founder and antiwar activist, Medea Benjamin, have visited with Venezuela president Hugo Chávez.[89]

Two other notable trustees are Robert Borosage, co-director of Campaign for America's Future, and Barbara Ehrenreich, about whom the authors previously wrote. Previously the editorial board included former SDSer and onetime Obama mentor, Tom Hayden.

The Nation magazine is worthy to note since, in what was described as a rare move, it endorsed Barack Obama's candidacy: "Interestingly, the last time *The Nation* endorsed a candidate was in 1988, when the magazine endorsed Jesse Jackson."[90]

Brenda J. Elliott wrote in October 2008:

> On February 7, 2008, *The Nation* editorial board proclaimed its support of Barack Obama's presidential candidacy, clearly stating "we support Obama for President." *The Nation*'s article also appeared on the CBS News website on February 8th, headlined "Obama For President. Editors Say Democrat's Ability to Forge Progressive Majority Makes Him the Best Choice."[91]

The Nation and Progressive Democrats of America "team[ed] up to host 'Progressive Central,' a five-day gathering for activists, journalists and DNC delegates during DNC week [August 25–28, 2008] in downtown Denver."[92]

Featured speakers included Congressional Democratic Caucus co-chairs Barbara Lee and Lynn Woolsey, both Democratic Congresswomen from California, and CDC members John Conyers (D-Mich.) and Robert Wexler (D-Fla.), "plus such other well-known activists" as *The Nation* editor and co-owner Katrina Vanden Heuvel, Tom Hayden, Jim Zogby, Medea Benjamin, and Jim Hightower. Lee, Woolsey, Conyers, Hayden, and Hightower are all members of Progressive Democrats of America's advisory board.[93]

One other group that supported Barack Obama's presidential campaign, and which shares a similar "socialist" agenda, is the Communist Party USA.

"It is getting increasingly difficult to distinguish between the agenda of the Democratic Party, and the agenda of the Communist Party," Henry Lamb wrote October 8, 2007, at *Canada Free Press*.[94]

Lamb quoted Joelle Fishman, chairman of the Communist Party USA Political Action Committee, and chairman of the Connecticut Communist Party, who said:

> Our Party has an important role to play in keeping the focus on the fight for a new direction in our country for jobs, healthcare and an end to the war. That is how the 2008 elections will be won.
>
> We should get involved in voter registration in every club, and involving every member. We can inspire voter registration and turnout by relating the elections to ending the war, achieving universal single-payer health care, and measures to respond to the economic crisis.

Lamb added:

> Should the 2008 elections go to the Democrats, as the Communist Party USA is working to accomplish, the direction of the nation will change dramatically. The direction will not be toward individual freedom, free enterprise, private property rights, and the pursuit of individual happiness. The direction will be toward the values of communism, which holds the state as the grantor of all rights, including socialized medicine through universal health care; amnesty for all illegal aliens

who want to come to America; cradle-to-grave education by the state; surrender in Iraq; and acquiescence to all threats of violence; no right to own guns; and a state-assigned job for everyone.

In June 2008, the CPUSA endorsed Barack Obama's candidacy. Fishman said:

> Big political shifts are under way. . . . Thousands of grassroots union volunteers are already in motion as part of the largest-in-history labor mobilization, visiting co-workers to talk about the issues. . . .
>
> The Obama campaign, drawing upon the candidate's community organizing experience, is also looking toward the grassroots. Unity for Change house parties across the country on June 28 will bring neighbors together for voter registration and getting out the vote. . . .
>
> As AFL-CIO Executive Vice President Arlene Holt Baker told the Coalition of Black Trade Unionists convention, "This election . . . must be about working people's vision—our vision of a new direction for our country. A vision that includes universal health care, the elimination of poverty, good jobs and the passage of the Employee Free Choice Act. . . . [W]e are going to spark a movement of those who are ready to make their voices heard in shaping the new America. . . .
>
> The Communist Party USA's emergency program to repair, renew and rebuild America is a contribution toward this effort. . . .[95]

Fishman "made it very plain that the CPUSA was a part of the Obama Unity for Change movement."[96]

Fishman also maintained a presence for the Connecticut Communist Party on the official My.BarackObama.com website. By late November 2008, the Community page for her husband, Art Perlo, Chairman of the CPUSA Economics Commission, had been demoted to cache file status.[97]

Fishman was not the only CPUSA member involved in supporting Barack Obama's candidacy.[98] Two National Committee board members—Terry Albano and Rosalio Munoz—were listed with alleged duties associated with the Obama administration. Teresa (Terry) Albano, editor of CPUSA's Chicago-based newspaper, *People's Weekly World* (now

People's World), was "responsible for work with the Obama adminis-tration."[99] Albano endorsed Obama's candidacy January 31, 2008, in a blog post on the *PA* (*Political Affairs*) Editors Blog, in which she wrote: "Barack Obama's run for the White House has captured the imagina-tion of a wide swath of Americans. The question is, will progressives respond?" Albano added:

> The Progressive Democrats of America have said many favorable things in the wake of [Tom] Hayden's endorsement. Hayden is a PDA board member and many in the PDA are so excited to see the numbers of young people involved in Obama's campaign.[100]

Rosalio Munoz was listed as "responsible for work with Progressives for Obama." No direct contact has been found linking Munoz with P4O. Munoz wrote February 5, 2008, on the *PA* Editors Blog:

> I'm active in East LA Obama activities, outreach to the neighborhoods by phone and shoe leather is mushrooming Obama support, *manana* is here its time to get out the vote all day Super Tuesday.[101]

The following day, Trevor Loudon wrote of Munoz:

> Rosalio Munoz is no lowly party hack, but is one of the most influen-tial communist leaders in the USA.
>
> The fact that he is actively campaigning for Obama is significant. He has clearly been entrusted by the CPUSA to get out the Latino vote for Obama and the Democrats.[102]

In her November 15, 2008, report to her National Election Commit-tee, Joelle Fishman "described the Nov. 4th election as 'an extraordinary and history-making election.'"[103]

> The consensus among labor and the people's movement, Fishman emphasized, is that the election is not the change that we need by itself, but it gives us the chance the make the change we need. . . .

The Communist Party, Fishman concluded, has to develop the correct tactics and strategy to build on the election victory and strengthen and deepen the movement that puts the wind at Obama's back.

The "movement that puts the wind at Obama's back"! That "movement" was there for anyone to see—who knew what it was they were seeing—as long ago as primary election night in New Hampshire.

It was no illusion, regardless of how mystified the news media seemed to be, that the "social movement based on the working class concept of 'yes we can' and 'si se puede'" was in evidence everywhere.[104]

Obama had not borrowed the "movement"; the "movement" was empowering Obama.

10

OBAMA'S TOP GUNS EXPOSED

I N THE SEPTEMBER 6, 2009, speech announcing his resignation as Barack Obama's "Green Jobs Czar," radical activist Van Jones blamed his downfall on a "smear campaign:"

> On the eve of historic fights for health care and clean energy, opponents of reform have mounted a vicious smear campaign against me. They are using lies and distortions to distract and divide.[1]

Jones' resignation—from the post of Special Advisor to President Obama for Green Jobs, Enterprise and Innovation, at the White House Council on Environmental Quality—came after revelations that Jones had founded a radical communist organization and signed on to a petition accusing the Bush administration of possible involvement in the 9/11 terrorist attacks.[2]

Of course, Jones' crocodile tears over "lies and distortions" and "smears" were empty, unless we redefine a smear campaign to mean factually reporting on the extremist activities and views of any Obama administration official. A quick review of the Jones case is instrumental. His was not an isolated incident. Indeed, Jones reportedly was screened by a top Obama adviser; he was and is of a piece with the same radical nexus that can be found throughout the Obama administration. And, crucially, Jones is just one of scores of radical White House officials with agendas that may be far different from what they are made to appear.

In April 2009, Aaron Klein reported at *WorldNetDaily* that Jones was a founder and leader of the communist revolutionary organization STORM—Standing Together to Organize a Revolutionary Movement. That organization had its roots in a grouping of black activists protesting the 1991 Gulf War. STORM was formally founded in 1994, eventually becoming one of the most influential and active radical groups in the San Francisco Bay area.[3]

Speaking to the *East Bay Express* in 2005, Jones said he first became radicalized in the wake of the 1992 Rodney King riots, during which time he was arrested. "I was a rowdy nationalist on April 28th, and then the verdicts came down on April 29th," he said. "By August, I was a communist. I met all these young radical people of color—I mean really radical: communists and anarchists. And it was, like, 'This is what I need to be a part of.' I spent the next 10 years of my life working with a lot of those people I met in jail, trying to be a revolutionary," he said.[4] He boasted to the *East Bay Express* that his current environmental activism was really a means to fight for racial and class "justice."

Jones went on to found the Ella Baker Center for Human Rights in 1996, named after a little-known civil rights firebrand and socialist activist.

Jones' STORM organization worked with known communist leaders. Its official manifesto, "Reclaiming Revolution," had been published on the Internet until Klein and others wrote articles and blog entries linking to the online publication.[5]

A review of the 97-page treatise found that the manual describes Jones' organization as having a "commitment to the fundamental ideas of Marxism-Leninism." "We agreed with Lenin's analysis of the state and the party," reads the manifesto. "And we found inspiration in the revolutionary strategies developed by Third World revolutionaries like Mao Zedong and Amilcar Cabral."

Cabral was a neo-Marxist revolutionary theoretician, and leader of Guinea-Bissau and the Cape Verde Islands in their independence movement from Portugal, then afterward as prime minister. Jones named his son after Cabral and reportedly concludes every e-mail with a quote from the African leader.[6]

One section of the official STORM manifesto describes a vigil that Jones' group held September 12, 2001, at Snow Park in Oakland, CA. That event drew hundreds and articulated "an anti-imperialist line," according to STORM's own description. The radical group's manual boasted that its 9/11 vigil was held to express solidarity with Arab and Muslim Americans and to mourn the civilians killed in the terrorist attacks "as well as the victims of U.S. imperialism around the world."

Jones' routine involvement in anti-government activism included a 2002 keynote speech at a rally at People's Park in Berkeley, CA, to mark the national launch of a Maoist, terrorist-supporting, antiwar group, Not In Our Name, founded by Revolutionary Communist Party member C. Clark Kissinger. The antiwar rally urged "resistance" against the U.S. government." [7]

Subsequent revelations about Jones include that he signed a statement for 911Truth.org in 2004 demanding an investigation into what the Bush Administration may have done that "deliberately allowed 9/11 to happen, perhaps as a pretext for war." In a 2005 conference, Jones characterized the United States as an "apartheid regime" that civil rights workers helped turn into a "struggling, fledgling democracy." Jones signed a petition calling for nationwide "resistance" against police, accusing them of using the 9/11 attacks to carry out policies of torture. Amazingly, just days before his White House appointment, Jones used a forum at a major youth convention to push for a radical agenda that included "spreading the wealth" and "changing the whole system."[8]

The mainstream media predictably ignored the Jones revelations— right up until the moment of his resignation on September 5, 2009. Much of the investigation into Jones had been conducted over the Internet, including reporting by Aaron Klein, Brenda J. Elliott, and Trevor Loudon, a New Zealand blogger. Fox News Channel's Glenn Beck picked up the reports and released new information about Jones, hammering away at the story for weeks, until finally Jones was forced to step down.

This "Green Jobs Czar" of Barack Obama's did not live in some sort of vacuum. Jones is tied to radical groups that are by now familiar to readers of this book. Jones was a longtime member of the board of the Apollo

Alliance, a far-left coalition of labor, business, environmental, and community leaders. Chapter 13 details the involvement of Apollo in several Obama administration initiatives, including the writing of the $787 billion so-called stimulus bill. Apollo's New York office is directed by Jeff Jones, who was a founding and leading member of the Weather Underground. Jeff Jones founded the Weatherman with Bill Ayers and Mark Rudd in 1969, when the three signed an infamous manifesto calling for revolution against the American government, both inside and outside the country, to fight and defeat what the group termed U.S. imperialism.

Separately, Van Jones' environmental center was named after Ella Baker, who participated in a 1976 conference organized by Jennifer Dohrn, sister of Weatherman leader Bernardine Dohrn. The Chicago conference, called "Hard Times," was designed by the Weatherman to unite the U.S. far-left into a new communist party.[9]

Jones' appointment to a senior position in the Obama administration had not required Senate confirmation; as with the proliferation under Obama of so many such "czars," they avoided the kind of vetting Cabinet officials are usually put through. (Still, some "czars" to be discussed in this chapter were confirmed by Congress.)

After Jones' resignation, administration officials claimed that his controversial past had caught the White House off guard.[10]

But at the time they hired Jones, Obama's top adviser, Valerie Jarrett, had struck a decidedly different note, gushing, "We were so delighted to be able to recruit him into the White House. We've been watching him really—he's not that old—for as long as he's been active out in Oakland and all of the ways and creative ideas that he has."[11]

COMMUNIST SYMPATHIZER INTRODUCED VALERIE JARRETT?

Valerie Jarrett has been described as Obama's most trusted adviser. An official from Obama's presidential campaign told the New York Times, "If you want him to do something, there are two people he's not going to say no to: Valerie Jarrett and Michelle Obama." The president confirmed his deep relationship with Jarrett when he told Times reporter Robert Draper, "I trust her completely. . . . She is family." The president said he trusts Jarrett "to speak for me, particularly when we're dealing with delicate issues."[12]

"We have kind of a mind meld," Jarrett, in turn, said about Obama. "And chances are, what he wants to do is what I'd want to do."[13]

With a level of trust verging on telepathy, it is no surprise that Jarrett has been central to the White House process of recruiting cabinet officials. What is surprising, however, is the string of radicals Jarrett has brought to the administration, especially Obama's "Regulatory Czar," Cass Sunstein—whom we will profile later in this chapter. Jarrett also reportedly helped convince Obama to create the position of Chief Diversity Officer within the Federal Communications Commission, a position filled by Mark Lloyd, who is discussed at length in the next chapter.

Jarrett's background, her family, and her initial introduction to Obama all tie her to the by now familiar radical milieu of this administration.[14]

Jarrett's father-in-law, Vernon Jarrett, was an associate of Frank Marshall Davis, the controversial labor movement activist who has been identified as an early influence on Obama. Vernon Jarrett worked with Davis in 1940 in the Communist Party–dominated organization, Citizen's Committee to Aid Packing House Workers. The group's own correspondence, previously uncovered by the *New Zeal* blog, describes its communist influence. Many of its leaders were tied to the Communist Party USA.[15]

Davis and Vernon Jarrett also frequented the South Side Community Art Center, which was dominated by communists. In addition, Davis and Jarrett both worked in the late 1940s on the communist-influenced, black-run *Chicago Defender* newspaper.[16]

In 1948, Jarrett started a radio show, *Negro Newsfront*, and went on to become the *Chicago Tribune's* first black syndicated columnist.

A May 2004 *Washington Post* obituary for Jarrett notes he "stoked the political embers in Chicago that led to the 1983 election of the city's first African-American mayor, Harold Washington." "Vernon Jarrett was a key influence in Washington's decision to run for the Chicago mayoralty and remained a key supporter through his four-year tenure," the *Post* reported. Obama has cited Washington's victory as a prime motive for his relocation to Chicago from New York. Mayor Washington, among other things, was involved in communist-dominated circles in Chicago.[17]

Vernon Jarrett clearly observed Obama's rise as an activist. When Obama worked for Project VOTE! to register black voters with the intent of aiding the senatorial campaign of Carol Moseley Braun, Jarrett took note. Obama later took over Braun's senate seat.

Writing in the *Chicago Sun-Times* in 1992, Jarrett noted: "Good news! Good news! Project Vote, a collectivity of 10 church-based community organizations dedicated to black voter registration, is off and running. . . . If Project Vote is to reach its goal of registering 150,000 out of an estimated 400,000 unregistered blacks statewide, 'it must average 10,000 rather than 7,000 every week,' says Barack Obama, the program's executive director."[18]

Valerie Jarrett married Vernon's son, William Robert Jarrett, in 1983. By 1987 she had gotten her start in politics, working for Mayor Washington as deputy corporation counsel for finance and development. She was also deputy chief of staff for Mayor Richard Daley, during which time she hired Michelle Robinson, who was by then engaged to Obama.

Jarrett moved on to work in a senior capacity at Habitat, a real estate firm headed by Daniel Levin. A profile of Jarrett by Chicago journalist Lynn Sweet notes: "activist public affairs consultant with close ties to City Hall Marilyn Katz introduced Jarrett to Levin."[19] Katz was an aide to Mayor Washington from 1983 to 1987. She later served on the national finance committee of Obama's presidential campaign and, according to Public Citizen, Katz raised at least $50,000 for the Obama '08 campaign.[20]

ANOTHER SDSER, AYERS ASSOCIATE FACILITATES OBAMA'S RISE

A *Discover the Networks* profile describes Katz in the 1960s providing "security" for the Students for a Democratic Society, from which Ayers' Weatherman later splintered. Katz had known Ayers since she was 17 years old. During the SDS's "Days of Rage" riots in October 1969, Katz's "security" duties evidently included introducing protesters to a new weapon to deploy against police: a cluster of nails sharpened at both ends and fastened in the center. Indeed, police later reported being hit by golf balls with nails through them, as well as by excrement. Katz would insist years later that her "guerrilla nails" were merely "a defensive weapon" to prevent "possible bad behavior by the police."[21]

By 1983, Katz was in the public relations business, founding MK Communications, Inc., and representing a who's who of left-liberal activists, including the American Civil Liberties Union, Amnesty International, Chicagoans Against War & Injustice, Human Rights Watch, and at least two groups with which Obama was intimately involved—Project VOTE! and the Joyce Foundation.

It was Katz and Chicagoan Bettylu Saltzman who organized the 2002 antiwar demonstration at which Obama, then a little-known senator, gave a now famous speech opposing the Iraq War, calling it a "stupid" conflict. This speech has been credited with Obama's meteoric rise on the national political scene.

Katz worked closely with former SDS national secretary Carl Davidson, who was also a founding member of the socialist New Party—a group whose involvement with Obama we detailed in Chapter 6. Katz and Davidson together founded Chicagoans Against the War in Iraq. The two also co-authored a 2004 article, "From Protest to Politics," urging radicals to support Democrat John Kerry for president. One year later they collaborated in a book, *Stopping War, Seeking Justice: Essays in a Time of Empire*. Davidson helped Katz and Saltzman organize the 2002 antiwar rally.

Discover the Networks points out that Obama initially met Katz through his first job at a law firm run by Judd Miner. None other than the *New York Times* reported that the introduction to Katz "gave him [Obama] entry into another activist network: the foot soldiers of the white student and black power movements that helped define Chicago in the 1960s."[22]

After Obama assumed the presidency, Katz was reportedly involved in trying to convince Illinois governor Rod Blagojevich to appoint Valerie Jarrett to Obama's open U.S. Senate seat. The *Times* describes Katz as "a friend" of Jarrett's who encouraged the latter to step out of Obama's shadow and "be the sun."[23]

Katz was also close with Obama's top political adviser David Axelrod, who, we shall see, was mentored by Katz's former SDS comrade, Don Rose.[24]

The whole episode of Obama's decision to participate in the 2002 Chicago antiwar rally, organized by Katz and Saltzman, is worthy of closer scrutiny. The event was coordinated by the two activists' small group,

Chicagoans Against the War & Injustice. The rally was staged to "protest the United States' impending invasion of Iraq."[25]

Bettylu Saltzman, by then a "Democratic doyenne from Chicago's lakefront liberal crowd," had first met Obama in 1992 when he was in charge of Project VOTE!'s registration drive for the election. (See Chapter 8 for more information on Project VOTE!) Saltzman was reportedly "so impressed that she immediately took [Obama] under her wing, introducing him to wealthy donors and talking him up to friends like [David] Axelrod."[26]

In 2002, with "just a few days to go before the rally," Saltzman says that, when she had not heard back from Obama, she left word with his wife, Michelle. And before responding, Obama "dialed up some advice" from Axelrod.[27]

Because Obama had his sights on a possible run for the United States Senate, he wanted to speak with Axelrod and others about the ramifications of broadcasting opposition to a war the public was fast getting behind. An antiwar speech would play to his Chicago liberal base, and could help him in what was expected to be a hotly contested primary, they told him, but it also could hurt him in the general election.

"This was a [phone] call to assess just how risky was this," said Pete Giangreco, a partner in The Strategy Group who served as "lead direct mail consultant to Obama for President during the Democratic primary season.[28] Giangreco, along with Axelrod, described the conversation. When Obama tossed out the idea of calling it a "dumb war," Mr. Giangreco said he cringed. "I remember thinking, 'this puts us in the weak defense category, doesn't it?'"

So Obama did indeed accept Katz and Saltzman's fateful invitation to deliver an antiwar speech at the October 2, 2002, rally, with nearly 2,000 in attendance, at Chicago's Federal Plaza, but not before clearing it with his confidante, David Axelrod.[29]

DAVID AXELROD'S COMMUNIST MENTOR

And Axelrod was the ultimate busy man. Axelrod's heavy client load and the impending midterm elections might explain the time lapse between the 2002 invitation and Obama's acceptance. Among the many high-profile clients served in 2001 by his firms, Axelrod & Associates of Chicago, and AKP&D Message and Media of Washington, D.C., were Iowa Governor Tom Vilsak, D.C. Mayor Anthony Williams, Houston Mayor Lee Brown, Detroit Mayor Dennis Archer, U.S. Representatives Ken Bentsen of Texas and Rod Blagojevich of Illinois, the AFL-CIO, and the League of Conservation Voters.[30]

Axelrod had already been a significant player in Chicago politics for more than a decade, having been part of the team, in 1989, that put William Daley into city hall. "Prominent liberal activist" David Axelrod told Doug Ireland of *The Nation* in February 1997 that the team was "stuck together as a kind of mutual admiration society who promote and support each other." Ireland described Axelrod as a "media consultant who fancies himself Chicago's David Garth, turning his hand to everything from writing speeches to making political strategy as well as commercials—and, once the election is won, advising on appointments and policy."[31]

Axelrod's official profile reads like a conventional American story—though unusually precocious and successful—of working himself up the ladder of mainstream political jobs.

A profile from 2000 relates that Axelrod worked for Robert Kennedy's 1964 senatorial campaign and John Lindsay's mayoral campaign the following year. New York's unusual party structure "allowed Axelrod to avoid any GOP support" even though Lindsay was a Republican. Axelrod said: "I worked out of Liberal Party headquarters, I didn't want to work for a Republican." [32]

While at the University of Chicago, Axelrod "became a journalist, eventually working for the *Chicago Tribune* for almost a decade after he graduated in 1976, and spending most of that time covering politics." Axelrod left the *Tribune* to serve as press secretary, later becoming campaign manager, for Paul Simon's 1984 run for the U.S. Senate from Illinois.[33]

The 2001 client list of Axelrod's detailed above was only a small sampling of his political relationships. In 2000 he was reported to have "worked for almost every recently successful Illinois Democrat, from Mayors Harold Washington and Richard M. Daley to Senators Carol Moseley Braun and Paul Simon, as well as for unsuccessful gubernatorial candidate Adlai Stevenson." Between campaigns, Axelrod stayed on as an adviser to Chicago Mayors Harold Washington and Richard Daley. Outside of Illinois his client list included New York's Mario Cuomo and California's Gray Davis.[34]

Nor was the Obama-Biden 2008 ticket the first time "electioneering businessman" Axelrod had represented Joe Biden. In 1988 he worked for both Biden and Paul Simon. In the next presidential election, in 1992, he worked for Bill Clinton in the primaries and for the Clinton-Gore ticket in the general election.[35]

Axelrod "ran the independent expenditure media program" for the Democratic Congressional Campaign Committee in 2006, also serving as media adviser to now-Governor Deval Patrick, Massachusetts' "first Democratic governor in 16 years and the state's first-ever African American governor." In 2004 Axelrod served as top adviser for Obama's U.S. senatorial campaign, helping "him defeat a primary field of six other Democrats and go on to a landslide win in his U.S. Senate campaign."[36]

Today Axelrod serves as Senior Advisor to the president. Besides serving as top adviser for Barack Obama's 2004 U.S. senatorial campaign, he was Senior Strategist for Obama's 2008 presidential campaign, and Senior Advisor to the Obama-Biden Presidential Transition.[37]

So much for the conventional Axelrod resume. Now let us take a look under its veneer—which reveals a much more radical past.

"Who Is Behind the Man Behind Obama?" asked New Zealand blogger Trevor Loudon just days before the 2008 election. In questioning the "Axelrod axis" Loudon wrote:

> Axelrod was born in New York in 1955 to leftish parents Joseph and Myril Axelrod.
>
> In the 1940s Myril Axelrod wrote for a left-leaning magazine PM. Though not officially a communist publication, several Marxists (including labour editor Leo Huberman) and Communist Party members worked on the paper. [38]

Citing a Traditional Values Coalition report from March 4, 2008, Loudon notes:

Former Communist Eugene Lyons, writing in *The Red Decade: The Stalinist Penetration of America*, noted that PM's staff included a former editor of the Daily Worker; another was former editor of *The Communist*; a third was a leader of the Communist Youth League; a fourth was a Soviet government official; and a fifth was the former staff cartoonist for the *Daily Worker*, the official newspaper of the Communist Party, USA.[39]

"*PM's* Washington, D.C. correspondent I.F. Stone was later identified as involved in Soviet Intelligence operations," Loudon adds.

Besides the radical associations of his mother, David Axelrod's own mentor was a well-known Chicago journalist/political activist named Donald C. Rose, a member of a Communist Party front, the Alliance to End Repression, in the sixties, whom Axelrod met while studying political science at the University of Chicago.[40]

Loudon notes:

> Rose hired Axelrod to write for a small newspaper he edited and co-owned called the *Hyde Park Kenwood Voices*. The paper's radical tone suited the neighbourhood. It tended to follow the Communist Party line campaigning, for example, to abolish the House Committee on Un-American Activities. The *Voice's* co-owner, the late David S. Canter, had personal experience with the committee, being hauled before it and named as a Communist Party member in the late 1960s.

Don Rose actually contacted Marc Canter, the son of David S. Canter, in response to Loudon's article. Marc Canter then posted their exchange on the Web. In the exchange Rose confirmed David Axelrod's connection with both Canter [senior] and himself:

> Just for the historical record, David Axelrod did not work for the *Voices* at any point. He was a reporter for the *HP Herald* while attending U of C, appearing on the scene first in 1975, just after the *Voices* folded—but he was familiar with our paper as a student before he got the *Herald* job. Your dad and I "mentored" and helped educate him politically in that capacity, which is perhaps why you may recall seeing him hanging around the house. I later

wrote a reference letter for him that helped him win an internship at the *Tribune*, which was the next step in his journalism career.[41]

Marc Canter's posting also noted that Rose, like Axelrod, had represented Carol Moseley Braun and Paul Simon, and was also an organizing member of Chicagoans Against the War in Iraq, the group that invited Barack Obama to speak at its October 2, 2002, antiwar rally in Chicago.[42]

Loudon writes:

> In 1968 Rose was asked to serve as press secretary to the Chicago Mobilization Committee—the Students for a Democratic Society/Communist Party-influenced alliance that wreaked havoc at the Chicago Democratic Party Convention. It was during these violent times that Rose coined the famous phrase "the whole world is watching."
>
> Through the Mobilization Committee, Rose met Marilyn Katz, the SDS security officer for the demonstrations.[43]

Loudon's information about Rose and Canter was otherwise on target, as confirmed by Marc Canter, who wrote:

> This journalist—Trevor Loudon and his buddy (Brenda J. Elliott's The Real Barack Obama blog) produced some great stuff—which hopefully they won't take down. These two articles chronicle the history of my father and grandfather (and many of their colleagues) and with just a slight correction to statements like he was "an identified member of the Communist Party USA, a registered agent of the Soviet Union and a paid disseminator of Soviet black propaganda"—most of the stuff is basically true.[44]

Loudon writes:

> In 1982 David S. Canter and nine others invited black Democratic Congressman Harold Washington to stand for the Chicago mayoralty. Washington had a long history with Chicago's communists and socialists. When he accepted, the Communist Party and DSA formed a multiracial alliance behind Washington.

Rose, Katz and Canter all worked on the successful campaign and all later secured jobs in Washington's administration.

In 1987 Washington successfully re-stood, aided by a young political adviser named David Axelrod.

Though Washington died in office shortly after, the communist/socialist alliance lived on.

In 1992 the alliance elected the Communist/DSA friendly Carol Moseley Braun to the U.S. Senate.

In 2004 it helped put Barack Obama into the same Senate seat. In 2008 it is campaigning hard to put Obama in the White House.

Loudon published a follow-up article on November 1, 2008—"The Paid Soviet Agent Behind Axelrod and Obama"—in which he showed that David Axelrod "once worked for a man who was an identified member of the Communist Party USA, a registered agent of the Soviet Union and a paid disseminator of Soviet black propaganda."[45] The man is the late Chicago lawyer, David Simon Canter, 1923–2004, Loudon writes. Canter was once a "key Chicago political fixer who helped elect communist linked politicians including the late Chicago mayor Harold Washington and former U.S. Senator Carol Moseley Braun."

Canter's father, Harry, Loudon adds, was an "activist with the International Workers of the World who later became secretary of the Boston Communist Party. . . . While the Communist Party candidate for Massachusetts secretary of state, Canter was arrested for carrying a placard [reading] 'fuller—murderer of sacco and vanzetti,' attacking Governor Fuller for the execution of anarchists Sacco and Vanzetti. Harry Canter was tried, convicted and jailed for a year for criminal libel in May 1929."

In 1948 David Canter was editor of the University of Chicago student newspaper, *Maroon*, and in 1958 he graduated from the John Marshall Law School. David Canter also edited the Packinghouse Workers Union *Champion* newspaper.

Loudon cites Communist historian Max Friedman, who wrote on June 13, 2008, in the *Augusta Free Press*:

The Packinghouse Workers Union was a long time CPUSA-influenced, if not controlled union that later merged with the Meatcutters to form the CPUSA-run Amalgamated Meatcutters & Butcherworkmens' Union, lead [sic] by identified CPUSA labor leader Abe Feinglass, who was also a VP of the Soviet-KGB front, the World Peace Council.[46]

By the late sixties, Loudon writes, David Canter was "publishing a small politically oriented Chicago neighbourhood newspaper *Hyde Park Kenwood Voices*." And Canter's partner, the paper's editor, was Don Rose, a journalist active in at least two Communist Party fronts. In one of them—the Alliance to End Repression—Rose worked with Quentin Young, Timuel Black, and Rabbi Arnold Jacob Wolf—all now personal friends and supporters of Barack Obama.

Fast forward to the late eighties, as Loudon reports, and Don Rose and David Axelrod are both working for Harold Washington's mayoral campaign: "Rose served as an adviser to the mayor, while Axelrod served as a campaign consultant." Rose and Axelrod worked together again, running the 1992 U.S. senatorial campaign of longtime Communist Party/Democratic Socialists of America "associate" Carol Moseley Braun. While Canter, Rose, and Axelrod "played senior roles in the successful campaign," Barack Obama "ran the highly successful voter registration drive," Project VOTE!, that "secured Moseley Braun's victory."

As stated above, David Canter knew Barack Obama and was a "key member" of Independent Voters of Illinois, "which endorsed Barack Obama in his 2004 US Senate race." Additionally, both Barack Obama and his wife, Michelle Obama, were active members of IVI, Loudon writes, which was "once investigated by the FBI over claims of communist infiltration."[47]

Who is the official David Axelrod?

According to *Newsweek* of December 20, 2008:

As the campaign's chief strategist, Axelrod was at Obama's side at every critical moment of the protracted election, giving Axelrod broad influence over political positioning, TV advertising and the day-to-day message. Inside the White House, the soft-spoken Axelrod will have direct control over communications, the press office and speechwriting. . . . More than anyone else, Axelrod will be the guardian of Obama's image and voice.[48]

EXPOSING THE EXTREMIST CZARS

Axelrod and Jarrett are by no means the only highly placed Obama officials with ties to extremists. Even if Van Jones was forced to resign his White House position, the Obama administration still maintains an unprecedented number of "czars" and top advisers whose exact power and positions of influence have yet to be fully disclosed, just as their political backgrounds have yet to be fully exposed. Here we present investigative profiles of some of the Obama administration's top officials, as well as other members of the government whose political ties merit attention.

CAROL M. BROWNER, ENERGY/CLIMATE CZAR

OFFICIAL PROFILE: Browner is Assistant to the president for Energy and Climate Change.

Earlier Browner served as Environmental Protection Agency administrator during the Clinton administration and was Florida Secretary of the Environment. Browner founded and continues to serve as a principal of The Albright Group LLC, the global strategy firm led by former Secretary of State Madeleine Albright, and is a principal of Albright Capital Management, an investment advisory firm that concentrates on emerging markets.[49]

EXTREMIST AGENDA: Socialist activist.

The story about Carol Browner's socialist connections developed over a week's time, beginning January 3, 2009, when blogger Omri revealed at *Mere Rhetoric* that Browner was a member of the Commission for a Sustainable World Society at Socialist International.[50] *Discover the Networks* describes the Socialist International as the "umbrella group for 170 'social democratic, socialist and labor parties' in 55 countries."

SI's "organizing document" cites capitalism as the cause of "devastating crises," "mass unemployment," "imperialist expansion," and "colonial exploitation" worldwide. Browner worked on SI's Commission for a Sustainable World Society, which contends that "the developed world must reduce consumption and commit to binding and punitive limits on greenhouse gas emissions."

By January 7, 2009, Nick Loris at the Heritage Foundation's *The Foundry* blog noted, "As of today, however, [Browner's] bio was taken off the site." Loris added: "Maybe it's just a coincidence and maybe she didn't have time to be a commission member of a socialist organization now that she's an energy czar."[51]

A *Washington Examiner* editorial reported January 9, 2009, that both Browner's picture and biography had been scrubbed from SI's site but that her name was "still listed next to the photo-biographies of her 14 colleagues on the commission."

> [There] is no question about the socialism . . . but The Socialist International is no group of woolly-headed idealists. It is an influential assembly of officials from across the international community whose official Statement of Principles describes an agenda of gaining and exercising government power based on socialist concepts.[52]

On January 12, 2009, Stephen Dinan expanded on the story in the *Washington Times*:

> Until last week, Carol M. Browner, President-elect Barack Obama's pick as global warming czar, was listed as one of 14 leaders of a socialist group's Commission for a Sustainable World Society, which calls for "global governance" and says rich countries must shrink their economies to address climate change.
>
> By Thursday, Mrs. Browner's name and biography had been removed from Socialist International's Web page, though a photo of her speaking June 30 to the group's congress in Greece was still available.[53]

The *Washington Examiner* commented on what this meant regarding the Obama administration:

By appointing Browner to a White House post, Obama has at the least implicitly endorsed an utterly radical socialist agenda for his administration's environmental policy. The incoming chief executive thus strengthens critics who contend environmental policies aren't really about protecting endangered species or preserving virgin lands, but rather expanding government power and limiting individual freedom.[54]

Dinan also wrote in January 2009 that, at the time of her selection, Browner was on the "board of directors for the National Audubon Society, the League of Conservation Voters, the Center for American Progress and former Vice president Al Gore's Alliance for Climate Protection."[55]

The Center for American Progress is the George Soros–funded, John Podesta–led extremist organization whose fingers are found throughout the Obama administration, as the authors have illustrated in this book.

Some organizations moved quickly to distance themselves from Browner. Dinan reported that her name was "removed from the Gore organization's Web site list of directors, and the Audubon Society issued a press release about her departure from that organization."[56] The Gore organization's reaction is interesting in that Browner served as legislative director to then-Senator Gore.[57]

Commented New Zealand blogger Trevor Loudon on January 13, 2009:

Browner's membership in a senior SI body should not be downplayed. While once the SI was staunchly anti-communist this has changed dramatically in recent years. Since the fall of communism, several former and "still existing" communist parties, including those of Laos, Cuba and China, now actively participate in the International. In many ways, the SI has replaced the old Communist international as a key driver of socialist change.[58]

Loudon added in September 2009 that Browner worked in the seventies for Citizen Action, founded by "former Students for a Democratic

Society radicals, Steve Max and Heather Booth," both later affiliated with Democratic Socialists of America.[59]

The Heritage Foundation's Ben Lieberman quipped: "The old joke that environmental activists are like watermelons—green on the outside but red on the inside—isn't so funny anymore."[60]

SAMANTHA POWER—FOREIGN POLICY, UN, AND INTERNATIONAL AGENCIES

OFFICIAL PROFILE: Power, an Irish American journalist, writer, and Harvard professor, is the National Security Council's senior director for multilateral affairs.[61] Power is married to Obama Regulatory Czar, Cass Sunstein. Her position at Harvard is the Anna Lindh Professor of Practice of Global Leadership and Public Policy at the Carr Center for Human Rights Policy at the Kennedy School of Government. She was noted in August 2007 as being among Barack Obama's "key advisers" who spoke for him on matters of foreign policy.[62]

EXTREMIST AGENDA: Foreign policy apologist.

"Barack Obama's judgment is right; the conventional wisdom is wrong. We need a new era of tough, principled and engaged American diplomacy to deal with 21st century challenges," Power wrote in an August 3, 2007, memo published in the *Washington Post*, entitled "Conventional Washington versus the Change We Need."[63]

Taking her praise even further, in a May 2008 interview with History News Network's Robin Lindley, Power described Barack Obama as a "globalized being."[64]

This is not the first time Power has advised Obama. In 2005, after Obama was elected to the U.S. Senate, Power left her position at Harvard for a year to work for Obama. In 2008 Power married Obama's friend, and now Regulatory Czar, Cass Sunstein, whom the authors will discuss in this chapter and the next.[65]

Just how close is the Power-Obama relationship? The *Weekly Standard* quipped in March 2008: "Power is a card-carrying member of the Obamaphile elite—she plays basketball with George Clooney and claims that Sen. Obama sometimes text-messages her in the middle of the night."[66]

Power stirred up controversy, and was forced to resign as Obama campaign adviser in March 2008, after she called Obama's Democratic presidential primary opponent, Hillary Clinton, a "monster" in an interview in London with *The Scotsman*'s Gerri Peev:

> Power told the *Scotsman* newspaper [published January 9, 2008] that Clinton would stop at nothing to defeat Obama. "She is a monster, too," Power said in the interview. "She is stooping to anything." Power added that "the amount of deceit she has put forward is really unattractive."[67]

In an ironic twist of fate, following the general election in November 2008, Power returned to the fold, serving on the Obama transition team for the U.S. Department of State that was to be headed by Hillary Clinton.[68] Commented the *Politico*: "Power was close to Obama personally, so her return is not particularly surprising. Many of her friends thought it was a case of 'when,' not 'if.'"[69]

Power's foreign policy views also aroused concern during the 2008 primaries. The *American Thinker*'s chief political correspondent Richard Baehr, and its news editor, Ed Lasky, expressed their concerns about Power in February 2008. "[She] is very problematic regarding Israel, Iran, and for that matter, American supporters of Israel's role."

> The problem for those who favor a strong US-Israel relationship is that Power seems obsessed with Israel, and in a negative way. Much like the authors of the Baker-Hamilton report, she believes resolution of the Israeli-Palestinian conflict is central to solving other problems in the Middle East. And it is clear that her approach to addressing the Israeli-Palestinian conflict would be for the U.S. to behave in a more "even handed" fashion, which of course means withdrawing U.S. support for Israel, and instead applying more pressure on Israel for concessions.

Baehr and Lasky add:

> Power's views on the problems caused by the US-Israel relationship also place her in the same camp as Zbigniew Brzezinski and George Soros

(an influential billionaire supporter of Barack Obama), who also oppose the so-called "Israel lobby" and reject the participation of American supporters of Israel, including Christians, in the foreign policy discussion.[70]

Regarding Power's endowed chair at Harvard, Baehr and Lasky comment: "How appropriate: Anna Lindh, the late Swedish Foreign Minister, was a dedicated opponent of Israel."[71]

On the matter of Iran, Baehr and Lasky link to a piece Power wrote January 17, 2008, in *Time* magazine, "Rethinking Iran." The authors write, the "thrust of [Power's] rethinking involves the need to engage diplomatically the mullahs and pretend that the Iranian nuclear program is a figment of the paranoid imagination of the Bush administration."[72]

On the subject of withdrawing U.S. troops from Iraq, in a February 21, 2008, appearance on public television's *Charlie Rose Show,* Power played the role of campaign foreign policy apologist. She said Obama had "restricted his promises to '[saying] I'm going to try to have all the combat brigades out within 16 to 18 months' and is emphasizing that the United States will 'have to be more careful getting out of Iraq than it was getting in.'"[73]

In hedging the presidential candidate's antiwar utterances, Power uttered this priceless phrase: "Expectation calibration and expectation management is essential at home and internationally"—meaning the campaign intended to tightly control the message, which had already become a hallmark of the Obama campaign, as well as of his tenure so far in White House.[74]

Commenting on the Power interview, Paul Street observed at the leftist website Znet:

> Behind this disturbing application of elitist and technocratic language to the "management" of domestic and global opinion and hopes is an obvious (for those willing to detect it) admission: Obama is as attached to the U.S. imperial project as Bush and this will dangerously disappoint hopeful masses at home and abroad in the event of an Obama ascendancy. Unenlightened humanity's naïve faith in "change we can believe in" needs to be downwardly "calibrated" as we cross into the post-Bush era of U.S. global dominance.[75]

In a follow-up to the Rose interview, Power appeared March 6, 2008, on BBC's HARDtalk. Power again stated that Obama's pledge to "have all U.S. combat brigades out of Iraq within 16 months" was a "best case scenario" that "he will revisit when he becomes President."[76]

Giving a bit more of the substance of Power's view, Eric Alterman reported March 20, 2008, on the website of *The Nation*, that Power came to Obama's defense during the presidential debates on the issue of "negotiating with America's enemies." Power wrote "in the form of a memo":

> American foreign policy is broken. It has been broken by people who supported the Iraq War, opposed talking to our adversaries, failed to finish the job with Al Qaeda, and alienated the world with our belligerence. Yet conventional wisdom holds that people whose experience includes taking these positions are held up as examples of what America needs in times of trouble. . . . We cannot afford any more of this kind of bankrupt conventional wisdom.[77]

JOHN HOLDREN, SCIENCE CZAR

OFFICIAL PROFILE: Holdren was appointed December 20, 2008, to serve as Assistant to the President for Science and Technology, Director of the White House Office of Science and Technology Policy, and Co-Chair of the President's Council of Advisors on Science and Technology (PCAST).[78]

Holdren is the Teresa and John Heinz Professor of Environmental Policy at Harvard's Kennedy School of Government, director of the environmental research group for the Woods Hole Research Center, and a past president of the American Association for the Advancement of Science.

EXTREMIST AGENDA: Globalist, climate alarmist, and conspiracy theorist who has advocated controlling the world population.

Holdren, among all of Barack Obama's appointees, is perhaps the most frightening to contemplate, considering the extent of his far-reaching powers combined with the extremism of his far-fetched beliefs.

In announcing Holdren's appointment, Obama described him as the man charged with "leading a new effort to ensure that federal policies are based on the best and most unbiased scientific information."[79] Commenting at *FrontPageMagazine.com*, managing editor Ben Johnson observed that, in Obama's nomination of Holdren, his words could scarcely have taken on a more Orwellian ring:

> Some critics have noted Holdren's penchant for making apocalyptic predictions that never come to pass, and categorizing all criticism of his alarmist views as not only wrong but dangerous. What none has yet noted is that Holdren is a globalist who has endorsed "surrender of sovereignty" to "a comprehensive Planetary Regime" that would control all the world's resources, direct global redistribution of wealth, oversee the "de-development" of the West, control a World Army and taxation regime, and enforce world population limits. He has castigated the United States as "the meanest of wealthy countries," written a justification of compulsory abortion for American women, advocated drastically lowering the U.S. standard of living, and left the door open to trying global warming "deniers" for crimes against humanity. Such is Barack Obama's idea of a clear-headed adviser on matters of scientific policy.[80]

Holdren's name and the precise words "surrender to sovereignty" do not appear online. However, we need look no further for an explanation than Johnson's key piece of information—that Holdren was part of the New Left:

> All of these positions are consistent with a man who began his career as a "dissident scientist." Peter Collier remembers Holdren working by day at a national laboratory and by night writing for *Ramparts*, the intellectual journal of the New Left.

Collier should know. He was *Ramparts'* co-editor.[81]

Jonathan Adler, in the January 7, 2009, edition of *National Review Online*, opined that Holdren was "unlikely to usher in an age of free and open scientific inquiry":

Though trained as a physicist, Holdren is best known for his work on energy and environmental policy. For the past few decades [he] has been among the nation's leading purveyors of ecological doom. Of more immediate concern, Holdren has exhibited an extreme intolerance to dissenting scientific and environmental views and a tendency to claim his politics are dictated by science.

Holdren cut his teeth on environmental issues in the 1970s, when he frequently collaborated with notorious doomster Paul Ehrlich, author of *The Population Bomb* which famously proclaimed "The battle to feed all of humanity is over. In the 1970s, the world will undergo famines— hundreds of millions of people are going to starve to death." In their many collaborations Holdren and Ehrlich made several equivalent, if less quotable, prophecies and called for draconian measures to stave off environmental ruin. He was, in his own words, a "neo-Malthusian."

In 1971, Holdren and Ehrlich decried humanity's "rapacious depletion of our fossil fuels" and called for "de-development" of industrialized nations. Writing with Anne Ehrlich in 1973 they called for "A massive campaign . . . to restore a high-quality environment in North America and to de-develop the United States." To achieve this end, they explained, "Resources and energy must be diverted from frivolous and wasteful uses in overdeveloped countries to filling the genuine needs of underdeveloped countries."[82]

"What is clear from the record going back over nearly four decades is that White House science czar John Holdren is a climate alarmist, even if he can't make up his mind whether the crisis is the Earth warming up or cooling down," Jerome Corsi wrote October 6, 2009, at *WorldNetDaily*.[83]

"But long before Holdren was the global warming Cassandra he is today, he was a global cooling alarmist predicting a new ice age," Corsi wrote. "The only consistency seems to be that Holdren has always utilized climate hysteria to argue that government must mandate public policy measures to prevent imminent and otherwise unavoidable climate catastrophes."[84]

Adler, at *National Review Online*, writes that Holdren is "equally intolerant of those who dispute his views on climate change. Holdren believes the media attention given climate skeptics is a 'menace . . . insofar as this delays the development of the political consensus that will be needed before society embraces remedies that are commensurate with the magnitude of the climate-change challenge.' According to Holdren, 'the science of climate change' dictates urgent action, and contrary views are 'dangerous.' Science tells us what to do, so there is nothing to debate."[85]

Corsi adds: "Still, Holdren remains a climate alarmist, now with an important government policy position as science czar in the Obama White House."[86]

Adler concedes that it should be expected that POTUS would pick someone who agreed with his own beliefs on climate change. But, Adler writes, Holdren's "climate policy views are not the issue. Rather it's his tendency to blur the lines between science and policy in pursuit of his agenda."

In light of social engineer Holdren's bizarre and alarming views on other ways to save the planet, "blurring the lines" is a gross understatement of his unsuitability for high office.

Holdren wrote in the seventies college textbook, *Ecoscience: Population, Resources, Environment*—co-authored with Paul and Anne Ehrlich— that "compulsory, government-mandated 'green abortions' would be a constitutionally acceptable way to control population growth and prevent ecological disasters, including global warming, because a fetus was most likely not a 'person' under the terms of the 14th Amendment," according to Jerome Corsi, writing September 23, 2009, at *WorldNetDaily*.[87]

Compulsory abortions would fit within the terms of the U.S. Constitution, according to Holdren and his co-authors. Corsi writes that "compulsory birth control methods" would be allowed, "including involuntary abortions, government-imposed sterilizations and laws limiting the number of children permitted to be born, as steps justified under the banner of 'sustainable well-being.'" [88]

Holdren "further suggested government-mandated population control measures might be inflicted in the United States against welfare recipients," Corsi wrote. "The authors argued involuntary birth-control measures, including forced sterilization, may be necessary and morally acceptable under extreme conditions, such as widespread famine brought about by 'climate change.'"[89]

If unwed women are unwilling to submit to government-mandated abortions, then the "illegitimate children" "could be taken by the government and put up for adoption," Corsi writes. Holdren believes that "'illegitimate childbearing could be strongly discouraged' as a socioeconomic measure imposed to control population growth."[90]

When the scandal broke that e-mails hacked from the Climatic Research Unit (CRU) at East Anglia University in the U.K. "show[ed] that some climate researchers declined to share their data with fellow scientists, conspired to rig data and sought to keep researchers with dissenting views from publishing in leading scientific journals," longtime climate alarmist John Holdren's name was found among the alleged conspirators.[91]

Canadian climatologist Dr. Tim Ball and Judi McLeod of the *Canadian Free Press* wrote November 24, 2009, that Holdren is "directly involved in CRU's unfolding Climategate scandal." According to Ball, the files reveal Holdren acted in what Ball termed "a truculent and nasty manner that provides a brief demonstration of his lack of understanding, commitment on faith and willingness to ridicule and bully people." Ball added: "Holdren's emails show how sincere scientists would be made into raw 'entertainment.'" [92]

CASS R. SUNSTEIN, REGULATORY CZAR

OFFICIAL PROFILE: Sunstein is the Administrator of the White House Office of Information and Regulatory Affairs. He is considered a scholar in the fields of constitutional law, administrative law, environmental law, and behavioral economics. He has taught for 27 years at the University of Chicago Law School and is a professor at Harvard Law School, where he is on leave while working in the Obama administration. A prolific writer, Sunstein has authored or co-authored over 30 books, including scholarly legal works and *New York Times* bestsellers. He is married to Samantha Power, the National Security Council's Senior Director for Multilateral Affairs.

EXTREMIST AGENDA: Sunstein openly promotes a socialist bill of rights, has petitioned to redistribute America's wealth, supports the abolition of marriage as a legal institution, and has pushed for a "New Deal Fairness Doctrine" to regulate the news media, among other radical goals.

In 2004 Sunstein penned a book, *The Second Bill of Rights: FDR'S Unfinished Revolution and Why We Need It More than Ever*, in which he advanced the notion that welfare rights, including some controversial new entitlements, be granted by the state. His inspiration for a new Bill of Rights came from President Roosevelt's 1944 proposal of a different, "new Bill of Rights." In his book, Sunstein laid out what he wants in his Second Bill of Rights:

- The right to a useful and remunerative job in the industries or shops or farms or mines of the nation;
- The right to earn enough to provide adequate food and clothing and recreation;
- The right of every farmer to raise and sell his products at a return which will give him and his family a decent living;
- The right of every businessman, large and small, to trade in an atmosphere of freedom from unfair competition and domination by monopolies at home or abroad;
- The right of every family to a decent home;
- The right to adequate medical care and the opportunity to achieve and enjoy good health;
- The right to adequate protection from the economic fears of old age, sickness, accident, and unemployment;
- The right to a good education.[93]

On one page in his book, Sunstein claims he is "not seriously arguing" his Bill of Rights be "encompassed by anything in the Constitution," but on the next page he states that "if the nation becomes committed to certain rights, they may migrate into the Constitution itself." Later in the book, Sunstein argues that "at a minimum, the second bill should be seen as part and parcel of America's constitutive commitments."

In April 2005, Sunstein opened up a conference at Yale Law School entitled "The Constitution in 2020," which sought to change the nature and interpretation of the Constitution by that year.[94] Sunstein has been a main participant in the movement to create a "progressive" consensus as to what the U.S. Constitution should provide for by the year 2020. The group also suggests strategy for how liberal lawyers and judges might bring such a constitutional regime into being. Just before his appearance at the conference, Sunstein wrote a blog entry in which he explained he "will be urging that it is important to resist, on democratic grounds, the idea that the document should be interpreted to reflect the view of the extreme right-wing of the Republican Party."[95]

In *The Second Bill of Rights,* Sunstein also argued that an economic crisis can be used to usher socialism into the United States. Sunstein pointed to the precedent of the Great Depression to show that historic economic crises "provided the most promising conditions for the emergence of socialism in the U.S."

"With a little nudge or a slight change in emphasis, our culture could have gone, and could still go, in many different directions," Sunstein wrote. In the same book, Sunstein said the United States should move in the direction of socialism but that the country's "white majority" opposes welfare, since such programs would largely benefit minorities, especially blacks and Hispanics. "The absence of a European-style social welfare state is certainly connected with the widespread perception among the white majority that the relevant programs would disproportionately benefit African Americans (and more recently Hispanics)," Sunstein claimed.

Sunstein not only argues for bringing socialism to the United States, he even lends support to communism. "During the Cold War, the debate about [social welfare] guarantees took the form of pervasive disagreement between the United States and its communist adversaries. Americans emphasized the importance of civil and political liberties, above all free speech and freedom of religion, while communist nations stressed the right to a job, health care and a social minimum." Continued Sunstein: "I think this debate was unhelpful; it is most plausible to see the two sets of rights as mutually reinforcing, not antagonistic."

Sunstein claims the "socialist movement" did not take hold in the United States in part because of a "smaller and weaker political left or lack of enthusiasm for redistributive programs." He laments, "In a variety of ways, subtle and less subtle, public and private actions have made it most difficult for socialism to have any traction in the United States."

Sunstein has promoted the "desirable" redistribution of America's wealth to poorer nations. In a 2007 University of Chicago Law School paper, entitled "Climate Change Justice," Sunstein maintains that U.S. wealth should be redistributed to poorer nations. He uses terms such as "distributive justice" several times. The paper was written with fellow attorney Eric A. Posner.[96] "It is even possible that desirable redistribution is more likely to occur through climate change policy than otherwise, or to be accomplished more effectively through climate policy than through direct foreign aid," wrote Sunstein.

He posited:

> We agree that if the United States does spend a great deal on emissions reductions as part of an international agreement, and if the agreement does give particular help to disadvantaged people, considerations of distributive justice support its action, even if better redistributive mechanisms are imaginable.
>
> If the United States agrees to participate in a climate change agreement on terms that are not in the nation's interest, but that help the world as a whole, there would be no reason for complaint, certainly if such participation is more helpful to poor nations than conventional foreign-aid alternatives.
>
> If we care about social welfare, we should approve of a situation in which a wealthy nation is willing to engage in a degree of self-sacrifice when the world benefits more than that nation loses.[97]

Meanwhile, the U.S. government should abolish its sanctioning of marriage, wrote Sunstein and co-author Richard Thaler in their 2008 book, *Nudge: Improving Decisions about Health, Wealth and Happiness.* Sunstein proposes that the concept of marriage should become privatized, with the state only granting civil union contracts to couples wishing to enter into an agreement. He explains that marriage licensing is unnecessary, pointing out that people stay committed to organizations like country clubs and homeowner associations without any government interference. "Under our proposal, the word marriage would no longer appear in any laws, and marriage licenses would no longer be offered or recognized by any level of government." Marriages would instead be "strictly private matters, performed by religious and other private organizations. Governments would not be asked to endorse any particular relationships by conferring on them the term marriage," he wrote.

Sunstein slams government's current recognition of marriage as "an official license scheme." "When the state grants marriage it gives both maternal and symbolic benefits to the couples it recognizes. But why combine the two functions? And what is added by the term marriage?" he asked.

In *Nudge*, Sunstein and co-author Thaler also discuss multiple legal scenarios regarding organ donation. One possibility presented in the book, termed by Sunstein as "routine removal," posits that "the state owns the rights to body parts of people who are dead or in certain hopeless conditions, and it can remove their organs without asking anyone's permission."

"Though it may sound grotesque, routine removal is not impossible to defend," wrote Sunstein. "In theory, it would save lives, and it would do so without intruding on anyone who has any prospect for life."

Sunstein continued:

> Although this approach is not used comprehensively by any state, many states do use the rule for corneas (which can be transplanted to give some blind patients sight). In some states, medical examiners performing autopsies are permitted to remove corneas without asking anyone's permission.

Sunstein seems to miss the point that medical examiners remove corneas only from patients already declared deceased. After defending the position, Sunstein concedes the "routine removal" approach "violates a generally accepted principle, which is that within broad limits, individuals should be able to decide what is to be done with and to their bodies." Still, Sunstein does not say that the removal of organs from a living individual should be banned.

Also in the same book, Sunstein argues for removing organs from deceased patients who are not registered as organ donors, a policy not without precedent. Spain and some European Union countries have been debating the adoption of a law of implied consent. Writes Sunstein: "A policy that can pass libertarian muster by our standards is called presumed consent."

The Obama czar also has exhibited some strange views toward animals, cells, and abortion. In his 1993 book *The Partial Constitution*, Sunstein argues that any restriction on access to abortions would turn women's bodies into vessels to be "used" by fetuses. "A restriction on access to abortion turns women's reproductive capacities into something to be used by fetuses. . . . Legal and social control of women's sexual and reproductive capacities has been a principal historical source of sexual inequality," Sunstein wrote.

In the book, Sunstein posits that the government should be required to fund abortion in cases such as rape or incest. "I have argued that the Constitution . . . forbids government from refusing to pay the expenses of abortion in cases of rape or incest, at least if government pays for childbirth in such cases," Sunstein wrote.

In a review of the 2003 book, *Our Posthuman Future*, by Francis Fukuyama, Sunstein further argues there is no moral concern regarding cloning human beings since human embryos, which develop into a baby, are "only a handful of cells."

"If scientists will be using and cloning embryos only at a very early stage when they are just a handful of cells (say, before they are four days old), there is no good reason for a ban [on cloning]," Sunstein writes.

In addition to Sunstein's moral disregard for human embryos, the Obama czar several times has quoted approvingly from an author who likened animals to slaves and argued that an adult dog or a horse is more rational than a human infant and should, therefore, be granted similar rights.[98] A brief video on YouTube captures Sunstein at a 2002 event using the writings of Jeremy Bentham, an eighteenth-century social reformer and animal-rights pioneer.[99] "You've heard a reference to Bentham, so let's listen to him, shall we?" he begins in the video.[100] He then quotes from Bentham's 1789 primer, *Introduction to Principals of Morals and Legislation*, written just after slaves had been freed by the French but were still held captive in the British dominions:

> The day may come, when the rest of the animal creation may acquire those rights which never could have been withholden from them but by the hand of tyranny. The French have already discovered that the blackness of the skin is no reason why a human being should be abandoned without redress to the caprice of a tormentor.

Sunstein continues quoting Bentham: "A full-grown horse or dog is beyond comparison a more rational, as well as a more conversable animal, than an infant of a day or a week or even a month old. But suppose the case were otherwise." The rest of Bentham's sentence, not captured in the video, continued, "what would it avail? The question is not, can they [animals] reason or can they talk? But, can they suffer?"

While the YouTube video admittedly offers only a brief sound bite with no context, a review conducted by these authors of Sunstein's academic writings found that Sunstein uses the same verses from Bentham to push for animal rights. In the footnotes to a 2002 academic paper for Harvard University, "The Rights of Animals: A Very Short Primer," Sunstein expresses his approval of Bentham's arguments: "I suggest that Bentham and [J.S.] Mill were not wrong to offer an analogy between current uses of animals and human slavery," he wrote.[101] Several other works by Sunstein, including his books, quote approvingly from Bentham's statements comparing adult dogs and horses to human infants.[102] In the Harvard paper, Sunstein even suggests animals could be granted the right to sue humans in court. "We could even grant animals a right to bring suit without insisting that animals are in some general sense 'persons,' or that they are not property," he wrote.

Sunstein has also advocated worrying policies regarding media "fairness" and regulation that are detailed in the following chapter.

ROSA BROOKS, PENTAGON ADVISOR

OFFICIAL PROFILE: Brooks, a former *Los Angeles Times* columnist, is senior advisor to the Under Secretary of Defense for Policy, Michele Flournoy.

She is a law professor at the Georgetown University Law Center, where she also serves as Director of Georgetown Law School's Human Rights Center. She previously served as a foreign policy advisor to the John Kerry–John Edwards presidential campaign of 2004 and was special counsel to the president at George Soros' Open Society Institute. She worked for multiple human rights organizations, including Human Rights Watch, where she consulted, and Amnesty International USA, where she served as a board member.

EXTREMIST AGENDA: The daughter of a socialist activist, Brooks has blamed the 9/11 attacks on U.S. policies, blasted Republicans as "paranoid, rage-driven, xenophobic nuts," and largely faults Israel in the Mideast conflict.

Reportedly named after communist heroine Rosa Luxemburg, Brooks is the daughter of Barbara Ehrenreich, who is Honorary Chairwoman of the Democratic Socialists of America as well as a board member of the extremist, pro-socialist Movement for a Democratic Society. In her long leftist career, Ehrenreich has openly promoted Marxism and celebrated the re-release of the *Communist Manifesto* on its 150th anniversary in 1998.[103]

"I prefer to think of [my new position] as my personal government bailout," Brooks wrote of her new job at the Pentagon, in her swan song for the *Los Angeles Times*. In 2007, she called al-Qaeda "little more than an obscure group of extremist thugs, well financed and intermittently lethal but relatively limited in their global and regional political pull. On 9/11, they got lucky. . . . Thanks to U.S. policies, al-Qaeda has become the vast global threat the administration imagined it to be in 2001."[104]

Also that year, she called the surge in Iraq a "feckless plan" that is "too little too late" with "no enduring solution in Iraq." A year later, the surge was widely credited with helping to stabilize Iraq.

Brooks wrote that President Bush and Vice President Cheney "should be treated like psychotics who need treatment. . . . Impeachment's not the solution to psychosis, no matter how flagrant." She also penned a column about Bush entitled "Our torturer-in-chief" in which she implied that attacks against the United States were a result of torture policies. "Today, the chickens are coming home to roost," she fumed, but "the word 'accountability' isn't in the White House dictionary."[105]

Another column referred to the regimes of Iran and North Korea as "foreign authoritarians," while calling the Bush administration a "homegrown" authoritarian regime. Brooks compared the Bush administration's arguments for prosecuting the war on terrorism to tactics used by Hitler. According to Brooks: "How did such dangerously bad legal memos ever get taken seriously in the first place? One answer is suggested by the so-called Big Lie theory of political propaganda, articulated most infamously by Adolf Hitler. Ordinary people 'more readily fall victim to the big lie than the small lie,' wrote Hitler."

Brooks' departing column also argued for more "direct government support for public media" and government licensing of the news. Wrote Brooks: "Years of foolish policies have left us with a choice: We can bail out journalism, using tax dollars and granting licenses in ways that encourage robust and independent reporting and commentary, or we can watch, wringing our hands, as more and more top journalists are laid off."

A 2006 column blamed Israel's actions in the Middle East for fueling anti-American resentment from the Arab world. The column largely focused on Israel's war that year against the Hezbollah terrorist group. The conflict broke out when Hezbollah built rocket arsenals along the Israeli border and then launched a major border raid in which Hezbollah killed Israeli troops, kidnapped two more soldiers, and fired mortars and rockets into Jewish civilian population zones.

"Israeli policies are a major source of discord in the Islamic world, and anger at Israel usually spills over into anger at the U.S., Israel's biggest backer," Brooks wrote. "With resentment of Israeli policies fueling terrorism and instability both in the Middle East and around the globe, it's past time for Americans to have a serious national debate about how to bring a just peace to the Middle East," she recommends. "But if criticism of Israel is out of bounds, that debate can't occur—and we'll all pay the price."

In another piece, Brooks grossly distorts the historical record by claiming former Prime Minister Ariel Sharon was to blame for the failure of U.S.-brokered negotiations between Israelis and Palestinians that culminated in a summit at Camp David in 2000. The talks briefly continued into 2001 in Taba, Egypt, but broke down in late January after Palestinian leader Yasser Arafat refused an Israeli offer of a Palestinian state in the Gaza Strip, West Bank, and eastern Jerusalem. Instead, Arafat launched the "intifada," or terrorist war, aimed at liberating "Palestine" through violence.

Sharon, who is perceived as a defense hawk, was only elected prime minister two weeks after the talks had already collapsed and on the heels of a major Palestinian terrorist campaign. President Bill Clinton largely blamed Arafat. The Palestinians claimed that Israel's peace gestures, under Prime Minister Ehud Barak, had not gone far enough. But even the Palestinians did not blame Sharon's election for the talks' collapse. If anything, the collapse of the talks had helped bring about Sharon's election.

But according to Brooks, "Israel and the Palestinian Authority came achingly close to a final settlement, but talks broke down after Likud's Ariel Sharon was elected prime minister on Feb. 6, 2001."

Another piece, entitled "Israel can't bomb it's way to peace," continues, "Sharon refused to meet with Yasser Arafat, and newly inaugurated President George W. Bush had no interest in pushing Israel toward peace." In the same op-ed, Brooks slammed Israel's 22-day military campaign against Hamas in the Gaza Strip that ended January 2009. She claimed that "Israel has justified its bombardment of Gaza on the grounds that Hamas broke a fragile, temporary cease-fire . . . but the timing of the Israeli military offensive has more to do with politics than anything else."

The two sides were not on equal footing, Brooks wrote, allowing that as compared to Israel's military might, Hamas is "weak, and its weapons—terrorism, homemade rockets—are the weapons of the weak." But missing from Brooks' account is any acknowledgement that Hamas rocket-fire devastated Israeli towns over the past few years, killing Israelis and disrupting life for over 100,000 of its citizens. Hamas started launching the rocket attacks into Israel after the Jewish state unilaterally evacuated its citizens and its military from the Gaza Strip, leaving the strategic territory to Palestinian control.

Brooks went on to exaggerate the Gaza casualty count by failing to differentiate between civilians and terrorists. "The first day of the offensive, Israeli bombs killed at least 180 Palestinians. By Wednesday, the

Palestinian death toll exceeded 390," she wrote. According to the Israel Defense Forces, two-thirds of the casualties were Hamas fighters.

Brooks concluded:

It's time for the United States to wake up from its long slumber and reengage—forcefully—with the Middle East peace process. Only the U.S.—Israel's primary supporter and main financial sponsor—can push it to make the hard choices.

She pointed out that as long as Bush was in the White House, "Israel could count on a U.S. administration that wasn't merely 'supportive' of Israel but blindly, mindlessly so. Obama may be less willing to offer Israel blank checks."[106]

11

THE WHITE HOUSE AND "MEDIA JUSTICE"

What the hardcore *reformistas* really want, it seems,
is not diversity or an open debate but a media that promotes
their own vision of society and the world.

—Ben Compaine, author of *Who Owns the Media?*
at *Reason.com*, January 1, 2004.[1]

THE AGENDA OF the far left is not confined to redistributing wealth and political power in America. The goal of radicals is also to "redistribute" control of speech and First Amendment "rights." One website touting "Media Justice Now! Building the Next Generation of Media Resistance," gives a flavor of this agenda. It describes "media redistribution" as "part of a long legacy of struggle for a fair and just mass media." The "struggle" in question, of course, is that of "the masses versus the corporate media," which, they say, have been an "effective mouthpiece for corporate interests and ha[ve] blocked dialogue and debate on our publicly owned airways."[2]

In other words, the same agenda as ACORN, the SEIU, DSA, the Soros-funded groups, former SDSers, "liberation theologists"—not to mention their allies further to the left—for using unions, politicized churches, and shady voter-registration drives to gain power, should be applied to control of the American mass media.

This radical media agenda got a big boost when President Obama appointed a "Diversity Czar" at the Federal Communications Commission—officially designated the FCC's Associate General Counsel and Chief Diversity Officer—in July 2009.

Mark Lloyd is a senior fellow at the George Soros–funded Center for

American Progress, headed by John Podesta, the former chief of staff to President Bill Clinton who also oversaw Obama's presidential transition. At CAP, Lloyd "focus[es] on communications policy issues, including universal service, advanced telecommunications deployment, media concentration and diversity." Lloyd is also a consultant to Soros' Open Society Institute.[3]

The appointment of Lloyd coincided with Obama's designation of long-time personal friend and top campaign fundraiser Julius Genachowski as Chief Commissioner of the FCC. Also, the new Obama "Regulatory Czar" Cass Sunstein, as we shall see, has been outspoken on the "media diversity" and "redistribution" agenda.

With these appointments, the United States presumably entered "a new phase of struggle" for "media justice."

So let's have a closer look at Barack Obama's newly appointed "Diversity Czar" for the mass media. In 2007 Lloyd wrote an article for CAP called "Forget the Fairness Doctrine," in which he instructed liberals to file complaints with the FCC against conservative radio stations.

"What [his article] lays out is a battle plan to use the FCC to threaten stations' licenses with whom they do not agree politically," said Seton Motley, director of communications at the Media Research Center, in an August 14, 2009, interview on the *Glenn Beck Show*. "And now he's at the FCC waiting to take their calls. This is not about serving the local interest, it's about political opposition," Motley said.[4]

For his part, Lloyd attributes the "rise and influence of Rush Limbaugh and other conservative radio hosts" to "'relaxed ownership rules' and other pro-business regulation that destroyed localism," Motley told Glenn Beck.

Lloyd says he is not interested in reinstating the Fairness Doctrine, an FCC decree that at one time required broadcast stations to demonstrate "balance" to the FCC in the presentation of public issues. The doctrine was a legacy of the early days of television broadcasting, when there were only three or four stations in each major market. Ronald Reagan, whose career before politics had been in the mass media, effectively abolished the doctrine in 1983, which did, in fact, allow talk radio to emerge as a largely conservative medium, though this was not foreseen at the time.

But the doctrine's abolition also occurred when cable, satellite TV, and later the Internet, were dramatically expanding the diversity of information outlets. So even its advocates had trouble sustaining the original justification for the Fairness Doctrine, which, in 1949, could be argued that electronic mass media were "a limited public resource."

Instead of pushing to reinstate the Fairness Doctrine, Lloyd calls for "equal opportunity employment practices," "local engagement," and "license challenges" to "rectify" that "perceived imbalance," Fox reported. According to Lloyd, there is "nothing in there about the Fairness Doctrine."

In an intent clearly to provoke, Lloyd wrote: "The other part of our proposal that gets the 'dittoheads' upset is our suggestion that the commercial radio station owners either play by the rules or pay. In other words, if they don't want to be subject to local criticism of how they are meeting their license obligations, they should pay to support public broadcasters who will operate on behalf of the local community."

Lloyd "concluded that 91% of talk radio programming is conservative and 9% is 'progressive,'" reports Matt Cover at *CNSNews.com* (August 13, 2009). Lloyd's report "argued that large corporate broadcasting networks had driven liberals off the radio, and that diversity of ownership would increase diversity of broadcasting voices," Cover adds.[5]

Lloyd's prescriptions for media reform are more fully described in a book he wrote while still full-time with the Center for American Progress: *Prologue to a Farce: Communications and Democracy in America* (2007). In the book, among other things, he "presents the idea that private broadcasters (private business) should pay a licensing [fee] which equals their total operating costs so that public broadcasting [stations] can spend the same on their operations as the private companies do," according to George Fallon at *RightPundits.com* (August 14, 2009). Lloyd's intent was to use the funds to "improve the Corporation for Public Broadcasting"— whose budget is already $400 million for 2009.

Additionally, Lloyd writes that he did not just want to "redistribute private profits" but also wants to "regulate much of the programming on these stations to make sure they focus on 'diverse views' and government activities. Lloyd contends that large corporate broadcasting networks have "driven liberals off of radio" based on a belief that "diversity owner-ship will reflect in diversity programming," Cover says.[6]

Elsewhere in *Prologue to a Farce*, Lloyd states:

> The Corporation for Public Broadcasting (CPB) must be reformed along democratic lines and funded on a substantial level. Federal and regional broadcast operations and local stations should be funded at lev-els commensurate with or above those spending levels at which com-mercial operations are funded. This funding should come from license fees charged to commercial broadcasters. Funding should not come from congressional appropriations. Sponsorship should be prohibited at all public broadcasters.[7]

So Lloyd's target of choice is not merely conservative talk radio. Makani Themba-Nixon and Nan Rubin write in the November 17, 2003, *Wall Street Journal* that, although Lloyd's movement "calls itself media justice today," in reality he is just trying to go back to "civil rights roots" and the "issues and concerns of the civil rights movement."[8] Lloyd's objections then were race-based, as clearly shown in the title of his January 1998 *Community Technology Center Review* article, "Communications Policy Is a Civil Rights Issue."[9] A brief bio compiled by Fox News notes that, prior to Lloyd joining the FCC, Lloyd "most recently served as vice president for strategic initia-tives at the Leadership Conference on Civil Rights/Education Fund, where he specialized in media and telecommunications."[10]

But, to be clear, Lloyd is going after bigger game than conservative broadcasters, or even racial progress. He says of the Telecommunications Act of 1996, signed by President Bill Clinton in February of that year, that it was "created by and for a communications industry dominated by global conglomerates." And Lloyd links the "influence of this global industry over the national legislative process" with "international media magnate Rupert Murdoch."

In the final analysis, Lloyd co-mingles his anticorporatist, anticapital-ist stance—portraying private industry as not only owning but also in full editorial control of television, radio, the Internet, even long-distance telephone service—with his media justice, civil rights agenda. There is nothing bipartisan in Lloyd's diagnosis; he blames "the right" for it all:

> The work of the civil rights community has suffered through a sustained assault by the right. The core of that assault is to deny funding to civil rights work, silence liberal voices, and set the agenda of public debate by an opposition that is better funded, more organized, and more savvy about strategic communications. The assault on affirmative action, welfare, multi-cultural studies, immigration, and foundations supporting progressive causes has been carefully orchestrated. Combined with this assault is a relentless marketing of the failed dogma of laissez-faire economics.

And Lloyd's prescription is a return to the Communications Act of 1934, which embodies "the concepts of public trusteeship and diversity of expression":

> Broadcasters (to whom the public airwaves are licensed), telephone and cable and satellite oligopolies (which benefit from government regulation, support, and public rights-of-way) are all responsible for acting in "the public interest, convenience, and necessity." The failure of our representatives (and the expert regulators they appoint) in federal and state offices is not a failure of the public interest standard as such, but a failure of the public to demand a public-oriented definition of that standard and its enforcement.

Lloyd, therefore, urges the "civil rights community" to step up and demand it.

"FULL SUPPORT OF OBAMA"

And Lloyd's agenda appears to have the full support of President Obama. Two articles by Katrina vanden Heuvel, editor of *The Nation,* tell the tale. In "Obama Blasts FCC Media Ownership Decision," (December 18, 2007), she writes:

Just hours after FCC Chairman Kevin Martin rammed through a vote to remove a longstanding newspaper/broadcast cross-ownership ban— thereby ignoring the public will, undermining democratic diversity and bowing to the corrupting campaign contributions and high-powered lobbyists of the largest media companies, Barack Obama slammed the decision. "Today the FCC failed to further the important goal of promoting diversity in the media and instead chose to put big corporate interests ahead of the peoples' interests," he said in a statement.[11]

Vanden Heuvel refers to her blog post from the prior week:

As I wrote in my Editor's Cut, "On the Media" (posted 12/12/07), Obama has been a stalwart supporter of encouraging diversity in the ownership of broadcast media. An Obama presidency, he has pledged, will promote greater coverage of local issues and better responsiveness by broadcasters to the communities they serve; it would also push for better opportunities for minority, small business and women-owned media firms.

Fortunately the fight is far from over. Obama has co-sponsored a bill in the Senate that would nullify the vote. "Congress will not stand by and allow the FCC to move forward with these regulatory changes," Obama said this afternoon, "and I will urge my colleagues to push forward legislation that ensures any changes will be evaluated and modified in a transparent and inclusive process, and fully takes into account the interests of our women and minority-owned outlets and communities."[12]

Indeed, as a senator Obama was co-sponsor of S.2332: "Media Ownership Act of 2007," introduced November 7, 2007, by Senator Byron Dorgan (D-N.D.), with 24 co-sponsors. The bill "would prevent the Federal Communications Commission from voting on any new media-ownership rules until sometime in 2008 and open a separate proceeding on broadcast localism," wrote John Eggerton at *Broadcastingcable.com* (Nov. 7, 2007).[13]

Eggerton added: "Senator John Kerry (D-Mass.) said at the hearing that it appeared that the FCC was headed down the same ill-advised path as that 2003 rewrite, calling it a new attempt to consolidate the media while there is still unfinished business on minority and localism issues." The bill died in committee.[14]

On Nov. 7, 2007, Sens. John Kerry and Barack Obama wrote: "Media consolidation silences diverse voices," published online at *The Politico*:

> In recent years, we have witnessed unprecedented consolidation in our traditional media outlets. Large mergers and corporate deals have reduced the number of voices and viewpoints in the media market-place.
>
> At the same time, massive technological change and an explosion of Internet access have opened new avenues for information and new methods of discourse. One thing we can be sure of: Change is upon us.
>
> As we look toward the future, we must ensure that all voices in our diverse nation have the opportunity to be heard. One important way to do this is to expand the ownership stake of women-owned, minority-owned and small businesses in our media outlets. . . .
>
> For too long now, the FCC has been putting corporate interests ahead of the people's interests. It's time for that to change.
>
> We need to not only create the opportunity for minority-owned businesses to participate in the market, but also to help those who enter this business succeed. We will keep fighting until we have a free and open media that represents every American in our diverse nation.[15]

Sounds like Senators Kerry and Obama wanted to extend affirmative action rationales to media ownership. They also sound like a good fit for the anticorporatist media policies being planned by Obama's new Diversity Czar at the FCC, Mark Lloyd.

Media ownership expert Ben Compaine took issue with Senators Kerry and Obama, in his blog of November 9, 2007: "But they once again turned a blind eye to years of research that have failed to show any pervasive ill effects of the existing media ownership structure. They fall back on anecdotes and 'fear' of potential behavior while barely giving lip service to the inevitable and largely positive effects of a rapidly changing media landscape."[16]

Compaine continues: "[Proponents in Congress]—Democrats and Republicans—insist on the quaint notion of 'locally-owned' media, when there is no sustained body of research that demonstrates that locally owned newspapers, radio or a TV stations provide more, better or more diverse information than corporately owned media entities."

"The policy they are pursuing," Compaine writes, "is populist to be sure. Thanks to the efforts of the advocacy group, the Free Press, and the unexamined assumptions of many journalists, there is an overwhelming misperception that the mass media are becoming more concentrated, when the numbers show they are not."

"TOO MANY WHITE PEOPLE"

Returning to Lloyd's earlier emphasis on race-based—not necessarily conservative-versus-progressive equality over the airwaves—Seton Motley comments at *NewsBusters* (Sept. 23, 2009) that "Lloyd is a man myopically focused on race." Motley directs our attention to excerpts of Lloyd's "offerings at a May 2005 Conference on Media Reform: Racial Justice [which] reveals a man that finds great fault with our nation's power structure—as he defines and sees it." Motley writes, in Lloyd's "racially-warped, finite pie worldview, too many white people sit alone in the too few spots atop the heap. They're 'good white people,' mind you, but . . . [17]

> This . . . there's nothing more difficult than this. Because we have really, truly good white people in important positions. And the fact of the matter is that there are a limited number of those positions. And unless we are conscious of the need to have more people of color, gays, other people in those positions we will not change the problem.
>
> We're in a position where you have to say who is going to step down so someone else can have power.

"So white people," Motley comments, "good though they may be, must 'step down so' 'more people of color, gays' and 'other people' 'can have power.' And thereby 'change the problem' of whites running the show."

And who, Motley asks, "is 'in a position where you have to say who is going to step down so someone else can have power'? Why, Lloyd is."

And while Lloyd rails on about how "the right" controls the media and fails to promote diversity, he conveniently avoids mentioning the amount of influence constantly being exerted by the George Soros–funded liberal/progressive echo chamber—by whom Lloyd is gainfully employed—and the pervasiveness of the Congressional Progressive Caucus, Congressional Black Caucus, Congressional Hispanic Caucus, Democratic Socialists of America, and other left-wing groups prevalent in Congress. With this much power, "the right" is still in control?

Nor do we hear much from the new Diversity Czar at the FCC about protecting freedom of speech or of the press. Speaking of the First Amendment at a June 10, 2008, National Conference for Media Reform in Minneapolis, Lloyd said: "It should be clear by now that my focus here is not freedom of speech or the press. This freedom is all too often an exaggeration. At the very least, blind references to freedom of speech or the press serve as a distraction from the critical examination of other communications policies. . . . [T]he purpose of free speech is warped to protect global corporations and block rules that would promote democratic governance."[18]

"Note how Lloyd views the freedoms of speech and the press as just two of a number of 'communications policies,'" Seton Motley comments. "Ones that he appears to view as less than equal—and in fact impediments to—the others he seeks to see implemented in the interest of promoting 'democratic governance.'"

Lloyd, however, is not alone in his views among members of the Obama administration.

SUNSTEIN: CENSOR SEAN HANNITY, "RIGHT-WING" RUMORS

Cass Sunstein, the Obama administration's Regulatory Czar, writes in his most recent book, *On Rumors* (September 2009), that websites "should be obliged to remove 'false rumors' while libel laws should be altered to make it easier to sue for spreading such 'rumors,'" as Aaron Klein reported at *WorldNetDaily* after reviewing the book.[19]

Sunstein "specifically cited as a primary example of 'absurd' and 'hateful' remarks, reports by 'right-wing websites' alleging an association between President Obama and Weatherman terrorist Bill Ayers," Klein wrote. In particular, Sunstein "singled out radio talker Sean Hannity for 'attacking' Obama regarding the president's 'alleged associations.'"

The age of the Internet is of particular concern to Sunstein, who writes: "It has become easy to spread false or misleading rumors about almost anyone."

Some right-wing websites liked to make absurd and hateful remarks about the alleged relationship between Barack Obama and the former radical Bill Ayers; one of the websites' goals was undoubtedly to attract more viewers.

On the Internet as well as on talk radio, altruistic propagators are easy to find; they play an especially large role in the political domain. When Sean Hannity, the television talk show host, attacked Barack Obama because of his alleged associations, one of his goals might have been to promote values and causes that he cherishes.

Klein remarks: "Sunstein presents multiple new measures he argues can be used to stop the spread of 'rumors' and contends 'freedom usually works, but in some contexts, it is an incomplete corrective.'" The more "complete corrective" Sunstein has in mind is stark, Klein writes: Sunstein "proposes the imposition of a 'chilling effect' on 'damaging rumors'—or the use of strong 'corrective' measures to deter future rumormongers."

Regarding websites: "Sunstein suggests a 'right to notice and take down' in which 'those who run websites would be obliged to take down falsehoods upon notice.'" Sunstein "also argues for the 'right to demand a retraction after a clear demonstration that a statement is both false and damaging,'" Klein writes. "But he does not explain which agency would determine whether any statement is false and damaging." Sunstein "further pushes for 'deterrence' through making libel lawsuits easier to bring," Klein adds.

Mark Lloyd is not the only one who dances on the head of a pin regarding a "New Deal Fairness Doctrine." In his 1993 book, *The Partial*

Constitution, Sunstein draws up the radical proposal for a "First Amendment New Deal"—a new "Fairness Doctrine"—"that would include the establishment of a panel of 'nonpartisan experts' to ensure 'diversity of view' on the airwaves." This "received no news media attention and scant scrutiny" until Klein reported it (September 15, 2009).[20]

In an argument similar to that advanced by Lloyd, Sunstein "compared the need for the government to regulate broadcasting to the moral obligation of the U.S. to impose new rules that outlawed segregation."

Sunstein echoes Lloyd to a great degree. He "outwardly favors and promotes [reintroducing] the 'Fairness Doctrine,'" Klein writes, while Sunstein's "'First Amendment New Deal' to regulate broadcasting in the U.S." focuses "largely on television, includ[ing] a government requirement that 'purely commercial stations provide financial subsidies to public television or to commercial stations that agree to provide less profitable but high-quality programming,'" Klein writes, adding: Sunstein says it is "worthwhile to consider more dramatic approaches as well."

As does Lloyd, Sunstein proposes "compulsory public-affairs programming, right of reply, content review by nonpartisan experts or guidelines to encourage attention to public issues and diversity of view."

Nor does he see any Constitutional problems with his radical proposals. He does, however, slam the U.S. courts' "unwillingness to 'require something like a Fairness Doctrine' to be a result of 'the judiciary's lack of democratic pedigree, lack of fact-finding powers and limited remedial authority,'" Klein writes. But Sunstein insists "he is not arguing the government should be free to regulate broadcasting however it chooses."

"Regulation designed to eliminate a particular viewpoint would of course be out of bounds. All viewpoint discrimination would be banned . . . at the very least, regulative 'fairness doctrines' would raise no real doubts" constitutionally, Sunstein writes.

"NET NEUTRALITY"

A third Obama administration member and Mark Lloyd's new boss at the FCC, Julius Genachowski, was a classmate of Barack Obama's at both Columbia University and Harvard Law School, as the authors discussed in Chapter 2.

President Obama appointed Genachowski, his longtime friend and top fund-raiser (who personally raised over $500,000 for the presidential campaign), as Chairman of the Federal Communications Commission, on June 29, 2009. It was Genachowski's third stint at the FCC.[21]

After graduating from Harvard Law in 1985, Genachowski took the post-graduate clerkship Obama turned down and worked for federal appeals court Judge Abner Mikva. Genachowski also served as "a law clerk to U.S. Supreme Court Justice David H. Souter and, before that, to retired U.S. Supreme Court Justice William J. Brennan, Jr." He "worked in Congress on the staff of the Select Committee investigating the Iran-Contra Affair and also for then-U.S. Representative, now Senator, Charles E. Schumer." [22]

Genachowski's experience in the private sector includes co-founding and serving as managing director of digital media investment firm Rock Creek Ventures, and co-founding LaunchBox Digital, a "seed-stage investment program for web and mobile entrepreneurs." He also served in "senior executive positions for eight years at IAC/InterActiveCorp," an Internet company with over 50 websites across 40 countries, from *Ask.com* to *ZwinkyCuties*.[23]

During the Obama 2008 presidential campaign, Genachowski served as Obama's chairman of the Technology, Media and Telecommunications policy working group. TMT "created the Obama Technology and Innovation Plan" and "advised and guided the Obama campaign's innovative use of technology and the Internet for grassroots engagement and participation." Also on the campaign's behalf, Genachowski "spoke out on network neutrality," while he co-led the Technology, Innovation, and Government Reform Group for Obama's transition team.[24]

Of Genachowski, Tom Steinert-Threlkeld comments at *ZDNet* (January 13, 2009): "interestingly for the man who would be head of the commission that governs communications, there are few communications that indicate where he actually stands on any communication issues."[25]

Or as Matthew Lasar, of *Ars Technica* (and a former reporter at far-left Pacifica Radio) writes (December 2008): "You would think that, as the semi-official media broadband guru of the week, this Genachowski guy would have left some kind of paper trail as to what he thinks about stuff. You know, op-ed pieces, brilliant public statements, at least one book about how to get rich by saving the planet—but it's been slim pickings so far, search engine/library database-wise."[26]

Genachowski's blank slate, however, and his appointment as FCC chairman, did not disappoint the advocates of a highly controversial regulatory proposal known as "net neutrality." As Ryan Singel writes at *WIRED* (March 3, 2009), the new FCC chairman was "widely anticipated and quickly applauded by proponents of net neutrality, who hope an Obama FCC will move decisively to limit what telecoms can and cannot do with internet traffic on their networks."[27]

Genachowski's tech plan for the Obama transition team "called for the U.S. to increase its definition of 'high speed' Internet and reform a $7 billion federal phone-subsidy program, to help cover the costs of offering broadband in rural areas." It also called for "encouraging diversity in media ownership," according to Amy Schatz and Shira Ovide, writing in the January 15, 2009 *Wall Street Journal*. The authors interpreted Genachowski's tech plan as "a signal that efforts by big media companies to expand their empires could face tougher scrutiny."[28]

On the issue of "media diversity" it is unclear where Lloyd's boss stands vis-à-vis the affirmative action notions of his Diversity Czar—or even if they share the same definition of what media diversity is. Whereas Genachowski talks about media diversity in terms of implementation and application of existing FCC regulations, Lloyd is focused on media justice, including the mandated expansion of minority ownership of the mass media.

Genachowksi's leanings are unclear. For example, since early July 2009, Genachowski's press secretary has been Jen Howard, former press director at the liberal/left media think tank Free Press. This would be the same Free Press co-founded by Robert W. McChesney, about whom more follows, and on whose board sat avowed Marxist, and former Obama administration "Green Jobs Czar," Van Jones.[29] It is the same Free Press that, jointly with the Center for American Progress, co-published *The Structural Imbalance of Political Talk Radio*, of which Mark Lloyd was a co-author.[30]

Comments conservative activist and blogger Warner Todd Huston: "This slanted paper whines that AM talk radio is dominated by conservative views and suggests that liberal views should be forced upon the talk radio indus-try." Huston continues: "That left-wing idea, of course, is bad enough, but the group that Lloyd was working with to have the paper published shows ties to left-wingers, outright Marxists and other haters of this country and that connection should have disqualified Lloyd for service in the federal government."[31]

"For instance," Huston writes, "founder of the Free Press, Robert W. McChesney, has said some pretty harsh stuff against the U.S.A.,"[32] and, "at the end of September of 2001, right after the Twin Towers fell, McChesney said that the United States was the 'leading terrorist institu-tion in the world today.'"

In February of 2009, McChesney recommended that capitalism be "dismantled" in the United States. Adds Phil Kerpen, of the conservative think tank and activist group, Americans for Prosperity: "Free Press is the brainchild of Robert McChesney, who wrote a column last year advis-ing President Obama: 'In the end, there is no real answer but to remove brick-by-brick the capitalist system itself, rebuilding the entire society on socialist principles.'"

October 21, 2009, Kerpen "blasted the FCC for being in bed with Free Press, a group dedicated to advancing government control of the Internet and all media."[33] Kerpen was reacting to an email "sent out under FCC Spokeswoman Jen Howard's name by Free Press, discussing the FCC's intent to advance net neutrality regulations. Free Press is a well-known advocate of government intervention in the Internet, and Howard's attempt to have one foot in and one foot out of government at the same time is outrageous." Kerpen's reference to "one foot in and one foot out" is to Jen Howard's still being listed as with Free Press, while on the FCC payroll.

Prior to working at Free Press, Jen Howard worked at the Media Access Project, which describes itself as a "non-profit, public interest law firm and advocacy organization dedicated to promoting the public's First Amendment right to access a diverse marketplace of ideas in the mass media system."[34]

The Media Access Project traces its origin to the "landmark United Church of Christ litigation of the 1960s. Those cases . . . established that members of the viewing and listening public have the legal right, derived from the First Amendment, to participate in FCC proceedings."[35] Like other proponents of media reform, the Media Access Project touts its "unique role as a Washington thought leader in communications and technology policy. From leading efforts to convince the FCC to create the Low Power FM radio service to being among the first to advocate for open access and network neutrality."

"AVOWED MARXIST"

Howard's former boss, Robert McChesney, is a professor at the University of Illinois, and former editor of the Marxist journal, *Monthly Review.*

Blogger Raymond Pronk points out that McChesney is a self-avowed Marxist, whose Free Press started "having large influence and holding great sway in the development of policy for the Obama administration." McChesney "has a very distorted view of the first amendment," Pronk writes, viewing the "media marketplace in the same way [as] Mark Lloyd, the chief diversity officer." McChesney and Lloyd "don't believe in free speech," Pronk writes, and they are "proud of it."[36]

Aside from creating Free Press, McChesney served on the board of Norman Solomon's Institute for Public Accuracy, and "remains on the board of *Monthly Review*, which has a half-century history of supporting Communist movements and regimes."[37] Contributors to *Monthly Review* include "former Weather Underground terrorist Bernardine Dohrn; Marilyn Buck, another former Weather Underground member; convicted cop-killer Mumia Abu-Jamal; Bill Fletcher, Jr., a founder of Progressives for Obama; and [Professor Noam] Chomsky."[38]

Writes Matthew Vadum at *NewsRealBlog* (October 12, 2009): "Echoing President Obama's media diversity czar Mark Lloyd, McChesney supports Venezuela's Marxist strongman Hugo Chávez and that country's crackdown on the media. He even argued that owners of an opposition TV station that had been critical of Chávez should be arrested for treason."[39]

Regarding McChesney's idea of media reform, Adam Thierer writes at *TechLiberation.com* (August 10, 2009) that McChesney is the "godfather of the media *reformista* movement, the founder of Free Press, and an avowed socialist. And he has made his intentions in this regard abundantly clear throughout his prolific career. In his book *Rich Media, Poor Media*, he says that 'Media reform cannot win without widespread support and such support needs to be organized as part of a broad anti-corporate, pro-democracy movement.'" McChesney "casts everything in 'social justice' terms and speaks of the need 'to rip the veil off [corporate] power, and to work so that social decision making and power may be made as enlightened and as egalitarian as possible,'" Thierer writes.[40]

In a book called *Our Media, Not Theirs: The Democratic Struggle against Corporate Media*, written by *The Nation*'s John Nichols, McChesney "argues that media reform efforts must begin with 'the need to promote an understanding of the urgency to assert public control over the media.' They go on to state that, 'Our claim is simply that the media system produces vastly less of quality than it would if corporate and commercial pressures were lessened,'" Thierer notes.

SOROS-LINKED "INTERNET CZAR"

Obama administration connections to McChesney's Free Press do not end with "Diversity Czar" Mark Lloyd and FCC spokeswoman Jen Howard.

Meet Obama's "Internet Czar," Susan P. Crawford.

Crawford was chosen to head up the Obama transition's Federal Communications Commission Review team. After the inauguration, Obama named her Special Assistant to the President for Science, Technology, and Innovation Policy—or Internet Czar.

WIRED magazine calls Crawford "the most powerful geek close to the president," and notes that prior to her work for the administration, she was a "prolific" writer on Net Neutrality.[41] Crawford teaches cyber and telecommunications law at the University of Michigan, is a member of the National Economic Council, and served as a member of the board of ICANN, which assigns domain names on the Internet, from 2005 to 2008. She is the founder of OneWebDay, which seeks to "[deepen] a culture of participation in building a Web that works for everyone."[42]

Meanwhile, speaking at the recent "Free Press Summit: Changing

Media" held at the Newseum in Washington (May 14, 2009), Crawford advocated for newspaper subsidies.[43]

Crawford is controversial, as well, for her connection to ACORN. It was discovered in September 2009 that Crawford's "OneWebNow project lists Acorn as one of its 'participating organizations.' Crawford's One-WebNow participating organizations' page lists both ACORN and Free Press.[44] Crawford . . . also has a board member, Mitchell Kapor, who is an ACORN apologist."[45]

Crawford and Kevin Werbach, who co-directed the Obama transition team's Federal Communications Commission Review team, are advisory board members at Public Knowledge, a George Soros–funded public interest group.[46]

Public Knowledge claims to be bipartisan, working with groups from both sides of the aisle, including Free Press and the Open Society Institute.[47]

A third Public Knowledge advisory board member is Timothy Wu, who writes on his blog that in his "spare time," he is the chair of the "media reform organization Free Press." According to his Columbia University faculty profile, Wu is chairman of the board for Free Press, as well as a fellow at the New America Foundation.[48]

The New America Foundation is funded by what are now familiar usual suspects: George Soros' Open Society Institute, which appears in the wide-ranging $250,000 to $999,999 category, and Free Press and the Tides Foundation, listed in the $10,000 to $24,999 category.[49]

Wu is credited with "popularizing the concept" in his 2003 paper, *Network Neutrality, Broadband Discrimination*, presented at the Silicon Flatirons conference in Boulder, Colorado (February 3, 2003). Wu's paper is "believed to be the first use of the term."[50]

In June 2008, Wu held that the U.S. Constitution is "flawed because the founders did not anticipate the problem of 'the abuse of private power.'" The Bill of Rights, Wu says, "was merely designed to protect people against government and the founders were concerned about the exercise of 'public power.'"[51]

Cliff Kincaid at Accuracy in Media comments, regarding the National Conference for Media Reform held in June 2008, which "turned into a Barack Obama-for-President rally":

This is their rationale for using the powers of the federal government, through the FCC and Congress, to control the media. It is significant and telling that the Broadcaster Freedom Act, which would prevent the return of the Fairness Doctrine, was not endorsed by any speaker at the conference. The obvious reason is that the conference organizers want to use the government to silence voices objecting to their vision of what America should be.[52]

Wu was an early Obama supporter, posting December 11, 2006, on his blog: "It's beginning. . . New Yorkers for Obama." Wu's name appears as a signatory to the November 15, 2007, letter (posted on the Obama for America website) endorsing Obama the "day after he unveiled his innovation agenda at Google headquarters."[53]

Wu's support for Obama certainly has been well placed. As the president-to-be said at an April 21, 2008, campaign stop:

I'm committed to having the FCC review what our current policies are in terms of media diversification and part of what I want to do is to expand the diversity of voices in media or have policies that encourage that, taking into account that the nature of our media itself is changing so rapidly that the most important thing that we can probably do is to preserve the diversity that's emerging through the internet.[54]

And we now know who his advisors have been, as well.

12

COALITION OF EXTREMISTS PUSHING OBAMA AGENDA

THAT TEAM OBAMA ran a smooth, efficient, and winning presidential campaign in 2008 is universally acknowledged. Two of the architects of that campaign, and veterans of Obama's Illinois state and U.S. senatorial campaigns—David Axelrod and Valerie Jarrett—were discussed by the authors in detail in Chapter 10 of this book. Naturally, the campaign efforts of these two and the rest of Obama's staff were bolstered by various panels and advisory boards comprised of experts, academics, and specialists on foreign policy, economics, the environment, government regulations, minority issues, and health care, to name a few.

But unknown to the general public, the Obama campaign also included a loose coalition of extremists who, for the most part, remain the president's loyal supporters. Though infrequently seen, unless while networking with fellow travelers, they worked—and are still working—fervently behind the scenes with inside connections, as well as with less intimate acquaintances within the Obama circle, not only to propel Barack Obama to victory, but also to advance a radical agenda within Obama's presidency.

Sometime in spring 2008, or possibly earlier, unidentified Marxists, socialists, and communists "created a safe space" on the *Obama for America* official campaign website, where they could "congregate, exchange ideas—including a stated revolution against the U.S. 'oppres-sive' regime—and support their favored presidential candidate," as Aaron Klein reported at *WorldNetDaily* at the time.[1]

This online community, only one of numerous existing groups, or ones newly created, to support Obama's candidacy, called itself "Marxist/Socialists/Communists for Obama" on the *Obama for America* website. They declared:

> This group is for self-proclaimed Marxists/Communists/Socialists for the election of Barack Obama to the Presidency. By no means is he a true Marxist, but under Karl Marx's writings we are to support the party with the best interests of the mobilization of the proletariat. . . . We support Barack Obama because he knows what is best for the people![2]

Many of the actors in these groups are onetime members of the New Left that emerged in the sixties and late seventies. And many are still working to influence President Obama's policies.

The connection of the New Left to the Communist Party–affiliated Old Left of the 1910s through the 1950s was described in a Heritage Foundation report in 1978 on the role of the New Left in government. William T. Poole writes:

> Those who gave impetus to the New Left were often the offspring of Old Left activists, including members of the Communist Party, U.S.A., one of the principal Old Left Communist organizations. While there were major differences between the two broad movements, particu-larly as to ideological and organizational discipline, they also managed to coalesce around the great radical organizing causes of the period, including especially the Vietnam war; and, though often wracked by sectarian and tactical disputes, they were alike in their common rejec-tion of traditional American society and institutions and in their general preference for radical Marxist (and, in many cases, Marxist-Leninist) alternatives.
>
> [V]irtually every major anti-Vietnam war coalition, including those which initiated and carried out the massive protests in Washington,

D.C., in 1967, 1969, 1970, and 1971, was either dominated or controlled by functionaries and concealed members of either the CPUSA [Communist Party USA] or the SWP [Socialist Workers Party], very often working together toward their common goal of bringing about an American defeat and Communist victory in Southeast Asia. Other Communist groups, many of them created by former members of the CPUSA and SWP, also worked in this effort. To the extent that these other groups, including such avowedly Maoist organizations as the Progressive Labor Party and such other dissident Communist entities as the Workers World Party, are reflective of an openly Communist perspective on revolutionary change in our society, they should be considered inheritors of the Old Left tradition.[3]

Thirty years later, the New Left of the sixties and seventies has morphed into a New, New Left. As Andrew C. McCarthy observed on December 4, 2009, at *National Review Online*, many of them have become "Alinskyites," disciples of the radical theorist Saul Alinsky (see Chapter 4), who have well learned how to manipulate the weak points of American democracy in order to achieve radical results. As McCarthy, in describing President Obama, writes:

[T]he president is an Alinskyite, so steeped in the ideology of the seminal community organizer that he became a top instructor in Alinskyite tactics for other up-and-coming radicals.

. . . Alinksyites are fifth-column radicals. They have, in substance, the same goals as open revolutionaries: overthrowing the existing free-market republic and replacing it with a radical's utopia. That's why Obama could befriend such unrepentant former terrorists as Bill Ayers and Bernardine Dohrn, and take inspiration from Jeremiah Wright, a black-liberation theologist. But Alinskyites are more sophisticated, patient, and practical. They bore in, hollowing out the system from within, appropriating the appearance and argot of mainstream society. Their single, animating ambition is to overthrow the capitalist social order, which they claim to see as racist, corrupt, exploitative, imperialist, etc. Apart from that goal, everything else—from the public option to Afghanistan—is negotiable: They reserve the right to take any position on any matter, to say anything at any time, based on the ebb and flow of popular opinion. That keeps them politically viable while they radically transform society. Transform it into what, they haven't worked out in great detail — except that it will be perfect, communal, equal, and just.[4]

A large number of the New, New Leftists emerging from the sixties and seventies had been members of Students for a Democratic Society. The authors have discussed a number of former SDS members elsewhere in this book:

- Tom Hayden, principal organizer of Students for a Radical Society;
- Unrepentant terrorist couple, and Barack Obama's Hyde Park neighbors, Bill Ayers and Bernardine Dohrn, who went underground following the Days of Rage in Chicago;
- Bettylou Saltzman, who met Barack Obama in 1992 when he ran Project VOTE! and who introduced Obama to senior campaign adviser, David Axelrod, and Marilyn Katz;
- Marilyn Katz, longtime Obama supporter and bundler for the presidential election, who, along with Saltzman, was involved with avowed Maoist Carl Davidson in the group that, in October 2002, invited Obama to speak at the Chicago antiwar rally;
- Husband and wife team, Paul Booth and Heather Booth, co-founders of the Midwest Academy, long involved with various incarnations of USAction. Paul Booth was founding secretary-treasurer of SDS, and former president of Chicago's Citizen Action Program, "formed in 1969 by trainees" from Saul Alinsky's Industrial Areas Foundation, and is now executive assistant to AFSCME president Gerald McEntee. Paul and Heather Booth are both involved with Health Care for America Now;
- Jeffrey Blum, director of Health Care for America Now;
- Harry C. Boyte, an Obama campaign adviser and transition team member, and longtime associate of Heather Booth; and,
- Wade Rathke, the founder of ACORN and SEIU 100.[5]

It should be noted that both Tom Hayden and Bill Ayers have, since the January 2009 inauguration, in a sort of "unendorsement," spoken out against President Obama's war policies in Afghanistan. Ayers criticized POTUS on February 24, 2009, after Obama announced he would send an additional 17,000 troops to Afghanistan. In response to questions by Sean Hannity, on his Fox News Channel show, Ayers said: "It's a mistake. It's a colossal mistake."[6] Ayers turned to Hannity's co-host, Alan Colmes, and said: ". . . you know, we've seen this happen before, Alan. . . . We've seen a hopeful presidency, Lyndon Johnson's presidency, burn up in the furnace of war. . . . I fear that this brilliant young man, this hopeful new administration, could easily burn their prospect of a great presidency in the war in Afghanistan or elsewhere." Following Obama's December 1, 2009, announcement that he would send yet another 30,000 troops to Afghanistan, while promising in July 2011 to begin a drawdown of U.S. forces, Tom Hayden wrote in the *Nation* it was time for him to strip his Obama campaign bumper sticker from his car.[7]

> Obama's escalation in Afghanistan is the last in a string of disappointments. His flip-flopping acceptance of the military coup in Honduras has squandered the trust of Latin America. His Wall Street bailout leaves the poor, the unemployed, minorities and college students on their own. And now comes the Afghanistan-Pakistan decision to escalate the stalemate, which risks his domestic agenda, his Democratic base, and possibly even his presidency.

Hayden was joined in his disappointment by Ayers, who said in a videotaped interview "captured on the streets of Chicago" the last week of November 2009: "I am here demonstrating against the war because I am appalled and alarmed that once again we are escalating the war. The idea that there are benchmarks for getting out is a myth and a lie."

> The fact is that, you know, you cannot imagine a scenario where six months from now or 18 months from now the administration would say, well we didn't meet our benchmarks, therefore we're leaving. This is an absolute tragedy for the Middle East, for Afghanistan and us.[8]

But do not shed any tears for the bitter disappointment of Messrs. Hayden, Ayers, and their ilk. Rather, bear in mind the words of Andrew C. McCarthy, cited above, on the flexibility of tactics—that for the Alinskyites, everything "is negotiable," and "they reserve the right to take any position on any matter, to say anything at any time, based on the ebb and flow of popular opinion. That keeps them politically viable while they radically transform society."

The Alinskyist social/economic/racial democratic justice movement, which is how they view themselves, is not insignificant. It includes many more members who have either supported or who are currently involved with President Obama.

"OBAMA WORKS WITH SOCIALISTS WHO HAVE COMMUNIST BACKGROUNDS"

First, we have the support for Obama coming from the Movement for a Democratic Society. New Zealand blogger Trevor Loudon first exposed MDS in late September 2008. Only two years before, in early 2006, a "group of former SDS members and sympathisers," led by Democratic Socialists of America activist Paul Buhle, had "joined with some from a new generation of college students to re-found Students for a Democratic Society." MDS, Loudon discovered, had been formed as an SDS "support group for older activists." Moreover, Loudon learned, the new incarnation of SDS already claimed over 130 chapters countrywide.[9] As Loudon described it, the "SDS is the muscle behind the new protest movement and was very prominent in the recent violence at the Republican National Convention at St. Paul Minnesota. MDS is the brains behind the SDS brawn."[10]

The MDS board of directors, named in 2006, is a virtual who's who of radicals. Among them is found:

- Elliott Adams, leader of the Communist Party USA front, Veterans for Peace;
- Noam Chomsky, well-known linguist, writer, and far-left activist, as well as a member of both Democratic Socialists of America and Committees of Correspondence for Democracy and Socialism;
- Carl Davidson, an SDS founding member, later a Maoist activist, and leader of the New Party of which Obama was a participant;

- Bernardine Dohrn;
- Bill Fletcher, Jr., a former Maoist and leader of DSA and labor leader with the AFL-CIO;
- Bert Garskof, involved with SDS in the sixties and a close friend to Bill Ayers and Bernardine Dohrn;
- Tom Hayden;
- Gerald Horne, Professor of African American studies, University of North Carolina, Chapel Hill, editorial board of CPUSA theoretical journal *Political Affairs*;
- Robin D. G. Kelley, historian, Africana Studies, New York University, formerly with the Communist Workers Party, latterly close to CPUSA;
- Michael Klonsky, son of CPUSA member Robert Klonsky, and a former member of SDS, who later led the pro-Chinese Communist Party (Marxist-Leninist), and who works closely with Bill Ayers on educational projects;
- Ethelbert Miller, chairman of the board of the "notoriously leftist and Cuban linked Washington based think tank," Institute for Policy Studies;
- Charlene Mitchell, a CCDS leader and former high-ranking CPUSA member;
- Mark Rudd, a former SDS leader and member of the Weather Underground; and,
- Howard Zinn, a well-known Marxist historian.[11]

Loudon notes that historian Gerald Horne studied the Hawaiian Communist Party and was "first to publicly reveal the connection between Barack Obama and his boyhood mentor, secret Communist Party USA member Frank Marshall Davis."[12]

Other MDS founders, besides Paul Buhle, include Thomas Good (whom Loudon describes as a "former communist turned anarchist who has referred to himself as an 'unrepentant Weather supporter'"); former SDS activists David Hamilton and Thorne Dreyer; Marilyn Katz; Marxist academics Rosalyn Baxandall and Immanuel Wallerstein; and Cornel West, an "academic and DSA member who refers to Obama as his 'comrade.'"[13]

In October 2008, Bill Ayers found himself under attack by bloggers and some in the broadcast news media for his radical past and his associations with Barack Obama. To his rescue came Rosalyn Baxandall, of SUNY Old Westbury, who was among those signing a petition in Ayers' support, according to Brenda J. Elliott.[14] Baxandall, however, was not only one of the many endorsers of Obama's campaign at Progressives for Obama, which is discussed in the following paragraphs, but was also a member of Historians for Obama, and of New York Feminists for Peace and Barack Obama. A known Marxist, Baxandall wrote, along with her sister, Harriet Fraad, the chapter on "Red Sisters of the Bourgeoisie" in *Red Diapers*, a 1998 anthology of autobiographical writings by the children of American communists. She also wrote the chapter "Marxism and Sexuality: The Body as Battleground" in *Marxism in the Postmodern Age*, which is discussed in *Red Feminism*.

Writing of Bill Ayers at about the time Baxandall came to his defense, Sol Stern wrote in the October 6, 2008, *City Journal*, under the title, "The Bomber as School Reformer":

> Calling Bill Ayers a school reformer is a bit like calling Joseph Stalin an agricultural reformer. (If you find the metaphor strained, consider that Walter Duranty, the infamous *New York Times* reporter covering the Soviet Union in the 1930s, did, in fact, depict Stalin as a great land reformer who created happy, productive collective farms.) For instance, at a November 2006 education forum in Caracas, Venezuela, with President Hugo Chávez at his side, Ayers proclaimed his support for "the profound educational reforms under way here in Venezuela under the leadership of President Chávez. We share the belief that education is the motor-force of revolution. . . . *I look forward to seeing how you continue to overcome the failings of capitalist education as you seek to create something truly new and deeply humane.*" [15]

In a follow-up to Loudon's September 2008 article, Brenda Elliott reported that Movement for a Democratic Society had held its first "convergence" in November 2007 at Loyola University, with the participation of the newly inspired SDS.[16] Elliott also reported that, in February 2007, there was a change in MDS leadership, with Manning Marable elected as the organization's new chairman. Marable meanwhile retained his positions as co-chair of the Committees of Correspondence, a leader in the Chicago branch of the New Party, and a member of the Ida B. Wells–W.E.B. Du Bois Network.[17]

In a February 2008 article in *The Black Commentator*, of which he is an editorial board member, Marable "strongly endorsed" Obama, writing on "Barack Obama's Problem Along the Color Line—And Ours."[18] A leading Marxist, Marable claimed in the December 2008 issue of the British Trotskyist journal, *Socialist Review*, that then president-elect Obama had read some of Marable's books and "understands what socialism is." Marable also said Obama "works with socialists 'with backgrounds in the Communist Party,'"[19]

Marable wrote:

> Obama represents a generation of what might be called post-racial black politicians—by which I mean they espouse a politics that minimises matters of race. They do not like to talk about race and subsume it under the rubric of poverty and class. So they are generally left of centre, or liberal, on social and economic policy. Obama is a progressive liberal.
>
> What makes Obama different is that he has also been a community organiser. He has read left literature, including my works, and he understands what socialism is. A lot of the people working with him are, indeed, socialists with backgrounds in the Communist Party or as independent Marxists. There are a lot of people like that in Chicago who have worked with him for years. . . .[20]

In an interview with Aaron Klein, Marable declined to identify the individuals working with Obama whom he had written of as socialists with Communist Party backgrounds.[21] "I think the point I was making is that there are a number of people with left histories who were early participants in Obama's mobilization. They have a strong belief in Obama as a candidate with the possibility of changing the tenor of politics within the Democratic Party," he told Klein.

Loudon points out that, when Marable voted for Barack Obama in the presidential election, "he voted for him not as a Democrat, but on the New York Working Families Party (WFP) line. Manning Marable is a member of the WFP which is a direct descendant of the now defunct New Party."[22]

WEATHERMAN TERRORIST GROUP FOUNDER HELPING DRAFT OBAMA POLICIES

Besides Marable, among those seated on MDS's 2007 board of directors was former SDSer, and founding member of the radical Weather Underground, Jeff Jones.[23] Jones had come out of the 1969 SDS National Convention as one of the Weatherman's three leaders, along with Bernardine Dohrn and Mark Rudd.

Most recently, Jones was identified as head of the New York office of the Apollo Alliance.[24] The Alliance crafted portions of the $787 billion "stimulus" legislation (officially called the American Recovery and Reinvestment Act) that Obama signed into law in early 2009. The role the Alliance and its radical members play in the Obama administration is so extensive that the authors have dedicated Chapter 13 to the subject. Jones's bland official bio on the Apollo Alliance website, meanwhile, stated, "the activist campaigned to remove PCBs from the Hudson River, clean up toxic pollution in inner-city and rural neighborhoods, and reverse global warming."[25] Additionally, the bio stated that, from 1995 to 2005, Jeff Jones "served as the communications director of Environmental Advocates of New York. Previously, he was a reporter covering state politics and policy for a variety of news organizations."

Not mentioned is that Jeff Jones was a leading antiwar activist and terrorist-group founder, who spent time on the run from law enforcement agencies while his group carried out a series of bombings of U.S. government buildings. In 1969, Jeff Jones founded the Weatherman with Bill Ayers and Mark Rudd when the three signed a proclamation calling for a revolution against the American government.[26] Jeff Jones was a main leader and orchestrator of what became known as the Days of Rage, a series of violent riots in Chicago organized by the Weatherman. The culmination of the riots came when Jones gave a signal for the rowdy protestors to target a hotel that was the home of a local judge presiding over a trial of antiwar activists.

After failing to appear for a March 1970 court date to face charges of "crossing state lines to foment a riot and conspiring to do so," Jeff Jones went underground.[27] He moved to San Francisco with Ayers' wife, Bernardine Dohrn. That year, at least one bombing claimed by the Weatherman went off in Jones' locale at the Presidio Army base. Jones's Weatherman would take "credit" for multiple bombings of U.S. government buildings, including attacks against the U.S. Capitol on March 1, 1971, the Pentagon on May 19, 1972, and a 1975 bombing of the State Department building.

OBAMA HELPS FUND FORMER TOP COMMUNIST AYERS ASSOCIATE

Progressives for Obama is another organization with links to two of the founders of MDS, Bill Fletcher, Jr., and Tom Hayden. According to Trevor Loudon, MDS and Progressives for Obama "unite all the main radical strands behind the Obama movement"[28]—Democratic Socialists of America (DSA), Communist Party USA (CPUSA), Committees of Correspondence for Democracy and Socialism (CCDS), former members of the ultraradical Students for a Democratic Society (SDS), and its terrorist splinter the Weather Underground.

Fletcher and Hayden co-founded Progressives for Obama with two others, author/activist Barbara Ehrenreich and Hollywood actor Danny Glover.[29] All four co-founders authored an article entitled "Progressives for Obama," published March 24, 2008, at *The Nation*, in which they wrote: "All American progressives should unite for Barack Obama."

> We believe that Barack Obama's very biography reflects the positive potential of the globalization process that also contains such grave threats to our democracy when shaped only by the narrow interests of private corporations in an unregulated global marketplace. We should instead be globalizing the values of equality, a living wage and environmental sustainability in the new world order, not hoping our deepest concerns will be protected by trickle-down economics or charitable

billionaires. By its very existence, the Obama campaign will stimulate a vision of globalization from below. . . .

We intend to join and engage with our brothers and sisters in the vast rainbow of social movements to come together in support of Obama's unprecedented campaign and candidacy. Even though it is candidate-centered, there is no doubt that the campaign is a social movement, one greater than the candidate himself ever imagined. . . .

[I]t will be the Obama movement that will make it necessary and possible to end the war in Iraq, renew our economy with a populist emphasis, and confront the challenge of global warming.[30]

A former Maoist, Bill Fletcher, Jr., is the executive editor of *Black Commentator*, founder of the Center for Labor Renewal, and a leader of Democratic Socialists of America, Trevor Loudon writes. Fletcher was also a founding member in 1998 of the CPUSA/CCDS/DSA-dominated Black Radical Congress.[31]

Barbara Ehrenreich is a well-known democratic socialist, feminist, "social critic," political and antiwar activist.[32] "Candid about her affinity for Marxism, Ehrenreich is the Honorary Chairwoman of the Democratic Socialists of America," *Discover the Networks* documents.

When the *Communist Manifesto* was re-released on its 150th anniversary in 1998, Ehrenreich celebrated the event. She noted that in producing the Manifesto as a commercial product, capitalists were—as Lenin had once predicted—providing the rope that eventually would hang them.

"In a February 2008 blog appearing on *AlterNet*, Ehrenreich expressed her support for Senator Barack Obama's presidential bid," *Discover the Network* writes. Or in Ehrenreich's own torrid prose: "We, perhaps white people especially, look to him for atonement and redemption. All of us, of whatever race, want a fresh start. That's what 'change' means right now: *Get us out of here!*"[33]

A prolific author of more than a dozen books and countless magazine and newspaper articles, Ehrenreich serves on the editorial board of the Institute for Policy Studies organ, *The Nation*. She also maintains her own blog, *Barbara's Blog*, where she writes on a wide variety of topics.[34]

Film and television star and activist Danny K. Glover supports the Castro regime in Cuba and the Hugo Chávez regime in Venezuela, Brenda J. Elliott wrote in April 2009.[35] *Venezuelanalysis.com* reported January 8, 2004, on a trip AARP spokesman Danny Glover took to meet with Hugo Chávez:

> African-American activists Bill Fletcher, president of the TransAfrica Forum, actor Danny Glover, and SEIU union vice president Patricia Ford are heading a delegation on a week-long visit to Venezuela to see results of the peaceful revolutionary process led by President Hugo Chávez.[36]

David Horowitz's *Discover the Networks* reports:

> Shortly after the 9/11 attacks, Glover publicly stated that the U.S. was in no position to pass moral judgment on the terrorists responsible for those atrocities. "One of the main purveyors of violence in this world," said Glover, "has been this country, whether it's been against Nicaragua, Vietnam or wherever."
>
> On another occasion, Glover criticized Americans' "rabid [post-9/11] nationalism that has its own kind of potential of being maniacal, in some sense." . . .
>
> At a February 2003 anti-war rally in New York City, Glover charged that the Bush administration was composed of "liars and murderers."
>
> . . . On several occasions, Glover has visited Venezuela and made guest appearances on President Hugo Chávez's television and radio talk show, "Hello, President." Glover is a Board member of Venezuela's "TeleSUR" news network, which Chávez created in 2005.[37]

Rory Carroll reported May 21, 2007, from Caracas, that Venezuela was giving Glover "almost $18m (£9m) [from a recent bond sale with Argentina] to make a film about a slave uprising in Haiti . . . a biopic of Toussaint L'Overture, an iconic figure in the Caribbean who led an 18th-century revolt in Haiti."[38] Carroll described Glover as "a vocal critic of the Bush administration," a "regular visitor to Venezuela," and "a civil rights activist and supporter of Mr. Chávez's radical leftwing policies."

Politically, in the recent presidential election, Glover first publicly endorsed John Edwards, and then, after Edwards withdrew in January 2008, Glover endorsed Obama.

Danny Glover chairs the board of the TransAfrica Forum, an Institute for Policy Studies "partner organization." Tom Hayden is a long-term IPS associate, going back to the days of the Conference on Alternative State and Local Policies, Trevor Loudon writes. Ehrenreich is an IPS trustee and Fletcher is an IPS scholar.[39]

Loudon adds:

> Several people around Obama have IPS connections including his Chicago mentor, former Congressman Abner Mikva.
> In 1979 Don Rose, a mentor to Obama's right-hand man, David Axelrod, served in the leadership of the IPS spinoff Conference on Alternative State and Local Policies, with Miles Rapoport.

Loudon, writing in late September 2008 about the Movement for a Democratic Society, identified Ayers, Davidson, and Klonsky as the "Toxic Trio" linked to the pro-Obama organization, Progressives for Obama.[40] Loudon wondered, while Obama's "political opponents have been racing the clock to uncover the Senator's links to his radical friend and colleague. . . . Are there any current links between Ayers and organizations supportive of Obama?"

The answer, of course, is Progressives for Obama. Carl Davidson, who served on the Movement for a Democratic Society board after its founding, serves as Progressives for Obama webmaster. In the mid-nineties Davidson was a leader in the Chicago branch of the New Party, which publicly endorsed Barack Obama's run for the Illinois State Senate, and of which, evidence suggests, Obama may have been a member, as documented by the authors in Chapter 6.

Aaron Klein described in September 2008 how Barack Obama's official website had scrubbed a "series of user-generated blog postings" by former top communist activist, Mike Klonsky. Klein writes:

In a book, *Revolution in the Air*, author Max Elbaum, himself a former Maoist activist, recounts that in Beijing, Klonsky toasted the Chinese Stalinist leadership who, in turn, hailed the formation of his Communist Party group as "reflecting the aspirations of the proletariat and working people," effectively recognizing Klonsky's organization as the all-but-official U.S. Maoist party.[41]

In 1995, while Obama was chairman of the newly formed Chicago Annenberg Challenge, that board gave Klonsky's Small Schools Workshop, of which he is the director, a grant of $175,000, in addition to another $482,662 over the next few years. The Workshop is an "outreach program founded in 1991 by Ayers with the stated goal of providing support for teachers who want to create smaller learning environments. Ayers reportedly recruited Klonsky to head the Workshop," Klein wrote.[42] In a September 13, 2008, telephone interview with Klein, Klonsky "would not state whether he is still a communist," nor did he "deny his associations with Ayers or his communist activism in the 1970s."[43]

Another member of, and a signatory to, Progressives for Obama is Mark Rudd, one of the main Weatherman leaders, Aaron Klein wrote in late September 2008.[44] Rudd not only worked closely for years with Ayers, but was also a top member of SDS. Rudd led the "famed 1968 Columbia University strikes in which hundreds of students seized several university buildings. He also served as spokesman for the strikes, attracting international media attention."[45] Before going underground in 1970, Rudd traveled with the SDS to Cuba two years earlier, in 1968, "defying U.S. travel bans, where he says he was heavily influenced by the legacy of Che Guevara and by Cuban-style revolution. When he returned to the U.S., Rudd advocated for Columbia's chapter of the SDS to carry out militant, aggressive action, but he was turned down," Klein documented.[46]

In November 2005, Rudd wrote an editorial in the *Los Angeles Times* in which he lamented "the state of the anti[-Iraq] war movement in the U.S.":

What's hard to understand—given the revelations about the rush to war, the use of torture and the loss of more than 2,000 soldiers—is why the antiwar movement isn't further along than it is. Given that President

Bush is now talking about Iraq as only one skirmish in an unlimited struggle against a global Islamic enemy, a struggle comparable to the titanic, 40-year Cold War against communism, shouldn't a massive critique of the global war on terrorism already be underway?[47]

Klein points out that, while Rudd "condemned the Weatherman's decision to embark on an 'armed-struggle,' calling it 'stupid' since the violent acts led to the group's demise," Rudd did not "condemn the terrorism itself, only its contribution to the downfall of the Weatherman."[48]

The repentant former SDSer David Horowitz, who knew his fellow travelers well in the 1960s, wrote in his 2009 pamphlet, "Barack Obama's Rules for Revolution":

The *Alinsky Model*, words that are important to keep in mind whether you are viewing these extremists from an historical perspective or in connection with the radical goals they hope to achieve via the Obama presidency:

Guided by Alinsky principles, post-Communist radicals are not idealists but Machiavellians. Their focus is on means rather than ends, and therefore they are not bound by organizational orthodoxies in the way their admired Marxist forebears were. Within the framework of their revolutionary agenda, they are flexible and opportunistic and will say anything (and pretend to be anything) to get what they want, which is resources and power.[49]

13

ANTI-AMERICAN RADICALS DRAFTING OBAMA LEGISLATION

A LITTLE-KNOWN GROUP CALLED the Apollo Alliance is another of the Obama administration's radical components. Not only is Apollo the stealth architect of President Obama's "green jobs" programs, but it helped craft the president's $787 billion "stimulus bill" as well as his proposed new energy legislation.

In a now familiar pattern, Apollo board members are leaders at "progressive" organizations and labor unions, and are often tied to extremist groups. Yet one more plan to vastly increase control of the economy by the federal government, and straightjacket private business, is cloaked in innocuous-sounding proposals for "clean energy, good jobs programs." Unfortunately, Apollo's agenda has less to do with actually helping the environment than it does with using the environmental movement to advance its left-wing political and economic schemes.

According to his colleagues:

> Apollo co-founder Dan Carol deserves credit for having the "vision" to "[broaden] the coalition on climate and energy solutions through a focus on economic transformation . . . at the heart of a political movement that is finally emerging as a new politics for the country, linking

concern over climate change, national security, and energy to hope for good jobs, stronger communities, and a more robust democracy."[1]

These are the words of Apollo Alliance co-founder, Bracken Hendricks, and Jay Inslee (D-WA), in their 2007 book, *Apollo's Fire: Igniting America's Clean-Energy Economy*. Apollo's policy recommendations to the Obama administration—incorporating the above-mentioned "focus on economic transformation" and "new politics"—were developed in, and published as, "The New Apollo Program" and "The Apollo Economic Recovery Act" in 2008.[2]

Little attention was paid to the Apollo Alliance until August 2009 when, during a weeklong series of programs on his Fox News program, Glenn Beck focused on one of the Apollo Alliance's board members, Van Jones. Jones had been named Obama's "Green Jobs Czar" (Special Advisor for Green Jobs, Enterprise and Innovation on the White House Council on Environmental Quality) in March. At first it was Jones' identity as a San Francisco Bay Area radical agitator and avowed communist that garnered Beck's attention following reports, including from Aaron Klein, exposing Jones's extremist background.

As a direct result of the attention directed at Jones, it became known that, in February 2009, the Apollo Alliance had posted on its website that it was responsible for influencing "specific content of many of the [stimulus] bill's provisions." The Alliance also claimed "policy proposals" had originated in October 2008 in its New Apollo Program and Apollo Economic Recovery Act.[3]

Had it not been for the initial exposure of the radical Van Jones, in spring 2009, the role of the Apollo Alliance might still not be fully understood. The true measure of what was afoot had been discovered, and reported, in a November 2008 Heritage Foundation blog post by Conn Carroll:

> The lie goes something like this: "The Obama-Biden comprehensive New Energy for America plan will help create five million new jobs by strategically investing $150 billion over the next ten years to catalyze private efforts to build a clean energy future." Obama's plan to build "a

clean energy future" reads an awful lot like the union/enviro backed Apollo Alliance plan to "build America's 21st century clean energy economy" and create "5 million jobs." The only difference is that while Obama says he can create 5 million new "green collar jobs" with just $150 billion, The Apollo Alliance says it will take $500 billion to create the same 5 million jobs.

When asked to explain the discrepancy, why Obama claims he can create the same 5 million jobs with $350 billion less money, Apollo Alliance co-director (and self pro-claimed coiner of the "green collar jobs" term) Kate Gordon told the *Wall Street Journal*, "Honestly, it's just to inspire people."[4]

In the subsequent February 2009 news item on Apollo, it was revealed that Senate Majority Leader, Harry Reid (D-NV), was well aware of the Apollo Alliance's involvement with the Obama administration. Reid is quoted as saying: "We've talked about moving forward on these ideas for decades. The Apollo Alliance has been an important factor in helping us develop and execute a strategy that makes great progress on these goals and in motivating the public to support them."

Unfortunately, Reid does not identify the "we" to whom he is referring, although the story does refer to "the organization's founders." The Apollo founders are then identified as Dan Carol, Joel Rogers, Bob Borosage, and Bracken Hendricks, who "recruited an untraditional national coalition of labor, business, environmental and social justice organizations and leaders to advocate for clean energy and good jobs."

But are "clean energy" and "good jobs" the real goals of the Obama administration and the Apollo Alliance? Or have they become fig leaves to conceal a far-reaching agenda of "progressive social and economic justice programs"?

The following close-up of the four named Apollo Alliance co-founders will provide an unambiguous answer. What emerges is a group of decades-long fellow travelers now focused on a new progressive administration to implement an agenda far removed from promoting "domestic energy independence."

SOCIALIST PARTY FOUNDER

Dan Carol worked as a strategist for the Obama for America campaign. As Content & Issues Director, headquartered in Chicago, Carol "guided the launch of Obama's *NewEnergyforAmerica.com* plan and the 2008 Democratic Platform, Listening to America."[5]

Carol has been a "strategist for MoveOn, True Majority, and the Oregon Bus Project, among other innovative grassroots efforts." He served as a member of the unofficial environmental campaign team for 2004 presidential candidate, Senator John Kerry (D-MA), and worked for the Clinton-Gore debate team. In 1992 Carol was "one of the young bulls on Bill Clinton's vaunted rapid response team," and he was research director for the Democratic National Committee. He previously worked as a budget analyst at the Congressional Budget Office and is a founding partner of the progressive political and Internet consulting firm, Carol/Trevelyan Strategy Group (CTSG). He served as board chairman of Common Assets.[6]

According to one sympathetic observer of Carol's proposals:

> I do know that he'll be a major force in pushing one of Obama's signature ideas: a "Green Deal" that would enlist the American people themselves to build a green infrastructure all across America, creating millions of new conservation and renewable energy jobs, reviving our grassroots economy, and achieving energy independence.
>
> This would be a multibillion-dollar national effort derived from the successful community-based projects already underway through the Apollo Alliance. Such solid, progressive thinkers and activists as Van Jones of California and Joel Rogers of Wisconsin are also enlisted in this exciting aspect of Obama's campaign.[7]

In 2006 Carol was listed as a member of the Apollo Alliance steering committee. His name is no longer listed as a current board member. More importantly, however, is the fact Carol sits on the Tides board of directors, which is made up of directors from both the Tides Center and the Tides Foundation. More about Tides appears at the end of this chapter.[8]

In January 2006 the Apollo Alliance was described as 501c3 nonprofit organization, a joint project of the Institute for America's Future and the Center on Wisconsin Strategy (COWS).[9]

Joel Rogers served as the Apollo Alliance's first chairman. In 1992 Rogers founded COWS, described as "the strategy center for high-road (high wage, low waste, democratic) development." Rogers is a professor of Law, Political Science, and Sociology at the University of Wisconsin at Madison, and directs the Center for State Innovation.[10] Rogers is named on the 2006 Apollo Alliance steering committee as well as the current board of directors.[11]

John Nichols of *The Progressive* described Rogers as a "wunderkind" in the October 1996 issue. At the age of 21, Rogers graduated from Yale University "with a triple-major in economics, political science, and philosophy" before "sailing through" Yale Law School and "picking up" a Ph.D. in political science at Princeton University.[12]

Nichols adds that Rogers "watched the Reagan revolution stall the march toward economic and social justice, and began to hatch sophisticated theories for revitalizing the labor movement and reinvigorating American democracy."

In 1992 Rogers co-founded the "ACORN/Democratic Socialists of America initiated New Party"; in 1996 Rogers served as New Party national chair. The authors discuss Barack Obama's involvement with the New Party—a socialist party—in Chapter 6 of this book.[13]

"COMMUNIST FRONT GROUP"

Another organization named in January 2006 as being behind the founding of the Apollo Alliance is the Institute for America's Future (which will be more fully detailed in the next chapter), of which Robert Borosage is president.[14]

Borosage founded and currently chairs the Progressive Majority Political Action Committee, the "activist arm of a political networking organization, which has "one goal—to help elect as many 'progressive' politicians to federal, state, and local offices as possible," and "to lead the way against the anti-worker, anti-family, anti-environmental agenda being pushed by conservatives in power."[15]

The Progressive Majority's "six chief areas of concern" are economic justice, civil rights, health care, education, environment, and "reproductive freedom." Regarding the latter, at the April 25, 2004, "March for Women's Lives" held in Washington, D.C., Progressive Majority sought to "'identify and support candidates of color who [would] champion a broad progressive agenda' on behalf of abortion-on-demand."[16]

In 1989 Borosage was the co-founder and director of the Campaign for New Priorities, which "called for decreased federal spending on the military and greater allocations for social welfare programs."[17]

Earlier, between 1979 and 1988, Borosage was director of the influential Institute for Policy Studies, which, since its founding in 1963, has spawned a large number of spinoff organizations to promote leftist causes. Borosage still serves as an IPS trustee.[18]

Borosage claims to have founded the Center for National Security Studies in 1974, described as a "spinoff" from the Institute for Policy Studies. *Discover the Networks* reports that CNSS is "aligned" with the National Lawyers Guild, well known as an international communist front group. CNSS staff members come mostly from the IPS and the NLG, *Discover the Networks* reports. While also serving as director at IPS, Borosage helped CNSS founder, Morton Halperin, run the organization.[19]

It should be noted that Halperin is Senior Vice President of the Center for American Progress and director of George Soros' Open Society Policy Center.[20]

Borosage has advised "progressive" political campaigns, including those of Senators Carol Moseley Braun (D-IL), Barbara Boxer (D-CA), and the late Paul Wellstone (D-MN). Borosage was Senior Issues Advisor to 1988 presidential candidate Rev. Jesse L. Jackson.[21]

Borosage was a member of the 2006 Apollo Alliance steering committee. He is a member of the current Apollo Alliance board of directors.

The Institute for America's Future is a sister organization to another think tank, the Campaign for America's Future, of which Borosage is co-director. In March 2009 IAF's board of directors included John Sweeney of the AFL-CIO and Antonio Villaraigosa, mayor of Los Angeles. CAF's board, listed for April 2009, includes Leo Gerard of United Steelworkers and Eli Pariser of the George Soros–funded *MoveOn.org*. Serving on both boards are Borosage and Roger Hickey, who co-founded CAF in 1996 and IAF in 1999.[22]

John Sweeney, president of the AFL-CIO, is an avid Barack Obama supporter. Dick Meister reported May 13, 2009, in the Communist Party USA's *People's World*, that Sweeney responded, "Absolutely" when asked if President Obama was "delivering on his promise to lead a pro-union administration." The AFL-CIO had "played a major role in Obama's victory," spending "more than $450 million" and putting "more than a quarter-million volunteers to work in its campaigns for Obama and pro-labor congressional candidates, and turned out millions of union voters."

In January 2009 former Michigan Congressman and Obama economic adviser, David Bonior, first met with the leaders from "12 of the largest unions, along with rival federations AFL-CIO and Change to Win," to reunite "under a single, more powerful federation." Why? Because President-elect Obama had "signaled that it would prefer dealing with a united movement, rather than a fractured one that often had two competing voices."[23]

Among the union leaders was Anna Burger, chairwoman of Change to Win and secretary-treasurer of the Service Employees International Union (SEIU), who had recently been appointed to the president's Economic Recovery Advisory Board. Burger, who was a signatory to the radical Progressives for Obama, also served as an Apollo Alliance steering committee member in 2006.[24]

Another member of the Obama economic team was Los Angeles Mayor Villaraigosa, who was appointed by Obama after the November 2008 election to his Transition Economic Advisory Board. New Zealand blogger, Trevor Loudon, who has written about Villaraigosa's radical past, says that the appointment "was a gesture of solidarity to the California left, second only to Chicago as a crucible of the 'peoples movement' that brought Obama to power."[25]

As Richard Louv pointed out in the *San Diego Union Tribune* (June 26, 2004):

> The "political key" to the Apollo Alliance's "potential success is that its proponents are selling it as a jobs program. Leo Gerard, president of

United Steel Workers of America, and Carl Pope, executive director of the Sierra Club, have thrown their weight behind Apollo, as have 16 of the country's other big labor unions, along with major environmental groups."[26]

In fact, Leo Gerard, who served in 2006 on the Apollo Alliance's National Advisory Board, and serves on the Alliance's current board of directors, was the key union backer of the Apollo Alliance, according to Jim Grossfeld, writing October 2007 in the *American Prospect*.[27]

As president of the United Steelworkers, Gerard "has responded to the double challenge of disappearing middle-income jobs and the advent of global warming by linking the two causes. Under his leadership, the Steelworkers have become the principal union backer of the Apollo Alliance. . . . Gerard understood that Apollo could not only be a vehicle for the creation of green jobs, but could also become the big tent for labor and environmentalists," Grossfeld writes. "Gerard quickly set about making Apollo into a labor-enviro joint venture. Though the USW wasn't the first union to endorse it, Gerard's passionate support for Apollo gave it the credibility it needed in labor circles."

"One by one," Grossfeld wrote, "labor leaders began to buy Gerard's argument that Apollo was labor's best bet for ensuring that U.S. workers would become the beneficiaries, not the victims, of efforts to reduce greenhouse gas emissions. Gerard's backing for Apollo not only won it the support of the AFL-CIO's Industrial Union Council but also helped it gain the endorsement of its Building and Construction Trades Department and, eventually, the AFL-CIO itself."

The last of the Apollo Alliance founding four, Bracken Hendricks, now a Senior Fellow at the Center for American Progress, was the founding executive director of the Apollo Alliance.[28]

Hendricks is also director of the New Growth Initiative, a joint project of the Institute for America's Future and the Center on Wisconsin Strategy. In May 2003 he penned an article, "An Energy/Jobs Program," in *The Nation*, the online organ of the Institute for Policy Studies. The article borders on the comical in its mention over six years ago of the need for both an economic "stimulus" and "budget relief":

America needs jobs, and working families are hurting. At the same time, the war in Iraq has heightened awareness of our dependence on foreign oil and the vulnerability of our energy system.

The time is right for a national commitment to energy independence on the scale of John Kennedy's Apollo Project, which put a man on the moon. A bold program to advance energy efficiency and promote renewable energy, like wind and solar power, and drive investment into new technology and public infrastructure would create 2 million jobs and offer stimulus to our flagging economy.[29]

Reading further, it becomes clear that the New Growth Initiative of May 2003 (the Apollo Alliance, Hendricks wrote, was "now forming") sounds pretty much like the American Recovery and Reinvestment Act introduced in January 2009—a "bold $300 billion plan for the next ten years." The New Growth Initiative, Hendricks proposed at the time:

[W]ould be broad-based, sharing the benefits of investment widely across the economy while insuring that no single sector bears all the costs. And it would be immediate, deploying proven and cost-effective technologies that exist today, not placing all our hopes on long-term R&D, like the Bush plan for a hydrogen "freedom car."

[The Initiative] would promote renewable energy sources like wind and solar. It would convert assembly lines to put American-made cars using advanced technology on the road. It would help older plants improve their environmental performance, preserving domestic manufacturing jobs. It would deploy new technology for pollution control as well as research how to capture carbon from coal plants, and it would invest in research and development to deploy hydrogen fuel cells.

[Additionally, the Initiative] would promote high-performance "green" building and push a new generation of energy-efficient appliances to market—driving up efficiency without driving jobs overseas. It would support smart growth and mass transit, increase brownfield redevelopment and rebuild transportation and water infrastructure, relieving municipal budget pressures. And an Apollo project would strengthen, not repeal, regulatory protections for consumers, workers and the environment.

Unsurprisingly, Hendricks' Center for American Progress profile relates that he served as an advisor to the Obama for America campaign, as well as on Obama's transition team. Hendricks claims to have been an "architect" of the "clean-energy portions" of the stimulus bill.[30]

Previously, Hendricks served in the Bill Clinton administration as special assistant to the Office of Vice President Al Gore; with the Department of Commerce's National Oceanic and Atmospheric Administration; and with the President's Council on Sustainable Development. He has also served as "an energy and economic advisor to the AFL-CIO, Pennsylvania Governor Ed Rendell's Energy Advisory Task Force, and numerous other federal, state, and local policymakers and elected officials."[31]

In a second article, published May 2004, in *Yes* magazine, Hendricks made it clear that the scope for "The Apollo Project" far exceeded "domestic energy independence."[32]

The Apollo Project, Hendricks wrote, would "help rebuild our manufacturing base, converting assembly lines to make clean cars and efficient appliances and building demand for these products, creating jobs here in the U.S.," and would "increase investment in the neglected infrastructure" in American cities.

Hendricks proposed spending "$300 billion over 10 years, creating or retaining 3 million jobs that are more sustainable and more likely to be union, while making the economy more competitive and more productive."

Many have wondered about the source of President Obama's numerous references to 3 million jobs "created" or "saved." Now it is clear. It comes straight from the Apollo Alliance's plans.

Hendricks' May 2004 article also explains a little more about the entities who have been involved with the Apollo Alliance for the past five years or so. Many have been represented on either the Apollo Alliance steering committee or the current board, or both.

[The plan] has already been supported by 12 labor unions, representing 5.5 million members, including the International Association of Machinists and Aerospace Workers, the Steelworkers, the UAW, and others. The project has been praised by the heads of the Sierra Club and the Natural Resources Defense Council, and we continue to build alliances with labor, environmental, community, and faith groups, and progressive policy advocates of all stripes.

This version of the Apollo Alliance history, however, leaves out a few facts about how the organization actually came about—and how the agenda has changed.

We begin with an April 2007 interview for the environmental website *Grist,* with former Apollo Alliance steering committee member, Representative Jay Inslee, who said that he had "focused on energy issues since the early 1970s and amassed a wonk's expertise." Indeed, since 1999, when he began serving in Congress, Inslee co-founded the Climate Change Congress; served as a member of the Renewable Energy Caucus; and serves on both the House Committee on Energy and Commerce and House Committee on Natural Resources, as well as the Subcommittee on Energy and Air Quality.[33]

Inslee wrote in a January 2007 press release:

> In a December 2002 column for [the *Seattle Post-Intelligencer*], I named my vision for a new energy future the New Apollo Project because our race for clean, domestic energy sources closely parallels the space race. First, our national security and technological pre-eminence are on the line. Second, success depends on decisive action, bold leadership, focused federal resources, optimism and the genius of American entrepreneurs and innovators.[34]

In February 2003, Inslee presented his New Apollo Project to local Washington residents. The Project "call[ed] for creating a new U.S. shift to clean-energy production, rather than remaining dependent on fossil-fuel energy."[35]

Inslee wrote that his plan contained "three key objectives": First, "reducing America' dependence on foreign oil. . . . The second objective of his plan [is] an attempt to alleviate accelerating rates of global warming. . . . Finally, the proposal should spark tremendous benefits for the U.S. economy, by ensuring its involvement in the technologies crucial in the future global economy."

The following month, in March 2003, Inslee presented his "New Apollo Energy Project" to the Democratic Caucus "in hopes that the Democratic Party will adopt such a plan as their 'alternative' energy bill." Inslee had networked with a "core group of about 30 members of Congress to develop the proposal."[36]

Among the presenters at the event was current Apollo Alliance board member, John Podesta, president and CEO of the Center for American Progress and former White House chief of staff to President Bill Clinton, and later the head of Barack Obama's transition team. In 2003 Podesta founded the Center for American Progress as a "liberal counterweight to the heavyweight policy centers of the right like the Heritage Foundation and the Cato Institute," with $20 million provided by wealthy progressive funders Herb and Marion Sandler.[37]

According to grant information for 2006, the Center for American Progress also received a three-year, $3 million grant from George Soros' Open Society Institute to be used for "general support." The Center is also funded in part by individuals who are members of Soros' Democracy Alliance—a major funder of ACORN. Two Democracy Alliance board members are SEIU's Anna Burger and Tides Foundation founder, Drummond Pike, who also serves as Democracy Alliance treasurer.[38]

In April 2003, Inslee introduced an amendment, "The New Apollo Energy Independence Act," as "a comprehensive alternative to the Republican-sponsored energy bill."[39]

The scope of Inslee's proposed Project/Act seems to have changed a bit over time. According to Inslee's press release cited above, it has taken on the tones of a cap-and-trade bill—it "sets energy performance goals for the country." Additionally, the scope of the legislation had been expanded to include "environmental health issues."

The amendment did not pass. In April 2004 Inslee tried again, posting a detailed "Conceptual Legislation." This was followed up in fall 2004 with a forum held in Seattle focusing on the New Apollo Energy Project.[40]

The Project was described as a "10-year, $300 billion initiative designed to create incentives for developing clean and renewable energy sources such as solar- and wind-generated power and fuel recycled from municipal and agricultural waste." The program, sponsored by Inslee and

Senator Maria Cantwell (D-WA), was "to meet 20 percent or more of the nation's power needs by 2020 with resources other than imported fossil fuels, thereby reducing global warming and dependence on foreign oil."

It was also reported that University of California, Berkeley, researcher Daniel Kammen, a professor in nuclear engineering and public policy, a member of the Energy and Resources Group, and founding director of the Renewable Appropriate Energy Laboratory, had "been working with legislators and policymakers on this project since 2001, when he testified in Congress about the need for an organized federal approach to the power grid that would promote energy independence in the U.S."[41]

In 2005 Inslee presented yet another amendment, as well as the New Apollo Energy Act, with Democratic Illinois co-sponsors Representatives Jesse Jackson, Jr., Jan Schakowsky, and Rahm Emanuel. But there was still no success in passing the legislation. Inslee tried again in June 2007 with a second version of his New Apollo Energy Act, which likewise failed to earn enough votes.[42]

A few months later, in October 2007, *Apollo's Fire: Igniting America's Clean Energy Economy*, co-authored by Inslee and Bracken Hendricks, was released. Hendricks, then a senior fellow with Podesta's Center for American Progress, was identified as the former executive director of the Apollo Alliance.[43]

But there is another layer to this story—in the activities of two Apollo Alliance co-founders and original national board members: Michael Shellenberger, a "progressive" public relations man, and Ted Nordhaus, a pollster. Shellenberger and Nordhaus are also co-founders of the Breakthrough Institute.

Reports on the Breakthrough Institute website support the Apollo Alliance founding date as sometime in 2002. This date lines up with Inslee's December 2002 article in the *Seattle Post-Intelligencer* when he "named his vision for a new energy future the New Apollo Project." This begs the question as to which came first—Inslee's "vision" or Shellenberger and Nordhaus' Apollo Alliance?[44]

One possible answer comes from a September 2005 article in the Center for American Progress' *American Prospect*. The Apollo Alliance "was publicly unveiled in June 2003, at a time when other organizations were forming on the heels of the events of September 11, 2001, and concern for America's energy future."[45]

VAN JONES

Another question is, how did the good intentions in 2002 by Shellenberger and Nordhaus and Inslee all end up as part of the shell game involving Van Jones, John Podesta, George Soros, Drummond Pike, and Tides, among others?

The authors don't want to jump to conclusions here. However, it is beginning to look a lot like all the great ideas got away from their creators and wound up in the hands of very different folks with a very different agenda.

The trail begins with the November 2, 2005, *East Bay Express* article, "The New Face of Environmentalism," in which Eliza Strickland reported from her interview with Van Jones at the October Bioneers Conference.

It seems that Jones came to be a board member on the Apollo Alliance through his connection in 2005 with Michael Shellenberger, who co-authored the paper, "The Death of Environmentalism: Global Warming Politics in a Post-Environmental World," with Ted Nordhaus. Strickland writes that the paper itself was "primarily an assault upon the strategies of the left," while Shellenberger and Nordhaus "praised a few people and projects." Among these was Van Jones, "whom the authors called an 'up-and-coming civil-rights leader,' extolling his vision of a broad alliance between environmentalists, labor unions, civil-rights groups, and businesses. His focus on investment, they said, pointed the way to the environmental movement's future."[46]

Strickland adds that Jones, Shellenberger, and Nordhaus "became close allies who brainstormed ideas for the new shape of the environmental movement." Jones and Shellenberger "worked together" on the Apollo Alliance, and it was Shellenberger "who convinced alliance leaders to include Jones on the national board."

Strickland indicates that Jones knew well on which side to butter his bread. After Jones joined the Alliance board there was a "shakeup," as Jones began to criticize the Shellenberger-Nordhaus paper.

Strickland writes that Jones said that his quarrel did not lay with Shellenberger and Nordau's "ideas but [with] their tactics." Jones felt "their critique of the status quo was an assault on national environmental organizations, which leaders such as Sierra Club executive director Carl Pope greeted with anger. 'It was a smart document, but it was not wise,' Jones said. 'You don't ambush allies. You don't shame elders.'"

Shellenberger and Nordhaus, however, said Jones had "merely adopted the same tack as most of the progressive left. He has embraced their paper's feel-good ideas, but renounced the dialogue and arguments that helped get to that point."

Strickland reports that Shellenberger and Nordhaus "complain that Jones didn't begin critiquing their paper until he was surrounded by its detractors at the Apollo Alliance, a group whose strong ties to the Sierra Club guaranteed that it would take a stance against the two upstarts."

"Jones's emphasis on solidarity only increased his cachet among environmental leaders," Strickland writes. "But Nordhaus believes Jones is taking the easy route by avoiding confrontations with the progressive movement's old guard. It may allow him to be a more popular leader in the short term, Nordhaus said, but ultimately prevent the movement from undergoing the self-scrutiny it needs to regain a place in the national debate."

When Jones' Ella Baker Human Rights Center, named after a little-known socialist firebrand, relocated to Oakland, it took the California Apollo Alliance with it. The "shakeup" became a complete separation.

Strickland reports that Jones' Ella Baker Center was "one of the first groups to act upon the ideas espoused by the Apollo Alliance." Jones "approached the Apollo organizers because he believed that their original formulation of environmentalists plus labor unions wasn't ambitious enough."

Although Jones was "already working on the Ella Baker Center's own environmental program," Strickland writes, he "saw the Apollo Alliance as a useful partner, with a national platform."

The Apollo Alliance Oakland website spells out Jones' agenda clearly:

> a national example of transformation that shifts the country's beliefs about what is possible on these issues . . . starts with proving that our

unique coalition—environmentalists + organized labor + social justice activists + business—can come together across lines of race and
issue area to create real change. Then we leverage that success as a new
national model for change.[47]

As for the outcome of the Shellenberger-Nordhaus-Jones fallout,
Strickland writes: "while Jones continues to advance the ideas he developed along with the Apollo Alliance, the organization's cofounders Shellenberger and Nordhaus were both forced to remove themselves from
the national board because of the controversy they stirred up."[48]

Bracken Hendricks left the Apollo Alliance, as well, reports Amanda
Little in her 2005 article for *Grist*. In spring 2005 Hendricks resigned
from the executive director position but remained on the steering committee. He is reported to divide his time between his fellowship at the
Center for American Progress and as a strategic consultant for the Breakthrough Institute.[49]

Little's article suggests that disagreement among the board members contributed to the failure of Inslee's bill in the House, and possibly Obama's in the Senate. She writes: "the alliance could not throw
its weight behind Representative Inslee's New Apollo Energy Project—the only federal-level initiative yet proposed that embodies the
alliance's mission—because one of its members objected to a fuel-
economy provision."[50]

COLLABORATION WITH OBAMA

Inslee and Obama sponsored another related piece of federal legislation,
called the "Health Care for Hybrids" Act, which also involved the Breakthrough Institute.[51]

Little writes that the Apollo Alliance's focus is on "maintaining consensus," while the Breakthrough Institute "aims to compete on the ter-
rain of concrete and controversial legislative proposals." The Institute
"has been collaborating with the office of Senator Barack Obama on a
bill it hopes he will propose later this year known as the Automotive
Competitiveness and Accountability Act," Little writes.

According to Hendricks, Little writes, this "would relieve the pressure on U.S. automakers to bankroll the rising costs of legacy health insurance—an expense that doesn't burden their foreign competitors—and, in exchange, obligate them to invest heavily in energy-efficiency technologies and comply with substantially more aggressive fuel-economy standards." Hendricks added, in "offering a bailout to the [auto industry] from these hugely debilitating health costs, they're grappling with but linking it to an accountability for achieving public purposes."

This may sound familiar as well. Little wrote in her September 2005 article: "The hope is that Obama and other progressive leaders could characterize anyone who votes against the Automotive Competitiveness and Accountability Act as an opponent of national security, job creation, and public health. . . ."[52]

It was Shellenberger and Nordhaus, PR man and pollster, respectively, who charted this strategy. In a January 2005 interview, Shellenberger told Little:

> Take the proposal for a new Apollo Project. We cofounded the Apollo Alliance by starting first with core values to unify labor, community, civil-rights, and environmental movements around a vision of a new American future based on revitalizing our economic competitiveness and creating good jobs for millions of Americans. And whether or not it passes Congress right away doesn't matter—Apollo can be used to put anti-environmentalist, anti-labor forces on the defensive. Those who vote against it will confront public scrutiny: "You voted against a program to create 3 million jobs?"
>
> . . . The usefulness of any legislative proposal should be determined not just by whether it's going to reduce the level of carbon in the atmosphere, but also whether it's going to create a cultural environment where much more dramatic and sweeping transformations can take place in the future.[53]

SOROS, ACORN

Although we now know quite a bit about the coalition behind the Apollo Alliance—and the agenda that has evolved—we know next to nothing about its funding. The watchdog website, *Undue Influence*, identifies the Apollo Alliance as a project of the Tides Center. As was mentioned earlier, Tides Center founder Drummond Pike serves as treasurer of the Soros-funded Democracy Alliance.[54]

Undue Influence reports that the Apollo Alliance, as a project of the Tides Center, does not have an independent tax exemption; nor is the Apollo Alliance listed in IRS Publication 78, the federal index of exempt organizations. Nor does the Apollo Alliance have a federal employer identification number; it uses that of the Tides Center. Additionally, the Apollo Alliance does not have any financial records. *Undue Influence* reports that the Tides Center "does not release financial data on its individual projects."[55]

According to David Horowitz's *Discover the Networks*:

> The Tides Foundation was established in 1976 by Drummond Pike as a "public charity" to receive money from donors, many of which "groups are quite radical," and then "funnels" the money "to the recipients of their choice. . . . By letting the Tides Foundation, in effect, 'launder' the money for them and pass it along to the intended beneficiaries, donors can avoid leaving a 'paper trail.' Such contributions are called 'donor-advised,' or donor-directed, funds." In 1996 the Foundation established a second entity, the Tides Center, also headed by Drummond Pike, which "functions as a legal firewall insulating the Tides Foundation from potential lawsuits filed by people whose livelihoods or well-being may be harmed by Foundation-funded projects."[56]

Seated on both boards is Wade Rathke, founder of the radical group ACORN. Also seated on the Tides Center's board is Maya Wiley, the daughter of George A. Wiley, founder of the National Welfare Reform Organization, the man who both trained and sent Rathke to Arkansas to launch what became ACORN.[57]

Thus it is nearly impossible to follow—or even find, if you knew where to look—the Apollo Alliance's money.

14

EXTREMISTS BEHIND HEALTH CARE FOR AMERICA NOW

In 1999, Roger Hickey, then with the Social Security Information project, noted, "combining private investments with public guarantees is the perfect formula for 'lemon socialism': the government absorbs the downside risks ('lemons') and the private sector is assured the upside gains ('socialism')."[1]

ENTRAL TO BARACK Obama's success in winning the Presidency in 2008 was his promise to provide "affordable, universal health care" to every American. The desire by "progressives" to finally implement this goal—dating back at least to Franklin Roosevelt's New Deal—was a driving issue in support of Obama's candidacy. Many Americans, without knowing what it would really mean, thought the vague objective of "affordable, universal health care" would be desirable. But what would "universal health care" look like? How would it be structured? Was federal government control of health care really an improvement over what most Americans then had? And, perhaps most of all, who would pay for it?

In this chapter, we will expose, among other things, how the Health Care plan, masked by moderate, populist rhetoric, was pushed along and partially crafted by extremists, while the plan seems intended to achieve corporate state goals and a vast increase in government powers.

Over the years, a number of liberal groups—as well as some prominent extremists—had pushed various proposals that would come to form the basis of Obama's health care policy. To truly understand these proposals, and who has been pushing them, we need to explore the history of Health Care for America Now, or HCAN—the so-called national grassroots campaign for quality, affordable health care.

In 2006, Nancy Pelosi was still the House Democratic minority leader. But she was eagerly anticipating a Democratic win in the 2006 midterm Congressional elections. The first 100 hours of the next Congress, she famously announced in early October, would be sufficient "to begin to 'drain the swamp' after more than a decade of Republican rule." On day one, she claimed, Congress would create new rules to "break the link between lobbyists and legislation."[2]

No surprise, as it turned out, the lobbyists and legislators whose "link" Pelosi intended to "break" were principally Republicans and their allies. Pelosi and the Democrats were able, as she predicted, to capitalize on public disgust with a widely perceived—and news media–hyped—Republican "culture of corruption," connected with disgraced House Republican leader Tom DeLay and convicted corrupt lobbyist Jack Abramoff.[3]

Washington's K Street is a major thoroughfare known as home to an endless proliferation of lobbying and advocacy groups. During the latter years of the George W. Bush administration the K Street label had become synonymous with corrupting "special interests." But less than 30 days into the reign of the newly-sworn-in and now–Democrat controlled Congress, "progressive" lobbying and advocacy groups had begun making themselves comfortable in their new offices on K Street.[4] In particular, 1825 K Street had, by mid-February 2007, become "Ground Zero for 'progressive' groups subsidized by anti-war, anti-GOP, Big Nanny special interests," commented conservative author and blogger Michelle Malkin.[5]

1825 K Street, housed on the "boulevard of dreams for lobbyists and influence peddlers," now became the influence-seeking headquarters for such liberal/left groups as Campaign for America's Future, Progressive Majority Political Action Committee, and the Ballot Initiative Strategy Center, where they joined "two other progressive groups, Americans United for Change and USAction, in the building," reported Jeff Patch in the February 26 *Politico*.[6]

Campaign for America's Future—co-founded by Robert Borosage and Roger Hickey— "supports welfare bloat, socialized medicine, income redistribution, gun control, and open borders," according to *Discover the Networks*.[7] (Borosage was discussed in the previous chapter.) CAF's list of advisers "reads like a who's who of Democratic Party activists. Jesse Jackson, former Senator

Howard Metzenbaum of Ohio, former California State Senator Tom Hayden, Jim Hightower of Texas, and Clinton-era Secretary of Labor Robert Reich lead a host of union leaders and academics who have all stumped for Democrats," commented HotAir.com blogger Ed Morrissey in February 2007. CAF soon took on a few tenants of its own at 1825 K Street, including Americans Against Escalation in Iraq, a "coalition directed by Thomas Matzzie, who is also the Washington director of MoveOn.org Political Action."

An inside view of the new K Street operation was provided by Jeffrey H. Birnbaum of the *Washington Post* on May 7, 2007. There is, he writes, on weekdays a "rolling meeting with staffers from each of the organizations mixing with one another on such issues as lowering prescription drug prices and increasing funding for children's health programs." CAF's co-director Roger Hickey "called this clustering of a critical mass of these groups 'a happy accident,' and a very useful one." Added USAction's executive director, Jeff Blum, "We believe in synergy."[8]

Hickey is a veteran liberal/left activist, co-founding a number of "progressive" organizations over the last 25 years, including, with Robert Borosage, CAF's sister organization, Institute for America's Future, in March 1996. In December 1998, IAF was the major force behind the creation of the "now-defunct New Century Alliance for Social Security, an umbrella of leftist groups that collaborated 'to protect Social Security from schemes that "privatize" America's retirement system by reducing guaranteed benefits to fund private investment accounts.'"

Hickey is also former vice president of an AFL-CIO "front group," according to one source—the Economic Policy Institute. EPI was reportedly established in 1986 due to "frustration with the failure of the AFL-CIO's Industrial Union Department to attract media interest in its studies." Evidently Hickey was brought in when union officials wanted to create an organization "that was committed to their principles and ideas but not tainted directly by their label."[9]

PATH TO UNIVERSAL HEALTH CARE

On February 27, 2001, newly elected President George W. Bush delivered his inaugural address to Congress. The very next day, Hickey and Borosage used Campaign for America's Future to "[pull] together in Washington roughly 500 people, mostly leaders in a wide range of progressive groups and unions, to discuss 'the next agenda,'" according to David Moberg, writing for *In These Times*, the magazine linked to the Chicago-based Democratic Socialists of America. The group had been formed earlier, Moberg wrote, "in part to counterbalance the influence of the conservative Democratic Leadership Council, [and] had planned the gathering to prod a future President Gore to the left." Instead, they were confronting a new Republican administration. Speakers at the gathering included "AFL-CIO President John Sweeney and Congressional Democrats like Paul Wellstone, Dick Durbin, Jan Schakowsky, Jesse Jackson Jr., Dennis Kucinich, George Miller and Maxine Waters."[10]

According to Moberg, "the next agenda" group did not technically originate with the Campaign for America's Future. Rather Borosage and Hickey had already co-edited *The Next Agenda Blueprint for a New Progressive Movement*, published in 2001. "This is a blueprint for small 'd' democrats, an agenda that progressives can unite around and fight for universal health care, empowering workers, moving towards an environmentally sustainable economy, getting big money out of politics," as the late Senator Paul Wellstone (D-MN) wrote in his cover blurb for the book.[11]

By mid-2007, then, many elements of the "next agenda" group were well entrenched at 1825 K Street. Though Hickey claimed the confluence there of like-minded organizations was a "happy accident," in reality he and Borosage had been working to bring that "accident" into being for the better part of a decade. Indeed, by 2007 the group not only possessed a well-defined "next agenda," but, as we shall see, had also honed aggressive new tactics designed to push its implementation.

And so, on July 7, 2008, the Campaign for America's Future unveiled a brand-spanking-new lobby (though careful to call itself a "coalition")—Health Care for America Now—HCAN.

HCAN's launch was announced at a press conference at the National Press Club by Jeffrey D. Blum, the director of USAction, who conceived of the initiative as a coordinated "all-out" assault.[12] In an HCAN press release, communications director Jacki Schechner announced a new national campaign in "52 cities across the country, including 38 state capitals . . . by more than 100 national and state-based groups that represent labor, community organizations, doctors, nurses, women, small businesses, faith-based organizations, people of color, netroots activists, and think tanks" to bring together "millions of Americans to demand quality, affordable health care for all."[13]

As might be expected, the lead organizations in the HCAN coalition were identical to many of the new K Street occupants and their funders: ACORN, AFSCME, Americans United for Change, Campaign for America's Future, Center for American Progress Action Fund, Center for Community Change, MoveOn.org, National Education Association, National Women's Law Center, Planned Parenthood Federation of America, SEIU, United Food and Commercial Workers, and USAction.[14]

HCAN's steering committee was a virtual cross-section of the "progressive" Democrat left:

Richard Kirsch (Health Care for America Now);
Maude Hurd (ACORN);
Gerald McEntee (AFSCME);
Caren Benjamin (Americans United for Change);
Roger Hickey (Campaign for America's Future);
Elizabeth Edwards (Center for American Progress Action Fund);
Eli Pariser (MoveOn.org);
Reg Weaver (National Education Association);
Marcia Greenberger (National Women's Law Center);
Cecile Richards (Planned Parenthood);
Anna Burger (SEIU);
Joseph Hansen (United Food and Commercial Workers);
Jeff Blum (USAction);
David T. Tayloe, Jr., MD FAAP (American Academy of Pediatrics); and
David White (small business owner).[15]

Comprised of Obama backers, HCAN arrived just in time to promote the administration's proposed health care ambitions.

Note that, in February 2009, Brad Woodhouse, former president of

Americans United for Change, became communications director for the Democratic National Committee under Barack Obama. Woodhouse previously served as communications director for USAction and helped run Americans Against Escalation in Iraq.[16]

The national campaign director for Campaign for America's Future, Richard Kirsch, has also, since its founding in 2008, served as national campaign director for HCAN.[17]

Kirsch has a long career of working for health care reform. Following graduation from the University of Chicago business school, from 1980 to 1982, Kirsch served as financial director of the Illinois Public Action Council. There he "worked with two young Illinois Democrats," Rahm Emanuel and Jan Schakowsky. (It should surprise no one that Obama's White House chief-of-staff, Emanuel, "began his public career with the consumer rights organization Illinois Public Action.")[18]

In 1982 Kirsch moved to the East Coast where he founded a USAction (Illinois Public Action) affiliate, New Jersey Citizen Action. In those days, Kirsch's "primary areas of focus were progressive tax and housing policy, and he worked on elections and community organizing related to both."[19]

Sometime in 1985 Kirsch opened New York Citizen Action in Albany, where he stayed "for more than two decades." Kirsch's "main priority was reforming health care at the state level." In 1991 he "helped New York pass Child Health Plus, one of the first programs to provide public health coverage to children," which, along with a similar program in Rhode Island, "served as models for national State Children's Health Insurance Program legislation." Also, as early as 1992, Kirsch "and his team helped push a plan for a full-financed single-payer health insurance bill through one house of the New York state legislature." Kirsch's bill eventually failed to pass in either house of the legislature, though his proposed bill is heralded as "the first of its kind in the nation to make it that far."[20]

"FASTER ROAD TO GOVERNMENT-RUN HEALTH CARE"

After the failure in 1993 of the Clinton administration's health care reform plan, Kirsch "focused on passing legislation to regulate managed care companies." He co-authored in 1995, with Ruth Finkelstein and Cathy Hurwit, *The Managed Care Consumers' Bill of Rights: A Health Policy Guide for Advocates*. "The book became like the template that state legislatures used around the country to write managed care bills," Kirsch said.[21]

Kirsch and Hurwit knew one another from when he served as Executive Director of Citizen Action in New York and she was with National Citizen Action. Hurwit has served as Representative Jan Schakowsky's (D-IL) chief of staff since 2000 and serves on the board of directors at Heather Booth's "progressive" Midwest Academy.[22]

When Borosage and Hickey co-edited their manifesto *The Next Agenda* in 2001, the chapter on achieving "universal health care" was contributed by high-profile academics Jonathan B. Oberlander and Theodore R. Marmor. Oberlander is Assistant Professor of Social Medicine at the School of Medicine, University of North Carolina, Chapel Hill, and Marmor is Professor Emeritus of Public Policy and Management and Professor Emeritus of Political Science at the Yale School of Management.[23]

Oberlander and Marmor recounted the historical barriers to health care reform in their article, based their recommendations on the Bradley plan—the proposals of 2000 Presidential candidate Bill Bradley, whom they called the only candidate who focused "on the need for comprehensive health reform."[24]

(It should be mentioned here that, while Barack Obama was an undergraduate at Occidental College in Los Angeles, he was involved with Students for Economic Democracy, the student affiliate of Tom Hayden's Campaign for Economic Democracy. Bradley, who endorsed Barack Obama's candidacy in January 2008, was coordinator for CED's political action team. See Chapter 2 for more information.)

According to Oberlander and Marmor, Bradley's plan was attacked from left and right, including by Physicians for a National Health Program, led by Obama neighbor, physician, mentor, DSA member, and avid single-payer advocate, Dr. Quentin D. Young. Young's organization complained that Bradley's plan was "not ambitious enough" and "too similar to the Clinton administration's reliance on managed competition, and for leaving the current arrangements of an increasingly profit-oriented health care system largely intact."[25]

The Bradley plan, according to Young's PNHP, "had four core components":

> First, it required that all children be covered by health insurance, either through their parents' plans or private plans under the [Federal Employees Health Benefits Plan] FEHBP. Premium costs would be subsidized according parental income, with children in low- and moderate-income families having their premiums fully subsidized. Second, adults were given two choices: They could continue to participate in their current insurance plan or join one of the private plans in the FEHBP. Again, premium subsidies would vary according to income. Third, Bradley sought to "mainstream" Medicaid by providing all current recipients with a subsidy to join one of the private plans under the FEHBP as well. Finally, Bradley proposed to expand Medicare insurance to cover outpatient prescription drugs, with no cap on total claims.[26]

The Federal Employees Health Benefits Plan (FEHBP) is a "federally managed pool of private insurance plans presently available only to federal employees and their families."

Oberlander and Marmor were skeptical that the Bradley plan "[a]ttempts to build support for a new health reform plan that appeal[s] to both the right and the left [but] may leave you standing in the middle, with no support from either side."[27] They also noted its "reliance on private insurance for coverage and on the federal surplus for financing [which] had obvious political advantages over raising taxes to pay for a public insurance program." One "major flaw," they wrote, "was the plan's reliance on the FEHBP, which at that time was turning in its worst financial performance in a decade, with spending far exceeding growth rates in Medicare." The future cost projections, and method of payment, under the Bradley plan could obviously not succeed today based upon nothing more than the staggering growth in the federal deficit under the Obama administration.[28]

The "second fundamental problem," they wrote, "was that the plan Bradley proposed contained no measures to reliably control the costs of medical care." A third problem was that, "despite its label as universal insurance, the plan left at least 15 million Americans uninsured. Bradley advisers argued that many of those left uncovered would be young, healthy adults who would decide not to accept the new coverage."[29]

If all this is beginning to sound like déjà vu—it is. The same arguments Oberlander and Marmor were confronting in 2000 were still circulating in the halls of Congress throughout the fall of 2009.

Oberlander and Marmor criticized Bradley for falling "victim to the same infatuation with managed competition, and the same exaggerated promises made on its behalf by some health economists, that President Clinton did."[30] And they proposed a "Federalist Option" as an alternative plan, which permitted "states to choose how to organize their own medical care arrangements while encouraging them financially to provide universal coverage and broad benefits." This would allow a "decentralized emergence of multiple models" and offer an "opportunity to unify advocates of reform who agree on the goal of universal coverage but disagree on which plan should be adopted to reach that goal." The Federalist Option, they wrote, had been endorsed by Senator Wellstone, the Universal Health Care Access Network, and the SEIU.[31]

But the biggest drawback they foresaw was that "a federalist health system would be inequitable. Such a system would be unfair, in critics' view, because citizens' access to medical care services would be a function of the health system chosen by the state in which they reside."[32]

Another "possible alternative for health policy reform" proposed by Oberlander and Marmor was called the "pincer strategy." This would extend Medicare eligibility "downward to age 55, while expanding Medicaid, CHIP, and other insurance sources both for children and for working adults." The pincer strategy, they wrote, is "more incremental than either the federalist or single-payer approaches. Instead of creating a new medical care system, it seeks to build on existing institutions, gradually moving toward universal coverage."[33] The downsides to the pincer strategy, they wrote, are questions about "the effectiveness of Medicaid" and that it "would do little to control costs."[34]

The final alternative plan Oberlander and Marmor suggest is single-payer health care—the so-called public option.

Again, if any of this sounds at all familiar, it is. Both the House and the

Senate got to the point in December 2009 that they were throwing almost any and all options to see which one—if any—of them might stick.

On December 7, 2009, President Obama held a Democrats-only meeting on health care. Two days later, on December 9, Senate Majority Leader Harry Reid announced a "new compromise," a "Medicare 'buy-in' for people from ages 55 to 64 has overcome the liberal-moderate impasse over the 'public option.'" Reid let slip, "Let's say that I proposed a plan that moved to a single-payer system. . . ."

The *Wall Street Journal* remarked that "if anything, this gambit is an even faster road to government-run health care:"

> Mr. Reid's buy-in simply cuts out the middle man. Why go to the trouble of creating a new plan like Medicare when Medicare itself is already handy? A buy-in is an old chestnut of single-payer advocate Pete Stark, and it's the political strategy liberals have tried since the Great Society: Ratchet down the enrollment age for Medicare, boost the income limits to qualify for Medicaid, and soon health care for the entire middle class becomes a taxpayer commitment.[35]

Representative Pete Stark (D-CA), a member of the radical Congressional Progressive Caucus, introduced his health care reform plan, AmeriCare Health Care Act of 2007 (H.R. 1841), in March 2007 and repitched the plan, which guarantees universal health care, on January 6, 2009—two weeks ahead of Obama's inauguration.[36]

Stark has introduced his bill in several sessions of Congress. Regarding "single payer," and Medicare, Stark's "proposal establishes AmeriCare as secondary to Medicare but mandates that Medicare benefits conform to AmeriCare coverage." In the states, "Medicaid remains in place."

A second "blueprint" dates from March 2003 when Richard Kirsch, who had worked on the Clinton health care proposal, penned the lengthy proposal for health care reform, "Will It Be Déjà Vu All Over Again? Renewing the Fight for Health Care for All Tales, Hopes and Fears of a Battle-Scarred Organizer."

At the time of this writing, Kirsch's 2003 proposal bears a strong resemblance to a compromise of issues being debated in the U.S. Senate. He wrote:

So here's my proposal, in a nutshell: provide everyone in the country with the option, and the means of paying for, coverage through Medicare or through private insurance. Such a proposal achieves the two core goals outlined above; is built on two familiar systems; allows institutional forces to protect, and even expand, what they have now; and provides room for both sides of the ideological divide.

. . . Such a system would provide all Americans with comprehensive coverage based on the ability to pay, and would establish a national health insurance for Americans of all ages and incomes, while providing financing for private insurance plans to compete with the national health insurance program. It would be sold as providing all Americans a choice of two approaches that works now, assuring that all Americans have affordable access to the best of the American health care system.

Kirsch wrote July 15, 2008, on HCAN's website, that, a year before HCAN was officially launched, he had written an article detailing its points and advancing a strategy for its adoption.[37] Kirsch's experience of more than two decades focusing on health care reform make it clear why he was the one invited in 2008 by HCAN to "lead the drafting of an 895-page campaign plan for passing meaningful health-care reform under the next president" and to "move to Washington to lead the campaign."[38]

As it turns out, the liberal assessments by Oberlander and Marmor in June 2000—and Kirsch's 2003 plan—were not the only sources for HCAN's campaign plan. In 2008 Kirsch had a much more radical "blueprint" to consult while drafting it.

A SCANDAL AND A RADICAL PLAN

At the height of the public furor over health care reform, a chance discovery poured gasoline onto the fires of political controversy.

The discovery was made by Joel B. Pollak, a Republican who had announced he was challenging Illinois Congresswoman Jan Schakowsky in the 2010 midterm elections. In early December 2009, Pollak revealed that Schakowsky's husband, left-wing political consultant Robert Creamer, had written a "lengthy political manual" while in prison.

Creamer called his book: *Listen to Your Mother: Stand Up Straight! How Progressives Can Win*. The congresswoman's husband was incarcerated in a federal penitentiary in 2006 after being "sentenced to five months in prison after pleading guilty to bank fraud and withholding taxes while heading" Citizen Action of Illinois.[39]

Pollak detailed his discovery in an article headlined: "Was Democrats' Health Care Strategy Written in Federal Prison?" At the height of the battle over health care reform, Pollak revealed that Creamer's manifesto contained a "ten-point plan for foisting universal health care on the American people in 2009." Naturally, the discovery of Creamer's book set off a blogger firestorm.

A section of Creamer's book called "Progressive Agenda for Structural Change" contained the following ten points:

"We must create a national consensus that health care is a right, not a commodity; and that government must guarantee that right."

"We must create a national consensus that the health care system is in crisis."

"Our messaging program over the next two years should focus heavily on reducing the credibility of the health insurance industry and focusing on the failure of private health insurance."

"We need to systematically forge relationships with large sectors of the business/employer community."

"We need to convince political leaders that they owe their elections, at least in part, to the groundswell of support of [sic] universal health care, and that they face political peril if they fail to deliver on universal health care in 2009."

"We need not agree in advance on the components of a plan, but we must foster a process that can ultimately yield consensus."

"Over the next two years, we must design and organize a massive national field program."

"We must focus especially on the mobilization of the labor movement and the faith community."

"We must systematically leverage the connections and resources of a massive array of institutions and organizations of all types."

"To be successful, we must put in place commitments for hundreds of millions of dollars to be used to finance paid communications and mobilization once the battle is joined."

According to Pollak, "Creamer added: 'To win we must not just generate understanding, but emotion—fear, revulsion, anger, disgust.'"

Pollak believes that President Obama and the "Democrats have followed Creamer's plan to the letter. They have claimed our health care system is in crisis despite polls showing the overwhelming majority of Americans are happy with the care they receive. They have—with the help of President Obama—circulated false horror stories about Americans dying for lack of health care and health insurance."

Pollak also reported that Creamer's plan, written in 2006, "explicitly propos[ed] that it be carried out in 2009, once a 'progressive Democrat is elected President' and once Democrats could count on 60 votes in the Senate." More recently, Pollak noted, Creamer wrote about his "broader aim . . . laid out in his book . . . the 'democratization of wealth' in America and 'progressive control of governments around the world.'"

As Pollak wrote, in a November 19, 2009, *Huffington Post* article, "Crashing the Gates of the Status Quo," Creamer said: "If we succeed in winning health insurance reform we will have breached the gates of the status quo. We will demonstrate that fundamental change is possible. Into that breach will flow a wave of progressive change."[40] Creamer's book, Pollak wrote, "was endorsed by leading Democrats and their allies, including SEIU boss Andy Stern—the most frequent visitor thus far to the Obama White House—and chief Obama strategist David Axel-rod, who noted that Creamer's tome 'provides a blueprint for future victories.'"[41]

EXTREMIST ENDORSEMENTS: OBAMA'S SELECTION

The authors of this book found a number of familiar names among "Testimonials" cited for Creamer's book on his Strategic Consulting Group website:

Heather Booth (about whom more follows);
Jim Hightower of Progressives Democrats of America, PDA;
Senator Dick Durbin (D-IL);
Tom Hayden;
Greg Galluzzo, one of Barack Obama's mentors at the
    Gamaliel Foundation;
Roger Hickey;
USAction's Jeff Blum and William McNary;
Miles Rapoport of Demos, on whose advisory board Barack Obama
    once served;
Robert Borosage; and
Brad Woodhouse, who serves as communications director for the Democratic National Committee.[42]

Pollak wrote that Creamer's impressive client list includes such groups as ACORN and SEIU. The authors also found Campaign for America's Future, Heather Booth's Midwest Academy, and USAction on the list, as well as a number of state Democratic political parties. The *Undue Influence* website shows Creamer as having served circa 1999–2000 as a member of the Academy's board of directors.[43]

Creamer appears to have been in hot water over his handling of Citizen Action of Illinois funds well before 2005. *Illinois Issues* reported in its July/August 1997 issue that, after two decades heading the group, Creamer had "abruptly ended his tenure" with Citizen Action of Illinois the previous month, "amid a federal investigation into the group's financial affairs." Creamer wrote in a prepared statement that his departure was due to his "inability to serve as an effective leader and spokesman." The *Chicago Tribune* reported Creamer had "met with federal agents about a $1 million overdraft in an organization account."[44]

A decade later, Creamer was Obama's choice to head his GOTV (getting out the vote) training program, a sort of "Camp Alinsky-Obama."[45]

Obama's selection of Creamer for this job was no accident. A May 1, 1999, *Campaigns and Elections* article about the growing influence of soft money employed in "interest group- and party-centered campaigns" reported that Creamer's Chicago-based consulting firm, Strategic Consulting Group, had provided "training and setup" of the Democratic Party's soft money–funded 17th District Victory Fund, which was "designed to help" U.S. Representative Lane Evans (D-IL) and "state and local Democrats win re-election." The "campaign school" operated on a budget of "roughly $300,000 and [employed] 18 full-time volunteers (with no salaries but expenses paid)." Volunteers "focused on phone calling and door-to-door canvassing to reach tens of thousands of voters, culminating in a GOTV effort on election day."[46]

Campaigns and Elections wrote that Lane's challenger, Mark Baker, "attacked this group repeatedly, calling it 'Lane's imported labor' and 'political mercenaries.'" Evans claimed that the Victory Fund was separate from his campaign, defending it "repeatedly by comparing it to the 'Freedom Riders' of the 1960s, noting that its goal was to register and get people to vote."

An October 3, 2008, editorial in *Investor's Business Daily* said Obama's "campaign school," Camp Obama, had dirty street-fighting at its heart. While Obama "stands above the fray," *IDB* wrote, "his minions at ACORN are threatening, intimidating, confronting and even committing voter fraud," adding that Obama needed "more agitators" and therefore "set up these camps to train them." In Chicago alone Creamer's Camp Obama had trained "some 2,000 agitators to go back to their college campuses and reproduce more Obama clones."[47]

"DISTRIBUTION OF WEALTH AND POWER"

In a July 10, 2009, *Huffington Post* article, Creamer wrote that "progressives" needed to remember seven things to succeed. Foremost among them, that "the critical battles being fought in 2009 are not about 'policies'—they are about the distribution of wealth and power."[48] Creamer wrote that the money to pay for "exploding health care costs for families" should come from the pockets of insurance and pharmaceutical companies and that they, the companies, will fight to maintain the status quo. More ominously, Creamer said that if "every member of Congress" does not understand what is expected of them, "deliver on health care reform, a path towards energy independence, regulatory reform, and immigration reform in 2009," they will not return to Washington in 2010.

The sort of agitation tactics Creamer spelled out in his article immediately bring to mind Camp Obama: "That will require millions of phone calls from constituents, angry town meetings, lobby days, protests, letters, email, TV ads—and cornering Members of Congress in the grocery store. It will require intensity. It will require a massive progressive mobilization that won't take 'no' for an answer."

Creamer was a "political force in his own right, having consulted for Chicago Mayor Richard M. Daley and Illinois Governor Rod Blagojevich in past political campaigns, among others," added John Ruberry at *Marathon Pundit*.[49] Creamer's circle of influence includes his wife, Representative Jan Schakowsky, who, with Representative Tammy Baldwin (D-Wisc.), were speakers at the USAction November 1999 founding convention.[50] According to *Union Corruption Update*—the National Legal and Policy Center's Organized Labor Accountability Project—dated January 17, 2000, Citizen Action members Schakowsky and Baldwin were "allegedly 'nurtured' into candidates by Citizen Action."[51]

Other attendees at the USAction founding included "two militant unions," SEIU and AFSCME, "as well as other prominent leftist organizations such as the U.S. Student Association, Midwest Academy and Progressive Action Network." At the time USAction's statewide groups claimed "700,000 members, more than 100 full-time staff and combined annual budgets of $15 million to $20 million."

Creamer's 1997 departure from Citizen Action was obviously related to the corruption issue mentioned in *Update*. It was reported that the "once powerful, far-left Citizen Action virtually committed suicide in 1996 when it became a key player in the Teamsters' money-laundering scandal"—

taking "two 'donations' of $475,000 and $150,000 and rout[ing] $110,000 and $100,000, respectively," back to Union President Ron Carey's reelection campaign.[52]

Despite the debacle, *Update* reported that many "old guard" members "strongly" defended Citizen Action, including USAction Executive Director, and Citizen Action's transportation lobbyist, Jeff Blum, who "insisted that the new group would be more democratic and accountable." Blum said, "there would be no more of the old budget sleight-of-hand."

USAction President William McNary added that his group "must avoid Citizen Action's mistake of becoming a conduit for unions and trial lawyers' money and messages."

A year earlier, in December 1997, Illinois Public Action had reorganized and changed its name to Citizen Action of Illinois.[53]

Again, this links to Schakowsky and Creamer. Tom Roeser wrote on his blog on July 12, 2007, that Creamer had "a multiple group of organizations that received money, the best known being the 'Illinois Public Action Council,' a left-wing group on which his wife, Jan Schakowsky, was a board member while the manipulating was going on. She was already in Congress when he pleaded guilty; she was not charged."[54]

In the January/February 1998 issue of *New Ground*, Democratic Socialists of America announced that Citizen Action of Illinois had been reconfigured. Its board members would serve double duty, with the additional duty of Policy Council. The familiar names of DSA members—and Obama friends—Alice Palmer and Quentin Young are listed on the boards.[55] *New Ground* also reported Citizen Action of Illinois "appears to be on sound financial footing after its troubles last year which resulted in the resignation of long-time director and founder Bob Creamer."

The source for this financial "sound" footing was none other than unions. *New Ground* reported: "Major contributors include UNITE, SEIU, ATU, the Illinois State Council of Carpenters, as well as individuals such as Cook County Clerk David Orr."

Schakowsky's and Obama's connections with Citizen Action, and its successor, USAction, are unsurprising, as they are often found in similar—as well as each other's—political company. Both have shared some of the same backers along the way—Democratic Socialists of America, the New Party,

AFSCME, and SEIU. In August 2004 USAction President McNary, Representative Schakowsky, and then-Illinois State Senator Obama all appeared on the same podium at an Illinois Action event to honor Illinois trial attorney Phillip Corboy, with Schakowsky introducing keynote speaker Obama.[56]

COMMUNISTS, SOCIALISTS, SDS ACTIVISTS

In a July 8, 2008, press release HCAN announced its immediate plans to spend "an initial $1.5 million on national television, print, and online advertising" and send out "an email blast to more than 5 million people." HCAN's future plan was to "spend $25 million in paid media, have 100 organizers in 45 states," and ask members of Congress, "Which side are you on?" for the following five months.[57]

As Birnbaum wrote in May 2007: "Big money from unions such as the Service Employees International Union and the American Federation of State, County and Municipal Employees, as well as the Internet-fueled MoveOn, has provided groups like those at 1825 K Street the wherewithal to mount huge campaigns."[58]

The relationship between all of the groups and individuals behind the creation of HCAN is, to say the least, an interesting one—one which has been in the making for decades.

Nowhere else is clearer proof to be found that HCAN is a front group than its State Contact List, which is dominated by addresses and contacts for ACORN, SEIU, and USAction and its state affiliates.[59]

To understand the evolution of this group dynamic, we begin in September 2007 when USAction merged with True Majority, another MoveOn-style organization founded by Ben Cohen of Ben & Jerry's ice cream fame, to form True Majority Action, a netroots organization with an email list containing hundreds of thousands of names.[60]

It should come as no surprise to learn that USAction Fund for a True Majority supported Barack Obama's presidential campaign—to the tune of $64,766.75. Without a doubt, those "hundreds of thousands of names" on True Majority's email list also came in handy.

USAction Fund's president is Obama's friend, longtime colleague, and political supporter, William McNary.[61]

New Zealand researcher and blogger, Trevor Loudon, writes September 3, 2008, that McNary previously served for twelve years as Legislative Director of Illinois Public Action, now known as Citizen Action/ Illinois. Both USAction and IPA, Loudon writes, are "heavily infiltrated by Marxists—several of whom have close connections to Barack Obama, including his long-time friend, Democratic Socialists of America member Dr. Quentin D. Young, and Young's one-time boss, Communist Party USA 'front activist' and long-time Obama supporter, Alice Palmer, 'DSA friendly' Democratic Congresswoman Jan Schakowsky, and Obama supporting linked unionist Tom Balanoff."[62]

Loudon asks: How close are Obama and McNary? Close. McNary, commented May 1, 2008, at the *Huffington Post*: "I am also a voter. And in this election, I am supporting Barack Obama, whom I've known and worked with for years. I am also an elected delegate to the Democratic Convention for Barack Obama."[63]

Obama "has certainly worked with McNary for some years," Loudon adds.

David Moberg, the writer for the Chicago DSA–linked magazine *In These Times*, wrote Spring 2007 that Obama "collaborated" with United Power for Action and Justice, a "metropolitan Chicago faith-based organization formed in 1997" by the Alinsky-founded Industrial Areas Foundation, to "expand children's health insurance in Illinois."[64]

The collaboration benefited both Obama and the UPAJ, which, Moberg writes, "gave Obama a prominent platform to address its multiracial, metropolitan membership during his 2004 bid for the U.S. Senate." McNary commented: "Barack was not just willing to meet with community-based groups, not only to be a good vote for us, but he also strategized with us to help move our position forward."

Moberg wrote in the September 17, 2007, issue of *In These Times*, that McNary "personally—but not organizationally" supports Obama as a "genuine progressive" who will "expand the boundaries of American democracy" and "heal the rupture with the rest of the world Bush caused with the war in Iraq."[65]

Next we have USAction founder and vice president, former Students for a Democratic Society member, Heather Tobis Booth. In 1973

Booth and her husband, Paul Booth, co-founded the Midwest Academy, a "training organization . . . for a variety of leftist causes and organizations," which "describes itself as 'one of the nation's oldest and best known schools for community organizations, citizen organizations and individuals committed to progressive social change.'"[66]

Paul Booth is a founder and the former National Secretary of Students for a Democratic Society and former president of Chicago's Citizen Action Program, formed in 1969 by trainees from Saul Alinsky's Industrial Areas Foundation, according to *Discover the Networks*. Currently, Paul Booth is an assistant to Gerald McEntee, president of the public employees union AFSCME.[67]

Then we have Jeffrey David Blum, identified in July 2008 as the founder and co-chair of Health Care for America Now. Blum is also executive director of USAction.

Jeffrey Blum was a low dollar contributor to Obama for America. Beginning in 2001, Blum made a number of contributions to loyal Obama supporter Jan Schakowsky.[68]

The speaker's profile for Jeffrey Blum, USAction's executive director and Health Care for America Now's founder and president, is quite impressive, as well.[69]

Blum is an Executive Committee member for America Votes; an advisor to Progress Now; and a former steering committee member for Americans United to Protect Social Security (launched by Institute for America's Future).

Blum previously founded and directed Pennsylvania Citizen Action; worked for the People's Coalition for Peace and Justice, Massachusetts Fair Share, People for the American Way (where he co-coordinated the campaign to establish AmeriCorps), Surface Transportation Policy Project, Chesapeake Bay Foundation and Citizens Fund; was Transportation Policy Director for Citizen Action; served as president of Maryland Citizen Action, founder and member of the Advisory Board (with Heather Booth) of the Jewish Fund for Justice and as a member of the board of Citizens for Tax Justice. Additionally, Blum was the Northeast Pennsylvania Regional Director of the Clinton/Gore Campaign in 1992.[70]

He received his BSN from Boston University and says he attended the University of Chicago and the University of Warwick, England.

As head of USAction, Blum is no slouch at GOTV, either. *The Hill* wrote, in February 2005, Blum reported that USAction "by its own estimates mobilized 20,000 volunteers to register and turn out low-income minority voters."[71]

What is not found among Blum's remarkable credentials are his connections with Students for a Democratic Society.

An August 1976 declassified FBI report on members and activities of Bill Ayers' Weather Underground to date provides a profile of Jeffrey David Blum of Baltimore, Maryland, who, as of September 1969, was considered by the FBI as one of the activists of the Chicago Regional, Weatherman Faction of SDS (Students for a Democratic Society).[72]

Blum's name is found on the Chicago Police Department, Statistical Section of the Records Division, list dated October 17, 1969, of those who had been arrested during WUO's "Days of Rage" riots in Chicago, October 8–11, 1969.[73]

The previous year Blum was issued a passport on May 2, 1968, in Chicago, where he listed his proposed travel for a number of countries to include England, France, West Germany, Belgium, Netherlands, Norway, Denmark, Sweden, Finland, Yugoslavia, Italy, Hungary, Romania, Austria, Czechoslovakia, and the Union of Soviet Socialist Republics. Blum stated he planned to travel to these countries via Trans Globe Airways about June 14, 1968.

Although the FBI's report does not specifically state it, it is most likely Blum was one of those who accompanied WUO leader Bernardine Dohrn to Europe during the summer of 1968.

In 1973, Kirkpatrick Sale wrote in *SDS: The Rise and Development of the Students for a Democratic Society* that after the Democratic National Convention in 1968, Jeff Blum, Gerry Long, Bernardine Dohrn, John Jacobs, Bob Tomashevsky, and Peter Clapp shared an apartment in Chicago. This clearly puts Dohrn and Blum together.[74]

Dohrn wrote in the October 2006 issue of the Marxist journal, the *Monthly Review*, that the SDS "took delegations of youth to meet with the Vietnamese in Budapest, Montreal, and Havana. We met with New Left activists across Europe at an international new left conference in Ljubljana, stopping in Prague, Frankfurt, Stockholm, and Paris—seeking common ground and finding inspiration."[75]

An article at Knology.net adds that, after the 1968 Democratic National Convention, "approximately twenty-eight Americans including nine individuals who had participated in the Chicago demonstrations traveled to Budapest, Hungary for a conference. (Bernardine Dohrn who had departed for a month-long trip to various countries earlier also attended this conference.) They met for five days with five Vietcong and North Vietnamese representatives."[76]

This information is confirmed by the August 1976 FBI report, which cites from a September 21, 1968, *Washington Post* article that reported on the "trip of 28 American war foes who traveled to Hungary to meet with representatives of North Vietnam and the National Liberation Front to discuss strategy on U.S. campuses." The article stated that nine of the above-mentioned 28 individuals took part in demonstrations at the Democratic National Convention. However, Blum's name is not specified as having taken part in the DNC demonstrations.

The WUO's last open meeting prior to their submergence into underground status was the Flint, Michigan, War Council, held December 27–31, 1969. During this meeting the WUO decided to go underground and engage in guerrilla warfare against the U.S. government. Jeffrey Blum was known to have attended this meeting.

Additionally, the records of the Flint, Michigan, Police Department show that a vehicle registered to Jeffrey Blum was at this meeting. Although several others were, Blum's vehicle was not stopped and searched by the police.

In fact, many of the same people from the sixties, Jeffrey Blum, Heather Booth, and a number of former members of Students for a Democratic Society, have been plying the same shell game practically from the day SDS split into two factions. The one is represented by the likes of Bill Ayers and Bernardine Dohrn, who chose the visible path of violence to force social change. The other faction, represented by Blum and the Booths, chose the more subtle, less visible path of working within the system to social-economic-racial justice via Saul Alinsky–inspired activism.

"MARXIST": "I TURNED OBAMA INTO SINGLE-PAYER ADVOCATE"

Ezra Klein, the former associate editor at *American Progress*, a Center for American Progress organ, who is now a columnist at the *Washington Post*, wrote November 15, 2009, in "The path to single-payer," that President Harry Truman "sought single-payer" but failed. Presidents John F. Kennedy and Lyndon B. Johnson only managed to extend health care to "poor families and the elderly." Health reform efforts by President Richard M. Nixon were "entirely based around private insurers and government regulation"; President Jimmy Carter "favored an incremental, and private, approach"; and President Bill Clinton "sought [to] reform the system by putting private insurers in a market that would be structured and regulated by the government."[77]

Ezra Klein blames Clinton's failure for birthing President Barack Obama's "much less ambitious proposal, which attempts to reform not the health care system, but the small group and nongroup portions of the health care system by putting a small minority of private insurance plans into a market that's structured and regulated by the government, and closed off to most Americans."

Single-payer health care is the goose who will lay the golden egg so dearly sought by progressives.

In remarks to the Congressional Progressive Caucus in June 2009, the late Nick Skala, former Research Director for Physicians for a National Health Program, told the CPC they had a choice to make. Would they "maintain their unflinching support for single-payer" or "accede to intense political pressure to support the plan currently being developed in Congress under the direction of President Obama: a mandate for Americans to purchase an insurance plan from a massive new regulatory 'exchange,' with one plan potentially being a 'public option.'"[78]

Skala told the CPC that they had a "better chance to pass single-payer than Lyndon Johnson had when he passed Medicare. Unlike the public option, single-payer—because it holds the potential to finally realize universal, equitable health care—can be a vehicle to inspire the American people for progressive change."[79]

Physicians for a National Health Program is the organization co-founded in 1987 by Dr. Quentin D. Young, Barack Obama's neighbor, longtime friend, physician, and health care mentor. Dr. Young is a former PNHP president and currently serves as PNHP National Coordinator.[80]

Dr. Young has been the subject of a number of articles by New Zealand blogger Trevor Loudon. Loudon writes that, for nearly three decades, Young "has been the US's most active proponent of 'single payer' or socialized healthcare, firstly through his medical committee for Human Rights, then his Physicians for a National Health Program and his Health and Medicine Policy Research Group," which he founded in 1980 and of which he is currently chairman.[81]

The influential Dr. Young is a "practicing internist in Hyde Park, a Clinical Professor of Preventive Medicine and Community Health at the University of Illinois Medical Center and Senior Attending Physician at Michael Reese Hospital." In 1998 he served as president of the American Public Health Association.[82]

Dr. Young's PNHP profile clearly states his Marxist leaning: "Dr. Young has chosen to limit his medical practice in order to spend more time fighting the corporate takeover of medicine in America."[83]

Loudon writes that Young, a member of Democratic Socialists of America, was a "member of the Young Communist League in his teens." Young, Loudon writes, was "also accused of membership of the Bethune Club of the Communist Party (a party doctor's group) by a government commission investigating the 1968 Democratic Party Convention riots in Chicago."[84]

Young and "his DSA comrades and his allies in Committees of Correspondence for Democracy and Socialism (CCDS) and the Communist Party USA, all want socialized healthcare as a major stepping stone to a socialist America," Loudon writes.[85]

The Health and Medicine Policy Research Group was co-founded in 1981 by Dr. Young and John McKnight, one of Barack Obama's Alinskyite mentors at the Gamaliel Foundation. (McKnight also provided Obama with a letter of support for his application to Harvard Law School.)[86]

On March 7, 2008, Loudon writes, the Health and Medicine Policy

Research Group "organized an 85th birthday tribute dinner for Quentin Young in Chicago, themed 'Rebel without a pause.'" Invited guests included Illinois Senator Dick Durbin and Illinois Governor Pat Quinn.

Of greater interest are the radicals and Democratic Socialists of America members on the birthday celebration's host committee, which included longtime friend and Obama supporter, and Black Radical Congress founder, Timuel Black, who was formerly with the Socialist Party USA; Illinois Representative and former New Party member, Danny K. Davis; "close friend and supporter of Barack Obama," William McNary, who "has close ties to the Communist Party," whom the authors discussed in this chapter; longtime Obama supporter and campaign contribution bundler, Bettylu Saltzman, who was instrumental in Obama presenting his 2002 antiwar speech in Chicago; and Representative Jan Schakowsky, longtime Obama supporter and wife of Robert Creamer, both of whom are discussed by the authors in this chapter.[87]

One of the event's key speakers was Representative John Conyers (D-MI), a "leading proponent of 'single payer' healthcare." Conyers, Loudon writes," praised Quentin Young, Danny Davis, and Jan Schakowsky for their efforts on the health issue.

Loudon stated that "'we' were pushing 'single payer' long before Barack Obama came out in favor of the idea while still an Illinois State Senator. . . . He also makes it very clear that he and [his] comrades will not be satisfied with anything but fully socialized healthcare."[88]

Indeed. It was none other than Dr. Quentin Young himself who took credit March 11, 2009, on Amy Goodman's *Democracy Now!* program, for "turning Barack Obama into a 'single payer' advocate when the President was an Illinois State Senator."[89]

AGITATING AND ASTROTURFING

Many of HCAN's proposals echo those that President Obama advocated during his campaign, who signed on to the group's proposals during his 2008 campaign. HCAN has pledged to ensure Congress will pass a plan based on those principles.

— *WhoRunsGov.com*[90]

Camp Obama and HCAN agitation expert Robert Creamer wrote August 3, 2009, in the *Huffington Post* of the plan of action for what he deemed the "August Offensive" to define the health care debate during the Congressional recess:

> A potentially decisive battle to define this year's health care debate— and the Obama Presidency—will take place in town hall meetings, little league bleachers, and conversations on door steps near you during the August Congressional recess. . . .
>
> Well-organized progressive coalitions like Health Care for America Now (HCAN), and Obama's field operation—Organize for America— have been preparing for this engagement for months. They have been accumulating resources, testing public opinion, organizing grassroots field operations—all in preparation for this decisive battle.[91]

Another example of a propaganda tactic employed by HCAN, of which community activist Saul Alinsky would approve, is modern day astroturfing.[92] Author and blogger Michelle Malkin, in June 2009, likened the "Obamacare Astroturf Campaign" headquartered at 1825 K Street NW to that of the decades-old "welfare reform" astroturf campaign housed at 1024 Elysian Fields, the New Orleans headquarters of the radical group ACORN. As the authors have written elsewhere, Barack Obama has been associated with ACORN since at least 1982.[93]

Astroturf, defined as "apparently grassroots-based citizen groups or coalitions that are primarily conceived, created and/or funded by corporations, industry trade associations, political interests or public relations firms," is an accurate term for HCAN's health care reform campaign.[94]

As these authors have shown in great detail, there is nothing "grassroots" about HCAN. It is a well-oiled machine run by well-funded and well-seasoned political operatives.

Only a couple of examples will clearly demonstrate just how expertly the HCAN freight train operates.

It is highly unlikely that you've heard of Jason Rosenbaum, unless you frequent political blogs and have been intently followed President Obama's health care town halls.

On July 2, 2009, the day following President Obama's staged health care town hall at Northern Virginia Community College in Annandale, Virginia, the *Washington Post* reported: ". . . of the seven questions the president answered, four were selected by [White House] staff from videos submitted to the White House Web site or from those responding to a request for 'tweets.'" And the three audience members he called on randomly? The *Post* says they "all turned out to be members of groups with close ties to his administration: the Service Employees International Union, Health Care for America Now, and Organizing for America, which is a part of the Democratic National Committee." [95]

The White House transcript for the town hall shows the following exchange:

Question: Jason Rosenbaum . . .

Obama: What do you do, Jason?

Question: I work for a group called Health Care for America Now.

(APPLAUSE)

Obama: I think the—he knows something about health care. This is like . . . [96]

The *Washington Times'* Greg Pierce characterized the exchange as *embarrassing*: "The questioner declared that he worked 'for a group called Health Care for America NOW,' a group that basically supports the president's plans. 'I think he knows something about health care,' said Mr. Obama." [97]

What's even more embarrassing is the fact that Jason Rosenbaum's full resume has been overlooked by the mainstream media.

For example, Rosenbaum is a contributor to the progressive *National Journal*, which identifies him as Deputy Director of Online Campaigns, Health Care for America Now. [98]

Rosenbaum operates an online blog, *The Sentinel*, which has joined the Firedoglake blog family. In addition to his HCAN connection, we learn:

Jason Rosenbaum is a writer and musician currently residing in Washington D.C. He is interested in the intersection of politics and culture, media consolidation issues, and making sense out of our foreign policy disasters.[99]

The Sentinel, according to a April 2005 article in the Chicago Tribune, is a "Chicagocentric hip-hop and urban culture monthly" started by "six college students from DePaul and Northwestern, [is] a mix of concert reviews, interviews and essays." A student at Northwestern, Rosenbaum was then a "music technology major who plays guitar."

Rosenbaum's 2008 Netroots Nation speaker's profile makes his role with HCAN clear. Rosenbaum is a Washington, D.C., blogger, web designer, and "new media organizer" who blogs on "media issues, retroactive immunity and the presidential race." Rosenbaum and his co-authors at The Sentinel have built a "community around the blog using social media outreach." Rosenbaum "currently works for Progressive Media USA" and as "remnant manager" for CommonSense Media.[100]

Progressive Media USA is the pro-Obama PR war room that was coordinated by John Podesta's Center for American Progress through its Center for American Progress Action Fund, and Media Matters.[101]

Progressive Media USA was initially formed by "Tom Matzzie, a leader of the liberal group MoveOn.org" and "David Brock [Media Matters for America], once a conservative journalist who is now a liberal media critic . . . pledging to raise $40 million and lead the attack on McCain," the Washington Post reported May 14, 2008.[102]

A year later, Progressive Media's focus shifted. In May 2009 Greg Sargent reported at The Plum Line that the "Democratic operatives running the project are already holding a daily early morning call with dozens of operatives from liberal groups—labor, health care, the environment—to coordinate messaging and to deliver usable talking points for the day, according to liberal operative Jennifer Palmieri, who's the project's communications director."[103]

"The new war room," Sargent wrote, "represents a serious ratcheting up of efforts to present a united liberal front in the coming policy wars. The goal of the war room will be to do hard-hitting research that boils down complex policy questions into usable talking points and narratives that play well in the media and build public support for the White House's policy goals."

Sargent wrote that the war room was to be "headed by well-known liberal operative Tara McGuinness, who worked on John Kerry's presidential campaign and was a major player in the anti-war movement during the Bush years."

Sargent reported the "morning calls are key to the effort to present a united liberal front—something that the Obama White House had already been working to build among outside groups." Palmieri said the "coordination call" was to "get our content out and to coordinate people so they can fire up for the day," "adding the group will work with the White House 'only informally.'"

Although Rosenbaum posts on his LinkedIn online profile that he only worked at Progressive Media for less than a year, in 2008, we now have a clearer picture of who he is and how it came about that he was "selected" to pose a canned question to President Obama at a tightly orchestrated town hall.[104]

A second example of how Health Care for America Now's astroturf campaign controls the message for the White House is HCAN's four-page Playbook for Thwarting Town Hall Protests. Of these Saul Alinsky would have been most proud.[105]

In light of the July 1, 2009, staged town hall kabuki dance at Northern Virginia Community College between President Obama and HCAN employee Jason Rosenbaum, one brief paragraph in the Handbook leaps out:

> In many cases protesters will show up at events and meetings you don't recognize but are participating in as an attendee or a sponsor. You can still influence the outcome of these events or meetings, and it's important for HCAN organizers and leaders to be ready to encounter these protesters in order to make sure that our volunteers and activists respond appropriately as well as capitalize on opportunities to also move our message, work with Members, and educate the public.

Rosenbaum's question was a single paragraph in length:

> I've been—obviously I read the news a lot, and I've been hearing a lot about the price tag of health reform and how people are very

concerned that it's going to cost a trillion dollars, and we're trying to keep it under a certain number. I'm most concerned about making it affordable, folks like me, the American people. So what do you—and like you said, you're committed to making this deficit-neutral. So I hope you could talk a little bit about affordability and what your plans are for that.

President Obama delivered what appeared to be a lengthy prepared speech in response.

We know Rosenbaum was obviously not participating in the town hall to handle protesters. What he was doing was taking advantage of a planned situation on behalf of HCAN leadership. Rosenbaum was nothing more than a HCAN shill.

LEGISLATION PASSES FIRST HURDLES

After 25 straight days of debate, on December 24, 2009, in a 60-to-39 party-line vote, Senate Democrats passed legislation that brought them "a step closer to a goal they have pursued for decades," Robert Pear reported in the *New York Times*.[106]

This "clears the way for negotiations" with the House, which, on November 7, 2009, passed the Affordable Health Care for America Act, a "broadly similar bill," by a 220-to-215 vote, Pear wrote.[107]

After the vote, President Obama said "the health care bill was 'the most important piece of social legislation since the Social Security Act passed in the 1930s' and that together with the House bill, represented 'the toughest measures ever taken to hold the insurance industry accountable,'" Pear wrote.

Richard Kirsch, HCAN's national campaign manager, made a statement from which one can only conclude that HCAN's guiding hand will stay the course until the health care reform bill becomes law.

Kirsch said the "nation has moved one big step closer to comprehensive health care reform," and that HCAN "will work to get the strongest bill to the President's desk, one that provides good, affordable coverage to all and holds insurance companies accountable."[108]

Kirsch said that employers should be "required to help pay for good coverage for their workers," that premiums should be "affordable to families," that tax benefits should not be taxed, "that we enact tough insurance regulations, and that we offer the choice of a public health insurance option."

"The bill would require most Americans to have health insurance, would add 15 million people to the Medicaid rolls and would subsidize private coverage for low- and middle-income people, at a cost to the government of $871 billion over 10 years, according to the Congressional Budget Office," Robert Pear reported at the *Times*. The CBO "estimates that the bill would provide coverage to 31 million uninsured people, but still leave 23 million uninsured in 2019. One-third of those remaining uninsured would be illegal immigrants," he wrote.

The bill's passing was not welcomed by all, including many Democrats. David S. Broder at the *Washington Post* remarked that the "health-care reform bill coming out of the Senate presents a real dilemma for spectators: How do you applaud while holding your nose?"[109]

"Six decades after FDR's death, one of his Four Freedoms will, at long last, be guaranteed to almost all Americans. And the shame of this affluent society tolerating the denial of health care to its citizens will be largely lifted," Broder wrote. "But Lord, what a load of embarrassment accompanies this sense of satisfaction! What should have been a moment of proud accomplishment for the Senate, right up there with the passage of Social Security and the first civil rights bills, was instead a travesty of low-grade political theater—angry rhetoric and backroom deals."

Broder is referring to Democratic antics the week preceding the bill's passage, when Senate Majority Leader Harry Reid was cutting deals with Senate Democrats to entice reluctant members to cast a "yea" vote. Most egregious of these shenanigans was Senator Ben Nelson's "Cornhusker Kickback," which guarantees Nebraska will never have to bear the burden of supporting Medicaid; American taxpayers will pick up the tab in perpetuity. Additionally, non-profit insurance companies in Nelson's Nebraska and Senator Carl Levin's Michigan "will be exempt from a new, nearly $7 billion tax to pay for Demcare," Michelle Malkin wrote on her blog.[110]

David L. Bahnsen, a man well-versed in Wall Street financial planning and investment management services, remarked that this bill "makes no one happy." A debate, he wrote, which "started around one major issue: a public option for health care run by and paid for [by] the government . . . is dead and gone."[111]

Days before the vote, "progressive" blogger and lawyer Jane Hamsher at Firedoglake outlined ten good reasons the Senate bill should be killed, all inconvenient financial facts Democratic lawmakers did not want voters to know.

1. Forces you to pay up to 8% of your income to private insurance corporations—whether you want to or not.
2. If you refuse to buy the insurance, you'll have to pay penalties of up to 2% of your annual income to the IRS.
3. Many will be forced to buy poor-quality insurance they can't afford to use, with $11,900 in annual out-of-pocket expenses over and above their annual premiums.
4. Massive restriction on a woman's right to choose, designed to trigger a challenge to Roe v. Wade in the Supreme Court.
5. Paid for by taxes on the middle class insurance plan you have right now through your employer, causing them to cut back benefits and increase co-pays.
6. Many of the taxes to pay for the bill start now, but most Americans won't see any benefits—like an end to discrimination against those with preexisting conditions—until 2014 when the program begins.
7. Allows insurance companies to charge people who are older 300% more than others.
8. Grants monopolies to drug companies that will keep generic versions of expensive biotech drugs from ever coming to market.
9. No re-importation of prescription drugs, which would save consumers $100 billion over 10 years.

10. The cost of medical care will continue to rise, and insurance premiums for a family of four will rise an average of $1,000 a year—meaning in 10 years, your family's insurance premium will be $10,000 more annually than it is right now.[112]

At this juncture, the two versions of the health care bill must next be reconciled into a single document and voted on again.

NOTES

1: OBAMA TIED TO BILL AYERS...AT AGE 11!

1 Ron Grossman, "Setting the record straight on Obama's neighborhood: Hyde Park, where the left and the right have one thing in common: an uncommon obdurance," *Chicago Tribune*, August 2, 2008, http://archives.chicagotribune .com/2008/aug/02/travel/chi-obama-hydepark_bd03aug03.

2 Dinita Smith, "No Regrets for a Love of Explosives; In a Memoir of Sorts, a War Protester Talks of Life With the Weatherman," *New York Times*, September 11, 2001, http://www.nytimes.com/2001/09/11/books/no-regrets-for-a-love-of-explosives&st-nyt.

3 Full Transcript: Obama and Clinton Debate, ABC News, April 16, 2008, http:// abcnews.go.com/Politics/DemocraticDebate/story?id=4670271.

4 Ibid.

5 Ben Smith, "Ax on Ayers," Politico, February 26, 2008, http://www.politico.com/ blogs/bensmith/0208/Ax_on_Ayers.html.

6 Daniel Nasaw, "Obama and Bill Ayers," *Guardian UK*, February 26, 2008, http:// www.guardian.co.uk/world/deadlineusa/2008/feb/26/obamaandbillayers. Smith, February 26, 2008.

7 Aaron Klein, "Obama worked with terrorist: Senator helped fund organization that rejects 'racist' Israel's existence," WorldNetDaily, February 24, 2008, http://www.wnd. com/index.php?pageId=57231.

8 Andrew Walden, "Obama's other controversial church," Hawaii Free Press, June 4, 2009, available online at http://hawaiifreepress.com/Main/ArticlesMain/tabid/56/ article Type/ArticleView/articleId/815/Obamas-Other-Controversial-church.aspx.

9 Aaron Klein, "Obama tied to Ayers . . . at age 11: Anti-military congregation attended as boy in Hawaii linked to radical's organization," WorldNetDaily, June 19, 2009, http://www.wnd.com/index.php?fa=PAGE.view&pageId=101566.

10 Dinita Smith, "No Regrets," September 11, 2001.

11 Klein, "Obama tied to Ayers," June 19, 2009.

12 Ibid.

13 Ben Smith, "Obama on Ayers: 'I assumed that he had been rehabilitated,'" Politico, October 9, 2008, http://www.politico.com/blogs/bensmith/1008/Obama_on_ Ayers_I_assumed_he_had_been_rehabilitated.html.

14   Susan Chira, "Bernadine Dohrn; Same Passion, New Tactics," *New York Times*,
     November 18, 1993, http://www.nytimes.com/1993/11/18/garden/at-home-with-
     bernadine-dohrn-same-passion-new-tactics.html.

15   "A chip off the old 'Weatherbureau' block," Dateline D.C./*Pittsburgh Tribune*,
     December 22, 2002, http://www.pittsburghlive.com/x/pittsburghtrib/s_108950.
     html; Carol Brightman, "Running on Empty," *The Nation*, December 18, 2003,
     http://www.thenation.com/doc/20040105/brightman; Federal Bureau of Prisons
     Inmate Locator for Bernardine Dohrn, released 12-23-1982, http://www.bop.gov/
     iloc2/InmateFinderServlet?Transaction=NameSearch&needingMoreList=false&Fi
     rstName=Bernardine+&Middle=&LastName=Dohrn&Race=U&Sex=U&Age=&x
     =62&y=16.

16   Brian DeBose, "Obama's Early Near-Miss; 2008 Hopeful Initially Rejected
     for Chicago Job," *Washington Times*, July 26, 2007, http://www.questia.com/
     read/5021924446?title=Obama's%20Early%20Near-Miss%3b%202008%20
     Hopeful%20Initially%20Rejected%20for%20Chicago%20Job. Gregory A.
     Galluzzo, "Gamaliel and the Barack Obama Connection," Gamaliel.org, undated
     (post–general election), http://www.gamaliel.org/Obama%20Gamalie%20
     lConnection.htm.

17   Lynn Sweet, "Obama's book: What's real, what's not," *Chicago Sun-Times*,
     February 20, 2007 (reprint from August 8, 2004), http://blogs.suntimes.com/
     sweet/2007/02/sweet_column_reprise_obamas_bo.html.

18   Stephanie Block, "The Chickens Have Come Home to Roost: Obama, ACORN, and
     the Catholic Campaign for Human Development," *CatholicCitizens.org*, September
     28, 2008, http://catholiccitizens.org/press/pressview.asp?c=48125.

19   Marilyn J. Gittell, *Strategies for School Equity: Creating Productive Schools in a Just
     Society* (Hartford, Conn.: Yale University Press, 1998), 215.

20   Mary O'Connell. "School Reform Chicago Style, Designs for Change. How Citizens
     Organized to Change Public Policy." A special issue of *The Neighborhood Works*
     (Chicago: Center for Neighborhood Technology, Spring 1991), 40, http://www
     .designsforchange.org/pdfs/SchlRfrmChgoStyle.pdf, funded by Woods Charitable
     Fund. Pauline Lipman, *High Stakes Education: Inequality, Globalization, and Urban
     School Reform* (RoutledgeFalmer, 2003), 34.

21   O'Connell, "School Reform Chicago Style," 1.

22   A detailed discussion of the role of the Chicago business community in school
     reform can be read in Dorothy Shipps' unpublished doctoral dissertation, "Big
     business and school reform: The case of Chicago, 1988" (Palo Alto, Calif.: Stanford
     University, 1995), which chronicles the activities of the Civic Committee and its
     satellite organizations, Chicago United and Leadership for Quality Education, in
     the mobilizing for reform.

23   Ibid.

24   Lipman, *High Stakes Education*, 34; O'Connell, "School Reform Chicago Style,"
     40.

25   Ben Joravsky, "The Long, Strange Trip of Bill Ayers," Chicago Reader,
     November 9, 1990, https://securesite.chireader.com/cgi-bin/Archive/abridged2.
     bat?path=1990/901109/AYERS1&search=%22bill%20ayers%22.

26   Aaron Klein, "Obama cited Ayers job as qualification to run. Interview during
     2000 congressional race contrasts with effort to separate self from domestic

terrorist," WorldNetDaily, September 15, 2008, http://www.wnd.com/index.
php?fa=PAGE.view&pageId=75384.

27   William Ayers, Warren Chapman, and Anne Hallet, "A booster shot for Chicago's
public schools," *Chicago Tribune*, January 31, 1995, http://pqasb.pqarchiver.com/
chicagotribune/access/20680871.html?dids=20680871:20680871&FMT=ABS&F
MTS=ABS:FT.

28   Stanley Kurtz, "Chicago Annenberg Challenge Shutdown? A cover-up in the
making? " National Review Online, August 18, 2008, http://article.nationalreview.
com/?q=MTgwZTVmN2QyNzk2MmUxMzA5OTg0ODZlM2Y2OGI0NDM=.

29   Stanley Kurtz, "Obama and Ayers Pushed Radicalism On Schools," *Wall Street Journal*,
September 23, 2008, http://online.wsj.com/article/SB122212856075765367.html.

30   October League (Marxist-Leninist), Building a new Communist Party in the U.S.,
October League (Marxist-Leninist), Los Angeles, 1973. Aaron Klein, "Obama
worked closely with terrorist Bill Ayers. Records show collaboration on funding
leftists despite claim he's just 'a guy' in neighborhood," WorldNetDaily, September
23, 2008, http://www.wnd.com/index.php?pageId=76022.

31   Stanley Kurtz, "Obama and Ayers pushed radicalism on schools," Wall Street
Journal, September 23, 2008; available online at http://online.wsj.com/article/
SB122212856075765367.html.

32   "Bill Ayers. Radical Educator" in Ron Chepesiuk, *Sixties Radicals, Then and Now:
Candid Conversations with Those Who Shaped the Era*, 1995, 92ff, http://books
.google.com/books?id=hqbM4eyLyx8C&pg=PA92&lpg=PA92&dq=%E2%80%9C
Ron+Chepesiuk%22,+Ayers&source=bl&ots=5_MzLnsdov&sig=OU_ydAjQtfT6
hxxQfSbrAFiJjHI&hl=en&ei=J0gNS4zSG8bulAfP3NCZBA&sa=X&oi=book_resul
t&ct=result&resnum=2&ved=0CAoQ6AEwAQ#v=onepage&q=&f=false.

33   Klein, "Obama cited Ayers job," September 15, 2008.

34   Ibid.

35   Joe Klein, "The Fresh Face," *Time*, October 15, 2006, http://www.time.com/time/
magazine/article/0,9171,1546362-1,00.html.

36   Peter Osnos, "The Making of the Book That Made Obama," Daily Beast, January
27, 2009, http://www.thedailybeast.com/blogs-and-stories/2009-01-27/the-making-
of-the-book-that-made-obama.

37   Summary: "Who wrote 'Dreams from My Father'?" WorldNetDaily, n.d., http://
www.wnd.com/index.php?fa=PAGE.view&pageId=79392.

38   Jack Cashill, "Book confirms: Ayers wrote Obama's book," WorldNetDaily,
September 23, 2009, http://www.wnd.com/index.php?fa=PAGE
.view&pageId=110781. See also Christopher Andersen, *Barack and Michelle:
Portrait of an American Marriage*, (William Morrow Press, September 2009)

39   Jack Cashill, "A Closer Look at Obama's Odyssey," American Thinker, October 11,
2009, http://www.americanthinker.com/2009/10/a_closer_look_at_obamas_
odysse.html.

40   "See Klein 'Obama worked with terrorist.'"

41   Ibid.

42   "Should a child ever be called a 'super predator'? A panel at the University of
Chicago debates the merits of the juvenile justice system," University of Chicago,
November 4, 1997, http://www-news.uchicago.edu/releases/97/971104.juvenile
.justice.shtml.

2: UNMASKING THE MYSTERIOUS COLLEGE YEARS

1   David Mendell, *Obama: From Promise to Power* (Harper Collins Publishers), 2007, 56.

2   Barack Obama, *Dreams from My Father: A Story of Race and Inheritance* (Three Rivers Press, 1995), 100.

3   Adam Schatz, "'Frantz Fanon': The Doctor Prescribed Violence," *New York Times*, September 2, 2001, http://www.racematters.org/doctorwhoprescribedviolence. htm.

4   Margo Mifflin, "The Occidental Tourist," *New York Times*, January 17, 2009, http://www.nytimes.com/2009/01/18/opinion/18mifflin .html?scp=1&sq=Occidental%20College,&st=cse.

5   See also William E. Rivers, "Politics, Ethics, and Corporate Policy: U.S. Corporations' 1986 Position Papers on South Africa," *Journal of Business Communication* 37 (2000).

6   Obama, *Dreams*, 105.

7   Ibid., 105, 106, 107.

8   Serge F. Kovalkeski, "The Long Run: Few From Obama's Youth Remember His Drug Use," *New York Times*, February 9, 2008, http://www.nytimes .com/2008/02/09/us/politics/09obama.html?pagewanted=print.

9   Roy H. Campbell, "Occidental Still in Standoff Over Divestment," *Los Angeles Times*, June 5, 1986, http://articles.latimes.com/1986-06-05/news/gl-9692_1_ occidental-college-republicans.

10 Jane Jaquette, Account of early phase of the anti-apartheid movement on campus based on a 2008 senior thesis written by History major Caitlin Croall, based on documents in the College archives, http://departments.oxy.edu/dwa/ JaquetteDIVESTPostere.pdf.

11 Roger Boesche teaches history of European and American political thought at Occidental College; faculty profile available online at http://departments.oxy .edu/politics/faculty/BOESCHE.HTM. Among his many writings on Alexis de Tocqueville's liberalism, Boesche is also the author of "How White People Riot: Quietly, at the Ballot Box," *Baltimore Sun*, October 15, 1995, 3F.

12 Larry Gordon, "Occidental recalls 'Barry' Obama," *Los Angeles Times*, January 29, 2007, http://articles.latimes.com/2007/jan/29/local/me-oxy29. Curriculum vitae for Roger Boesche, Occidental College, http://departments.oxy.edu/politics/ boesche/fall%2007%20cv.htm.

13 Oliver Haydock, "Expert Opinions: Meet Roger Boesche, Who Knew 'Barry Obama' in Passing at Occidental," *Observer* UK, April 3, 2008, http://www.observer. com/2008/expert-opinions-meet-roger-boesche-who-knew-barry-obama-passing-occidental. What Mendell writes (page 60) is that "a friend of Obama's said that one Occidental professor in particular played an enormous role in Obama's intellectual revolution. Roger Boesche taught two classes taken by Obama: American Political Thought and Modern Political Thought." Mendell reports from an unnamed "friend" as his source. Mendell next comments, lacking proof, "The latter [course] had a lasting effect."

14 Haydock, "Expert Opinions,"April 3, 2008.

15 Tyler Kearn and Aidan Lewis, "Retracing Obama's Legacy: An exclusive insider's scoop on President-elect Barack Obama's two years at Occidental and the

environment that molded the young sociopolitical activist," *Occidental Week*, November 25, 2008, http://media.www.oxyweekly.com/media/storage/paper1200/news/2008/11/25/Features/Retracing.Obamas.Legacy-3561358.shtml.

16 Gary Chapman is a professor at the University of Texas; his UT profiles are available online at http://www.utexas.edu/lbj/faculty/gary-chapman and http://www.utexas.edu/lbj/21cp/bio.html. In 1985 Chapman became Executive Director of Computer Professionals for Social Responsibility; his profile is available online at http://cpsr.org/prevsite/publications/newsletters/old/1980s/Winter1985.txt/view.

17 The New American Movement (NAM) is described thusly by Scott Sherman in "Class Warrior: Barbara Ehrenreich's Singular Crusade," *Columbia Journalism Review* 42 (November–December 2003): "New American Movement (NAM), which arose from the ashes of Students for a Democratic Society. NAM was a melting pot of New Leftists and former communists, and the group engaged in strike support and union organizing, political strategizing and consciousness-raising."

18 Maurice Isserman, "A Brief History of the American Left," Democratic Socialists of America website, undated, http://www.dsausa.org/about/history.html. Louis Proyect, "Maurice Isserman versus the new SDS," LouisProyect.com, March 1, 2007, http://louisproyect.wordpress.com/2007/03/01/maurice-isserman-versus-the-new-sds. Proyect describes Isserman as a "revisionist" historian of the CPUSA. Faculty profile for Maurice Isserman of Hamilton College: http://academics.hamilton.edu/history/home/misserma.html.

19 Isserman, "A Brief History."

20 The New Deal Coalition "brought together liberal interest groups and voting blocks that supported the New Deal and voted for Democratic presidential candidates from 1932 until approximately 1966," according to the Conservapedia, http://www.conservapedia.com/New_Deal_Coalition.

21 *American Red Groups*, last updated July 11, 2002, http://reds.linefeed.org/groups.html.

22 Max B. Sawicky, April 23, 1998 list-serv entitled "RE: Richard Rorty," http://www.mail-archive.com/pen-l@galaxy.csuchico.edu/msg25204.html. Reference is made to Harry C. Boyte, *The Backyard Revolution—Understanding the New Citizen Movement*, Temple University Press, August 1981, http://www.amazon.com/Backyard-Revolution-Understanding-Citizen-Movement/dp/0877222290/ref=sr_1_1?ie=UTF8&s=books&qid=1241470884&sr=8-1. "Harry C. Boyte: Just another radical Alinskyite Obama supporter," *TheRealBarackObama*, May 4, 2009, http://therealbarackobama.wordpress.com/2009/05/04/harry-c-boyte-just-another-radical-alinskyite-obama-supporter.

23 Profile: Harry C. Boyte, *The Broker*, circa December 2008, http://www.thebrokeronline.eu/en/archive/authors/Boyte-Harry-C. Finding Aid for the Register of the Boyte Family Papers, 1941–1981, Duke University Libraries, http://library.duke.edu/digitalcollections/rbmscl/boyte/inv.

24 Jim Tranquada, "Barack Obama '83 Elected President," Occidental College, November 4, 2008, http://www.oxy.edu/x8270.xml.

25 CV for Larry T. Caldwell, Occidental College, http://departments.oxy.edu/politics/caldwell/cv.htm. Larry Caldwell, "First strike, preventive war would be radical departure from American history," *PasadenaStarNews.com*, September 25, 2002, available online (cache file) at http://cache.zoominfo.com/CachedPage/?archive_id=0&page_id=330644212&page_url=%2f%2fwww.pasadenastarnews.com%2f

Stories%2f0%2c1413%2c206%257E11851%257E882492%2c00.html&page_last_u
pdated=9%2f26%2f2002+6%3a37%3a54+AM&firstName=Larry&lastName=C
aldwell. Sarah Schmidt, "Experts divided on tactics used by Russian forces. Several
other hostage incidents have ended badly," *National Post*, October 28, 2002, available
online (cache file) at http://cache.zoominfo.com/CachedPage/?archive_id=0&page_
id=344392605&page_url=%2f%2fwww.nationalpost.com%2futilities%2fstory.
html%3fid%3d%7bCD7B3F3B-1F83-4112-9855-E1E6CE54CE43%7d&page_last_
updated=10%2f29%2f2002+7%3a01%3a32+AM&firstName=Larry&lastName=
Caldwell.

26 Peterson's college guidebook for entry on Occidental College, http://www
.petersons.com/collegeprofiles/Profile.aspx?inunid=7921&reprjid=12&sponsor=
1&tabid=10005. Occidental College's undergraduate population today is less than
2,000 students, with only 6 percent identified as African American. In a best case
scenario there might have been 100 to 120 members of the Black Student Alliance.
It is unknown whether Students for Economic Democracy (SED) had a chapter on
campus, although it has been widely reported on the Internet that Barack Obama
joined SED. The information originated with a single source that provides no
documentation to back up the claim.

27 Tom Hayden profile at NNDB.com, http://www.nndb.com/people/153/000024081.

28 Port Huron Statement of the Students for a Democratic Society, 1962,
provided courtesy of office of Senator Tom Hayden, http://coursesa.matrix.msu
.edu/~hst306/documents/huron.html. See Mark E. Kann, "From Participatory
Democracy to Digital Democracy" at *Fast Capitalism* for an updated view of
Hayden's student thesis, http://www.uta.edu/huma/agger/fastcapitalism/1_2/kann.
html. Tom Hayden, "The Problem Is Empire," *ZNet*, September 4, 2008, http://
www.zmag.org/znet/viewArticle/18693. Douglas Linder, "The Chicago Seven,"
Jurist, February 2000, http://jurist.law.pitt.edu/trials2.htm.

29 Myra MacPherson, *Vietnam and the Haunted Generation* (Anchor Books/Doubleday,
1984), 466–467. Vicky Allan, "THE FAT CONTROLLERS: As the Battle of the
New Year Bulge Begins, Vicky Allan Weighs Up the Lives Behind the Diets,"
RedOrbit, January 10, 2006, http://www.redorbit.com/news/health/352491/the_
fat_controllers_as_the_battle_of_the_new_year.

30 "The Filthy Fight: Berkeley's April l981 Election," *Berkeley in the 70s*, University
of California Berkeley, April 1981, http://berkeleyinthe70s.homestead.com/
files/81camp.htm. John Wiener wrote in the November 29, 1986, issue of *The
Nation* (abstract), http://www.thenation.com/archive/detail/13836950: "Tom
Hayden, searching for 'a new political center for the Democratic Party,' has
closed down his ten-year-old Campaign for Economic Democracy (CED) and
has established a new organization, Campaign California. At its height, in the
late 1970s and early 1980s, CED, had thirty chapters and 8,000 members; it
was California's largest single organized force on the left. Hayden came up with
the idea for the group in 1975, arguing that Watergate and the U.S. defeat in
Vietnam had created an opening in electoral politics that the left should explore.
His campaign for the Senate the following year was a test of that theory. The
organization attacked corporations for endangering the environment with toxic
emissions; it organized renters to fight landlords, argued that research and
development of solar energy were being thwarted by the energy multinationals,
and made pro-choice politics a top priority."

31 William T. Poole, "Campaign for Economic Democracy Part I: The New Left in Politics," Heritage Foundation, September 19, 1980, n.p., http://www.heritage.org/ Research/GovernmentReform/IA13.cfm.

32 Congress, House, Committee on Un-American Activities, Subversive Involvement in Disruption of 1968 Democratic Party National Convention, Part 2, 90th Congress, 2d Session, December 1968 (Washington, D.C.: US Government Printing Office, 1968), http://historymatters.gmu.edu/d/6464. Full text of "Subversive involvement in disruption of 1968 Democratic Party National Convention. Hearings, Ninetieth Congress, second session," December 2 and 3, 1968, http://www.archive.org/stream/subversiveinvolv02unit/ subversiveinvolv02unit_djvu.txt.

33 Ibid.

34 Tom Hayden, Advisory Board, Progressives Democrats of America, http:// pdamerica.org/about/board.php. "A Progressive Plan to Change America," *Progressive Democrats of America* 1, no. 2 (October 2004), http://pdamerica.org/ newsletter/2004-10/planchange.php. Profile: Progressive Democrats of America, *Discover the Networks*, http://www.discoverthenetworks.org/groupProfile. asp?grpid=7123.

35 Trevor Loudon, "Has Trevor Loudon found the Ayers-Dohrn-Obama 'smoking gun'? Meet the Movement for a Democratic Society," *RBO*, September 21, 2008, http://therealbarackobama.wordpress.com/2008/09/21/has-trevor-loudon-found-the-ayers-dohrn-obama-smoking-gun-meet-the-movement-for-a-democratic-society/2.

36 Trevor Loudon, "Reds, Radicals, Terrorists and Traitors—Progressives for Obama," *RBO*, September 11, 2008, http://therealbarackobama.wordpress .com/2008/09/11/loudon-reds-radicals-terrorists-and-traitors-progressives-for-obama. Progressives for Obama blog, http://www.progressivesforobama.blogspot.com.

37 Tom Hayden, "Bobby and Barack," *Huffington Post*, June 5, 2008, http://www .huffingtonpost.com/tom-hayden/bobby-and-barack_b_105406.html.

38 Poole, "Campaign for Economic Democracy Part I."

39 Visit of Ron Dellums: Institute of International Studies, University of California, Berkeley, circa 1999, http://globetrotter.berkeley.edu/people/Dellums/Dellums .html. "The Story of Cesar Chávez" (1927–1993), *Las Culturas*, undated, http:// www.lasculturas.com/biographies/214-civil-rights/112-cesar-chávez. Michael Dieden, Advisory Board, USC Center for Sustainable Cities, http://college.usc .edu/geography/ESPE/profile_mdieden.html. Profile for David Hilliard, "Black Panther," http://w1.1559.telia.com/~u155900373/black.htm.

40 David Hilliard, "Barack Obama as president symbolises change," *Socialist Review* (December 2008), http://www.socialistreview.org.uk/article. php?articlenumber=10624.

41 Poole, "Campaign for Economic Democracy Part I." Jon Weiner, "Tom Hayden's New Workout," *Nation* 243, November 29, 1986. Harold Johnson wrote in "Clinton's Left Coast," *National Review*, 44, September 14, 1992, that Shearer was "present at the creation" of CED. Joel Bleifuss, "Keep the Heat on Obama," *In These Times*, August 19, 2008, http://www.inthesetimes.com/article/3854/keep_the_ heat_on_obama.

42 Profile: Derek Shearer, Occidental College, http://departments.oxy.edu/ globalaffairs/Shearer.htm. Peter Y. Hong, "Professor Offers Class a Personal

View of President," *Los Angeles Times*, November 17, 2004, http://articles.latimes .com/2004/nov/17/local/me-class17.

43 "Bill Bradley Backs Barack Obama," *The Radar*/ABC News, January 5, 2008, http:// blogs.abcnews.com/politicalradar/2008/01/bill-bradley-ba.html.

44 Weiner, "Tom Hayden's New Workout," September 14, 1992.

45 "Students Protesting," UPI in the *Ellensburg Daily Record*, February 12, 1980, http:// news.google.com/newspapers?nid=860&dat=19800212&id=UzAQAAAAIBAJ&sji d=lo8DAAAAIBAJ&pg=5371,2594857.

46 Poole, "Campaign for Economic Democracy Part I." For a review of this influence as it developed in the anti–Vietnam War movement, see Heritage Foundation Institution Analysis No. 11, "The Anti-Defense Lobby: Part II, 'The Peace Movement, Continued,'" September 1979.

47 Richard Flacks, "Richard Flacks on Tom Hayden," *Truthdig*, June 12, 2008, http:// www.truthdig.com/arts_culture/item/20080613_richard_flacks_on_tom_hayden. Flacks also says of the Port Huron Statement: "Tom Hayden wasn't the originator of this breakthrough (if any single person deserves credit, it's Al Haber—a fellow Ann Arborite, who actually created SDS out of the remnants of the old Student League for Industrial Democracy and recruited Tom and other student leaders to the project). But Tom's writing and speaking enabled a genuinely new political voice and outlook to come into being. He was, appropriately enough, elected first president of the new formation at that meeting."

48 Kyle-Anne Shiver, "Obama's Radical Revolution: Alinsky Roots and Global Vision," *American Thinker*, October 15, 2008, http://www.americanthinker.com/2008/10/ obamas_radical_revolutionits_a.html. Hayden, "Bobby and Barack."

49 Greg Waldmann, "Education of Barack Obama," *OpenLettersMonthly.com*, October 2008, http://openlettersmonthly.com/issue/oct08-education-of-barack-obama.

50 Tranquada, "Barack Obama '83 Elected President," November 4, 2008.

51 Waldmann, "Education of Barack Obama," October 2008.

52 Lysandra Ohrstrom, "The Local: Obama on Morningside Heights, Morningside Heights on Obama," *New York Observer*, September 12, 2008, http://www.observer .com/2008/real-estate/local-obama-morningside-heights-morningside-heights-obama. Janny Scott, "Obama's Account of New York Years Often Differs From What Others Say," *New York Times*, October 30, 2007, http://www.nytimes .com/2007/10/30/us/politics/30obama.html.

53 Ohrstrom, "The Local," September 12, 2008.

54 Aaron Klein, "Is Obama hiding something from his college days? Some link mystery years to Ayers, others believe affirmative action at play," *World Net Daily*, September 29, 2008, http://www.wnd.com/index.php?fa=PAGE .view&pageId=76504.

55 Matt Welch, "Wayne Allyn Root's Million-Dollar Challenge: The Libertarian VP candidate wants Barack Obama to release his grades," *Reason.com*, September 7, 2008, http://www.reason.com/news/show/128461.html.

56 Ibid.

57 About the Black Students Organization (BSO), Columbia University, http://www .columbia.edu/cu/bso/history.html.

58 Ohrstrom, "The Local," September 12, 2008. "Obama's Account of New York Years,"

59 Ohrstrom, "The Local," September 12, 2008.

60 "Have You Heard from Johannesburg?" presented by the Columbia Palestine Forum, *BarnardColumbiaISO.com*, March 31, 2009, http://barnardcolumbiaiso .wordpress.com/2009/03/31/thursday-730pm-have-you-heard-from-johannesburg-presented-by-the-columbia-palestine-forum.

61 Eric L. Hirsch, "The Columbia Divestment Campaign: A Case Study," in Jeff Goodwin and James M. Jasper, eds., *The Social Movements Reader: Cases and Concepts* (Wiley-Blackwell, 2003), 96. Columbia Coalition for a Free South Africa, African Activist Archive, http://africanactivist.msu.edu/organization .php?name=Columbia%20Coalition%20for%20a%20Free%20South%20Africa *.The Observer, Student Review of the School of General Studies*, Columbia University, Fall 1998, 8, http://www.columbia.edu/cu/observer/archive/observer98fall.pdf.

62 *The Observer*, Fall 1998, 8.

63 Paul Rogat Loev, *Generation at the Crossroads: Apathy and Action on the American Campus* (Rutgers University Press, 1995), 171–172.

64 Eric L. Hirsch, "The Columbia Divestment Campaign: A Case Study," in Jeff Goodwin and James M. Jasper, *The Social Movements Reader: Cases and Concepts* (Wiley-Blackwell, 2d Ed., 2009), 98, 99.

65 John Everett Bird and Sherrell Farnsworth, "The Hamilton Blockade," Chapter 1, *The Observer* (Fall 1998), 8–9, http://www.columbia.edu/cu/observer/archive/ observer98fall.pdf.

66 Samantha Sharf, "The Race for the White House. Profile of Senator Barack Obama," *Daily Pennsylvanian*, November 3, 2008, http://thedp.com/node/57440. Samantha Sharf is a "rising College sophomore from Long Island" and a Design Editor for *The Daily Pennsylvanian*.

67 Sarah A. Soule, "The Student Divestment Movement in the United States and Tactical Diffusion: The Shantytown Protest," *Social Forces* 75 (1997), http:// www.questia.com/read/95699685?title=The%20Student%20Divestment%20 Movement%20in%20the%20United%20States%20and%20Tactical%20 Diffusion%3a%20the%20Shantytown%20Protest.

68 Kim Parks and Sandra V. Williams, "The Heat is On," *Blackworld* 9, no. 5 (April 18, 1985), 1. http://dspace.sunyconnect.suny.edu/bitstream/1951/42836/1/ Blackworld,%20V.%2012g,%20i.%2005%20(V.%2011,%20i.%2005)%20-%20 19850418.pdf.

69 Curriculum Vitae for Barbara Ransby, University of Illinois-Chicago, http://www .uic.edu/depts/hist/Faculty/ransby.html.

70 Program: "Intellectuals: Who Needs Them?" A public gathering sponsored by the Center for Public Intellectuals and the University of Illinois–Chicago, April 19–20, 2002, http://www.uic.edu/classes/las/las400/conferencealt.htm.

71 Letter to the *Chicago Tribune* from Barbara Ransby, Beth E. Richie, Lisa Yun Lee, February 29, 2008, http://billayers.wordpress.com/2008/05/07/february-29-2008.

72 Trevor Loudon, "Black Radicals for Obama," *RBO*, October 12, 2008, http:// therealbarackobama.wordpress.com/2008/10/04/loudon-black-radicals-for-obama.

73 "What Is The Black Radical Congress (BRC)? From the Black Radical Congress, 19–21 June 1998, "LISTSERV from Arm The Spirit, June 15, 1998; http://www. hartford-hwp.com/archives/45a/228.html.

74 Ibid.

75 Bird and Farnsworth, "The Hamilton Blockade," 8.

76   The Potomac Officers Club, "Virginia Governor Tim Kaine and Julius
      Genachowski, Co-Founder of LaunchBox Digital and Obama Advisor, to Speak
      to The Potomac Officers Club," BusinessWire, http://www.businesswire.com/
      portal/site/home/permalink/?ndmViewId=news_view&newsId=2008101700559
      7&newsLang=en. Tom Lowry, "The Short List for US Chief Technology Officer,"
      BusinessWeek, October 20, 2008, http://benton.org/node/17990.

77   Michael Luo and Christopher Drew, "Big Donors, Too, Have Seats at Obama
      Fund-Raising Table," New York Times, August 8, 2008, http://www.nytimes.com/
      2008/08/06/us/politics/06bundlers.html. Bundler: Julius Genachowski,
      $500,001, WhiteHouseForSale, http://www.whitehouseforsale.org/bundler
      .cfm?Bundler=13024.

78   Biography of Chairman Julius Genachowski, Federal Communications
      Commission, http://www.fcc.gov/commissioners/genachowski/biography.html.

79   Andrew McCarthy, "Why Won't Obama Talk About Columbia?" National Review
      Online, October 7, 2008, http://article.nationalreview.com/?q=NjY4YzdhMDBk
      ZGQ3ZmU2MTUzYjdkMzc5ZjUzYmViZWM=):. Ali Abunimah, "How Barack
      Obama learned to love Israel," The Electronic Intifada, March 4, 2007, http://
      electronicintifada.net/v2/article6619.shtml.

80   Bird and Farnsworth, "The Hamilton Blockade," 8.

81   Steve Gilbert, "Co-Workers: Obama Inflated His Resume," Sweetness & Light,
      September 14, 2008, http://sweetness-light.com/archive/did-obama-turn-down-a-
      wall-street-career.

82   Charles Krauthammer, "The Perfect Stranger," Washington Post, August 28,
      2008, http://www.washingtonpost.com/wp-dyn/content/article/2008/08/28/
      AR2008082802852.html.

83   Janny, "Obama's Account of New York Years," October 30, 2007.

84   Ibid.

85   Ibid.

86   Ibid.

87   "President Barack Obama's Work History as an Organizer with the New York
      Public Interest Research Group," New York Public Interest Research Group," n.d.,
      http://www.nypirg.org/goodgov/obama.html.

88   Jason Fink, "Obama stood out, even during brief 1985 NYPIRG job," New York Daily
      News, November 9, 2008, http://www.newsday.com/news/new-york/obama-stood-
      out-even-during-brief-1985-nypirg-job-1.885513.

89   Ibid.

90   Hirsch, "The Columbia Divestment Campaign," 100.

3: "OBAMA WAS QUITE RELIGIOUS IN ISLAM"

1   Barack Obama, Call to Renewal Conference, sponsored by the progressive
      Christian magazine Sojourners, June 28, 2006, http://www.factcheck.org/
      askfactcheck/did_obama_say_we_are_no_longer.html.

2   Aaron Klein, "Obama: America is 'no longer Christian.' Democrat says nation also
      for Muslims, nonbelievers," WorldNetDaily, June 22, 2008, http://www.wnd.com/
      index.php?fa=PAGE.view&pageId=67735.

3   David Brody, "Obama to CBN News: We're no Longer Just a Christian Nation,"
      CBN News, July 30, 2007, http://www.cbn.com/CBNnews/204016.aspx.

4   "Transcript: Barack Obama's Inaugural Address," *New York Times*, January 20, 2009, http://www.nytimes.com/2009/01/20/us/politics/20text-obama.html.

5   Interview of the President by Laura Haim, Canal Plus, Office of the White House Press Secretary, June 1, 2009, http://www.whitehouse.gov/the_press_office/transcript-of-the-interview-of-the-president-by-laura-haim-canal-plus-6-1-09.

6   Michael Goldfarb, "Obama: America 'One of the Largest Muslim Countries in the World,'" *Weekly Standard*, June 2, 2009, http://www.weeklystandard.com/weblogs/TWSFP/2009/06/obama_america_one_of_the_large_1.asp.

7   Daniel Pipes, "How many Muslims in the United States?" *DanielPipes.com*, April 22, 2003, http://www.danielpipes.org/blog/2003/04/how-many-muslims-in-the-united-states.

8   Jodi Kantor, "Barack Obama's search for faith," *New York Times*, April 30, 2007, http://www.nytimes.com/2007/04/30/world/americas/30iht-30obama.5501905.html.

9   Lisa Miller and Richard Wolffe, "Finding His Faith: So much has been made about Barack Obama's religion. But what does he believe, and how did he arrive at those beliefs?" *Newsweek*, July 12, 2008, http://www.newsweek.com/id/145971.

10   Aaron Klein, "Obama was 'quite religious in Islam': Contemporaries, records dispute campaign claim that he was never 'practicing Muslim,'" *WorldNetDaily*, April 3, 2008, http://www.wnd.com/index.php?fa=PAGE.view&pageId=60559.

11   Ibid.

12   Ibid.

13   Barack Obama, *Dreams from My Father* (Three Rivers Press, 1995, 2004), 154.

14   Lao, "Tracking Down Obama in Indonesia - Part 5," *An American Expat in Southeast Asia*, January 28, 2007, http://laotze.blogspot.com/2007/01/tracking-down-obama-in-indonesia-part-5.html. "Obama's childhood records vindicate Corsi book: Photo shows candidate registered 'as an Indonesian citizen and a Muslim,'" *WorldNetDaily*, August 17, 2008, http://www.wnd.com/index.php?fa=PAGE.printable&pageId=72667.

15   The original publication, *Banjarmasin Post*, is no longer available online; corroboration comes from Daniel Pipes's April 29, 2008, FrontPageMagazine.com article, "Barack Obama's Muslim Childhood," http://www.danielpipes.org/5544/barack-obamas-muslim-childhood.

16   The *Los Angeles Times* article, as well as the *Baltimore Post* reprint, are no longer publicly available. Corroboration comes from Aaron Klein, "Obama anti-smear site: 'He was never a Muslim.' But contemporaries, records indicate candidate once 'quite religious in Islam,'" *WorldNetDaily*, June 12, 2008, http://www.wnd.com/index.php?fa=PAGE.view&pageId=66981; and Daniel Pipes, "Obama and Islam," FrontPageMagazine.com, December 26, 2007, http://97.74.65.51/readArticle.aspx?ARTID=29314.

17   Kimberly West, "Campaign Now Says Barak Hussein Obama Never a Practicing Muslim Despite Claims of Childhood Friends and Teachers," *Associated Content*, March 17, 2007, http://www.associatedcontent.com/article/179905/campaign_now_says_barak_hussein_obama.html?cat=37.

18   Kim Barker, "History of schooling distorted," *Chicago Tribune*, March 25, 2008.

19   Daniel Pipes, "Confirmed: Barack Obama practiced Islam," *FrontPageMagazine.com*, January 7, 2008; reprint available at: http://www.danielpipes.org/5354/confirmed-barack-obama-practiced-islam.

20   "Report: Obama's Muslim grandmother among Mecca pilgrims," *Earth Times*, November 25, 2009, http://www.earthtimes.org/articles/show/296278,report-obamas-muslim-grandmother-among-mecca-pilgrims.html.

21 Aaron Klein, "Obama: U.S. 'one of largest Muslim countries.' President makes inaccurate statement as White House stresses his Islamic roots," *WorldNetDaily*, June 3, 2009, http://www.wnd.com/index.php?pageId=100019.

22 "Odinga says Obama is his cousin. Kenyan opposition leader Raila Odinga has said he is a cousin of US presidential hopeful Barack Obama," *BBC*, January 8, 2008, http://news.bbc.co.uk/2/hi/7176683.stm.

23 University of Pennsylvania, African Studies Centre, East Africa Living Encyclopedia: Kenya: IRIN Election Briefing, December 13, 1997.

24 Mark Hyman, "Obama's Kenya ghosts," *Washington Times*, October 12, 2008, http://www.washingtontimes.com/news/2008/oct/12/obamas-kenya-ghosts/print.

25 Ibid.

26 "Kenyan Government calls Obama 'stooge' for Odinga," *LiveLeak.com*, January 5, 2008, http://www.liveleak.com/view?i=149_1199587542.

27 Sam Gale Rosen, "Obama Wades Into Kenya Fray: Candidate tells opposition leader in father's homeland he's worried about violence," *Newser*, January 8, 2008, http://www.newser.com/story/15900/obama-wades-into-kenya-fray.html.

28 Joe Klein, "Obama's Other Life," *Time*, January 7, 2008, http://swampland.blogs .time.com/2008/01/07/obamas_other_life. "Kenya's election seen as badly flawed," Reuters, September 18, 2008, http://africa.reuters.com/world/news/usnLI387861 .html.

29 Aaron Klein, "Christians copy Christ killers, says Obama pastor's magazine. 'George Bush, unwitting prophets of Baal distort true practice of Gospel of Jesus,'" *WorldNetDaily*, May 20, 2008, http://www.wnd.com/index.php?fa=PAGE .view&pageId=64828.

30 James H. Cone, *A Black Theology of Liberation*, 2nd anniversary ed. (Orbis Books, 1990).

31 Stanley Kurtz, "Left in Church: Deep inside the Wright *Trumpet*," *National Review Online*, May 20, 2008, http://article.nationalreview.com/?q=MjRhNDQ4MGFlYjk 0YzUwNDk0MzYyNTE1ZDkwYmNmNDc=.

32 Ibid.

33 Ibid.

34 Aaron Klein, "Obama's church newsletter: Israel making 'ethnic bomb'," WorldNetDaily.com, March 25, 2008. Available online at http://www.wnd.com/ index.php/index.php?fa=PAGE.view&pageId=59884 <http://www.wnd.com/ index.php/index.php?fa=PAGE.view&pageId=59884>.

35 Aaron Klein, "Obama church published Hamas terror manifesto: Compares charter calling for murder of Jews to Declaration of Independence," *WorldNetDaily*, March 20, 2008, http://www.wnd.com/index.php?pageId=59456.

36 "Obama's church reprinted ethnic bomb claim," Sweetness & Light blog, March 24, 2008, http://sweetness-light.com/archive/obamas-church-published-anti-israel-letter.

37 Profile: Rashid Khalidi, *Discover the Networks*, http://www.discoverthenetworks .org/individualProfile.asp?indid=1347; Profile: Rashid Khalidi, BarackBook, http://www.barackbook.com/Profiles/RashidKhalidi.htm. BarackBook includes numerous article links about Khalidi.

38 Evan R. Goldstein, "Rashid Khalidi's Balancing Act," The Chronicle of Higher Education, March 6, 2009. Available online at http://chronicle.com/article/Rashid-Khalidi-s-Balancing/7866.

39 Aaron Klein, "Another day, another terror tie for Obama. Professor friend has long history with Arafat's PLO," *WorldNetDaily*, October 30, 2008, http://www.wnd.com/index.php?pageId=79568.

40 Ibid.

41 Aaron Klein, "Obama worked with terrorist," *WorldNetDaily*, February 4, 2008, http://www.wnd.com/index.php?pageId=57231.

42 Alyssa A. Lappen and Jonathan Calt Harris, "Columbia U's Radical Middle East Faculty," *FrontPageMagazine.com*, March 18, 2003, http://97.74.65.51/readArticle.aspx?ARTID=19234.

43 Aaron Klein, "Obama worked with terrorist."

44 " Peter Wallsten/LAT refuses to release Barack Obama/Rashid Khalidi videotape," *24Ahead.com*, October 24, 2008, http://24ahead.com/blog/archives/008220.html.

45 Ibid.

46 Aaron Klein, "Obama raised funds for Islamic causes. Speeches for Palestinian refugees called code for Israel's destruction," *WorldNetDaily*, February 25, 2008, http://www.wnd.com/index.php?fa=PAGE.view&pageId=57341.

47 "Where do the presidential contenders stand on the issue of the Israeli–Palestinian conflict?" Democracy Now!, January 24, 2008, http://www.democracynow.org/2008/1/24/where_do_the_presidential_contenders_stand.

48 The original piece has been removed from the Electronic Intifada website, but the quotes are documented by *WorldNetDaily* online at: http://www.wnd.com/index.php?fa=PAGE.view&pageId=87454.

49 Ibid.

50 Ali Abunimah, "How Barack Obama learned to love Israel," *The Guardian*, March 5, 2007, http://www.guardian.co.uk/commentisfree/2007/mar/05/howbarackobamalearnedtolo.

51 Ibid.

52 "Batchelor & Klein Interview Hamas's Ahmed Yousef," *JohnBatchelorShow.com*, October 19, 2008, http://johnbatchelorshow.com/podcasts/2008/10/batchelor-klein-interview-hamass-achmed-yusef.

4: OBAMA'S RADICAL ALINSKY TRAINERS

1 David Alinsky, "Son sees father's handiwork in convention," *Boston Globe*, letters section, August 31, 2008, http://www.boston.com/bostonglobe/editorial_opinion/letters/articles/2008/08/31/son_sees_fathers_handiwork_in_convention/?s_campaign=8315.

2 Profile of Saul Alinsky, *Discover the Networks*, http://www.discoverthenetworks.org/individualProfile.asp?indid=2314.

3 Saul Alinsky, DtN. Jeff G., "Alinsky, Obama, and the progressive turn," *Protein Wisdom*, September 11, 2008, http://proteinwisdom.com/?p=13245.

4 Todd Gitlin, Columbia University faculty profile, http://www.journalism.columbia.edu/cs/ContentServer/jrn/1165270069177/JRN_Profile_C/1165270081547/JRNFacultyDetail.htm.

5 Gary Starr, "The Great Leftist Con Game—How the New Left is Hijacking the U.S. in Plain Sight and How to Fix It," The Neville Awards, October 17, 2008, http://www.nevilleawards.com/leftist_con.shtml.

6   David Horowitz, *Barack Obama's Rules for Revolution: The Alinsky Model*, David
     Horowitz Freedom Center, 2009, 29,: http://www.americanpatrol.com/OBAMA-
     BARACK/2009-2010/PDF/Rules-for-Revolution091120.pdf. Gary Starr, "The Great
     Leftist Con Game-How the New Left is Hijacking the U.S. in Plain Sight and How
     to Fix It," The Neville Awards, October 17, 2008, http://www.nevilleawards.com/
     leftist_con.shtml. See Radical Son (Magill Book Reviews), http://www.enotes.
     com/radical-son-salem/radical-son.

7   PlentyMag.com, "Coal and clear skies: Obama's balancing act. An investigative
     report of presidential hopeful Barack Obama's environmental philosophy," Mother
     Nature Network, April 8, 2009: http://www.mnn.com/earth-matters/politics/
     stories/coal-and-clear-skies-obama's-balancing-act.

8   Horowitz, *Barack Obama's Rules for Revolution*, 5.

9   Ibid., 5–6.

10   Ibid., 6–7.

11   Ryan Lizza, "The Agitator," *The New Republic*, March 9, 2007, http://www
     .discoverthenetworks.org/Articles/bobamasunlikelypoliticaledu.html.

12   *Barack Obama's Rules for Revolution*, 7.

13   Lizza, "The Agitator."

14   Robert Wuthnow and John H. Evans, *The Quiet Hand of God: Faith-Based Activism
     and the Public Role of Mainline Protestantism* (University of California Press, 2002),
     78: http://www.questia.com/read/105962643?title=The%20Quiet%20Hand%20
     of%20God%3a%20%20Faith-Based%20Activism%20and%20the%20Public%20
     Role%20of%20Mainline%20Protestantism. Gregory A. Hession, "Alinsky: A
     Radical Who Matters: Barack Obama Has Been Greatly Influenced by Saul
     Alinsky's Radical Theories of Political Organizing. What Effect Is This Likely to
     Have on an Obama Presidency?" *The New American* 24 (November 10, 2008).

15   "The Gamaliel Foundation's Faith and Democracy Platform," Gamaliel Foundation,
     http://www.gamaliel.org/Platform.htm. Carmen Sirianni and Lewis Friedland,
     *Civic Innovation in America: Community Empowerment, Public Policy, and the Movement
     for Civic Renewal* (University of California Press, 2001), 54–55. Information comes
     from *Gamaliel Foundation, Jubilee: A Time for Metropolitan Equities and the Common
     Good* (Chicago: Gamaliel Foundation, 1999).

16   Brian DeBose, "Obama's Early Near-Miss; 2008 Hopeful Initially Rejected
     for Chicago Job," *Washington Times*, July 26, 2007, http://www.questia.com/
     read/5021924446?title=Obama's%20Early%20Near-Miss%3b%202008%20
     Hopeful%20Initially%20Rejected%20for%20Chicago%20Job. Gregory A.
     Galluzzo, "Gamaliel and the Barack Obama Connection," Gamaliel.org, undated
     (post–general election), http://www.gamaliel.org/Obama%20Gamalie%20
     lConnection.htm.

17   Galluzzo, undated. Barack Obama, "Why Organize? Problems and Promise in
     the Inner City?" *Illinois Issues* (July/August 1988), http://www.edwoj.com/Alinsky/
     AlinskyObamaChapter1990.htm. The essay was included as a chapter in *After
     Alinsky: Community Organizing in Illinois* (Chicago: University of Illinois), 35–40.

18   "Obama's McKnight in Shining Armor," *Investor's Business Daily*, September 29,
     2008, http://www.investors.com/NewsAndAnalysis/Article.aspx?id=495268&amp
     ;Ntt=Obama's+McKnight+In+Shining+Armor.

19   Danny Duncan Collum, Organizing Hope, *Sojourners Magazine* 37 (April 2008).

20   Horowitz, *Barack Obama's Rules for Revolution*, 8–9.

21 Lizza, "The Agitator."

22 Galluzzo, "Gamaliel and the Barack Obama Connection."

23 Obama, July/August 1988. Woods Fund of Chicago Evaluation of the Fund's Community Organizing Grant Program: Executive Summary and Findings and Recommendations of the Evaluation Team. April 1995, 5, http://www.nfg.org/cotb/42woods.pdf.

24 Galluzzo, "Gamaliel and the Barack Obama Connection." *Investor's Business Daily*, September 29, 2008. Profile for John L. McKnight, *Discover the Networks*: http://www.discoverthenetworks.org/Articles/johnmcknight.html.

25 *Investor's Business Daily*, September 29, 2008.

26 Galluzzo, Gamaliel and the Barack Obama Connection." *Investor's Business Daily*, September 29, 2008.

27 Editorial, "Fairness Down Your Throat," *Investor's Business Daily*, August 28, 2008.

28 Ibid.

29 Lizza, "The Agitator."

30 Charlotte Allen, "From Little ACORNs, Big Scandals Grow. Barack Obama: torn between two models of community organizing," *The Weekly Standard*, November 3, 2008, http://www.weeklystandard.com/Content/Public/Articles/000/000/015/746zemwq.asp?pg=1.

31 The American Monetary Institute speaker's profile for Ed Chambers, AMI 2009 Monetary Reform Conference: http://www.monetary.org/2009schedule.html; and AMI 2008 Monetary Reform Conference, http://www.monetary.org/2008schedule.html.

32 Zeik Saidman, "What's wrong with community organizers?" *Rocky Mountain News*, October 23, 2008, http://m.rockymountainnews.com/news/2008/Oct/23/saidman-whats-wrong-community-organizers.

33 Edward T. Chambers, *Roots for Radicals: Organizing for Power, Action, and Justice* (Continuum International Publishing Group, 2003), 27.

34 "Michelle Obama's plea for education," TED, April 2009, http://www.ted.com/talks/michelle_obama.html. Includes video and transcript.

35 Saul D. Alinsky, *Rules for Radicals: A Pragmatic Primer for Realistic Radicals* (Random House, 1971), xix.

36 Barack Obama, "After Alinsky: Community Organizing in Illinois," *Illinois Issues*, University of Illinois at Springfield, 1990, http://www.edwoj.com/Alinsky/AlinskyObamaChapter1990.htm.

37 Irene Sege, "Community organizers fault comments at GOP gathering," *Boston Globe*, September 6, 2008, http://www.boston.com/news/nation/articles/2008/09/06/community_organizers_fault_comments_at_gop_gathering.

38 "Ernesto Cortés, Jr.," Summit Documents, undated, http://74.125.93.132/search?q=cache:tXp_JxdwBe0J:www.hispaniccsc.org/2007%2520Summit/Documents/ERNIEBIO.DOC+%22United+Neighborhoods+Organization%22&cd=34&hl=en&ct=clnk&gl=us.

39 Peter Dreier and Marshall Ganz, "We Have the Hope: Now Where's the Audacity? Kennedy passed the liberal torch to Obama. Let's run with it," *Washington Post*, August 30, 2009, http://www.washingtonpost.com/wp-dyn/content/article/2009/08/28/AR2009082801817_pf.html.

40 Geoffrey Kurtz, "Obama and the Organizing Tradition," *Logos* 7, no. 2 (2008), http://www.logosjournal.com/?q=node/76. Profile for Marshall Ganz, John F.

Kennedy School of Government, Harvard University, http://www.hks.harvard.edu/ about/faculty-staff-directory/marshall-ganz.

41   Zack Exley, "Obama Field Organizers Plot a Miracle," *Huffington Post*, August 27, 2007, http://www.huffingtonpost.com/zack-exley/obama-field-organizers-pl_b_61918.html.

42   Profile for Peter Dreier, Dr. E.P. Clapp Distinguished Professor of Politics, and director of the Urban & Environmental Policy Program, at Occidental College in Los Angeles, http://departments.oxy.edu/politics/faculty/dreier.htm. Curriculum vitae for Peter Dreier: http://departments.oxy.edu/politics/dreier/fall%20o7%20cv .htm.

43   Ibid.

44   Curriculum vitae for Peter Dreier. Trevor Loudon, "Exclusive! Obama, the Communist Van Jones and the Demos Connection," *RBO*, August 17, 2009, http:// therealbarackobama.wordpress.com/2009/08/17/loudon-exclusive-obama-the-communist-van-jones-and-the-demos-connection.

45   "The Credit Crunch," *New Ground* 115.3, Chicago Democratic Socialists of America, January 3, 2008, http://www.chicagodsa.org/ngarchive/ng115.html#anchor355839. Mike Pattberg, "Convention Notes," *The Yankee Radical. Institute for Democratic Socialism*, March 2006, 9, http://www.dsaboston.org/yradical/yr2006-03.pdf. Progressives for Obama website, http://progressivesforobama.net/tag/carl-davidson.

46   Gretchen Reynolds, "Vote of Confidence," *Chicago Magazine*, January 1993, http:// www.chicagomag.com/Chicago-Magazine/January-1993/Vote-of-Confidence.

47   Ibid.

48   Suzanne Perry, "Fired Up and Ready to Grow. Youth group's Obama link raises its profile nationwide," *The Chronicle of Philanthropy*, April 14, 2008, http://www .publicallies.org/atf/cf/%7BFBE0137A-2CA6-4E0D-B229-54D5A098332C%7D/ Chronicle%20Articles%20April%2014%202008.pdf.

49   Ibid.

50   Ibid.

51   Fact Sheet About Public Allies and the Obamas, Public Allies, 2008, http://www .publicallies.org/site/c.liKUL3PNLvF/b.3960231.

52   Ibid.

53   Ibid.

54   Ibid.

55   Steven Malanga, "Organizer in Chief: Barack Obama's Controversial Roots," *New York Post*, September 8, 2008, http://www.manhattan-institute.org/html/miarticle .htm?id=2960.

56   Gene Birmingham, "United Power: Alinsky Comes Home to Chicago," *New Ground* 55, Chicago DSA, Nov/Dec 1997, http://www.chicagodsa.org/ngarchive/ng55.html.

57   Ibid.

58   Ibid.

59   David Moberg, "Back to Its Roots: The Industrial Areas Foundation and United Power for Action and Justice," chapter 19 in John P. Koval, Larry Bennett, Michael I. J. Bennett, Fassil Demissie, Roberta Garner, and Kiljoong Kim, *The New Chicago: A Social and Cultural Analysis* (Temple University Press, 2006), 241, http://www .questia.com/read/113460305?title=The%20New%20Chicago%3a%20%20A%20 Social%20and%20Cultural%20Analysis. Profile, David Moberg, *In These Times*, http://www.inthesetimes.org/community/profile/11.

60   Moberg, "Back to Its Roots," 241. See Illinois' FamilyCare website for program
     details, http://www.familycareillinois.com.

61   Ibid.

62   David Moberg, "Obama carried lessons he learned as a community organizer to
     the political arena: Both organizers and politicians would be wise to study them
     closely," NHI.org, Spring 2007, http://www.nhi.org/online/issues/149/obama.html.

63   Hession, "Alinsky: A Radical Who Matters."

64   Malanga, "Organizer in Chief."

5: ISSUES OF ELIGIBILITY

1   "Obama's half brother: Our father was abusive. New novel 'Nairobi to Shenzhen'
     is patterned in part on Barack Obama Sr.," Associated Press, November 4, 2009,
     http://www.msnbc.msn.com/id/33608282/ns/today-white_house.

2   Text of the Act is available at: http://www.enotes.com/major-acts-congress/
     naturalization-act.

3   Alexander Heard and Michael Nelson, *Presidential Selection* (Duke University Press,
     1987), 123.

4   Emmerich de Vattel, *The Law of Nations* (1758), 1999 Digital Edition available
     online at http://www.constitution.org/vattel/vattel-01.htm

5   John Bingham in the United States House on March 9, 1866 (Cong. Globe, 39th,
     1st Sess., 1291 ([1866]).

6   Text of decision available online at http://www.loc.gov/rr/program/bib/ourdocs/
     DredScott.html.

7   Text of the case is available online at: http://caselaw.lp.findlaw.com/cgi-bin/
     getcase.pl?court=US&vol=88&invol=162.

8   A PDF version of the resolution is available online here: http://www.scribd.com/
     doc/23193397/S-RES-511-of-04-30-2008-A-Resolution-Recognizing-That-John-
     Sidney-McCain-III-Is-a-Natural-Born-Citizen.

9   Affidavit of Ron McRae, Philip G. Berg, Esq. v. Barack Hussein Obama et al., U.S.
     District Court for the Eastern District of Pennsylvania, October 27, 2008, http://
     www.wethepeoplefoundation.org/PROJECTS/Obama/Evidence/AFFIDAVIT-
     Bishop.pdf.

10   Ibid.

11   Tim Jones, "Barack Obama: Mother not just a girl from Kansas. Stanley Ann
     Dunham shaped a future senator," *Hartford Courant*, March 27, 2007, http://www
     .courant.com/news/nationworld/world/chi-0703270151mar27-archive,0,2145571
     .story?page=4.

12   Chelsea Schilling, "Kenya: 'I don't know' if Obama born in U.S.. Ambassador
     suggests question be put to American government," *WorldNetDaily*, November 26,
     2008, http://www.wnd.com/index.php?fa=PAGE.view&pageId=82060.

13   Steve Baldwin, "The Mystery of Barack Obama Continues," Exclusive to Western
     Center for Journalism, n.d., http://www.westernjournalism.com/?page_id=3255.

14   See Section 57- 9, 18, 19, & 20 of the Territorial Public Health Statistics Act in the
     1955 Revised Laws of Hawaii, which was in effect in 1961

15   See Section 57-40 of the Territorial Public Health Statistics Act in the 1955
     Revised Laws of Hawaii, which was in effect in 1961.

16 "[§338-17.8] Certificates for children born out of State," Vol. 6, Ch. 321/HRS 338, State of Hawaii, http://www.capitol.hawaii.gov/hrscurrent/vol06_ch0321-0344/HRS0338/HRS_0338-0017_0008.htm.

17 A PDF of Chiyome Fukino's statement is available on the Hawaii Department of Health website at http://hawaii.gov/health/about/pr/2009/09-063.pdf.

18 Dan Nakaso, "Hawaii: Obama Birth Certificate Is Real. Hawaii's health director has reiterated that she has personally seen Obama's birth certificate in the Health Department's archives," *Honolulu Advertiser*, July 28, 2009, http://abcnews.go.com/Politics/story?id=8191566&page=1.

19 Bob Unruh, "Republican senator says Snopes settled 'eligibility': Arizona's Kyl cites website that assumes Hawaiian birth," *WorldNetDaily*, March 6, 2009, http://www.wnd.com/index.php?fa=PAGE.view&pageId=90843.

20 Aaron Klein, "Was young Obama Indonesian citizen? Document, travel suggest 'Barry Soetero' member of world's largest Muslim country," *WorldNetDaily*, August 17, 2008, http://www.wnd.com/index.php?fa=PAGE.view&pageId=72656.

21 Ibid

22 Ibid.

23 Mayhill Fowler, "Obama: No Need For Foreign Policy Help From V.P.," *Huffington Post*, April 7, 2008, http://www.huffingtonpost.com/mayhill-fowler/obama-says-no-to-foreign_b_95357.html.

24 Jake Tapper, "Obama's College Trip to Pakistan," *Political Punch*/ABC News, April 8, 2008, http://blogs.abcnews.com/politicalpunch/2008/04/obamas-college.html.

25 See Klein, "Was young Obama Indonesian citizen?"

26 Lawyer Search: Attorney's Registration and Public Disciplinary Record, State of Illinois, http://www.iardc.org/ldetail.asp?id=986412167.

6: OBAMA PARTICIPATED IN SOCIALIST PARTY

1 Barack Obama, *Dreams from My Father* (Three Rivers Press, 1995, 2004), 122.

2 Erick Erickson, "Barack Obama sought the New Party's endorsement knowing it was a radical left organization," *RedState.com*, September 9, 2008, http://archive.redstate.com/stories/elections/2008/barack_obama_sought_the_new_partys_endorsement_knowing_it_was_a_radical_left_organization.

3 Ibid. Trevor Loudon, "More On Barack Obama and the Socialist New Party," *RBO*, October 27, 2008, http://therealbarackobama.wordpress.com/2008/10/27/loudon-more-on-barack-obama-and-the-socialist-new-party.

4 See New Party website at www.newparty.com.

5 See Chicago DSA's *New Ground* 38 Jan/Feb 1995; *New Ground* 39 March/April 1995; *New Ground* 42 Sep/Oct 1995; and *New Ground* 47 July/August 1996, http://www.chicagodsa.org/ngarchive/index.html.

6 "The Organization," Democratic Socialists of America, http://www.dsausa.org/about/index.html.

7 "The New Party Principles," *ThirdWorldTraveler.com*, undated, http://thirdworldtraveler.com/Political/NewParty_Principles.html.

8 Ibid.

9 See *New Ground* 42 Sep/Oct 1995.

10 Zach Polett, "Fair Housing Drives New Party Growth in Little Rock," NHI.org, September/October 1998, http://web.archive.org/web/20011217021708/www.nhi .org/online/issues/101/polett.html.

11 See *New Ground* 47, July/August 1996.

12 Trevor Loudon, "Documentary Evidence Obama Was New Party member," *RBO*, October 23, 2008, http://therealbarackobama.wordpress.com/2008/10/23/loudon-documentary-evidence-obama-was-new-party-member.

13 See *New Ground* 47 July/August 1996.

14 Aaron Klein, "Obama participated in socialist party: Activist recalls president's time with radical Chicago political group," *WorldNetDaily*, August 23, 2009, http:// www.wnd.com/index.php?fa=PAGE.view&pageId=107731.

15 Profile: Carl Davidson, *Discover the Networks*, http://www.discoverthenetworks.org/ individualProfile.asp?indid=2322.

16 See *New Ground* 45, March/April, 1996.

17 See organization's newsletter, *Democratic Left*, Summer 2006 edition, http:// www.dsausa.org/dl/Summer_2006.pdf. Brenda J. Elliott, "New Party candidates Danny Davis and Barack Obama talk to the Teamsters in Chicago in 2004": *RBO*, October 24, 2008, http://therealbarackobama.wordpress.com/2008/10/24/ new-party-candidates-danny-davis-and-barack-obama-talk-to-the-teamsters-in-chicago-in-2004/. Trevor Loudon, "Danny K. Davis—Obama's Socialist Ally Joins Powerful Congressional Committee," *RBO*, December 17, 2008, http:// therealbarackobama.wordpress.com/2008/12/17/loudon-danny-k-davis-obamas-socialist-ally-joins-powerful-congressional-committee.

18 Loudon, "Danny K. Davis," December 17, 2008.

19 Aaron Klein, "Communist Party hails role of labor unions in Obama win. Socialist activist pledges 'no let down' in helping White House bring 'change we need,'" *WorldNetDaily*, November 13, 2008, http://www.wnd.com/index. php?pageId=80925.

20 "Quentin Young, Early Supporter of Obama, Now Disappointed and Saddened," *Corporate Crime Reporter* 5, January 28, 2008, http://www.corporatecrimereporter .com/obama012808.htm.

21 Loudon, October 23, 2008. Also see Brenda J. Elliott, "Just your everyday Hyde Park radicals—Obama, Ayers, Dohrn, Young," *RBO*, October 27, 2008, http:// therealbarackobama.wordpress.com/2008/10/27/just-your-everyday-hyde-park-radicals-obama-ayers-dohrn-young.

22 Trevor Loudon, "Black Radicals for Obama," *RBO*, October 4, 2008, http://thereal barackobama.wordpress.com/2008/10/04/loudon-black-radicals-for-obama.

23 Trevor Loudon, "Obama 'Understands What Socialism Is.' Works With 'Socialists With Backgrounds in the Communist Party,'" *RBO*, January 13, 2009, http:// therealbarackobama.wordpress.com/2009/01/13/loudon-obama-understands-what-socialism-is-works-with-socialists-with-backgrounds-in-the-communist-party.

24 Aaron Klein, "Obama's team 'socialists with communist backgrounds': Prof with ties to radical White House associates says president understands socialism," *WorldNetDaily*, September 10, 2009, http://www.wnd.com/index .php?pageId=109486.

25 Trevor Loudon, "Former Weatherman Terrorists, Marxists, New Party Veterans, Unite Behind Obama," *RBO*, October 27, 2008, http://therealbarackobama

.wordpress.com/2008/10/27/loudon-former-weatherman-terrorists-marxists-new-party-veterans-unite-behind-obama. Movement for a Democratic Society website, http://movementforademocraticsociety.org.

26   Aaron Klein, "Obama's law firm led charge benefiting socialist party: Evidence indicates Democratic candidate was member of radical political group," *WorldNetDaily*, October 27, 2008, http://www.wnd.com/index.php?fa=PAGE .view&pageId=79285.

7: OBAMA'S TIES TO NATION OF ISLAM AND BLACK RADICALS

1   "Farrakhan Praises Obama as 'Hope of Entire World,'" Associated Press, February 25, 2008, http://www.foxnews.com/politics/elections/2008/02/25/farrakhan-praises-obama-as-hope-of-entire-world.

2   Democratic Presidential Debate on MSNBC, Cleveland, Ohio, February 26, 2008; transcript provided by the Federal News Service and CQ Transcriptions via the Associated Press, http://www.nytimes.com/2008/02/27/world/americas/27iht-26textdebate.10457266.html?_r=1.

3   Profile: Nation of Islam, *Discover the Networks*, http://www.discoverthenetworks .org/groupProfile.asp?grpid=6600.

4   Manya A. Brachear, "Rev. Jeremiah A. Wright, Jr.: Pastor inspires Obama's 'audacity,'" *Chicago Tribune*, January 21, 2007, http://www.chicagotribune.com/news/chi-070121-relig_wright-archive,0,4593486.story.

5   Ariel Sabar, "Barack Obama: Putting faith out front. How the Illinois senator came to embrace religion in his life," *Christian Science Monitor*, July 16, 2007, http://www .csmonitor.com/2007/0716/p01s01-uspo.htm.

6   About Us: "Our History," Trinity United Church of Christ, Chicago, Illinois: http://www. trinitychicago.org/index.php?option=com_content&task=view&id=12&Itemid=27.

7   Barack Obama, "Obama Says You Gotta Have Faith," *AlterNet*, June 28, 2006, http://www.alternet.org/story/38260/obama_says_you_gotta_have_faith.

8   TBlumer, "Attention Stanley Kurtz Re Obama, Wright, Trumpet: I've Got You Covered," BizzyBlog.com, May 12, 2008, http://www.bizzyblog.com/2008/05/12/attention-stanley-kurtz-re-obama-wright-trumpet-ive-got-you-covered.

9   Stanley Kurtz, "Jeremiah Wright's 'Trumpet.' The content of the magazine produced by Barack Obama's pastor reveals the content of his character," *Weekly Standard*, May 19, 2008, http://www.weeklystandard.com/Content/Public/Articles/000/000/015/082ktdyi.asp.

10   Amanda Carpenter, "5 Most Anti-American Rev. Wright Quotes. Video clips of Obama's former spiritual adviser's most controversial remarks," Townhall.com, May 1, 2008, http://townhall.com/video/TheFivewithAmandaCarpenter/1450_031708Past. Jeffrey Weiss, "Obama pastor Jeremiah Wright's incendiary quotes illuminate chasm between races," *Dallas Morning News*, April 8, 2008, http://www .dallasnews.com/sharedcontent/dws/dn/religion/stories/040808dnmetwrightchas m.442a11fb.html.

11   "Obama: I never heard my pastor's trash talk. Democrat senator 'denounces' anti-American, racist rhetoric," *WorldNetDaily*, March 14, 2008, http://www.wnd .com/index.php?fa=PAGE.view&pageId=58954. BarackObamaDotCom, "Obama

Denounces Controversial Remarks," YouTube, posted March 14, 2008, http://www.
youtube.com/watch?v=_7piGy0u43c. Barack Obama, "A More Perfect Union"
(transcript), Constitution Center, Philadelphia, Pennsylvania, March 18, 2008,
http://www.npr.org/templates/story/story.php?storyId=88478467.

12 Brenda J. Elliott, "Did Obama lift his 'More Perfect Union' speech from Farrakhan's
Million Man March speech?" *RBO*, April 4, 2008, http://therealbarackobama.
wordpress.com/2008/04/04/one-degree-of-separation-did-obama-lift-his-more-
perfect-union-speech-from-farrakhans-million-man-march-speech.

13 Ben Smith, "Obama denounces Wright," *The Politico*, April 29, 2008, http://www
.politico.com/blogs/bensmith/0408/Obama_denounces_Wright.html. Ben Smith,
"Obama leaves Trinity," *Politico*, May 31, 2008, http://www.politico.com/blogs/
bensmith/0508/Reports_Obama_resigns_Trinity.html.

14 Justin McCarthy, "Sherri Shepherd: Reverend Wright's Words 'Taken Out of
Context,'" *NewsBusters*, March 19, 2008, http://newsbusters.org/blogs/justin-
mccarthy/2008/03/19/sherri-shepherd-reverend-wrights-words-taken-out-
context. Ronald Kessler, "Obama Attended Hate America Sermon," Newsmax
.com, March 16, 2008.

15 Kurtz, "Jeremiah Wright's 'Trumpet,'" May 19, 2008.

16 Debbie Schlussel, "EXCLUSIVE—Obama's Nation of Islam Staffers, Edward Said
& 'Inflexible Jews' Causing Mid-East Conflict: An Obama Insider Reveals the
Real Barack," *DebbieSchlussel.com*, January 30, 2008, http://www.debbieschlussel
.com/3356/exclusive-obamas-nation-of-islam-staffers-edward-said-inflexible-jews-
causing-mid-east-conflict-an-obama-insider-reveals-the-real-barack.

17 Aaron Klein, "Obama strategist raises money for Hillary's 'I'm white!' pastor:
Black liberation theology church hosted Farrakhan, also well-known hotbed of
anti-American sermons," *WorldNetDaily*, June 1, 2008, http://www.wnd.com/index
.php?fa=PAGE.view&pageId=65924.

18 Brit Hume, "Reverend Michael Pfleger's Hard Lesson on Public Life," *FoxNews
.com*, June 3, 2008, http://www.foxnews.com/story/0,2933,362722,00.html.

19 Aaron Klein, "Obama campaign dumps 'Hillary supremacist' priest: Minister
who served as Dem candidate's faith adviser said Clinton thought being white
entitled her to victory," *WorldNetDaily*, May 29, 2008, http://www.wnd.com/index
.php?pageId=65663.

20 Ken Dilanian, "Priest who ridiculed Clinton backed Obama," *USA Today*, May 30,
2008, http://abcnews.go.com/Politics/story?id=4966839&page=1.

21 Brenda J. Elliott, "'They Owe Us'—Obama and reparations," *RBO*, May 23, 2008,
http://therealbarackobama.wordpress.com/2008/05/23/one-degree-of-separation-
they-owe-us-obama-and-reparations-updated-2x.

22 Dr. Conrad Worrill, "An International Day of Action Against Racism," *Final Call*,
September 4, 2001, http://www.finalcall.com/perspectives/against_racism09-04-2001.
htm. Tom Robb, "Worrill, Farrakhan and Castro meet in Cuba: Carruthers Center
director travels to Havana for disaster relief conference," *Northeastern Illinois University
Independent*, October 10, 2006, http://media.www.neiuindependent.com/media/
storage/paper1122/news/2006/10/10/News/Worrill.Farrakhan.And.Castro.Meet
.In.Cuba-2340763.shtml.

23 Peter Wallsten, "Obama defined by contrasts: He has cultivated associations
with disaffected figures while keeping his own views on race issues," *Los Angeles*

Times, March 24, 2008, http://articles.latimes.com/2008/mar/24/nation/na-obama24.

24   Aaron Klein, "Meet the man at center of Obama's race controversy," WorldNetDaily.com, July 24, 2009. Available online at: http://www.wnd.com/index.php/index.php/index.php?fa=PAGE.view&pageId=104938 <http://www.wnd.com/index.php/index.php/index.php?fa=PAGE.view&pageId=104938>.

25   Laura D. Roosevelt, "A conversation with Skip Gates," *Martha's Vineyard Magazine*, August 2008 edition, http://www.mvmagazine.com/article.php?17721.

26   Aaron Klein, "Obama's radical pal slams 'racist American empire,'" *WorldNetDaily*, August 2, 2009; http://www.wnd.com/index.php?pageId=105780.

27   See http://www.youtube.com/watch?v=EEOm3NiNCAc&NR=1; video also transcribed at http://www.wnd.com/index.php?pageId=105780

28   See http://www.youtube.com/watch?v=63MjK7MlA7I&feature=related, video also transcribed at http://www.wnd.com/index.php?pageId=105780.

29   Aaron Klein, "Gates lawyer was young Obama's mentor," *WorldNetDaily*, July 24, 20090, http://www.wnd.com/index.php?pageId=104928.

30   Ibid.

31   Ibid.

32   Ibid.

33   Aaron Klein, "Obama website yanks 'Black Panthers' plug: 'It's part of the game,' says anti-white, anti-Jew leader," *WorldNetDaily*, March 19, 2008, http://www.wnd.com/index.php?fa=PAGE.view&pageId=59398.

8: THE ACORN PRESIDENT

1   Transcript of the third McCain-Obama Presidential Debate, Hofstra University, Hempstead, New York, October 15, 2008, http://www.debates.org/pages/trans2008d.html.

2   Richard Poe, "Project Vote: Extended Profile," *Discover the Networks*, 2005, http://www.discoverthenetworks.org/Articles/pvextprofile.html. Ollie A. Johnson III and Karlin L. Stanford, *Black Political Organizations in the Post-Civil Rights Era* (Rutgers University Press, 2002), 184, http://www.questia.com/read/103151521?title=Black%20Political%20Organizations%20in%20the%20Post-Civil%20Rights%20Era.

3   Jarol B. Manheim, *The Death of a Thousand Cuts: Corporate Campaigns and the Attack on the Corporation* (Lawrence Erlbaum Associates, 2001), 139, http://www.questia.com/read/107010881?title=The%20Death%20of%20a%20Thousand%20Cuts%3a%20%20Corporate%20Campaigns%20and%20the%20Attack%20on%20the%20Corporation.

4   Ibid.

5   Johnson and Stanford, *Black Political Organizations*, 184. Manheim, *Death of a Thousand Cuts*, 139.

6   Manheim, *Death of a Thousand Cuts*, 138–139.

7   Manheim, *Death of a Thousand Cuts*, 139, cites ACORN co-founder Gary Delgado, *Organizing the Movement: The Roots and Growth of ACORN* (Philadelphia: Temple University Press, 1986), 43.

8   *ACORN People's Platform*, 1990, http://web.archive.org/web/20010615002306/www.acorn.org/people's_platform.html. Scott L. Cummings, "Community

Economic Development as Progressive Politics: Toward a Grassroots Movement for Economic Justice," *Stanford Law Review* 54 (2001), http://www.questia.com/read/5000947762?title=Community%20Economic%20Development%20as%20Progressive%20Politics%3a%20Toward%20a%20Grassroots%20Movement%20for%20Economic%20Justice.

9   Manheim, *Death of a Thousand Cuts*, 140.

10   Ibid.

11   Ibid. In footnote 18 Manheim writes that the information was found on a now inactive web page, http://www.igc.org/community/reports/acornrep06.1998.content.html.

12   Manheim, *Death of a Thousand Cuts*, 140. Kim Moody, "Organizing Poor Whites," ERAP Publication, Next Left Notes—New Left Archive, undated, http://www.antiauthoritarian.net/sds_wuo/erap_organizing_poor.

13   Third McCain-Obama Presidential Debate, October 15, 2008.

14   Terry H. Anderson, *The Movement and the Sixties* (Oxford University Press, 1996), 386, http://www.questia.com/read/22777836?title=The%20Movement%20and%20the%20Sixties.

15   Sol Stern, "ACORN's Nutty Regime for Cities," *City Journal* (Spring 2003), http://www.city-journal.org/html/13_2_acorns_nutty_regime.html.

16   Toni Foulkes, "Case Study: Chicago—The Barack Obama Campaign," *Social Policy* 34, Nos. 2 & 3 (Winter–Spring 2003), http://econopundit.com/toni.pdf. Foulkes is a former ACORN board member.

17   Michael J. Gaynor, "Americans: Focus on Obama, Not Obama Appointees," *WEBCommentary.com*, September 9, 2009, http://www.webcommentary.com/php/PrintArticle.php?id=gaynorm&date=090909.

18   Foulkes, "Case Study: Chicago," 49, 50. Gretchen Reynolds, "Vote of Confidence," *Chicago Magazine* (January 1993), http://www.chicagomag.com/Chicago-Magazine/January-1993/Vote-of-Confidence.

19   Poe, *DtN*, 2005. Profile: Richard Andrew Cloward, *Wikipedia*, http://en.wikipedia.org/wiki/Richard_Cloward. Timo Kokko, "Cloward-Piven—Now it makes sense," *LSJ Blogs: People's Politics*, July 13, 2009, http://noise.typepad.com/peoples_politics/2009/07/clowardpivennow-it-makes-sense.html. Richard Cloward and Frances Fox Piven, *The Politics of Turmoil: Essays on Poverty, Race and the Urban Crisis* (New York: Vintage, 1965; 1975), 71.

20   Leon Trotsky, "The League of Communist Youth," Chapter 8 in *Platform of the Joint Opposition* (1927), http://www.marxists.org/archive/trotsky/1927/opposition/ch08.htm.

21   Reynolds, "Vote of Confidence," January 1993. Poe, *DtN*, 2005. "Zach Polett" in "Who's Who: Key Leaders of Independent Groups," NPR.org, September 23, 2009, http://www.npr.org/templates/story/story.php?storyId=93351993. Profile: America Votes, SourceWatch, http://www.sourcewatch.org/index.php?title=America_Votes. Profile: Voting For America, Inc., Zachary Polett, president, Manta.com, http://www.manta.com/company/mm2xx4b. Michael Slater, Executive Director, Letter (no subject), Project Vote, July 17, 2008, http://matthewharrington.files.wordpress.com/2009/05/project-vote-letter-to-funders-7-18-08.pdf. Slater writes that Zach Polet served part-time as Project VOTE!'s executive director until June 2008.

22   Kokko, "Cloward-Piven." Profile: Cloward-Piven Strategy, *Discover the Networks*, http://www.discoverthenetworks.org/groupProfile.asp?grpid=6967. James Simpson, "Barack Obama and the Strategy of Manufactured Crisis," *American*

Thinker, September 28, 2008, http://www.americanthinker.com/2008/09/barack_obama_and_the_strategy.html.

23 Gilbert Y. Steiner, *The State of Welfare* (Brookings Institution, 1971), 16, http://www.questia.com/read/65667334?title=The%20State%20of%20Welfare.

24 Cloward-Piven Strategy, *Dtn*.

25 Kokko, "Cloward-Piven." Cloward-Piven Strategy, *Dtn*.

26 Poe, *Dtn*, 2005.

27 Frances Fox Piven and Richard Cloward, *Regulating the Poor* (New York: Vintage Books, 1971), xiii, 348. Robert E. Weir, *Class in America: An Encyclopedia* (Greenwood Publishing, 2007), 616.

28 Poe, *Dtn*, 2005. Richard A. Cloward and Frances Fox Piven, "Trying to Break Down the Barriers," *Nation* 241 (November 2, 1985).

29 Cloward-Piven, "Trying to Break Down the Barriers." Frederic I. Solop, Nancy A. Wonders, "The Politics of Inclusion: Private Voting Rights under the Clinton Administration," *Social Justice* 22 (1995).

30 Vernon Jarrett, "Project VOTE! Brings Power to the People—Obama," *Chicago Sun-Times* (Archives), August 11, 1992. [Posted November 11, 2008, at *FreeRepublic*.com, http://www.freerepublic.com/focus/f-news/2103573/posts.]

31 Jarrett, "Project VOTE!"

32 Reynolds, "Vote of Confidence."

33 Keith Kelleher, "Growth of a Modern Union Local: A People's History of SEIU Local 880," *Just Labour: A Canadian Journal of Work and Society* 12 (Spring 2008), http://www.docstoc.com/docs/11484473/Obamas-Ties-to-Chicago-SEIU-Local-880-ACORN-Project-VOTE!

34 Foulkes, "Case Study: Chicago," 49, 50. Ryan Lizza, "Making It: How Chicago shaped Obama," *New Yorker*, July 21, 2008, http://www.newyorker.com/reporting/2008/07/21/080721fa_fact_lizza?currentPage=all.

35 Simpson, "Manufactured Crisis."

36 Sam Graham-Felsen, "ACORN Political Action Committee Endorses Obama," Organizing for America, February 21, 2008, http://my.barackobama.com/page/community/post/samgrahamfelsen/gGC7zm.

37 "Obama Never Organized with ACORN," *Fight the Smears*, October 2008, http://www.fightthesmears.com/articles/20/acornrumor.

38 Aaron Klein, "Obama website lies about ACORN ties: Campaign tries to distance senator from group convicted of voter fraud," *WorldNetDaily*, October 12, 2008, http://www.wnd.com/index.php?fa=PAGE.view&pageId=77813.

39 Keith Kelleher and Madeline Talbott, "The People Shall Rule: Holding public officials accountable in Chicago," *Shelterforce Online*, November/December 2000, http://www.nhi.org/online/issues/114/kelleher.html.

40 Anita MonCrief, "ACORN'S Layers: Mullis Was Right," *AnitaMonCrief.com*, January 15, 2009, http://anitamoncrief.blogspot.com/2009/01/acorns-layers-mullis-was-right.html.

41 Stephanie Strom, "Acorn Report Raises Issues of Legality," *New York Times*, October 21, 2008, http://www.nytimes.com/2008/10/22/us/22acorn.html?_r=2.

42 *Barnett v. Daley*, 32 F.3d 1196 (7th Cir. 1994). Anonymous Attorney, "Obama's Early Legal Career: Heavy on Advocacy for Blacks," *VDARE.com*, May 9, 2008, http://blog.vdare.com/archives/2008/05/09/obamas-early-legal-career-heavy-on-advocacy-for-blacks/print.

43 *Buycks-Roberson v. Citibank Federal Savings Bank*, 94 C 4094 (N.D. Ill. 1994), http://clearinghouse.wustl.edu/detail.php?id=10112&search=source%7Cgeneral; caseCat%7CFH;orderby%7CcaseName.

44 John Fund, "A Victory Against Voter Fraud," *Wall Street Journal*, April 29, 2008, http://online.wsj.com/public/article_print/SB120943129695651437.html.

45 Foulkes, "Case Study: Chicago," 50. *ACORN v. James R. Edgar et al.*, 880 F. Supp. 1215 (N.D. Ill. 1995). ACORN v. Edgar, 56 F.3d 791 (7th Cir. Ill. 1995). *ACORN, Equip for Equality, Inc., et al. v. Illinois State Bd. of Elections*, 75 F.3d 304 (7th Cir. 1996).

46 Frank De Zutter, "What Makes Obama Run?" *Chicago Reader*, December 8, 1995, https://securesite.chireader.com/cgi-bin/Archive/abridged2 .bat?path=1995/951208/OBAMA.

47 Ibid.

48 Stanley Kurtz, "Inside Obama's ACORN," *National Review Online*, May 29, 2008, http://article.nationalreview.com/print/?q=NDZiMjkwMDczZWl5ODdjOWYxZT IzZGIyNzEyMjE0ODI=. Madeline Talbott, "BarackBook," http://www.barackbook .com/Profiles/MadelineTalbott.htm.

49 Madeline Talbott, "BarackBook."

50 Ibid.

51 Mona Charen, "Guilty Party," *National Review Online*, September 30, 2008, http:// article.nationalreview.com/373054/guilty-party/mona-charen.

52 Foulkes, "Case Study: Chicago," 50, 51.

53 Carla Marinucci, "ACORN comes out swinging," *San Francisco Chronicle*, October 16, 2008, http://www.sfgate.com/cgi-bin/blogs/nov05election/detail?blogid=14&entry_ id=31565.

54 Jennifer Rubin, "Obama and the Woods Fund," *Pajamas Media*, September 13, 2008, http://pajamasmedia.com/blog/obama-and-the-woods-fund/2.

55 Stanley Kurtz, "Obama and Ayers Pushed Radicalism on Schools," *Wall Street Journal*, September 23, 2008, http://online.wsj.com/article/SB122212856075765367 .html?mod=rss_opinion_main.

56 Grants: 1997: by Chicago Annenberg Challenge, October-December, http://www .catalyst-chicago.org/guides/index.php?id=87#cac. Grants 1998: by Chicago Annenberg Challenge, October–December, *Catalyst Chicago*, http://www.catalyst-chicago.org/guides/?id=86. IRS Form 990-PF, Return of Private Foundation, Chicago Annenberg Challenge 1998, http://sonatabio.com/CAC/1999.pdf. IRS Form 990-PF, Return of Private Foundation, Chicago Annenberg Challenge 2001, http://sonatabio.com/CAC/2001.pdf. Fred Lucas, "Obama-Run Foundation Gave Millions to Liberal Groups, Including One Run by Bill Ayers," CNSNews.com, October 13, 2008, http://www.cnsnews.com/news/article/37441.

57 John Kifner, "28-Year-Old Snapshots Are Still Vivid, and Still Violent," *New York Times*, August 26, 1996, http://www.nytimes.com/1996/08/26/us/28-year-old-snapshots-are-still-vivid-and-still-violent.html?sec=&spon=&pagewanted=all. Mark Alper, "The Legacy of S.D.S. and Its Relevance to Today's Activists," *Next Left Notes*, circa 2006, http://antiauthoritarian.net/NLN/archive/sds.html. David J. Garrow, "Mao Mix," *Village Voice*, July 2, 2002, http://www.villagevoice.com/2002-07-02/books/mao-mix. Stephen Diamond, "Who 'sent' Obama?" *Global Labor and Politics*, October 13, 2008, http://globallabor.blogspot.com/2008/04/who-sent-obama.html.

58   Mike Klonsky's *Small Talk* blog no longer includes this August 2, 2006, article.

59   Diana Nelson, "Guilt by association is wrong," *Chicago Tribune*, October 13, 2008, http://archives.chicagotribune.com/2008/oct/13/nation/chi-oped1013ayersoct13.

60   "The Community Renewal Society presents Here's to You. CATALYST's 10th Anniversary Prom, October 12, 2000," *Catalyst Chicago*, http://web.archive.org/web/20010124111600/www.catalyst-chicago.org/10-99/109prom.htm.

61   Program: "Going Beyond Taking Back Our Country," 48th Annual Dinner honoring Rev. Calvin Morris, Executive Director, Community Renewal Society, Eugene V. Debs–Norman Thomas–Michael Harrington Dinner, April 28, 2006, Chicago, Illinois, http://www.chicagodsa.org/d2006/2006book.pdf.

62   Linda Lenz, "Annenberg Challenge a radical enclave? Gimme a break! There is nothing to condemn about Ayers' leadership over the past 20 years," *Chicago Sun-Times*, August 30, 2008 available online at: http://www.freerepublic.com/focus/f-news/2071891/posts.

63   Stanley Kurtz, "Obama's Acorn Problem," *National Review Online*, August 22, 2008, http://corner.nationalreview.com/post/?q=MDQ0MDBmMjQwZmYxYzhlZjc 3ZGFkZjlkOWJlMTk2MWE=. David M. Brown, "Obama to amend report on $800,000 in spending," *Pittsburgh Tribune-Review*, August 22, 2008, http://www .pittsburghlive.com/x/pittsburghtrib/news/election/s_584284.html.

64   Brown, "Obama to amend report," August 22, 2008.

65   Katrina vanden Heuvel, "ACORN: Obama Gets It," *The Nation*, February 23, 2008, http://www.thenation.com/blogs/state_of_change/289192.

66   Ibid.

67   Press Release: "ACORN's Political Action Committee Endorses Obama," *ACORN.org*, February 21, 2008, http://www.acorn.org/index.php?id=8540&tx_ ttnews%5bpointer%5d=7&tx_ttnews%5btt_news%5d=21759&tx_ttnews%5bback Pid%5d=8359&cHash=c9638cbd58.

68   Brown, "Obama to amend report."

69   Ibid.

70   Charlotte Allen, "From Little ACORNs, Big Scandals Grow. Barack Obama: torn between two models of community organizing," *Weekly Standard*, November 3, 2008, http://www.weeklystandard.com/Content/Public/ Articles/000/000/015/746zemwq.asp?pg=1.

71   Harry C. Boyte, *The Backyard Revolution: Understanding the New Citizen Movement* (Philadelphia: Temple University Press, 1980), 93.

72   Ibid.

73   Ibid., 94.

74   Ibid.

75   Ibid.

76   Sam Graham-Felsen, "ACORN Political Action Committee Endorses Obama," Organizing for America, February 21, 2008, http://my.barackobama.com/page/ community/post/samgrahamfelsen/gGC7zm.

77   Transcript of the Third McCain-Obama Presidential Debate, October 15, 2008.

78   Charen, "Guilty Party." Deroy Murdock, "Obama Squirrels Away His Links to ACORN. But the truth is, they are old and dear friends," *National Review Online*, October 16, 2008, http://article.nationalreview.com/?q=ZGY1MWNhZDVlYWY2 YzhmZTIwMmE0NTNmODU3YzZjNDE=.

9: OBAMA'S SOCIALIST-LED UNION ARMY

1   Ben, "Members of ACORN's Advisory Board," *The Political Inquirer*, September 24, 2009, http://politicalinquirer.com/2009/09/24/members-of-acorns-advisory-board.

2   Union Membership: Largest Unions (2003), *WorkingLife.org*, www.workinglife .org/wiki/index.php?page=Union+Membership%3A+Largest+Unions+(2003).

3   Brenda J. Elliott, "POTUS and SEIU: 'as tight as Heidi Klum and a new pair of jeans'? " RBO, September 27, 2009, http://therealbarackobama.wordpress .com/2009/09/27/potus-and-seiu-as-tight-as-heidi-klum-and-a-new-pair-of-jeans.

4   Old Marine, "The Shadow Menace (Part 2 – SEIU's Andrew Stern)," A Scream in the Wilderness/Townhall.com blog, August 31, 2009, http://ascream.blogtownhall .com/2009/08/31/the_shadow_menace_part_2_–_seiu's_andrew_stern.thtml.

5   Chelsea Schilling, "Obama: 'We're going to paint nation purple with SEIU.' Explains how he 'built political power on south side of Chicago,'" *WorldNetDaily*, October 13, 2009, http://www.wnd.com/index.php?pageId=112780.

6   Schilling, "Obama." "Breitbart tv » Uncovered Video Obama Leads SEIU Chant After Vowing to Paint the Nation Purple," YouTube, posted October 12, 2009, http://www.youtube.com/watch?v=DQj-xBH30-I.

7   "In Final 72-Hour Push, SEIU Members Get Out the Vote for Barack Obama and Other Working Family Candidates Across the Country," *SEIU.org*, October 31, 2008, http://www.seiu.org/2008/10/in-final-72-hour-push-seiu-members-get-out-the-vote-for-barack-obama-and-other-working-family-candid.php.

8   Peter Nicholas, "Obama's curiously close labor friendship: SEIU chief Andy Stern enjoys unusual access to the White House, but some in the fractious labor movement question its value," *Los Angeles Times*, June 28, 2009, http://74.125.113.132/search?q=cache:7FkZ55HVHUUJ:articles.latimes .com/2009/jun/28/nation/na-stern28+Stern+L.A.+Times+visits+the+White+ House+about+once+a+week.&cd=1&hl=en&ct=clnk&gl=us.

9   Foon Rhee, "Obama gets big union nod," *Boston Globe*, February 15, 2008, http:// www.boston.com/news/politics/politicalintelligence/2008/02/obama_poised_ to.htm.

10   Michael Gaynor, "Stern nomination would expose SEIU fraud," *Union News* blog, November 10, 2008, http://theunionnews.blogspot.com/2008/11/stern-nomination-would-expose-seiu.html. Mike Allen, "Dems sketch Obama staff, Cabinet," *The Politico*, October 31, 2008, http://dyn.politico.com/printstory .cfm?uuid=542710E6-18FE-70B2-A8A346B36828470E.

11   "Follow the Money: ACORN, SEIU and their Political Allies," Staff Report, U.S. House of Representatives, 111th Congress, Committee on Oversight and Government Reform, February 18, 2010; http://republicans.oversight.house.gov/images/stories/Re ports/20100218followthemoneyacornseiuandtheirpoliticalallies.pdf.

12   Nicholas, "Obama's curiously close labor friendship."

13   Profile: Andrew Stern, *Discover the Networks*, http://www.discoverthenetworks.org/ individualProfile.asp?indid=1830.

14   Ben Johnson, "Communists Against the Military," *FrontPageMagazine.com*, July 14, 2005, http://97.74.65.51/readArticle.aspx?ARTID=7938.

15   Profile: Michael Harrington, *Discover the Networks*, http://www.discoverthenetworks .org/individualProfile.asp?indid=1165.

16   "Obama Caught Between Two Masters—Goldman Sachs & SEIU—Part 2. SEIU," *BigNews.
       biz*, September 24, 2009, http://www.bignews.biz/?id=815841&keys=Goldman-
       SEIU-Obama-healthcare. Ponte, July 14, 2004.

17   Comment #102 by michael098762001, *Firedoglake.com*, February 19, 2009,
       http://christyhardinsmith.firedoglake.com/2009/02/19/cocktails-with-obama-last-
       nights-guest-list-shows-focus-on-efca/comment-page-1/#comment-2510. "Stern
       calls on CEOs to solve health care," LBO ListServ, July 21, 2006, http://mailman
       .lbo-talk.org/2006/2006-July/013850.html. Profile: Andrew Stern, *Discover the
       Networks*.

18   Lowell Ponte, "How Socialist Unions Rule the Democratic Party," *FrontPageMag
       .com*, July 14, 2004, http://97.74.65.51/readArticle.aspx?ARTID=12216. Old
       Marine," August 31, 2009.

19   Jerry White, "Divisions among union officials over 'reform' of AFL-CIO," World
       Socialist Website, January 14, 2005, http://www.wsws.org/articles/2005/feb2005/
       afl-f14.shtml.

20   Ibid.

21   Ibid.

22   Pete Winn, "Unions Continue to Push Card Check Legislation; Senate Fate
       Uncertain," *CNSNews.com*, February 2, 2009, http://www.cnsnews.com/PUBLIC/
       Content/Article.aspx?rsrcid=42822.

23   Old Marine, August 31, 2009.

24   Profile: Andrew Stern, *Dtn*. Profile: Shadow Party, *Discover the Networks*, http://
       www.discoverthenetworks.org/groupProfile.asp?grpid=6706.

25   *United States of America v. Rod R. Blagojevich and John Harris* (N.D. Ill. 2008),
       http://www.chicagotribune.com/media/acrobat/2008-12/43789434.pdf.

26   John Kass, "Governor has one choice left: Sing?" *Chicago Tribune*, December 9,
       2008, http://archives.chicagotribune.com/2008/dec/09/news/chi-kass-blago-
       extradec09.

27   Ben Smith, "Source: 'SEIU official' was Stern," *Politico*, December 9, 2008, http://
       www.politico.com/blogs/bensmith/1208/Source_SEIU_official_was_Stern.html.

28   Jennifer Rubin, "The Plot Thickens," *Commentary Magazine*, December 9, 2008,
       http://www.commentarymagazine.com/blogs/index.php/rubin/46122.

29   Clare Ansberry, "Blagojevich and Union Have Longstanding Ties,"
       Wall Street Journal, December 13, 2008, http://online.wsj.com/article/
       SB122912760515203213.html.

30   Profile: Tom Balanoff, *SEIU.org*, http://www.seiu1.org/aboutlocal1/officersandstaff/
       president/default.aspx.

31   Stephen Diamond, "Who is Tom Balanoff? Obama, SEIU and the Senate For Sale
       Scandal," *Global Labor and Politics*, December 14, 2008, http://globallabor.blogspot
       .com/2008/12/who-is-tom-balanoff-obama-seiu-and_7794.html.

32   Robert McChesney, Discover the Networks; http://www.discoverthenetworks.org/
       individualProfile.asp?indid=2227.

33   Profile: Tom Balanoff, *SEIU.org*.

34   Ron Baiman, "Reorganized Illinois Citizen Action," New Ground 56, January/
       February 1996, http://www.chicagodsa.org/ngarchive/ng56.html#anchor1041720.

35   Diamond, "Who is Tom Balanoff?" Josh Kalven, "PI @ DNC: Interview With
       Tom Balanoff," *Progress Illinois*, August 28, 2008, http://www.progressillinois
       .com/2008/08/28/pi-dnc-balanoff-interview.

36   Diamond, "Who is Tom Balanoff?" *100 Things You Should Know About Communism in the U.S.A.*, Committee on Un-American Activities, U.S. House of Representatives, Appendix: Principle officers and offices of the Communist Party, U.S.A., as of 1947 (Organizer South Chicago section—James Balanoff, Jr., page 22), http://debs .indstate.edu/u588o55_1948.pdf.

37   Program: Democratic Socialists of America, 44th Annual Dinner Honoring Tom Balanoff, SEIU Local 1; 2002 Debs–Thomas–Harrington Dinner, May 10, 2002, http://www.chicagodsa.org/2002Book.pdf. "You have been a fierce partisan for social and economic justice throughout your distinguished career as an advocate for working people."

38   Diamond, "Who is Tom Balanoff? Joseph K. Cooper, "Nevada: Tom Balanoff. Trailing with unions, Obama camp makes labor pitch to NV press," *Politicker.com*, December 3, 2007, http://www.politicker.com/nevada/tags/tom-balanoff.

39   Andy Stern, *A Country That Works: Getting America Back on Track* (Free Press, May 2006).

40   Glenn Beck, "The 223 year problem?" *GlennBeck.com*, November 13, 2009, http://www.glennbeck.com/content/articles/article/198/33075.

41   Interview: Andrew Stern with Maria Bartiromo, *CNBC.com*, November 6, 2009, http://www.cnbc.com/id/15840232?play=1&video=1324296007.

42   Meredith Jessup, "SEIU President Andy Stern Ready to 'Share the Wealth,' Solve America's '223-Year-Old Problems,'" Townhall.com, November 13, 2009, http:// townhall.com/blog/g/90353b37-eb09-4887-af70-dc7eb672141a.

43   Editors, "Q&A: SEIU President Andy Stern," *Policy Today*, September 8, 2005, http://www.policytoday.com/index.php?option=com_content&task=view&a mp;id=27&Itemid=149.

44   Stern, *A Country That Works*, 112.

45   Ben, "Members of ACORN's Advisory Board," *Political Inquirer*, September 24, 2009. "ACORN plans independent investigation, 'Pimp' video prompts examination of controversial advocacy group," Associated Press, September 16, 2009, http://www.msnbc.msn.com/id/32880434/ns/politics-more_politics. Andrew Breitbart, "AP Whitewashes My Public Statement on Whitewashed ACORN Investigation ," *BigGovernment.com*, December 7, 2009, http:// biggovernment.com/2009/12/07/ap-whitewashes-my-public-statement-on-whitewashed-acorn-investigation.

46   Signatories to Progressives for Obama, http://progressivesforobama.blogspot .com/2008/03/progressives-for-obama_25.html.

47   Nicholas, "Obama's curiously close labor friendship."

48   Leon Fink and Brian Greenberg, *Upheaval in the Quiet Zone. 1199 SEIU and the Politics of Health Care Unionism* (University of Illinois Press, 2009), http://www.press .uillinois.edu/books/catalog/38cge4gn9780252076053.html.

49   Brenda J. Elliott, "Hispanic radicals in Congress 'marching the nation inevitably toward its self-proclaimed socialist ideal' since 1996," RBO, May 1, 2009, available online at: http://therealbarackobama.wordpress.com/2009/05/17/hispanic-radicals-in-congress-marching-the-nation-inevitably-toward-its-self-proclaimed-socialist-ideal-since-1996. "SEIU Healthcare's Dennis Rivera: 'There's No Time to Waste,'" *SEIU.org*, March 5, 2009, http://www.seiu.org/2009/03/seiu-healthcares-dennis-rivera-theres-no-time-to-waste.php.

50   J. Gonzalez, "New York labor leader Dennis Rivera in shady Puerto Rico union

deal," *New York Daily News*, March 4, 2008, http://www.nydailynews.com/
news/2008/02/29/2008-02-29_new_york_labor_leader_dennis_rivera_in_s.html.

51 Brenda J. Elliott, "Obama superdelegate indicted," *RBO*, March 27, 2008, http://
therealbarackobama.wordpress.com/2008/03/27/one-degree-of-separation-obama-
superdelegate-indicted-updated.

52 Brenda J. Elliott, "Time for Rightie Bloggers to Give Glenn Beck Credit Where
Credit is Due," *RBO*, September 28, 2009, http://therealbarackobama.wordpress
.com/2009/09/28/time-for-rightie-bloggers-to-give-glenn-beck-credit-where-
credit-is-due.

53 Trevor Loudon, "Parallel Lives? Obama's 'Go To' Man, Patrick Gaspard and New
York Socialism," *RBO*, October 1, 2009, http://therealbarackobama.wordpress
.com/2009/10/01/loudon-parallel-lives-obamas-go-to-man-patrick-gaspard-and-
new-york-socialism.

54 David A. Patten, "Obama's Top Aide Gaspard Tied to ACORN," *Newsmax.com*,
September 28, 2009, http://www.newsmax.com/insidecover/obama_acorn_
gaspard/2009/09/28/265678.html.

55 Loudon, "Parallel Lives?"

56 Speaker's Profile: Anna Burger, International Secretary Treasurer, SEIU, Center
for American Progress, http://www.americanprogress.org/events/special_events/
commongood_bios.html/#burger.

57 "Obama Caught Between Two Masters—Goldman Sachs & SEIU—Part 2.
SEIU," *BigNews.biz*, September 24, 2009, http://www.bignews.biz/?id=815841
&keys=Goldman-SEIU-Obama-healthcare.

58 Speaker's Profile: Anna Burger, Center for American Progress.

59 Democratic Super Delegates, *Washington Post*, http://www.washingtonpost.com/
wp-srv/politics/interactives/campaign08/primaries/2008_superdelegates.html.

60 Brenda J. Elliott, "Accountability NOW—The radical OBORG arrives as
MoveOn.org, Left Blogistan and unions unite," *RBO*, February 26, 2009,
http://therealbarackobama.wordpress.com/2009/02/26/accountability-now-
the-radical-oborg-arrives-as-moveonorg-left-blogistan-and-unions-unite.
Press Release: "Progressive Activists Launch 2010 Accountability Campaign,"
Accountability Now, February 26, 2009, http://action.firedoglake.com/page/
content/2010accountability.

61 Accountability Now website, http://accountabilitynowpac.com.

62 Jim Rutenberg, "Bloggers and Unions Join Forces to Push Democrats to Left,"
New York Times, February 26, 2009, http://www.nytimes.com/2009/02/27/us/
politics/27web-liberals.html?_r=1&partner=rss&emc=rss.

63 BarbinMD, "Accountability Now PAC," DailyKos, February 26, 2009, http://www
.dailykos.com/storyonly/2009/2/26/123249/598/594/702147.

64 Petition: Sign-up to help re-defeat Joe Lieberman, Firedoglake, circa February
2009, http://action.firedoglake.com/page/s/DefeatLieberman.

65 Press Release: Health Care for America Now, "$40 Million Health Care Campaign
to Launch, Announce New National Ad," Reuters, July 7, 2008, http://www
.reuters.com/article/pressRelease/idUS167523+07-Jul-2008+PRN20080707.

66 Henry J. Pulizzi, "Obama Demands Action on Economy, Names Advisory
Panel," *Wall Street Journal*, February 6, 2009, http://online.wsj.com/article/
SB123391937985456623.html?mod=rss_topics_obama.

67 Tula Connell, "Trumka Named to Obama Economic Advisory Panel," AFL-CIO

Blog, February 6, 2009, http://blog.aflcio.org/2009/02/06/trumka-named-to-obama-economic-advisory-panel.

68 Signatories to Progressives for Obama.

69 DSA 2001 Convention Keynote Address. Eliseo Medina, International Executive Vice President, Service Employees International Union, http://www.dsausa.org/convention2k1/eliseo.html.

70 Our Structure, Democratic Socialists of America, http://www.dsausa.org/about/structure.html. "Eliseo Medina named an Honorary Chair of DSA," Democratic Socialists of America, August 9, 2004, http://www.dsausa.org/LatestNews/2004/medina.html.

71 Trevor Loudon, "Hilda Solis — Obama Labor Secretary's Socialist Connections," *RBO*, December 21, 2008, http://therealbarackobama.wordpress.com/2008/12/21/loudon-hilda-solis-obama-labor-secretarys-socialist-connections.

72 "Glenn Beck: Time to Re-found America," *GlennBeck.com*, September 15, 2009, http://www.glennbeck.com/content/articles/article/198/30536. There does not appear to be any other printed record of Obama's remarks.

73 "Latinos pin hopes of immigration reform on Obama. After helping Barack Obama win the election, Latinos seek to remind him to enact comprehensive immigration reform," McClatchy Newspapers, November 24, 2008, http://www.guardian.co.uk/world/2008/nov/24/latinos-immigration-reform-obama.

74 Joaquin Guerra, "Foundation Laid for Needed Immigration Reform," SEIU Blog, August 20, 2009, http://www.seiu.org/2009/08/foundation-laid-for-needed-immigration-reform-1.php.

75 Apollo Alliance Board of Directors, http://apolloalliance.org/about/board.

76 Gerald Hudson, "SEIU VP Explains Strategy: Build a Progressive Movement with Labor at Its Core," *Talking Union*, January 22, 2009, http://talkingunion.wordpress.com/2009/01/22/building-a-new-progressive-movement-with-labor-at-its-core.

77 Brenda J. Elliott, "Unions and activists to Obama—You Owe Us," *RBO*, November 11, 2008, http://therealbarackobama.wordpress.com/2008/11/11/unions-and-activists-to-obama-you-owe-us/2. "Our Board," Center for Community Change, accessed November 11, 2009, http://www.communitychange.org/who-we-are/our-board.

78 Matthew Vadum, "Introducing Leftist Agitator Deepak Bhargava," *NewsRealBlog*, October 6, 2009, http://newsrealblog.com/2009/10/06/introducing-leftist-agitator-deepak-bhargava."Who We Are," Center for Community Change, http://www.communitychange.org/who-we-are/who-we-are.

79 Heartland Democratic Presidential Forum, December 1, 2007, CSPAN Video Library, http://www.c-spanvideo.org/program/id/184195. Quote from Investors' Business Daily cited by Jillian Becker, "Be afraid of an Obama presidency," *The Atheist Conservative*, October 14, 2008, http://www.theatheistconservative.com/2008/10/14/be-afraid-of-an-obama-presidency.

80 Trevor Loudon, "Deepak Bhargava 'Advancing Change in the Age of Obama,'" *RBO*, October 8, 2009, http://therealbarackobama.wordpress.com/2009/10/08/loudon-deepak-bhargava-advancing-change-in-the-age-of-obama.

81 Profile: Deepak Bhargava, Center for Community Change, http://www.communitychange.org/who-we-are/our-staff/bios/deepak-bhargava.

82 Deepak Bhargava, "Update on TANF [Temporary Assistance for Needy Families]," Democratic Socialists of America, published online in 2003, http://www.dsausa.org/lowwage/Documents/2003/TANF3.html.

83   Profile: Deepak Bhargava, Center for Community Change.

84   National Organizations Affiliated With UFPJ, *knology.net*, July 17, 2007, http://www.knology.net/~bilrum/UFPJGroups071607.htm.

85   Vadum, "Introducing Leftist Agitator Deepak Bhargava."

86   Board of Directors, Organizer's Forum, accessed November 11, 2009, http://organizersforum.org/index.php?id=352.

87   "Resolution on the 2008 Presidential Election," *Left*/Democratic Socialists of America, Summer 2008, http://www.dsausa.org/dl/Summer_2008.pdf.

88   Brenda J. Elliott, "Obama and the Marxist Socialist radical members of Congress," *RBO*, October 22, 2008, http://therealbarackobama.wordpress.com/2008/10/22/obama-and-the-marxist-socialist-radical-members-of-congress.

89   Elliott, "Obama and the Marxist Socialist radical members of Congress."

90   Board of Trustees, Institute for Policy Studies, http://www.ips-dc.org/about/trustees.

91   John Koblin, "*The Nation* (Sort Of?) Endorses Obama," *New York Observer*, January 31, 2008, http://www.observer.com/2008/nation-sort-endorses-obama.

92   Elliott, "Obama and the Marxist Socialist radical members of Congress."

93   Ibid.

94   Ibid.

95   Henry Lamb, "Are the Communists Coming?," Canada Free Press, October 8, 2007, http://www.canadafreepress.com/index.php/article/149.

96   Kurt Schulzke, "Communist Party USA PAC Chair endorses Obama," *Contraries*, October 12, 2008, http://iperceive.net/communist-party-usa-pac-chair-endorses-obama.

97   Dateline D.C., "The wrong kind of 'change,'" *Pittsburgh Tribune*, October 26, 2008, http://www.pittsburghlive.com/x/pittsburghtrib/opinion/columnists/datelinedc/s_595082.html.

98   Brenda J. Elliott, "CPUSA's expectations for Obama," *RBO*, November 20, 2008, http://therealbarackobama.wordpress.com/2008/11/20/cpusas-expectations-for-obama.

99   Brenda J. Elliott, "Communist Party USA Clubs 'springing up like dandelions with warm spring rains in Minnesota' — all in the 'era' of 'our friend' Obama," *RBO*, March 1, 2009, http://therealbarackobama.wordpress.com/2009/03/01/communist-party-usa-clubs-springing-up-like-dandelions-with-warm-spring-rains-in-minnesota-all-in-the-era-of-our-friend-obama.

100 Ibid.

101 Terry Albano, "Will progressives respond?" *PA (Political Affairs)* Editors Blog, January 31, 2008, http://paeditorsblog.blogspot.com/2008/01/will-progressives-respond.html.

102 Rosalio Munoz, "Southern California Latinos Rally for Obama," *PA (Political Affairs)* Editors Blog, November 5, 2008, http://paeditorsblog.blogspot.com/2008/02/southern-california-latinos-rally-for.html.

103 Trevor Loudon, "Communists Muster Latino Vote for Barack Obama," *New Zeal*, February 6, 2008, http://newzeal.blogspot.com/2008/02/obama-file-11-communists-muster-latino.html.

104 Joelle Fishman, "National Committee Election Report," *PA (Political Affairs)* Editors Blog, November 15, 2008, http://paeditorsblog.blogspot.com/2008/11/national-committee-political-report.html.

105 Ibid.

10: OBAMA'S TOP GUNS EXPOSED

1   Peter Wallsten, "Van Jones decries 'lies and distortions,' quits as Obama's environmental advisor," *Los Angeles Times*, September 7, 2009, http://www.latimes.com/news/nationworld/nation/healthcare/la-na-van-jones7-2009sep07,0,6923895.story.

2   Scott Wilson and Garance Franke-Ruta, "White House Adviser Van Jones Resigns Amid Controversy Over Past Activism," *Washington Post*, September 6, 2009, http://voices.washingtonpost.com/44/2009/09/06/van_jones_resigns.html?wprss=44.

3   Aaron Klein, "White House adviser immortalized socialist activist: Founded group named after leader with ties to Weatherman terrorists," *WorldNetDaily*, April 14, 2009, http://www.wnd.com/index.php?fa=PAGE.view&pageId=95013.

4   Eliza Strickland, "The New Face of Environmentalism," *East Bay Express*, November 2, 2005, http://www.truthout.org/article/eliza-strickland-the-new-face-environmentalism.

5   Aaron Klein, "Czar's 'communist manifesto' scrubbed from Net. Founded group with 'commitment to fundamental ideas of Marxism-Leninism,'" *WorldNetDaily*, August 30, 2009, http://www.wnd.com/index.php?fa=PAGE.view&pageId=108445.

6   Ibid.

7   Aaron Klein, "White House czar urged 'resistance' against U.S: Main speaker at rally sponsored by organization associated with Revolutionary Communist Party," *WorldNetDaily*, August 31, 2009, http://www.wnd.com/index.php?fa=PAGE.view&pageId=108553.

8   Aaron Klein, "Obama czar: U.S. was 'apartheid regime': Demands 'theology of resistance, liberation' to transform society," *WorldNetDaily*, September 3, 2009, http://www.wnd.com/index.php?fa=PAGE.view&pageId=108790. Aaron Klein, "Van Jones: 'Resist' against police. Anti-cop mission drawn up by Black Panther group," *WorldNetDaily*, September 4, 2009, http://www.wnd.com/index.php?fa=PAGE.view&pageId=108900. Aaron Klein, "Czar: 'Spread the wealth! Change the whole system.' Using White House position to push communist policies?" *WorldNetDaily*, August 30, 2009, http://www.wnd.com/index.php?fa=PAGE.view&pageId=108441. Amanda Carpenter, "Green jobs czar signed 'truther' statement in 2004," *Washington Times*, September 3, 2009, http://www.washingtontimes.com/weblogs/back-story/2009/sep/03/green-jobs-czar-signed-truther-statement-in-2004/?feat=home_blogs. "Van Jones at the Berkeley Conference on Spiritual Activism," Google Video, 2006, http://video.google.com/videoplay?docid=-275597845580120006&ei=mdWfSo4HhPTaApi0iJUH&q=%22van+jones%22&hl=en#. Aaron Klein, "Van Jones: 'Resist' against police: Anti-cop mission drawn up by Black Panther group," *WorldNetDaily*, September 4, 2009, http://www.wnd.com/index.php?fa=PAGE.view&pageId=108900. Note: as of this writing, the statement is available online at the Revolutionary Communist Party USA at http://www.rwor.org/a/066/022-en.html.

9   Klein, "White House adviser immortalized socialist activist."

10   Wilson and Franke-Ruta, "White House Adviser Van Jones Resigns."

11   "'Special Report' Panel on Green Jobs Czar Van Jones' Resignation," Special Report with Bret Baier, *FoxNews.com*, September 8, 2009, http://www.foxnews.com/story/0,2933,547920,00.html.

12   Robert Draper, "The Ultimate Obama Insider," *New York Times*, July 26, 2009,
      http://www.nytimes.com/2009/07/26/magazine/26jarrett-t.html.

13   Ibid.

14   Profile: Valerie Jarrett, *Discover the Networks*, http://www.discoverthenetworks.org/
      individualProfile.asp?indid=2418.

15   Trevor Loudon, "Barack Obama, Frank Marshall Davis, Vernon Jarrett—One
      Degree of Separation," *RBO*, October 18, 2008, http://therealbarackobama
      .wordpress.com/2008/10/18/loudon-barack-obama-frank-marshall-davis-vernon-
      jarrett-one-degree-of-separation.

16   Aaron Klein, "Van Jones: 'Resist' against police. Anti-cop mission drawn up by
      Black Panther group," *WorldNetDaily*, September 4, 2009, http://www.wnd.com/
      index.php?pageId=109222.

17   Yvonne Shinhoster Lamb, "Vernon Jarrett, 84; Journalist, Crusader," *Washington
      Post*, May 25, 2004, http://www.washingtonpost.com/wp-dyn/articles/A53239-
      2004May24.html.

18   Trevor Loudon, "Hard Evidence! Proof That Obama's Hawaii and
      Chicago Communist Networks Were Linked?" *RBO*, June 1, 2009; http://
      therealbarackobama.wordpress.com/2009/06/01/loudon-hard-evidence-proof-
      that-obamas-hawaii-and-chicago-communist-networks-were-linked.

19   Lynn Sweet, "Ms. Jarrett Goes To Washington," *Daily Beast*, November 24, 2008,
      http://www.thedailybeast.com/blogs-and-stories/2008-11-24/ms-jarrett-goes-to-
      washington/full.

20   Bundler: Marilyn Katz, WhiteHouseforSale/Public Citizen, http://www
      .whitehouseforsale.org/bundler.cfm?Bundler=13133.

21   Profile: Marilyn Katz, *Discover the Networks*, http://www.discoverthenetworks.org/
      individualProfile.asp?indid=2417.

22   Jo Becker and Christopher Drew, "Pragmatic Politics, Forged on the South
      Side," *New York Times*, May 11, 2008, http://www.nytimes.com/2008/05/11/
      us/politics/11chicago.html?pagewanted=2&_r=1&hp&adxnnlx=1210449878-
      vOvoJXUhZbK5cVCmk9NAkQ.

23   Jodi Kantor, "An Old Hometown Mentor, Still at Obama's Side," *New York Times*,
      November 24, 2008, http://www.nytimes.com/2008/11/24/us/politics/24jarrett .html.

24   John McCormick, "Blagojevich Says Emanuel Wanted to Reclaim House Seat,"
      Bloomberg News, August 31, 2009, http://www.bloomberg.com/apps/news?pid=2
      0601070&sid=aPeQzhEy32io.

25   Seth Gitell, "A Cog in the Chicago Machine?," *New York Sun*, July 8, 2008, http://
      www.nysun.com/opinion/a-cog-in-the-chicago-machine/81385.

26   Becker and Drew, "Pragmatic Politics," 5.

27   Ibid.

28   Ibid.

29   Ibid.

30   Dennis W. Johnson, *No Place for Amateurs: How Political Consultants Are Reshaping
      American Democracy* (Routledge, 2001), 260.

31   Doug Ireland, "Daley's Commerce: William Daley Seems to Fit Ron Brown's
      Shoes—a Master of 'Pinstripe Patronage,'" *The Nation*, Vol. 264, February 3, 1997.

32   "Movers and Shakers: David Axelrod," *Campaigns & Elections*, July 1994, 57. Cheryl
      Lavin, "Hooked on Politics: Media Consultant David Axelrod Now Shapes the
      News instead of Reporting It," *Chicago Tribune*, March 25, 1992, C1.

33   Ibid.

34   Ibid.

35   Ibid.

36   David Axelrod, Senior Advisor David Axelrod, White House Staff, *WhiteHouse.gov*, http://www.whitehouse.gov/administration/staff/david-axelrod.

37   Ibid.

38   Trevor Loudon, "The Axelrod Axis—Who Is Behind the Man Behind Obama?," *RBO*, October 30, 2008, http://therealbarackobama.wordpress.com/2008/10/30/loudon-the-axelrod-axis-who-is-behind-the-man-behind-obama.

39   "Who Is David Axelrod—Obama's Political Advisor?," Traditional Values Coalition, March 5, 2008, http://www.traditionalvalues.org/read/3275/who-is-david-axelrod--obamas-political-advisor.

40   Loudon cites: "David Canter, 81, lawyer, activist," *Chicago Sun-Times*, August 30, 2004, http://www.highbeam.com/doc/1P2-1547453.html.

41   Marc Canter, "My family has been outed—we're dam Commies—but we ain't paid to be," Marc's Voice, November 3, 2008, http://blog.broadbandmechanics.com/2008/11/03/my-family-has-been-outed-were-dam-commies-but-we-aint-paid-to-be.

42   Profile: Don Rose, *NegroArtist.com*, http://www.negroartist.com/writings/DON%20ROSE.htm.

43   Loudon, "The Axelrod Axis."

44   Canter, "My family has been outed."

45   Trevor Loudon, "The Paid Soviet Agent Behind Axelrod and Obama," *RBO*, November 1, 2008, http://therealbarackobama.wordpress.com/2008/11/01/loudon-the-paid-soviet-agent-behind-axelrod-and-obama.

46   Max Friedman, "A View From the Right: The Post and Me," *Augusta Free Press*, August 13, 2008, http://www.freerepublic.com/focus/f-news/2031236/posts.

47   "IVI-IPO Welcomes New & Returning Members," Action Bulletin, IVI-IPO, December 2003, http://www.iviipo.org/iviipodec2003-rev.pdf.

48   "Friends of Barack . . . David Axelrod and Valerie Jarrett will carry new weight in the White House," *Newsweek*, December 20, 2008, http://www.newsweek.com/id/176315.

49   Brad Haynes and T.W. Farnum, "Browner's Husband Lobbied on Energy Issues," *Wall Street Journal*, December 11, 2008, http://online.wsj.com/article/SB122903665464999775.html. Profile: Carol Browner, *Discover the Networks*, http://www.discoverthenetworks.org/individualProfile.asp?indid=2364.

50   Omri, "Of Course: Obama Energy Czar Carol Browner Sits on a Socialist International Commission," *Mere Rhetoric*, January 3, 2009, http://www.mererhetoric.com/archives/11275315.html.

51   Nick Loris, "Our Socialist Energy Czar," The Foundry/Heritage Foundation, January 7, 2009, http://blog.heritage.org/2009/01/07/our-socialist-energy-czar.

52   Editorial: "Browner is an environmental radical—and a socialist (seriously)," *Washington Examiner*, January 9, 2009,http://www.washingtonexaminer.com/opinion/Browner_is_an_environmental_radical__and_a_socialist_seriously_010809.html.

53   Stephen Dinan, "Obama climate czar has socialist ties," *Washington Times*, January 12, 2009, http://www.washingtontimes.com/news/2009/jan/12/obama-climate-czar-has-socialist-ties. "Socialist International Commission for a Sustainable World

Society," Socialist International, December 4, 2006, http://melbourne.indymedia
.org/news/2006/12/133110.php.

54 "Browner is an environmental radical, *Washington Examiner.*

55 Dinan, "Obama climate czar has socialist ties."

56 Ibid.

57 Profile: Carol Browner, *Discover the Networks.*

58 Trevor Loudon, "Obama's 'Energy Czar' and the Socialists—Foreign and Domestic,"
    RBO, January 13, 2009, http://therealbarackobama.wordpress.com/2009/01/13/
    loudon-obamas-energy-czar-and-the-socialists-foreign-and-domestic.

59 Trevor Loudon, "Obama's Socialist Appointees—Where is the Spotlight?," *RBO*,
    September 23, 2009, http://therealbarackobama.wordpress.com/2009/09/23/
    loudon-obamas-socialist-appointees-where-is-the-spotlight.

60 Ben Lieberman, "Obama's 'Extreme Team' on Energy," The Heritage Foundation,
    February 6, 2009, http://www.foxnews.com/story/0,2933,489476,00.html.

61 "Samantha Power '99 to join National Security Council," Harvard Law School,
    January 30, 2009, http://www.law.harvard.edu/news/2009/01/30_power.html.
    Profile: Samantha Power, *WhoRunsGov.com*, http://www.whorunsgov.com/Profiles/
    Samantha_Power.

62 Profile: Samantha Power, John F. Kennedy School of Government, Harvard
    University, http://www.hks.harvard.edu/about/faculty-staff-directory/samantha-
    power. Philip Giraldi, "Neolibs and Neocons, United and Interchangeable,"
    AntiWar.com, August 14, 2007, http://www.antiwar.com/orig/giraldi
    .php?articleid=11438.

63 Samantha Power, "Campaign Memo: 'Barack Obama Was Right,' *Washington
    Post*, August 3, 2007, http://blog.washingtonpost.com/44/2007/08/03/campaign_
    memo_barack_obama_was_1.html.

64 Robin Lindley, "Samantha Power Talks About Her New Book (Interview)," History
    News Network, May 12, 2008, http://hnn.us/articles/49504.html.

65 Richard Baehr and Ed Lasky, "Samantha Power and Obama's Foreign Policy Team,"
    American Thinker, February 19, 2008, http://www.americanthinker.com/2008/02/
    samantha_power_and_obamas_fore_1.html.

66 "Samantha Power, Cuban humor, etc.," *Weekly Standard*, March 17, 2008, http://
    www.weeklystandard.com/Content/Protected/Articles/000/000/014/858jhkph
    .asp.

67 Gerri Peev, "'Hillary Clinton's a monster': Obama aide blurts out attack in
    Scotsman interview," *Scotsman*, March 7, 2008, http://thescotsman.scotsman.com/
    latestnews/Inside-US-poll-battle-as.3854371.jp.

68 Matthew Lee, "Clinton critic Samantha Power preps State Department for
    senator: An adviser to Barack Obama's presidential campaign who was forced
    to resign after calling Sen. Hillary Rodham Clinton a 'monster' is working,"
    Associated Press, November 29, 2008, http://seattletimes.nwsource.com/html/
    politics/2008448571_power29.html.

69 "Samantha Power re-joins Obama," *Politico*, November 28, 2009, http://www
    .politico.com/news/stories/1108/16046.html.

70 Baehr and Lasky, "Samantha Power and Obama's Foreign Policy Team."

71 Ibid.

72 Ibid. Samantha Power, "Rethinking Iran," *Time*, January 17, 2008, http://www
    .time.com/time/magazine/article/0,9171,1704682,00.html.

73   Paul Street, "'Calibrating' HOPE in the Effort to 'Patrol the Commons': Samantha Power and the Hidden Imperial Reality of Barack Obama," ZNet, February 26, 2008, http://www.zcommunications.org/znet/viewArticle/16640.

74   Ibid.

75   Ibid.

76   "In a HARDtalk interview first broadcast on 6 March 2008, Stephen Sackur talks to Barack Obama's foreign policy adviser, Samantha Power," BBC, March 6, 2008, http://news.bbc.co.uk/2/hi/programmes/hardtalk/7281805.stm.

77   Eric Alterman, "The Ritual Sacrifice of Samantha Power," The Nation, March 20, 2008, http://www.thenation.com/doc/20080407/alterman.

78   Dave Rochelson, "The search for knowledge, truth and a greater understanding of the world around us," White House Newsroom Blog, December 20, 2008, http://change.gov/newsroom/entry/the_search_for_knowledge_truth_and_a_greater_understanding_of_the_world_aro.

79   White House Office of Science and Technology Policy, Executive Office of the President, http://www.ostp.gov.

80   Ben Johnson, "Obama's Biggest Radical," FrontPageMagazine.com, February 27, 2009, http://97.74.65.51/readArticle.aspx?ARTID=34198.

81   Profile: Peter Collier, SourceWatch.org, http://www.sourcewatch.org/index.php?title=Peter_Collier. Profile: Ramparts Magazine, SourceWatch.org, http://www.sourcewatch.org/index.php?title=Ramparts.

82   Jonathan H. Adler, "Obama's Political Science Adviser: John Holdren is unlikely to usher in an age of free and open scientific inquiry," National Review Online, January 7, 2009, http://article.nationalreview.com/?q=NTc4MGNiYmIxMGIyZWYwZjE3MTFmMGVlNDY0Nzc0NDU=.

83   Jerome R. Corsi, "Holdren warned of coming ice age: Science chief argued for population control to limit 'global cooling,'" WorldNetDaily, October 6, 2009, http://www.wnd.com/index.php?pageId=112073.

84   Ibid.

85   David Sassoon, "Obama Science Advisor a Home Run," SolveClimate.com, December 18, 2008, http://solveclimate.com/blog/20081218/obama-science-advisor-home-run. John P. Holdren, "Climate Change. Convincing the skeptics," New York Times, August 4, 2008, http://www.nytimes.com/2008/08/04/opinion/04iht-edholdren.1.14991915.html?_r=1.

86   Corsi, "Holdren warned of coming ice age."

87   Jerome R. Corsi, "Holdren: Sterilize welfare recipients: Obama boss suggested ways to save planet, said fetus not a person," WorldNetDaily, September 23, 2009, http://www.wnd.com/index.php?pageId=110768.

88   Jerome R. Corsi, "Holdren says Constitution backs compulsory abortion: Argued in writings: 'Quality of life demands fewer people,'" WorldNetDaily, September 22, 2009, http://www.wnd.com/index.php?fa=PAGE.view&pageId=110720.

89   Corsi, "Holdren: Sterilize welfare recipients."

90   Jerome R. Corsi, "Holdren: Seize babies born to unwed women: Proposed government force adoption if mother refused to get abortion," WorldNetDaily, September 30, 2009, http://www.wnd.com/index.php?pageId=111475.

91   Aaron Klein, "Meet Obama's climate change 'experts': Socialists, conspiracy theorists, supporters of spreading the wealth," WorldNetDaily, December 2, 2009, http://www.wnd.com/index.php?fa=PAGE.view&pageId=117804.

92　Dr. Tim Ball and Judi McLeod, "Obama's Science Czar John Holdren involved in unwinding 'Climategate' scandal," *Canada Free Press*, November 24, 2009, http://canadafreepress.com/index.php/article/17183.

93　Aaron Klein, "Obama's regulatory chief pushes new 'bill of rights': Cass Sunstein part of effort to change interpretation of Constitution by 2020," *WorldNetDaily*, September 11, 2009, http://www.wnd.com/index.php?fa=PAGE.view&pageId=109529.

94　Ibid.

95　"Post by Cass Sunstein," The Constitution in 2020 (blog), May 15, 2005, http://constitutionin2020.blogspot.com/2005/03/post-by-cass-sunstein.html.

96　Sunstein's paper is available at http://papers.ssrn.com/sol3/papers.cfm?abstract_id=1008958&rec=1&srcabs=375622.

97　Aaron Klein, "Cass Sunstein wants to spread America's wealth: Echoes Van Jones on using 'environmental justice' to redistribute money," *WorldNetDaily*, September 16, 2009, http://www.wnd.com/index.php?fa=PAGE.view&pageId=110031.

98　Aaron Klein, "Sunstein: Embryos are 'just a handful of cells': Argues cloning ban 'silly,' scoffed at those who find it morally repugnant," *WorldNetDaily*, September 14, 2009, http://www.wnd.com/index.php?pageId=109849.

99　"Cass Sunstein Ranks Animals Above Humans," posted September 10, 2009, on YouTube, http://www.youtube.com/watch?v=OoiHIbwRhSo.

100　Ibid.

101　Cass R. Sunstein, "The Rights of Animals: A Very Short Primer," Harvard University—Harvard Law School, August 2002, http://papers.ssrn.com/sol3/papers.cfm?abstract_id=323661.

102　Klein, "Sunstein: Embryos are 'just a handful of cells.'"

103　Profile: Barbara Ehrenreich, *Discover the Networks*, http://www.discoverthenetworks.org/individualProfile.asp?indid=1058.

104　Aaron Klein, "Pentagon official blames U.S. for al-Qaeda attacks: Worked for George Soros, argued for government control of media," *WorldNetDaily*, April 20, 2009, http://www.wnd.com/index.php?fa=PAGE.view&pageId=95630.

105　Ibid.

106　Aaron Klein, "Pentagon pick: Bush 'mindlessly' supported Israel. New top adviser warns Obama may not give Jewish state 'blank checks,'" *WorldNetDaily*, April 21, 2009, http://www.wnd.com/index.php?fa=PAGE.view&pageId=95746.

11: THE WHITE HOUSE AND "MEDIA JUSTICE"

1　Ben Compaine, "Domination Fantasies," *Reason.com*, January 1, 2004, http://reason.com/archives/2004/01/01/domination-fantasies.

2　Media Justice Now! Website, http://www.mediajustice.org.

3　Profile, Mark Lloyd, Associate General Counsel and Chief Diversity Officer, Federal Communications Commission, http://www.fcc.gov/ogc/lloyd.html. Profile: Mark Lloyd, Advisory Committee to the Congressional Internet Caucus, http://www.netcaucus.org/biography/mark-lloyd.shtml. Brenda J. Elliott, "Mark Lloyd: Redistribution of Wealth Czar at the FCC," *RBO*, August 17, 2009, http://therealbarackobama.wordpress.com/2009/08/17/mark-lloyd-redistribution-of-wealth-czar-at-the-fcc.

4   Seton Motley on Glenn Beck about Mark Lloyd: "Assault on Conservative and Christian Talk Radio," *FoxNews.com*, August 14, 2009, http://www.freerepublic .com/focus/news/2316678/posts. Mark Lloyd, "Forget the Fairness Doctrine," Center for American Progress, July 27, 2007, http://www.americanprogress.org/ issues/2007/07/lloyd_fairness.html.

5   Matt Cover, "FCC's Chief Diversity Officer Wants Private Broadcasters to Pay a Sum Equal to Their Total Operating Costs to Fund Public Broadcasting," *CNSNews.com*, August 13, 2009, http://www.cnsnews.com/news/article/52435.

6   George Fallon, "Mark Lloyd: FCC Chief Diversity Officer Seeks to Punish Conservative Broadcasters," *RightPundits*, August 14, 2009, http://www .rightpundits.com/?p=4608

7   Cover, August 13, 2009.

8   Makani Themba-Nixon and Nan Rubin, "Speaking for Ourselves: A Movement Led by People of Color Seeks Media Justice—Not Just Media Reform," *The Nation*, November 17, 2003.

9   Mark Lloyd, "Communications Policy Is a Civil Rights Issue," *Community Technology Center Review*, January 1998, http://www.comtechreview.org/winter-spring-1998/ r981lloy.htm.

10   Elliott, August 17, 2009.

11   Katrina vanden Heuvel, "Obama Blasts FCC Media Ownership Decision," *The Nation*, December 18, 2007, http://www.thenation.com/blogs/state_of_ change/261349.

12   Katrina vanden Heuvel, "On the Media," *The Nation*, December 12, 2007, http:// www.thenation.com/blogs/edcut/259249.

13   John Eggerton, "Dorgan, Obama, Others Sens. Move to Block FCC Media-Ownership Vote. Media Ownership Act of 2007 Introduced by Dorgan, Co-Sponsored by Lott, Obama, Feinstein, Cantwell, Snowe," Broadcastingcable.com, November 7, 2007, http://www.broadcastingcable.com/article/111119-Dorgan_ Obama_Others_Sens_Move_to_Block_FCC_Media_Ownership_Vote.php.

14   S. 2332: Media Ownership Act of 2007, 110th Congress, 2007–2008, http://www .govtrack.us/congress/bill.xpd?bill=s110-2332.

15   Sens. Barack Obama and John F. Kerry, "Media consolidation silences diverse voices," *Politico*, November 7, 2007, http://www.politico.com/news/ stories/1107/6758.html.

16   Ben Compaine, "Senate's Media Ownership Crusade: Ignores Research, Will Have Unintended Consequences," Who Owns the Media? blog, November 9, 2007, http://wotmedia.blogspot.com/2007/11/senates-media-ownership-crusade-ignores. html.

17   Seton Motley, "FCC's Diversity Czar: 'White People' Need to be Forced to 'Step Down' 'So Someone Else Can Have Power,'" *NewsBusters*, September 23, 2009, http://newsbusters.org/blogs/seton-motley/2009/09/23/fccs-diversity-czar-white-people-need-be-forced-step-down-so-someone-0. Seton Motley, "New FCC 'Chief Diversity Officer' Co-Wrote Liberal Group's 'Structural Imbalance of Political Talk Radio,'" *NewsBusters*, August 6, 2009, http://newsbusters.org/blogs/ seton-motley/2009/08/06/new-fcc-chief-diversity-officer-co-wrote-liberal-groups-structural-imb.

18   Seton Motley, "Video: FCC 'Diversity' Czar on Chávez's Venezuela: 'Incredible... Democratic Revolution,'" *NewsBusters*, August 28, 2009, http://newsbusters.org/

blogs/seton-motley/2009/08/28/video-fcc-diversity-czar-chávezs-venezuela-
incredible-democratic-revol.

19 Aaron Klein, "Cass Sunstein: Censor Hannity, right-wing rumors. Cites websites
for 'absurd' reports of Obama's ties to Ayers," *WorldNetDaily*, November 23, 2009,
http://www.wnd.com/index.php?pageId=116952.

20 Aaron Klein, "Cass Sunstein drafted 'New Deal Fairness Doctrine': Asserts
government should regulate broadcasting as it imposed end to segregation," *WorldNet
Daily*, September 15, 2009, http://www.wnd.com/index.php?pageId=109969.

21 Biography of Chairman Julius Genachowski, Federal Communications
Commission, http://www.fcc.gov/commissioners/genachowski/biography
.html. Profile: Julius Genachowski, FCC Chairman, Federal Communications
Commission, http://www.fcc.gov/commissioners/genachowski. Profile: Julius
Genachowski, *WhoRunsGov.com*, http://www.whorunsgov.com/Profiles/Julius_
Genachowski. Profile: Julius Genachoswki, *WhiteHouseforSale.org*, http://www
.whitehouseforsale.org/bundler.cfm?Bundler=13024%20.

22 Genachowski, *WhoRunsGov.com*. Profile: Julius Genachowski, Wikipedia, http://
en.wikipedia.org/wiki/Julius_Genachowski.

23 Ibid.

24 Ibid.

25 Tom Steinert-Threlkeld, "Julius Genachowski & the FCC: A Failure to
Communicate?" *ZDNet*, January 13, 2009.

26 Matthew Lasar, "In search of Julius Genachowski: Will Julius Genachowski take
over the FCC next year? And who is this guy, anyway?," *Ars Technica*, December
22, 2008, http://arstechnica.com/old/content/2008/12/in-search-of-julius-
genachowski.ars.

27 Ryan Singel, "Obama Nominates Net Neutrality Backer for FCC Chief," *WIRED*,
March 3, 2009, http://www.wired.com/epicenter/2009/03/obama-nominates.

28 Amy Schatz and Shira Ovide, "Obama's Pick for FCC Signals Change," *Wall Street
Journal*, January 15, 2009, http://online.wsj.com/article/SB123189367347579431.html.

29 Benton Foundation, "Jen Howard Named Genachowski's Press Secretary,"
Broadcasting & Cable, July 1, 2009, http://www.benton.org/node/26209.

30 John Halpin, James Heidbreder, Mark Lloyd, Paul Woodhull, Ben Scott, Josh Silver,
and S. Derek Turner, *The Structural Imbalance of Political Talk Radio*, Center for
American Progress and Free Press, June 20, 2007, http://www.americanprogress
.org/issues/2007/06/pdf/talk_radio.pdf.

31 Warner Todd Huston, "Another of Obama's Radical Appointees," *The Universal
Seduction*, undated, http://theuniversalseduction.com/articles/another-of-obamas-
radical-appointees. Jessica Clark, "Nattering Networks," How Mass Media Fails
Democracy" (an interview with Robert McChesney), *Lip Magazine*, September
24, 2001, http://www.lipmagazine.org/articles/featclark_138.shtml. John Bellamy
Foster and Robert W. McChesney, "A New New Deal under Obama?" *Monthly
Review*, February 2009, http://monthlyreview.org/090201foster-mcchesney
.php#fn1b.

32 Phil Kerpen, "FCC Official Spokeswoman Jen Howard Still Working for Radical
Left-Wing Group 'Free Press,'" Americans for Prosperity, October 21, 2009, http://
www.americansforprosperity.org/102109-fcc-official-spokeswoman-jen-howard-
still-working-radical-left-wing-group-"free-press".

33   Benton Foundation, "Jen Howard Named Genachowski's Press Secretary," *Broadcasting & Cable*, July 1, 2009, http://www.benton.org/node/26209. "About," Media Access Project, http://www.mediaaccess.org/about.

34   "About," MAP.

35   Raymond Pronk, "Network Neutrality–FCC Julius Genachowski–Tim Wu–Free and Open Internet Or Slow and Stupid Internet?," *Pronk Palisades*, October 8, 2009, http://raymondpronk.wordpress.com/2009/10/08/network-neurtrality-fcc-julius-genachowski-tim-wu-free-and-open-internet-or-slow-and-stupid-internet.

36   Matthew Vadum, "Robert McChesney's War on the First Amendment," NewsRealBlog, October 12, 2009, http://newsrealblog.com/2009/10/12/robert-mcchesneys-war-on-the-first-amendment.

37   Cliff Kincaid, "Controversial New Video of Obama's Pastor," Accuracy in Media, November 1, 2009, http://www.aim.org/aim-column/controversial-new-video-of-obamas-pastor.

38   Matthew Vadum, "Robert McChesney's War on the First Amendment," NewsRealBlog, October 12, 2009, http://newsrealblog.com/2009/10/12/robert-mcchesneys-war-on-the-first-amendment.

39   Adam Thierer, "Free Press, Robert McChesney & the 'Struggle' for Media," *TechLiberation.com*, August 10, 2009, http://techliberation.com/2009/08/10/free-press-robert-mcchesney-the-struggle-for-media-marxism.

40   Profile: Susan P. Crawford, Wikipedia, http://en.wikipedia.org/wiki/Susan_P._Crawford.

41   Profile: Susan Crawford, Advisory Committee to the Congressional Internet Caucus, http://netcaucus.org/biography/susan-crawford.shtml. Crawford left her position of White House technology adviser in January 2009 to return to the University of Michigan Law School, where she is a tenured professor. On the National Economic Council, Crawford advised Obama "on the development of broadband Internet networks and a net neutrality policy. Cecilia Kang, "Obama tech adviser Susan Crawford plans departure," *Washington Post*, October 27, 2009, http://voices.washingtonpost.com/posttech/2009/10/obama_tech_advisor_susan_crawf.html.

42   "Susan Crawford at Free Press Summit: Changing Media. Government intervention in newspapers and bandwidth," *Canada Free Press*, October 9, 2009, http://canadafreepress.com/index.php/article/15599. Transcript was expanded by the authors from the video tape posted with the article.

43   Participating organizations, OneWebDay.org, http://onewebday.org/participating-organizations.

44   "Obama's Internet Czar Susan Crawford has ties to ACORN," *FireAndreaMitchell.com*, September 27, 2009; http://www.fireandreamitchell.com/2009/09/27/obamas-internet-czar-susan-crawford-has-ties-to-acorn.

45   "Advisory Board," Public Knowledge, http://www.publicknowledge.org/about/who/advisors. "Funders and Supporters," Public Knowledge, http://www.publicknowledge.org/about/who/funders.

46   "Organizations We Work With," Public Knowledge, http://www.publicknowledge.org/about/who/organizations.

47   Profile: Tim Wu, TimWu.org, http://www.timwu.org/about.html. Faculty profile: Tim Wu, Columbia University, http://www.law.columbia.edu/fac/Timothy_Wu. Current Fellows, New America Foundation, http://www.newamerica.net/about/current_fellows.

48 Funding, New America Foundation, http://www.newamerica.net/about/funding.

49 "Tim Wu on Network Neutrality," Geek Entertainment TV, April 21, 2009, http://www.geekentertainment.tv/2009/04/21/tim-wu-on-network-neutrality. "Net Neutrality: A Historical Timeline," Sidecut Reports, November 16, 2008, http://www.sidecutreports.com/2008/11/16/net-neutrality-a-historical-timeline.

50 Cliff Kincaid, "'Media Reform' Activists Cheer Obama," Accuracy in Media, June 8, 2008, http://www.aim.org/aim-column/media-reform-activists-cheer-obama.

51 Ibid.

52 Tim Wu, "It's beginning. . . New Yorkers for Obama," What's New with Wu, December 11, 2006, http://www.timwu.org/log/archives/66. "Tech Leaders Announce Support for Barack Obama," Organizing for America/Obama for America, November 15, 2007, http://www.barackobama.com/2007/11/15/tech_leaders_announce_support.php.

53 David Brody, "Video: Obama in April 2008: I want to 'expand the diversity of voices in media,'" The Brody File/CBN.colm, March 3, 2009, http://blogs.cbn.com/thebrodyfile/archive/2009/03/03/video-obama-in-april-2008-i-want-to-expand-the.aspx.

12: COALITION OF EXTREMISTS PUSHING OBAMA AGENDA

1 Aaron Klein, "Obama site urges: 'Revolution' against U.S. 'oppressive' regime: Marxists, socialists, communists form group to plot on official campaign blog," WorldNetDaily, June 30, 2008, http://www.wnd.com/index.php?pageId=68462.

2 Community: "Marxists/Socialists/Communists for Obama," Organizing for America/Organizing for Obama, circa May 2008, http://my.barackobama.com/page/community/group/MarxistsSocialistsCommunistsforObama.

3 William T. Poole, "The New Left in Government: From Protest to Policy-Making," Heritage Foundation Reports—Institution Analysis No. 9, Heritage Foundation, November 1978, http://groups.google.com/group/soc.culture.vietnamese/msg/074f553b309310d9?hl=en&&q=William+Poole+new+left+government.

4 Andrew C. McCarthy, "Alinsky Does Afghanistan. Obama's radical inspiration would have loved his speech on the war," National Review Online, December 4, 2009, http://article.nationalreview.com/?q=MzRhOGIzZWNiN2FkZDIwNDEwOTcyYWY4OWJlYmNkNTg=.

5 Lowell Ponte, "How Socialist Unions Rule the Democratic Party," FrontPageMagazine.com, July 14, 2004, http://97.74.65.51/readArticle.aspx?ARTID=12216.

6 Abdon M. Pallasch, "Ayers on Obama's 'colossal mistake.' Rips Afghanistan troop buildup," Chicago Sun-Times, February 24, 2009, http://www.suntimes.com/news/politics/obama/1446301,CST-NWS-ayers24.article.

7 Tom Hayden, "Obama Announces Afghanistan Escalation," The Nation, December 1, 2009, http://www.thenation.com/doc/20091214/hayden.

8 Mark Silva, "Bill Ayers, Obama: Parting ways on war," The Swamp/Chicago Tribune, December 3, 2009, http://www.swamppolitics.com/news/politics/blog/2009/12/bill_ayers_obama_parting_ways.html. DogStar7, "Bill Ayers Breaks With Obama," YouTube, posted December 2, 2009, http://www.youtube.com/watch?v=Z1tr6JzzBro.

9   Trevor Loudon, "Has Trevor Loudon found the Ayers-Dohrn-Obama 'smoking gun'?"
    Meet the Movement for a Democratic Society," *RBO*, September 21, 2008, http://
    therealbarackobama.wordpress.com/2008/09/21/has-trevor-loudon-found-the-ayers-
    dohrn-obama-smoking-gun-meet-the-movement-for-a-democratic-society.

10 Ibid.

11 Ibid. Trevor Loudon, "Black Radicals for Obama," *RBO*, October 4, 2008, http://
    therealbarackobama.wordpress.com/2008/10/04/loudon-black-radicals-for-obama.

12 Loudon, "Has Trevor Loudon found the Ayers-Dohrn-Obama 'smoking gun'?"
    Gerald Horne, "Rethinking the History and Future of the Communist Party,"
    Political Affairs Magazine, March 28, 2007, http://www.politicalaffairs.net/article/
    articleview/5047/1/32.

13 Loudon, "Has Trevor Loudon found the Ayers-Dohrn-Obama 'smoking gun'?"

14 Brenda J. Elliott, "Support Bill Ayers," *RBO*, October 15, 2008, http://
    therealbarackobama.wordpress.com/2008/10/15/support-bill-ayers.

15 Sol Stern, "The Bomber as School Reformer," *City Journal*, October 6, 2008, http://
    www.city-journal.org/2008/eon1006ss.html.

16 Brenda J. Elliott, "More on the Movement for a Democratic Society and the
    "new" Students for a Democratic Society," *RBO*, September 22, 2008, http://
    therealbarackobama.wordpress.com/2008/09/22/more-on-the-movement-for-a-
    democratic-society-and-the-new-students-for-a-democratic-society. Thomas Good,
    "MDS Conference Elects Manning Marable Chair of MDS, Inc.," *Next Left Notes*,
    February 20, 2007, http://antiauthoritarian.net/NLN/?p=179.

17 Brenda J. Elliott, "An update on the Movement for a Democratic Society and the
    'new' SDS," *RBO*, September 25, 2008, http://therealbarackobama.wordpress
    .com/2008/09/25/an-update-on-the-movement-for-a-democratic-society-and-the-
    new-sds. Loudon, "Black Radicals for Obama."

18 Loudon, October 4, 2008. Manning Marable, "Barack Obama's Problem Along
    the Color Line—and Ours," The Black Commentator, February 2008, http://www
    .blackcommentator.com/267/267_along_the_color_line_obama.html.

19 Trevor Loudon, "Obama 'Understands What Socialism Is,' Works With 'Socialists
    With Backgrounds in the Communist Party,'" *RBO*, January 13, 2009, http://
    therealbarackobama.wordpress.com/2009/01/13/loudon-obama-understands-what-
    socialism-is-works-with-socialists-with-backgrounds-in-the-communist-party.

20 Manning Marable, "The four legged stool that won the US presidential election,"
    Socialist Review, December 2008, http://www.socialistreview.org.uk/article.
    php?articlenumber=10628.

21 Aaron Klein, "Obama's team 'socialists with communist backgrounds,'"
    WorldNetDaily, September 10, 2009; available at: http://www.wnd.com/index
    .php?pageId=109486.

22 Loudon, "Obama 'Understands What Socialism Is.'"

23 Good, "MDS Conference Elects Manning Marable."

24 Aaron Klein, "Obama's 'green jobs czar' worked with terror founder: Van Jones
    served on board of activist group where ex-Weatherman serves as top director,"
    WorldNetDaily, August 13, 2009, http://www.wnd.com/index.php?pageId=106653.
    Brenda J. Elliott, "Weatherman Dohrn," *RBO*, October 28, 2008, http://
    therealbarackobama.wordpress.com/2008/10/28/weatherman-dohrn.

25 The bio has been removed from the website as of this publication. Text of the

bio is available online on *WorldNetDaily.com* at http://www.wnd.com/index
.php?pageId=106653.

26 Aaron Klein, "Obama's 'green jobs czar' worked with terror founder,"
WorldNetDaily, August 13, 2009; available at: http://www.wnd.com/index
.php?pageId=106653.

27 Ibid.

28 Loudon, "Black Radicals for Obama."

29 Loudon, "Has Trevor Loudon found the Ayers-Dohrn-Obama 'smoking gun'?"

30 Tom Hayden, Bill Fletcher Jr., Danny Glover , and Barbara Ehrenreich,
"Progressives for Obama," *The Nation*, March 24, 2008, http://www.thenation.com/
doc/20080407/hayden_et_al.

31 Trevor Loudon, "Reds, Radicals, Terrorists and Traitors—Progressives For Obama,"
RBO, September 11, 2008, http://therealbarackobama.wordpress.com/2008/09/11/
loudon-reds-radicals-terrorists-and-traitors-progressives-for-obama.

32 Profile: Barbara Ehrenreich, *Discover the Networks*, http://www.discoverthenetworks
.org/individualProfile.asp?indid=1058.

33 Profile: Barbara Ehrenreich, *Discover the Networks*. Barbara Ehrenreich, "Obama's
Campaign: An Emotional Escape Hatch from the Bush Era," *AlterNet*, February 16,
2008, http://www.alternet.org/election08/77193/?comments=view&cID=835028
&pID=834823.

34 Barbara Ehrenreich, Barbara's Blog, http://ehrenreich.blogs.com.

35 Brenda J. Elliott, "Comradess Barbara Lee," *RBO*, April 20, 2009, http://
therealbarackobama.wordpress.com/2009/04/20/comradess-barbara-lee.

36 "Danny Glover, African-American Personalities Visit Venezuela to get Better
Vision of the Country," *Venezuelanalysis.com*, January 8, 2004, http://www
.venezuelanalysis.com/news/304.

37 Profile: Danny Glover, *Discover the Networks*, http://www.discoverthenetworks.org/
individualProfile.asp?indid=1119.

38 Rory Carroll, "Venezuela giving Danny Glover $18m to direct film on epic slave
revolt," UK *Guardian*, May 21, 2007, http://www.guardian.co.uk/world/2007/
may/21/film.venezuela.

39 Trevor Loudon, "Obama, the Communist Van Jones and the Demos Connection,"
RBO, August 17, 2009, http://therealbarackobama.wordpress.com/2009/08/17/
loudon-exclusive-obama-the-communist-van-jones-and-the-demos-connection.

40 Trevor Loudon, "Toxic Trio! Ayers, Davidson, Klonsky Linked to Pro-Obama
Organisation," *RBO*, September 27, 2008, http://therealbarackobama.wordpress
.com/2008/09/27/loudon-toxic-trio-ayers-davidson-klonsky-linked-to-pro-obama-
organisation.

41 Aaron Klein, "Meet Obama's new Bill Ayers associate. Ex-communist leader tied to
terrorist eliminated from campaign website," *WorldNetDaily*, September 14, 2008,
http://www.wnd.com/index.php?pageId=75282.

42 Ibid.

43 Ibid.

44 Aaron Klein, "Another Weatherman terrorist a player in Obama campaign:
Communists, socialists, anarchists also part of political organization,"
WorldNetDaily, September 26, 2008, http://www.wnd.com/index
.php?pageId=76234.

45 Ibid.

46 Ibid.
47 Mark Rudd, "Something Happening Here," *Los Angeles Times*, November 10, 2005, http://www.markrudd.com/?organizing-and-activism-now/pemby-mark-rudd-mark-rudd-who-led-the-student-uprising-at-columbia-university-in-1968-and-then-becam.html.
48 Klein, "Another Weatherman terrorist."
49 David Horowitz, "Barack Obama's Rules for Revolution. The Alinsky Model," David Horowitz Freedom Center, 2009, http://www.americanpatrol.com/OBAMA-BARACK/2009-2010/PDF/Rules-for-Revolution091120.pdf.

13: ANTI-AMERICAN RADICALS DRAFTING OBAMA LEGISLATION

1 Google books: Jay Inslee and Bracken Hendricks, *Apollo's Fire: Igniting America's Clean Energy Economy* (Island Press, 2007), 224.
2 Keith Schneider, "Clean Energy Is Foundation of Proposed Stimulus," Apollo News Service, January 15, 2009, http://apolloalliance.org/feature-articles/clean-energy-serves-as-foundation-for-proposed-reinvestment-bill. The New Apollo Program, Apollo Alliance, October 1, 2008, http://apolloalliance.org/programs/apollo-14. Apollo Economic Recovery Act, Apollo Alliance, undated, http://apolloalliance.org/programs/full-proposal.
3 Keith Schneider, "Apollo Weekly Update, 2/20/09: Clean Energy Breakthrough in Stimulus, Next Steps," Apollo News Service, February 20, 2009, http://www.cows.org/about_newsroom_detail.asp?id=970.
4 Conn Carroll, "Oh My God, They Admitted It," Heritage Foundation/The Foundry blog, November 12, 2008, http://blog.heritage.org/2008/11/12/oh-my-god-they-admitted-it.
5 Profile: Dan Carol, *LinkedIn.com*, http://www.linkedin.com/pub/dan-carol/5/298/a34.
6 "It Takes a Lot of Government Green to Create a Green Job," Institute for Energy Research, November 13, 2008, http://www.instituteforenergyresearch.org/2008/11/13/it-takes-a-lot-of-government-green-to-create-a-green-job. Miguel Llanos, "Kerry's environment aides start with family: Wife, stepson are key, activist groups aim for say," MSNBC.MSN.com, September 15, 2004, http://www.msnbc.msn.com/id/5772056. Profile: Dan Carol, LinkedIn.com. Jim Rutenberg, " Political Freelancers Use Web to Join the Attack," June 29, 2008, http://www.nytimes.com/2008/06/29/us/politics/29opposition.html. Jim Hightower, "We'll send him your picks for the pyramid of power: If Obama wins, who will be on his team—and who should be?," *Hightower Lowdown*, July 2008, http://www.hightowerlowdown.org/node/1690.
7 Hightower, "We'll send him your picks." Advisory Board, Progressive Democrats of America, http://pdamerica.org/about/board.php. Trevor Loudon, "Institute for Policy Studies and the Obama 'Movement,'" *RBO*, January 13, 2009, http://therealbarackobama.wordpress.com/2009/01/13/loudon-institute-for-policy-studies-and-the-obama-movement.
8 Steering Committee, Apollo Alliance, 2006, http://www.democraticunderground.com/discuss/duboard.php?az=view_all&address=115x37653. Board of Directors, Apollo Alliance, accessed October 25, 2009, http://apolloalliance.org/about/board.

Board of Directors, Tides Foundation, http://www.tides.org/about-us/board-of-directors/index.html.

9 The following Democratic Underground forum link is no longer publicly available: http://www.democraticunderground.com/discuss/duboard.php?az=view_all&address=115x37653.

10 Apollo Board of Directors, Apollo Alliance, July 14, 2008, http://www.apolloalliance.org/index.php?s=mcginty. Staff: Joel Rogers, COWS (Center on Wisconsin Strategy), http://www.cows.org/about_staff_detail.asp. Profile: Joel Rogers, Brookings Institution, http://www.brookings.edu/experts/rogersj.aspx. About page, Center on Wisconsin Strategy (COWS), http://www.cows.org/about_index.asp.

11 Apollo Board of Directors, Apollo Alliance, July 14, 2008.

12 John Nichols, "Joel Rogers—a founder of the New Party—Crashing the Parties" (Interview), *The Progressive*, October 1996, http://findarticles.com/p/articles/mi_m1295/is_n10_v60/ai_18710717.

13 Ibid. Trevor Loudon, "More on Barack Obama and the Socialist New Party," *RBO*, October 27, 2008, http://therealbarackobama.wordpress.com/2008/10/27/loudon-more-on-barack-obama-and-the-socialist-new-party. Erick Erickson, "Obama and the New Party," HumanEventsOnline, June 20, 2008, http://www.humanevents.com/article.php?id=26913.

14 The Democratic Underground forum link is no longer publicly available: http://www.democraticunderground.com/discuss/duboard.php?az=view_all&address=115x37653.

15 Profile: Progressive Majority, *Discover the Networks*, http://www.discoverthenetworks.org/groupProfile.asp?grpid=6489.

16 Ibid.

17 Profile: Robert Borosage, *Discover the Networks*.

18 Ibid. Trustees, Institute for Policy Studies, http://www.ips-dc.org/about/trustees. Profile: Institute for Policy Studies, *Discover the Networks*, http://www.discoverthenetworks.org/groupProfile.asp?grpid=6991.

19 Profile: Robert Borosage. Campaign for America's Future, http://www.ourfuture.org/user/4/full. Profile: Morton Halperin, *Discover the Networks*, http://www.discoverthenetworks.org/individualProfile.asp?indid=1682. Profile: National Lawyers Guild, *Discover the Networks*, http://www.discoverthenetworks.org/groupProfile.asp?grpid=6162.

20 Profile: Morton Halperin, *Discover the Networks*.

21 Apollo Board of Directors, Apollo Alliance, July 14, 2008.

22 Institute for America's Future Board Members (March 2009), Campaign for America's Future website, http://www.ourfuture.org/page/2009052122/institute-america-board-members. Campaign for America's Future Board Members (April 2009), Campaign for America's Future website, http://www.ourfuture.org/page/2009052122/campaign-americas-future-board-members .Apollo Board of Directors, Apollo Alliance, July 14, 2008. Profile: Robert Borosage, *Discover the Networks*, http://www.discoverthenetworks.org/individualProfile.asp?indid=1170.

23 Brenda J. Elliott, "Why is Barackistan HQ 'brokering' reuniting the unions?" *RBO*, February 28, 2009, http://therealbarackobama.wordpress.com/2009/02/28/why-is-barackistan-hq-brokering-reuniting-the-unions. Brenda J. Elliott, "Labor

'reunification,'" *RBO*, April 21, 2009, http://therealbarackobama.wordpress.com/2009/04/21/labor-reunification.

24   Elliott, "Why is Barackistan HQ 'brokering' reuniting the unions?"; Elliott, "Labor 'reunification'"

25   Trevor Loudon, "Obama, Antonio Villaraigosa and the Harry Bridges Connection," *RBO*, March 4, 2009, http://therealbarackobama.wordpress.com/2009/03/04/loudon-obama-antonio-villaraigosa-and-the-harry-bridges-connection.

26   Richard Louv, "US: A project for energy independence," *San Diego Union Tribune*, June 26, 2004, http://www.energybulletin.net/node/827.

27   Jim Grossfeld, "Leo the Linchpin: Steelworker President Leo Gerard Looks Like an Old-Time Union Leader, but He's Put Together a Labor-Environmentalist Alliance That Bridges Some Growing Democratic Fissures," *American Prospect* 18, October 2007.

28   Profile: Bracken Hendricks, Center for American Progress, http://www.americanprogress.org/experts/HendricksBracken.html.

29   Bracken Hendricks, "An Energy/Jobs Program," *The Nation*, May 22, 2003, http://www.thenation.com/directory/bios/bracken_hendricks.

30   Profile: Bracken Hendricks, Center for American Progress.

31   Ibid.

32   Bracken Hendricks, "The Apollo Project," *Yes Magazine*, May 20, 2004, http://yesmagazine.org/issues/government-of-the-people-shall-not-perish/636.

33   Jay Fever, "An interview with Rep. Jay Inslee, clean-energy champion from Washington state," *Grist*, April 11, 2007, http://www.grist.org/article/inslee.

34   Jay Inslee, "Energy bill boosts Apollo Project," *Seattle Post-Intelligencer*, January 25, 2007, http://www.house.gov/inslee/press/25january2007.html main.

35   Nick Koveshnikov, "Inslee presents energy options," *The Daily* (University of Washington), February 20, 2003, http://dailyuw.com/2003/2/20/inslee-presents-energy-options.

36   Jay Inslee, "The New Apollo Energy Project: Inslee Rallies Democrats Around Clean Energy Plan," Rep. Jay Inslee's Official House website, March 19, 2003, http://www.house.gov/inslee/issues/energy/apollo_rallydems.html main. Apollo Board of Directors, Apollo Alliance, July 14, 2008.

37   Profile: John Podesta, Center for American Progress, http://www.americanprogress.org/experts/PodestaJohn.html. Joe Nocera, "Self-Made Philanthropists," *New York Times*, March 9, 2008, http://www.nytimes.com/2008/03/09/magazine/09Sandlers-t.html?_r=1.

38   Grants, Scholarships and Fellowships View, Open Society Institute, 2006, http://www.soros.org/grants/research/detail.php?id=181. Democracy Alliance Board of Directors and Members, *SourceWatch.org*, http://www.sourcewatch.org/index.php?title=Democracy_Alliance#Board_of_Directors_and_Members.

39   Jay Inslee, "The New Apollo Energy Project: Inslee Offers Apollo Project Energy Amendment," Rep. Jay Inslee's Official House website, April 10, 2003, http://www.house.gov/inslee/issues/energy/apollo_amdt_update.html main.

40   Jay Inslee, "The New Apollo Energy Project: Conceptual Legislation," Rep. Jay Inslee's Official House website, undated 2004, http://www.house.gov/inslee/issues/energy/apollo_concept.html main.

41   "Clean energy generates jobs, Kammen team reports," *Forefront* (College of Engineering. University of California, Berkeley), Fall 2004, http://www.coe.berkeley.edu/forefront/fall2004/renewables.html.

42   Jay Inslee, "The New Apollo Energy Legislation. Inslee to offer New Apollo Energy
      Amendment to Energy Bill," Rep. Jay Inslee's Official House website, April 19,
      2005, http://www.house.gov/inslee/issues/energy/apollo_leg_2005.html main. Jay
      Inslee, "The New Apollo Energy Project. Inslee Introduces New Apollo Energy
      Act: *A Comprehensive Clean Energy Plan to Address Jobs, National Security and Climate
      Change*," Rep. Jay Inslee's Official House website, June 9, 2005, http://www.house
      .gov/inslee/issues/energy/new_apollo_energy_act.html main. Jay Inslee, "National
      Energy Issues. Inslee unveils hallmark bill during debate on energy independence,"
      Rep. Jay Inslee's Official House website, June 20, 2007, http://www.house.gov/
      inslee/issues/energy/inslee_unveils_apollo.html main.

43   Profile: *Apollo's Fire: Igniting America's Clean Energy Economy* listed under "Books
      that Focus on or Discuss Plug-In Hybrids (PHEVs)," *CalCars.org*, http://www
      .calcars.org/books.html#af.

44   Profile: Michael Shellenberger, President, The Breakthrough Institute, http://
      www.thebreakthrough.org/staff.shtml. Shellenberger's bio states both the Apollo
      Alliance and the Breakthrough Institute were founded in 2002. Jay Fever interview
      with Rep. Jay Inslee, April 11, 2007.

45   Amanda Griscom Little, "Shooting the Moon," *Grist*, September 18, 2005, http://
      www.prospect.org/cs/articles?article=shooting_the_moon.

46   Eliza Strickland, "The New Face of Environmentalism: Van Jones renounced his
      rowdy black nationalism on the way toward becoming an influential leader of
      the new progressive politics," *East Bay Express*, November 2, 2005, http://www
      .eastbayexpress.com/gyrobase/the_new_face_of_environmentalism/Content?oid=
      290098&showFullText=true.

47   Apollo Alliance Oakland website, http://apolloalliance.org/state-local/oakland.

48   Strickland, "the New Face of Environmentalism."

49   Little, "Shooting The Moon."

50   Ibid.

51   David Roberts, "Obama and Inslee propose to save the American auto industry
      by paying it to do the smart thing," *Grist*, February 8, 2006, http://www.grist.org/
      article/health-care-for-hybrids-a-smart-trade.

52   Little, "Shooting the Moon."

53   Amanda Little, "An interview with authors of the controversial essay 'The Death of
      Environmentalism,'" *Grist*, January 13, 2005, http://www.grist.org/article/little-doe.

54   Profile: Apollo Alliance, *UndueInfluence.com*, http://www.undueinfluence.com/
      apollo_alliance.htm. Democracy Alliance Board of Directors and Members,
      SourceWatch.org.

55   Profile: Apollo Alliance, *UndueInfluence.com*.

56   Profile: Tides Foundation, *Discover the Networks*, http://www.discoverthenetworks
      .org/funderprofile.asp?fndid=5184&category=79.

57   Ibid.

14: EXTREMISTS BEHIND HEALTH CARE FOR AMERICA NOW

1   Robert B. Hudson, "The Role of the Government in 'A Society for All Ages,'" *Health
      and Social Work* 24, 1999, http://www.questia.com/read/5001278123?title=The%20

Role%20of%20the%20Government%20in%20%22A%20Society%20for%20
All%20Ages.%22.

2   David Espo, "Pelosi Says She Would Drain GOP 'Swamp,'" Associated Press, October
     6, 2006, http://www.washingtonpost.com/wp-dyn/content/article/2006/10/06/
     AR2006100600056.html.

3   Profile: "Republican 'culture of corruption,'" SourceWatch: available online
     at http://www.sourcewatch.org/index.php?title=Republican_%27culture_of_
     corruption%27.

4   Jeff Patch, "Liberal Beachhead Established on K Street," *Politico*, February 26, 2007,
     http://www.politico.com/news/stories/0207/2894.html.

5   Michelle Malkin, "The Astroturf Drive for ObamaCare: How to Buy 'Grass-Roots
     Support,'" *New York Post*, June 24, 2009, http://www.nypost.com/p/news/opinion/
     opedcolumnists/the_astroturf_drive_for_obamacare_Yvpe7IHK0Tytb9P2OfEAzO.

6   Patch, "Liberal Beachhead."

7   Profile: Roger Hickey, *Discover the Networks*, http://www.discoverthenetworks.org/
     individualProfile.asp?indid=1183.

8   Jeffrey H. Birnbaum, "'The Other K Street': In the Concrete Canyon of the
     Business Lobby, a Pocket of Liberal Activists Settles In," *Washington Post*, May
     7, 2007, http://www.washingtonpost.com/wp-dyn/content/article/2007/05/06/
     AR2007050600892.html.

9   Richard Magat, *Unlikely Partners: Philanthropic Foundations and the Labor
     Movement* (Cornell University Press, 1999), 74. For Hickey's Profile: Institute
     for America's Future, *Discover the Networks*, http://www.discoverthenetworks.
     org/groupProfile .asp?grpid=7332. New Century Alliance for Social Security,
     Press Release: "Leaders of citizen groups unite to launch New Century Alliance
     to fight for Social Security; Civil Rights, Women, Labor, Senior, Disability,
     Religious, and Youth Leaders Release Principles for Social Security's Future,"
     CommonDreams.org, December 3, 1998, http://www.commondreams.org/
     pressreleases/Dec98/120398d.htm. Profile: Institute for America's Future,
     Inc., Green Tracking Library, accessed December 20, 2009, http://www
     .greentrackinglibrary.org/iaf.htm.

10   David Moberg, "Setting the Agenda," *In These Times*, April 1, 2001, http://www
     .inthesetimes.com/issue/25/09/edit2509.html.

11   Robert L. Borosage and Roger Hickey, *The Next Agenda: Blueprint for a New
     Progressive Movement* (Westview Press, 2001). Cover blurbs at Citizen Works,
     http://www.citizenworks.org/onlinestore/orderform.php.

12   Press Conference: Launch of Health Care for America Now by Jeffrey D. Blum,
     director, USAction, Washington, D.C., YouTube, August 8, 2009, http://www
     .youtube.com/watch?v=1xZ35qCKcTg.

13   Press Release, Health Care for America Now Launch, Health Care for America
     Now, July 8, 2008, http://healthcareforamericanow.org/site/content/health_care_
     for_america_now_launch_press_release.

14   Ibid. Profile: Brad Woodhouse, SourceWatch, http://www.sourcewatch.org/index
     .php?title=Brad_Woodhouse.

15   Press Release: "$40 Million Health Care Campaign to Launch, Announce New
     National Ad," Health Care for America Now, July 8, 2008, http://www.fcan.org/
     Press/HCAN%20Tampa%20Press%20Release.pdf.

16   Profile: Americans United for Change, SourceWatch, http://www.sourcewatch.org/
      index.php?title=Americans_United_for_Change.

17   Profile: Richard Kirsch, Health Care for America Now, http://healthcareforamerica
      now.org/site/content/richard_kirschr. Profile: Richard Kirsch, *WhoRunsGov.com*,
      http://www.whorunsgov.com/Profiles/Richard_Kirsch.

18   Profile: Richard Kirsch, *WhoRunsGov.com*. Stephen Kaufman, "Illinois
      Congressman Is Obama's First White House Appointment: White House chief
      of staff will juggle personnel, policy priorities," *America.gov*, November 6, 2008,
      http://www.america.gov/st/elections08-english/2008/November/20081106180912
      esnamfuak0.1655237.html.

19   Profile: Richard Kirsch, *WhoRunsGov.com*.

20   Ibid.

21   Ibid. Profile: Cathy Hurwit, Board of Directors, Midwest Academy, http://www
      .midwestacademy.com/board-directors.

22   Profile: Richard Kirsch, *WhoRunsGov.com*. Ruth Finkelstein, Cathy Hurwit, and
      Richard Kirsch, *The Managed Care Consumers' Bill of Rights: A Health Policy Guide for
      Advocates*, The Public Policy and Education Fund of New York in Cooperation with
      the Citizens' Fund, October 1995. The People's Business Show, October 19, 2000,
      Fiscal Policy Institute, http://www.fiscalpolicy.org/peoples_03.html.

23   Curriculum vitae, Jonathan B. Oberlander, September 2009, http://www.med.unc
      .edu/socialmed/files/cvs/Oberlander%20CV%202009%20September.pdf. Profile:
      Theodore R. Marmor, Yale School of Management, http://mba.yale.edu/faculty/
      profiles/marmor.shtml.

24   Jonathan Overlander and Theordore R. Marmor, "The Path to Universal
      Healthcare," in Robert L. Borosage and Roger Hickey, *The Next Agenda: Blueprint for
      a New Progressive Movement* (Westview Press, 2000), 104.

25   Ibid. Trevor Loudon, "Obama's Marxist Doctor Once Supported Google Health
      Advisor," *RBO*, December 10, 2009, http://therealbarackobama.wordpress
      .com/2009/12/10/loudon-obama's-marxist-doctor-once-supported-google-health-
      advisor.

26   Overlander and Marmor, "The Path to Universal Healthcare," 105.

27   Ibid.

28   Ibid., 106.

29   Ibid., 107.

30   Ibid., 106–107.

31   Ibid., 110.

32   Ibid., 112.

33   Ibid.

34   Ibid., 113–114.

35   "Worse Than the Public Option. Harry Reid's Medicare gambit," *Wall Street Journal*,
      December 11, 2009, http://online.wsj.com/article/SB100014240527487035144045
      74587981316751944.html.

36   Brenda J. Elliott, "Obama and the Marxist, Socialist, Radical Members of
      Congress," *RBO*, October 22, 2008, http://therealbarackobama.wordpress
      .com/2008/10/22/obama-and-the-marxist-socialist-radical-members-of-congress.
      "Pete Stark's AmeriCare Plan in Brief," ReformPlans.com, undated, http://www
      .reformplans.com/Plan-Briefs/Pete-Stark.html. Josh Richman, "Pete Stark
      re-pitches universal health care plans," *Contra Costa Times*, January 6, 2009,

http://www.ibabuzz.com/politics/2009/01/06/pete-stark-re-pitches-universal-health-care-plans.

37 Richard Kirsch, "Why not single-payer?," Health Care for America Now, July 15, 2008, http://healthcareforamericanow.org/site/blog/why_not_single_payer. "Health Care for America Now's strategy: Winning Quality Affordable Health Care for All," Health Care for America Now, circa 2007, http://hcfan.3cdn.net/0391625fb2a65ccfba_s6m6bxwjh.pdf.

38 Profile: Richard Kirsch, *WhoRunsGov.com*.

39 Joel Pollak, "Was Democrats' Health Care Strategy Written in Federal Prison?" *BigGovernment.com*, December 7, 2009, http://biggovernment.com/2009/12/07/was-democrats-health-care-strategy-written-in-federal-prison.

40 Robert Creamer, "Crashing the Gates of the Status Quo," *Huffington Post*, November 19, 2009, http://www.huffingtonpost.com/robert-creamer/crashing-the-gates-of-the_b_363622.html.

41 Pollak, "Was Democrats' Health Care Strategy Written in Federal Prison?"

42 Testimonials, Strategic Consulting Group website, http://www.stratcongroup.com/publication/testimonials.php.

43 Client list, Strategic Consulting Group, http://www.stratcongroup.com/clients.php.

44 "People," *Illinois Issues*, July/August 1997; Illinois Periodicals Online (IPO) digital imaging project at the Northern Illinois University Libraries, http://www.lib.niu.edu/1997/ii970833.html.

45 Brenda J. Elliott, "Camp Obama," *RBO*, October 4, 2008, http://therealbarackobama.wordpress.com/2008/10/04/camp-alinsky-obama.

46 The May 1, 1999, *Campaigns & Elections* article originally archived by The Free Library can no longer be located.

47 "Welcome to Camp Obama," *Investor's Business Daily*, October 3, 2008, http://doctorbulldog.wordpress.com/2008/10/03/investors-business-daily-picks-up-on-obamas-alinsky-method-of-indoctrination-and-change.

48 Robert Creamer, "How Progressives Can Deliver on the Promise of Change in 2009—Seven Rules for Success," *Huffington Post*, July 10, 2009, http://www.huffingtonpost.com/robert-creamer/how-progressives-can-deli_b_229305.html.

49 Brenda J. Elliott, "Jan Schakowsky: Obama's radical campaign co-chair—and replacement?" *RBO*, October 26, 2008, http://therealbarackobama.wordpress.com/2008/10/26/jan-schakowsky-obamas-radical-campaign-co-chair-and-replacement. John Ruberry, "Fundraiser tonight for admitted check-kiter and tax cheat Robert Creamer (husband of Congresswoman Jan Schakowsky)," *Marathon Pundit*, September 14, 2005, http://marathonpundit.blogspot.com/2005/09/fundraiser-tonight-for-admitted-check.html. Profile: Midwest Academy, *Undue Influence*, http://www.undueinfluence.com/midwest_academy.htm.

50 The November 1999 article, in the authors' possession, was originally published on the National Legal and Policy Center website, but cannot now be located. Check http://web.archive.org/web/20020505040833/http://www.nlpc.org/olap/UCU/03_02_09.htm.

51 Ibid.

52 Marianne Lavelle, "BIG MONEY. Citizen Action Spent $7 Million on Political Ads in the 1996 Campaign. When DoGooders Get Into Bad Trouble: The Teamster Connection at Citizen Action," *U.S. News & World Report*, October 13, 1997, http://www.laborers.org/USNWR_10-13-97.html.

53 Kaufman, "Illinois Congressman Is Obama's First White House Appointment."
54 Tom Roeser, "Personal Asides: Ever Wonder What Bob Creamer Is Doing Since Jail? Training Young People to Campaign for Obama . . . Pulido, Martire and Franks on 'Shootout' Sunday," *TomRoeser.com*, July 12, 2007, http://www.tomroeser .com/blogview.asp?blogID=24055.
55 Rod Baiman, "Reorganized Illinois Citizen Action," *New Ground* 56, January/ February 1998, http://www.chicagodsa.org/ngarchive/ng56.html#anchor1041720.
56 "Obama Speaks to Citizen Action/Illinois," *USAction Monthly Update*, August/ September 2004, 2, http://www.usaction.org/atf/cf/$7BB61F1B77-C265-416B-83EA-800FB44717CB$7D/August.September,%20Issue%205.pdf.
57 Press Release, HCAN, July 8, 2008.
58 Birnbaum, "'The Other K Street.'"
59 Health Care for America Now State Contact List, accessed December 4, 2009, http://www.scribd.com/doc/19925391/ACORNHealthcare-for-American-Now-State-Contact-List. The list is also posted on the ACORNCracked website, http://www.acorncracked.com/documents/HCANSTATECNTACTS1.15.09 .pdf. A state-by-state search engine for individual states is available at: http:// healthcareforamericanow.org/site/action_center/#state.
60 MattH, "TrueMajorityAction Merges with USAction!," True Majority Action/True Blog, September 27, 2007, http://www.truemajorityaction.org/blog/?p=16.
61 Trevor Loudon, "William McNary, Yet Another Obama Radical?" *RBO*, September 3, 2008, http://therealbarackobama.wordpress.com/2008/09/03/loudon-obama-file-26-william-mcnary-yet-another-obama-radical.
62 Loudon, Ibid. Trevor Loudon, "Socialist Octogenarians for Barack," *New Zeal*, February 20, 2008, http://newzeal.blogspot.com/2008/02/obama-file-15-socialist-octagenarians.html. Trevor Loudon, "Alice Palmer—Obama's Soviet Sympathizing Patroness," *New Zeal*, August 23, 2008, http://newzeal.blogspot.com/2008/08/ obama-file-23-alice-palmer-obamas.html. Trevor Loudon, "Jan Schakowsky— Barack Obama's Loyal Socialist Supporter," *New Zeal*, February 10, 2008, http:// newzeal.blogspot.com/2008/02/obama-file-12-jan-schakowsky-barack.html. Trevor Loudon, "Socialist Unionists Endorse Barack Obama," *New Zeal*, January 15, 2008, http://newzeal.blogspot.com/2008/01/obama-file-3-socialist-unionists.html.
63 William McNary, "News Articles, Press Releases and Media Advisories—William McNary Speaks Out in Support of WVWV," Women's Voices, Women Vote, May 1, 2008, http://wvwv.org/2008/5/1/statement-of-william-mcnary-president-of-usaction-co-executive-director-citizen-action-illinois-and-board-member-of-women-s-voices-women-vote.
64 Loudon, "William McNary, Yet Another Obama Radical?" David Moberg, "Obama's Third Way," *In These Times* (Spring 2007), http://www.nhi.org/online/issues/149/ obama.html.
65 Loudon, "William McNary, Yet Another Obama Radical?" David Moberg, "Obama's in the Eye of the Beholder: Can the junior senator from Illinois be both a stalwart progressive and a post-ideological unifier?" *In These Times*, September 17, 2007, http://www.inthesetimes.com/article/3329/obamas_in_the_eye_of_the_beholder.
66 Profile: Heather Booth, *Discover the Networks*, http://www.discoverthenetworks .org/individualProfile.asp?indid=1641.

67 Profile: Heather Booth, *Discover the Networks*.

68 Campaign Contributions for Jeffrey Blum, CampaignMoney.com, http://www
    .campaignmoney.com/political/contributions/jeff-blum.asp?cycle=08; and at
    NewsMeat.com, http://www.newsmeat.com/fec/bystate_detail.php?zip=20912&
    last=Blum&first=Jeffrey.

69 The speaker's profile for Jeffrey Blum posted at 21st Century Dems has been
    removed. Check http://www.21stcenturydems.org/SpeakerSeries/jeff-blum.

70 Not only are Jeff Blum and Heather Booth both advisory board members of the
    Jewish Fund for Justice, their names appear numerous times together on boards, as
    readily revealed in a Google search. Booth's name also previously appeared on the
    21stCenturyDems.org website as having been a trainer.

71 "Left allies regroup for battle: Coalition of progressive groups to oppose
    Social Security privatization," *The Hill*, February 1, 2005, http://www
    .usactioneducationfund.org/site/pp.asp.140.html.

72 Profile: Jeffrey David Blum, Federal Bureau of Investigation, "Weather
    Underground Organization (Weatherman)," 1976 Declassified Report, 61; http://
    foia.fbi.gov/weather/weath2a.pdf.

73 Ibid.

74 Kirkpatrick Sale, *SDS: The Rise and Development of the Students for a Democratic
    Society* (1973), 405, http://www.archive.org/details/SdsTheRiseAndDevelopment
    OfTheStudentsForADemocraticSociety.

75 Bernardine Dohrn, "Lessons for Leftists Old and New," *Monthly Review* (October
    2006), http://www.monthlyreview.org/1006dohrn.htm.

76 "National Lawyers Guild & Its Terrorist Network," Knology.net, http://www
    .knology.net/~bilrum/nlgterr.htm.

77 Ezra Klein, "The path to single-payer health care," *Washington Post*, November 15,
    2009, http://www.oregonlive.com/opinion/index.ssf/2009/11/the_path_to_single-
    payer_healt.html.

78 ralphbon, "Tragic Loss of a Health Reform Advocate: Nick Skala Dead at 27,"
    Firedoglake, August 11, 2009; http://seminal.firedoglake.com/diary/7134.
    Brandon Wu, "In Memory of Nick Skala, Former GTW Intern," PublicCitizen,
    August 14, 2009, http://citizen.typepad.com/eyesontrade/2009/08/in-memory-
    of-nick-skala-former-gtw-intern.html. Nick Skala, "Hold Out for Single-Payer,"
    SinglePayerNewYork.org, June 4, 2009, http://singlepayernewyork.org/news/
    holdout.php.

79 Skala, "Hold Out for Single-Payer."

80 Physicians for a National Health Program website, http://www.pnhp.org.

81 Trevor Loudon, "Obama's Marxist Doctor Once Supported Google Health Advisor,"
    RBO, December 10, 2009, http://therealbarackobama.wordpress.com/2009/12/10/
    loudon-obama's-marxist-doctor-once-supported-google-health-advisor. Profile:
    Quentin D. Young, Physicians for a National Health Program, http://www.pnhp
    .org/freshair/young_bio.php.

82 Profile: Quentin D. Young, PNHP.

83 Ibid.

84 Loudon, "Obama's Marxist Doctor."

85 Trevor Loudon, "Some Christmas Reading for Your Senators — Obama,

Conyers, Young and Socialized Healthcare," *RBO*, December 8, 2009, http://therealbarackobama.wordpress.com/2009/12/08/loudon-some-christmas-reading-for-your-senators-obama-conyers-young-and-socialized-healthcare.

86 Ibid.

87 Ibid.

88 Ibid.

89 Ibid. "Dr. Quentin Young, Longtime Obama Confidante and Physician to MLK, Criticizes Admin's Rejection of Single-Payer Healthcare," *Democracy Now!*, March 11, 2009, http://www.democracynow.org/2009/3/11/dr_quentin_young_obama_confidante_and.

90 Profile: Richard Kirsch, *WhoRunsGov.com*, http://www.whorunsgov.com/Profiles/Richard_Kirsch.

91 Robert Creamer, "August Offensive to Define Health Care Debate: Insurance Companies in the Bull's Eye," *Huffington Post*, August 3, 2009, http://www.huffingtonpost.com/robert-creamer/august-offensive-to-defin_b_249727.html.

92 "Rules for Radicals," http://vcn.bc.ca/citizens-handbook/rules.html.

93 Michelle Malkin, "Who's funding the Obamacare Astroturf campaign?" *MichelleMalkin.com*, June 24, 2009, http://michellemalkin.com/2009/06/24/who's-funding-the-obamacare-astroturf-campaign.

94 Profile: "Astroturf," SourceWatch, http://www.sourcewatch.org/index.php?title=Astroturf.

95 Michael D. Shear and Jose Antonio Vargas, "A Pitch on Health Care to Virginia And Beyond: Obama Hears from Guests and Twitter," *Washington Post*, July 2, 2009, http://www.washingtonpost.com/wp-dyn/content/article/2009/07/01/AR2009070100950.html.

96 "Remarks by the President in an Online Town Hall on Health Care," Northern Virginia Community College, Annandale, Virginia, Office of the White House Press Secretary, *WhiteHouse.gov*, July 1, 2009, http://www.whitehouse.gov/the_press_office/Remarks-of-the-President-in-an-Online-Town-Hall-on-Health-Care-Reform.

97 Greg Pierce, "Celebrities," *Washington Times*, July 3, 2009, http://www.questia.com/read/5029822387?title=Celebrities.

98 Contributor: Jason Rosenbaum, National Journal; http://healthcare.nationaljournal.com/contributors/Rosenbaum.php.

99 Profile: Jason Rosenbaum, *TheSeminal.com*, http://www.theseminal.com/author/j-ro.

100 Speaker profile, Jason Rosenbaum, Netroots Nation 2008, Austin, Texas, July 17–20, 2008, http://www.netrootsnation.org/downloads/program/NN_Program_2008_lores.pdf.

101 Profile: Progressive Media USA, SourceWatch, http://www.sourcewatch.org/index.php?title=Progressive_Media_USA.

102 Jonathan Weisman and Michael D. Shear, "Obama looks to control message: He tells his donors to shirk outside groups," *Washington Post*, May 18, 2008, http://www.concordmonitor.com/apps/pbcs.dll/article?AID=/20080514/FRONTPAGE/805140306/1013.

103 Greg Sargent, "Center for American Progress Launching Big War Room to Drive Obama Agenda," *The Plum Line*, March 10, 2009, http://theplumline.whorunsgov .com/labor/center-for-american-progress-launching-big-war-room-to-drive-obama-agenda.

104 Profile: Jason Rosenbaum, LinkedIn, http://www.linkedin.com/pub/jason-rosenbaum/4/153/592.

105 HCAN's Playbook for Thwarting Town Hall Protests: http://www.talkingpointsmemo.com/documents/2009/08/hcan-playbook-for-thwarting-town-hall-protesters.php?page=1.

106 Robert Pear, "Senate Passes Health Care Overhaul on Party-Line Vote," *New York Times*, December 24, 2009, http://www.nytimes.com/2009/12/25/health/policy/25health.html.

107 Ibid. "House passes health care reform bill," CNN, November 7, 2009, http://www.cnn.com/2009/POLITICS/11/07/health.care/index.html.

108 Jason Rosenbaum, "The Senate passes their health care bill," HCAN Blog, December 24, 2009, http://blog.healthcareforamericanow.org/2009/12/24/the-senate-passes-their-health-care-bill.

109 David S. Broder, "A health-care victory that stinks," *Washington Post*, December 23, 2009, http://www.washingtonpost.com/wp-dyn/content/article/2009/12/23/AR2009122302440.html.

110 Michelle Malkin, "Cash for Cloture: Demcare bribe list, Pt. II," *MichelleMalkin.com*, December 21, 2009, http://michellemalkin.com/2009/12/21/cash-for-cloture-demcare-bribe-list-pt-ii.

111 David L. Bahnsen, "What's Pork for the Goose Is Pork for the Gander: The Health Care Debacle Explained," *DavidBahnsen.com*, December 21, 2009, http://www.davidbahnsen.com/index.php/2009/12/21/whats-pork-for-the-goose-is-pork-for-the-gander-the-health-care-debacle-explained.

112 Jane Hamsher, "10 Reasons to Kill the Senate Bill," Firedoglake, December 21, 2009, http://fdlaction.firedoglake.com/2009/12/21/10-reasons-to-kill-the-senate-bill. The absolute accuracy of Hamsher's statements have not been verified due to the exhaustive volume of the bill itself and its unavailability at the time of this writing.

INDEX

AAAN (Arab American Action Network), 16–17, 47–48

ABCDI (Asset-Based Community Development Institute), 62

ABC News presidential primary debate, 2–3

ABCs Coalition (Alliance for Better Chicago Schools), 11

abortion-on-demand, 226

abortions, compulsory, 175–76

Abunimah, Ali, 49–50

Accountability Now PAC, 141

Acevedo Vilá, Anibal, 139–40

ACORN (Association of Community Organizations for Reform Now)
and CAC, 12, 118–20
and Crawford, 203
and Davis Miner, 116
and Gaspard, 140
and New Party, 81, 83–84
and Obama, 109–10, 113–23, 120–21
People's Platform, 107
and Project Vote!, 112–15
and Rathke, 105–7
voter fraud accusations, 121–22

ACORN Advisory Board, 138

"ACORN's Nutty Regime for Cities" (Stern), 108–9

ACT (American Coming Together), 131–32

Adams, Elliott, 210

Adi, Zulfin, 42

Adler, Jonathan, 173–75

Affordable Health Care for America Act (2009), 268

Afghanistan, 209–10

AFL-CIO
and ACORN, 107
and Apollo Alliance, 228
and CPUSA, 149
and Democratic Party, 131
and Economic Recovery Advisory Board, 142
and Obama, 226–27
and SEIU, 140

AFSCME (American Federation of State, County and Municipal Employees), 64, 132, 243, 254

Albano, Terry, 149–50

Albjerg Graham, Patricia, 12

Alinsky, L. David, 51

Alinsky, Saul, 9–10

Alinsky model, 51–55, 57–60, 122–23, 129–37, 207–8

Allen, Charlotte, 58

Alliance for Better Chicago Schools (ABCs Coalition), 11

Alterman, Eric, 172
American Coming Together (ACT), 131–32
American Federation of State, County and Municipal Employees (AFSCME), 64, 132, 243, 254
American New Left, 26
American Recovery and Reinvestment Act (2009), 81, 214, 222, 229–30
Americans Against Escalation in Iraq, 241
Amir, Rony, 42
Andersen, Christopher, 15–16, 66
Annenberg Foundation, 12
anti-apartheid movement, 20–23, 31–33
anti-Semitism, 89
Apollo Alliance, 81, 154–55, 214, 221–23, 228, 235–36
"Apollo Project, The" (Hendricks), 230–31
Apollo's Fire: Igniting America's Clean Energy Economy (Ensley and Hendricks), 222, 233
Aptheker, Herbert, 100
Arab American Action Network (AAAN), 16–17, 47–48
Arkansas Community Organization for Reform Now, 106. *See also* ACORN
Armstrong, Danny, 32, 36–37
Asset-Based Community Development Institute (ABCDI), 62
Association of Community Organizations for Reform Now. *See* ACORN
astroturf technique, 264, 267–68
Attiah, Mark, 32
Automotive Competitiveness and Accountability Act, 236–37
Axelrod, David, 3, 97–98, 158–63, 165–66
Ayers, Bill
  and Baxandall, 212
  and CAC, 12–14
  and *Dreams from My Father*, 14–16
  and GSIC, 119
  media response to first reports, viii
  and New New Left, 208, 209
  Obama on relationship with, 1, 2–3
  on panel with Obama and Ransby, 34
  and Weatherman, 5, 7–8, 87, 109, 155, 214

and Weather Underground, 5, 8, 110, 259–60
Ayers, Thomas, 10–11

Baehr, Richard, 169
Bahnsen, David L., 270
Baker, Mark, 253
Balanoff, Tom, 133–36
Ball, Tim, 176
Banjarmasin Post, 42, 283n15
Barack and Michelle (Anderson), 15–16, 66
"Barack Obama's Rules for Revolution" (Horowitz), 52–53, 220
Bartiromo, Maria, 136–37
Batchelor, John, ix
Baxandall, Rosalyn, 211, 212
Beck, Glenn, ix, 143, 154, 188, 222
Bentham, Jeremy, 181–82
Bernard, Elaine, 81
Bhargava, Deepak, 144, 145–46
Biden, Joe, 161
Biko Commons, Occidental College, 22
Bingham, John, 68–69
Birnbaum, Jeffrey H., 241, 256
birth certificate issue, 73–77
Black, Timuel, 263
Black Commentator, The, 213
Black Radical Caucus, 35
Black Radical Congress (BRC), 35
Black Student Alliance, 20–21, 278n26
Black Students Organization, 31, 32, 33–34
Black Theology of Liberation, A (Cone), 45–46, 92
Blagojevich, Rod, 132–33, 158, 254
Block, Stephanie, 9–10
Blum, Jeffrey D., 208, 242–43, 255, 258–59
Boesche, Roger, 23, 276n11, 276n13
"Bomber as School Reformer, The" (Ayers), 212
Bonior, David, 227
Booth, Heather Tobis, 208, 257–58
Booth, Paul, 208, 258
Borosage, Robert, 147, 223, 225–27, 240–42, 245, 252
Boudin, Katherine, 8
Boyte, Harry C., 24–25, 122–23, 208

Bradley, Bill, 28–29, 245
Bradley plan, 245–48
Braun, Carol Moseley, 114, 157, 164
BRC (Black Radical Congress), 35
Breakthrough Institute, 233
Breitbart, Andrew, 125
Broadcaster Freedom Act, 204
Brock, David, 266
Broder, David S., 269
Brooks, Rosa, 182–86
Brown, David M., 121
Brown, Stanley M., 120
Brown, Waverly, 8
Browne, Katrina, 62
Browner, Carol M., 166–69
Buhle, Paul, 211
Burger, Anna, 138, 140–42, 227
Bush, George W., 183–84, 185–86, 240
Business International Corporation
  (BIC), 37
Business International Money Report, 37

Cabral, Amilcar, 153–54
CAC (Chicago Annenberg Challenge),
  11–14, 118–20, 219
Caldwell, Larry T., 25
Campaign for America's Future (CAF),
  226–27, 240–41, 242
Campaign for Economic Democracy
  (CED), 28–30, 278n30
Campbell, Roy H., 21–22
Canter, David Simon, 162–66
Canter, Harry, 164
Canter, Marc, 162–65
Cantwell, Maria, 233
CAP (Center for American Progress), 168,
  187–88, 233–34, 266
Carol, Dan, 221–22, 223, 224–25
Carroll, Conn, 222–23
Cashill, Jack, 14–16
Catholic Campaign for Human
  Development, 9
CED (Campaign for Economic
  Democracy), 28–30, 278n30
Center for American Progress (CAP), 168,
  187–88, 233–34, 266
Center for Community Change (CCC),
  143–44

Center for National Security Studies
  (CNSS), 226
Certification of Live Birth (COLB), 73–75
CFSA (Coalition for a Free South Africa),
  32–33
Chambers, Edward T. "Ed," 55, 58–59,
  63–64, 122
Chapman, Gary, 23, 24, 25, 277n16
Charen, Mona, 117, 123
Chávez, César, 28, 123
Chávez, Hugo, 147, 201, 212, 217–18
Cheney, Dick, 183–84
Chepesiuk, Ron, 13
Chicago Annenberg Challenge (CAC),
  11–14, 118–20, 219
Chicagoans United to Reform Education
  (CURE or Chicago United), 10–11
Chicago School Reform Act, 10
Chicago School Reform Collaborative, 13
Chicago Sun-Times, 112–13
Chicago Tribune, 12–13, 43, 160
Chomsky, Noam, 81, 210
Citizen Action, 64, 168–69, 208, 244–45,
  254–55
Citizen Services, Inc., 120
"Climate Change Justice" (Sunstein),
  179
Climate Research Unit (CRU), 176
Clinton, Hillary, 1–2, 51, 97, 170
Cloward, Richard A., 106
Cloward-Piven strategy, 110–12
CNSS (Center for National Security
  Studies), 226
Coalition for a Free South Africa (CFSA),
  32–33
Cohen, Ben, 256
COLB (Certification of Live Birth), 73–75
Collier, Peter, 173
Collum, Danny Duncan, 55
Colmes, Alan, 209
Columbia College, New York, 30–32
Communications Act (1934), 191
"Communications Policy Is a Civil Rights
  Issue" (Lloyd), 190
communism, 53–54, 86, 178
Communist Party USA (CPUSA), 148–51
Compaine, Ben, 193–94
Cone, James, 45–46, 91–92

Congressional Progressive Caucus,
261–62
"Constitution in 2020, The" (Sunstein),
177–78
Conyers, John, 263
corporate broadcasting, 188–91
Corporate Campaigns, 130
corporate takeover of medicine, 262
Corporation for Public Broadcasting
(CPB), 189–90
Corsi, Jerome, 174, 175
Cortés, Ernesto, Jr., 60
Country That Works, A (Stern), 136
Cover, Matt, 188–89
CPUSA (Communist Party USA), 148–51
Crawford, Susan P., 202–3, 313n41
Creamer, Robert, 249–55, 264
CURE (Chicagoans United to Reform
Education), 10–11

Davidson, Carl, 81, 84–85, 158, 208,
210–11
Davis, Daniel K., 85–86
Davis, Frank Marshall, 11, 156–57, 211
Davis, Rennie, 26–27
Davis Miner law firm, 88, 116, 118
Days of Rage riots (SDS), 157, 214–15, 259
DCP (Developing Communities Project),
8–10, 55, 62–63
Dean, Howard, 122
"Death Angels," 90
Death of a Thousand Cuts, The (Manheim),
106–8
Democratic Party, 131–32, 147–48
Democratic Party Conventions, 4–5, 106
Democratic presidential primary
campaign, vii, 1–2, 28–29, 57, 170
Democratic Socialist Organizing
Committee (DSOC), 24
Democratic Socialists of America (DSA)
and Bhargava, 145
and CAP, 242
Debs–Thomas–Harrington Dinner, 135
and Dreier, 61
and NAM, 24
and New Party, 81–82
Obama endorsement, 146
online newsletter, 63

and SEIU, 142
Young's involvement, 262
Developing Communities Project (DCP),
8–10, 55, 62–63
Diamond, Stephen, 133–35
Dieden, Michael, 28
Dinan, Stephen, 167
Discover the Networks
on Cloward and Piven, 111–12
on Ehrenreich, 216
on IAF, 258
on Katz, 157
on Muhammad, 90, 91
on MWA, 128
on SDS and Weatherman, 4, 5
Socialist International, 166–67
on Stern, 132
on Tides Foundation, 238
Dohrn, Bernardine, 7, 8, 87, 109, 208,
211, 259–60
Dohrn children, 3
Dorgan, Byron, 192
Draper, Robert, 155–56
Dreams from My Father (Obama)
Ayers as possible ghost writer, 14–16
on head of DCP, 9
on Muslim school in Indonesia, 42
on Occidental College, 19–21, 30
on socialist conferences, 80
on Unitarian Church in Hawaii, 5
on wedding of his parents, 66
Dred Scot v. Sandford (1857), 69
Dreier, Peter, 60–61
Dreyer, Thorne, 211
DSA. See Democratic Socialists of
America
DSOC (Democratic Socialist Organizing
Committee), 24
Dunham, Stanley Ann, 65–67, 72
Duranty, Walter, 212

East Bay Express, 153
economic crises, utilizing for change, 178
Economic Policy Institute (EPI), 241
Ecoscience (Holdren), 175
Edgar, James, 116
Ehrenreich, Barbara, 81, 147, 183, 216–17
Ehrlich, Paul, 174

Ella Baker Center for Human Rights, 153, 235

Elliott, Brenda J., ix, 147, 212–13

Emanuel, Rahm, 233, 244

Employees Freedom of Choice Act/Card Check, 131, 143

"Energy/Jobs Program, An" (Hendricks), 228–29

EPI (Economic Policy Institute), 241

Evans, Jodie, 147

Evans, Lane, 253

Fairness Doctrine, 188–89, 197

Fallon, George, 189–90

Farrakhan, Louis, 89–99, 103–4

Federal Communications Commission (FCC), 188–93, 198–99, 200–201, 204

Federal Employees Health Benefits Plan (FEHBP), 246

Federalist Option in health care, 247

Financial Foreign Operations, 37

Finfer, Lew, 59–60

Fink, Jason, 38

Finkelstein, Ruth, 245

First Amendment, 187, 195, 197, 200–201

First Unitarian Church of Honolulu, Hawaii, 3–7

Fishman, Joelle, 148, 149, 150–51

Fitzgerald, Patrick, 132

Flacks, Richard, 30, 280n47

Fletcher, Bill, 81, 211, 216, 217

Fonda, Jane, 25, 26

Ford, Patricia, 217

"Forget the Fairness Doctrine" (Lloyd), 188

Free Press, 202–3

Friedman, Max, 164–65

Friends of Barack Obama PAC, 124–25

"From Protest to Politics" (Davidson and Katz), 158

Fugitive Days (Ayers), 7, 14–15, 36

Fukino, Chiyome, 76–77

Fund, John, 116

Galluzzo, Gregory, 53, 56, 57

Gamaliel Foundation, 54–57

Ganz, Marshall, 60

Gardner, Terri, 113

Garskof, Bert, 211

Gaspard, Patrick, 138, 140

Gates, Henry Louis, Jr., 99–101

Gaynor, Michael, 127

Genachowski, Julius, 35–36, 188, 198–99

Gerard, Leo, 227–28

Get Out the Vote efforts, 61, 109–16, 121–22, 126, 157, 253

Giangreco, Pete, 159

Gilbert, David, 8

Gilbert, Steve, 36

Gitlin, Todd, 52

Glover, Danny K., 217–18

Gonzales, Mary, 146

Good, Thomas, 211

Gordon, Larry, 23

Grassroots School Improvement Campaign (GSIC), 119

Gray, Young C., 6

Grossfeld, Jim, 228

guilt by association, xii

Halperin, Morton, 226

Hamas, ix, 47, 185–86

Hamilton, David, 211

Hamsher, Jane, 270–71, 327n112

Hannity, Sean, 196

Harrington, Michael, 128, 145

Harvard Law School, 59–60, 102

Hawaii, 70–73

Hayden, Tom, 25–28, 30, 150, 208–10, 241, 278n30, 280n47

Haydock, Oliver, 23

HCAN. See Health Care for America NOW

Health and Medicine Policy Research Group, 262–63

Health Care for America NOW (HCAN)
  federalist, pincer, and single-payer strategies, 244, 247–48, 261–63
  launch and members, 242–44
  legislation, 268–72
  overview, 239, 256–61
  principles, 263–68

Hendricks, Bracken, 222, 223, 228–31, 233, 237

Hendricks, Obery M., Jr., 46

Hershenov, Eileen, 37–38

vanden Heuvel, Katrina, 121, 191–92
Hickey, Roger, 227, 240–42, 245, 252
Hightower, Jim, 241
Hilliard, David, 28
Hirsch, Eric L., 33, 38
Hitler, Adolf, 184
Holdren, John, 172–76
Honolulu Star-Bulletin, 7
Horne, Gerald, 211
Horowitz, David, 51–56, 220. See also
    Discover the Networks
House Committee on Un-American
    Activities, 26–27
Howard, Jen, 199, 200–201
Hudson, Gerland "Gerry," 143–44
Huffington Post, The, 27–28, 30, 250–51,
    253–54, 264
Hurwit, Cathy, 245
Huston, Warner Todd, 199–200

IAF (Industrial Areas Foundation), 54,
    57–60, 64, 107, 258
IAF (Institute for America's Future), 225,
    241
Independent Voters of Illinois (IVI), 165
Indonesia, 41–43, 77–79
Industrial Areas Foundation (IAF), 54,
    57–60, 64, 107, 258
Inslee, Jay, 222, 231–33
Institute for America's Future (IAF), 225,
    241
Institute for Palestine Studies, 47–48
Institute for Policy Studies (IPS), 103,
    145, 218
International Workers of the World
    (IWW), 130
Internet-based libel lawsuits, 196
Investor's Business Daily, 57, 253
IPS (Institute for Policy Studies), 103,
    145, 218
Ireland, Doug, 160
Islam, 77–79. *See also* Nation of Islam
Israel, 16–17, 46–47, 49–50, 170–71,
    184–86
Isserman, Maurice, 24, 277n18
IVI (Independent Voters of Illinois), 165
IWW (International Workers of the
    World), 130

Jaquette, Jane, 22–23
Jarrett, Valerie, 155–56
Jarrett, Vernon, 112–13, 156–57
Jarrett, William Robert, 157
Jay, Father John, 68
Jessup, Meredith, 136–37
Johnson, Ben, 173
Jones, Jeff, 155, 214
Jones, Tim, 72
Jones, Van, ix, 152–55, 222, 224, 234–36
Joravsky, Ben, 11

Kammen, Daniel, 233
Kass, John, 132–33
Katz, Marilyn, 157–59, 208, 211
Kelleher, Keith, 113–14
Kelley, Alison, 38
Kelley, Robin D.G., 211
Kellman, Gerald "Jerry," 9
Kenya, Africa, 43–45, 70–73
Kerpen, Phil, 200
Kerry, John, 130–31, 192–93
Khalidi, Rashid, viii, 16–17, 47–49, 118
Kincaid, Cliff, 203–4
Kingsley, Elizabeth, 115
Kirsch, Richard, 244–45, 248–49,
    268–69
Kirsch, Vanessa, 62
Kissinger, C. Clark, 154
Klein, Ezra, 261
Klein, Joe, 45
Klonsky, Mike, 13, 119, 211, 218–19
Knauer, Brigada, 22
Kovalkeski, Serge F., 21
Krauthammer, Charles, 36
Kretzmann, Jody, 62
Kurtz, Stanley, 12, 46, 93, 95, 117, 118–19
Kyl, John, 77

labor unions
    and ACORN, 106, 107–8, 113–15
    and CAF, 226–27
    and Citizen Action, 255–56
    and Democratic Party, 131–32
    and United Powers, 63–64
    at USAction, 254–55
    See also AFL-CIO
Lamb, Henry, 148

Lasar, Matthew, 198–99
Lasky, Ed, 169
Latinos, 303n73
Law of Nations, The (de Vattel), 68
Leff, Deborah, 12
Lenin, Vladimir, 153
Lenz, Linda, 120
Levin, Carl, 269–70
Lieberman, Ben, 169
Lieberman, Joe, 142
Limbaugh, Rush, 188
Lincoln, Abraham, xii
Lindley, Robin, 169
Listen to Your Mother (Creamer), 249–55
Little, Amanda, 236–37
Living Wage Movement, 84–85, 107,
   111–12, 115
Lizza, Ryan, 54, 56, 58
Lloyd, Mark, 156, 187–92, 194–95
Loris, Nick, 167
Los Angeles Times, 42–43, 283n16
Loudon, Trevor
   on Axelrod, 161–62, 165
   on Bhargava, 145–46
   on BRC, 35
   on Canter, 163–64
   on Gaspard, 140
   on IPS, 218
   on Marable, 214
   on McNary, 257
   on MDS, 27, 210–13
   on Medina, 142–43
   on Munoz, 150
   on Obama and Davis, 211
   on Progressives for Obama, 27
   on Rose, 165
   on Villaraigosa, 227
   on Young, 262–63
Louv, Richard, 227–28
Lyons, Eugene, 162

MacPherson, Mary, 26
Malanga, Steven, 62–63, 64
Malcolm X, 90
Malkin, Michelle, 240, 264
Managed Care Consumers' Bill of Rights, The
   (Kirsch, Finkelstein, and Hurwit), 245
Manchurian Candidate, The (Condon), x

Manchurian Candidate, The (films), x
Marable, Manning, 86–87, 213
Marinucci, Carla, 118
Marmor, Theodore R., 245–48, 249
marriage sanctions, 179–80
Martin, Kevin, 192
Marxist/Socialists/Communists for
   Obama, 206
Marzook, Mousa Abu, 47
Mason, Jennifer, 96
Matzzie, Tom, 266
McCain, John, 70, 108
McCarthy, Andrew, 36, 207–8, 210
McChesney, Robert W., 200, 201–2
McDaniel, Martha D., 6
McFerren, Coretta, 11
McGuinness, Tara, 267
McKinney, Cynthia, 95
McKnight, John L., 56–57, 62
McLeod, Judi, 176
McNary, William, 64, 255, 256–57, 263
MDS (Movement for a Democratic
   Society), 27, 87, 210–13, 218–19
Media Access Project, 200–201
media diversity, 188, 199, 201, 204
Media Ownership Act (2007), 192
media redistribution, 187–90
Medina, Eliseo, 142–44
Meister, Dick, 227
Mendell, David, 19, 23, 276n13
Message to the Blackman in America
   (Muhammad), 90
Metzenbaum, Howard, 241
Midwest Academy (MWA), 128
Miller, Cynthia K., 96
Miller, Ethelbert, 211
Million Man March, 91, 94–95
Mitchell, Charlene, 211
Moberg, David, 63–64, 242, 257, 289n62
MonCrief, Anita, 115
Morrill, Barbara, 141–42
Morris, Calvin S., 120
Morrissey, Ed, 241
Motley, Seton, 188, 194–95
Movement for a Democratic Society
   (MDS), 27, 87, 210–13, 218–19
Muhammad, Elijah, 90
Muhammad, Khallid Abdul, 103

Munoz, Rosalio, 149–50
Murdoch, Rupert, 190
Murdock, Deroy, 123
MWA (Midwest Academy), 128

Nakba art exhibit, 17
NAM (New American Movement), 24–25, 129, 277n17
Napolitano, Janet, 143
Nation, The, viii–ix, 29, 110, 147–48, 215–16
National Legal and Policy Center, 254
National Living Wage Campaign Training Conference, 107
National Welfare Reform Organization (NWRO), 105–7, 108, 111–12, 123
Nation of Islam (NOI), 89–91, 95–96, 103
natural born citizen, defining, 67–70
Naturalization Act (1790), 68
Nelson, Ben, 269
Nelson, Diana, 119
Network Neutrality, Broadband Discrimination (Wu), 203
New America Foundation, 203
New American Movement (NAM), 24–25, 129, 277n17
New Apollo Energy Project, 231–33
New Black Panther Party, 103–4
New Deal Coalition, 277n20
"New Face of Environmentalism, The" (Strickland), 234–35
New Ground newsletter, 63, 81–82, 84
New Growth Initiative, 229
Newhall, Eric, 23
New Labor, 130–31
New Left, 173, 206
Newman, Sandy, 110
New New Left, 207–8
New Party, 35, 80–88, 225
New Party News, 84
news media's abdication of responsibility, vii–viii, 18–19
New York Citizen Action, 244
New York Public Interest Research Group (NYPIRG), 37–38
New York Times, 2, 6, 8, 36, 155–56, 158
Next Agenda Blueprint for a New Progressive

Movement, The (Borosage and Hickey, eds.), 242, 245
Nicholas, Peter, 127, 138–39
Nichols, John, 202, 225
NOI (Nation of Islam), 89–91, 95–96, 103
Nordhaus, Ted, 233, 234–36
Nudge (Thaler and Sunstein), 179–80
NWRO (National Welfare Reform Organization), 105–7, 108, 111–12, 123
NYPIRG (New York Public Interest Research Group), 37–38

Obama, Aoko, 66–67
Obama, Barack
   on ACORN and Project VOTE!, 114
   on CAC experience, 14
   on FCC and media diversification, 204
   on media consolidation, 193
   on Muslims, 40
   on relationship with Ayers, 1, 2–3
   on religion in America, 39–40
   on SEIU, 125–26
Obama, Barack, Sr., 65–67, 72
Obama, Michelle, 16–17, 58–59, 62, 102, 119–20
Obama, Roy, 43
Obama, Sarah, 43, 71–72
Obama for America website, 205–6
Obama: From Promise to Power (Mendell), 19, 23
Oberlander, Jonathan B., 245–48, 249
Occidental College, Los Angeles
   anti-apartheid movement, 21–23
   Obama on, 19–21, 30
   Obama's records from, 18–19
   overview, 22, 278n26
   speculation on influences, 23–30
Odinga, Raila Amollo, 44–45
Ogego, Peter N.R.O., 72
Ogletree, Charles, 101–3
O'Grady, Edward, 8
Ohrstrom, Lysandra, 31, 32
On Rumors (Sunstein), 195–96
Open Society Institute, 111, 203, 226, 232
organ donation, 180–81
Our Media, Not Theirs (Nichols), 202

Our Posthuman Future (Fukuyama), 181
Ovide, Shira, 199

Paige, Peter, 8
Pakistan, 79
Palestine Liberation Organization (PLO),
    16–17
Palestinian radicalism, 47–50
Palin, Sarah, viii, 147
Palmieri, Jennifer, 266–67
Parks, Kim, 34
Partial Constitution, The (Sunstein), 181,
    196–97
Pear, Robert, 268–69
Pelosi, Nancy, 240
People's Coalition for Educational Reform
    (PCER), 11
Pfleger, Father Michael, 97–98
Physicians for a National Health Program,
    245–46, 261–62
Pierce, Greg, 265
Pike, Drummond, 146, 238
pincer strategy for health care, 247
Pipes, Daniel, 43
Piven, Frances Fox, 81, 106, 110–12
Planetary Regime concept, 173
PM magazine, 161–62
Podesta, John, 138, 188, 232
Poe, Richard, 111–12
Polett, Zach, 110
Policy Today, 137
Politico website, 2–3, 169
Pollak, Joel B., 249–52
Ponte, Lowell, 129–31
Poole, William T., 29–30, 206–7
Pope, Carl, 228
Pope, Sandy, 81
Population Bomb, The (Ehrlich), 174
Posner, Eric A., 179
Power, Samantha, 169–72
"Progressive Agenda for Structural
    Change" (Creamer), 250–51
Progressive Democrats of America, 27,
    147–48, 150
Progressive Majority PAC, 225–26
Progressive Media USA, 266
Progressives for Obama
    Ayers, Davidson, and Klonsky, 218

Baxandall, 212
Burger, 142, 227
Dreier, 61
Fletcher, 201, 215
Hayden, 27, 215
Munoz, 150
overview, 27, 215–20
Rudd, 219
Stern, 138
Project VOTE! campaign, 61, 109–16,
    121–22, 157
Prologue to a Farce (Lloyd), 189–90
Public Allies Chicago, 62
Public Knowledge, 203

al-Qaeda, 183

Radical Son (Horowitz), 52
Ransby, Barbara, 32–33, 34–35
Rathke, Wade, 105–9, 122–23, 146, 208,
    238
Reason.com, 31
"Reclaiming Revolution" (STORM), 153
"Red Sisters of the Bourgeoisie"
    (Baxandall and Fraad), 212
Regulating the Poor (Cloward and Piven),
    112
Reich, Robert, 241
Reid, Harry, 223, 248, 269
religious pluralism, 39–40
"Rethinking Iran" (Power), 171
Reynolds, Gretchen, 113
Rezko, Antoin "Tony," ix, 96
Rich Media, Poor Media (McChesney),
    201–2
"Rights of Animals, The" (Sunstein), 182
*Rise and Development of the Students for a
    Democratic Society, The* (Sale), 259
Rivera, Dennis, 138, 139–40
Roach, The, 6
Roeser, Tom, 255
Rogers, Joel, 81, 223, 224, 225
Root, Wayne Allyn, 31
Roots for Radicals (Chambers), 58–59
Rose, Donald C., 162–64, 165
Rosenbaum, Jason, 264–66, 267–68
Ross, Fred, 122–23
Ruberry, John, 254

Rubin, Jennifer, 133
Rubin, Nan, 190
Rudd, Mark, 155, 211, 219–20
Rules for Radicals (Alinsky), 59
Russell, Alicia, 121
Rutenberg, Jim, 141

SAAS (Student Afro-American Society),
    31
Said, Edward, 36
Sale, Kirkpatrick, 259
Saltzman, Bettylu, 158–59, 208, 263
Sargent, Greg, 266–67
Sawicky, Max B., 24
SCAA (Student Committee Against
    Apartheid), 22–23, 25
Schakowsky, Jan, 254, 255, 263
Schatz, Amy, 199
Schechner, Jacki, 242–43
Scheer, Robert, 52
Schilling, Chelsea, 125–26
Schlussel, Debbie, 96
Scott, Janny, 31, 37
SDS (Students for a Democratic Society),
    4–5, 6, 26, 208
Second Bill of Rights, The (Sunstein), 177,
    178
SED (Students for Economic Democracy),
    20–21, 25–26, 278n26
SEIU. *See* Service Employees
    International Union
Sentinel, The (blog), 265–66
Service Employees International Union
    (SEIU)
    and ACORN, 113–14, 115
    Alinsky model, 129–37
    and Balanoff, 133–36
    convention mandate (2004), 137
    and Obama, 124–28, 131
    and Stern, 126–33, 134, 136–39, 144
Shabazz, Malik Zulu, 103–4
shantytown protests, 21–22, 33–34
Sharf, Samantha, 33
Sharon, Ariel, 184–85
Shearer, Derek, 28–29
Shellenberger, Michael, 233, 234–36, 237
Sherman, Scott, 277n17
Shipps, Dorothy, 10, 274n22

Shiver, Kyle-Anne, 30
SI (Socialist International), 166–69
Simpson, James, 110
single-payer health care, 244, 247–48,
    261–63
Siskind, Sarah, 81, 88
Sixties Radicals (Chepesiuk), 13
Skala, Nick, 261–62
Smerconish, Michael, 8
Smith, Ben, 3, 133
SOBU (Student Organization of Black
    Unity), 32
socialist agenda for America, 146–51
socialist bill of rights, 176–77
Socialist International (SI), 166–69
Socialist Workers website, 131
Soetoro, Barry, 41–43. *See also* Obama,
    Barack
soft money funding, 253
Soros, George, 132, 141, 187–88, 203,
    238. *See also* Open Society Institute
Soule, Sarah A., 34
Standing Together to Organize a
    Revolutionary Movement (STORM),
    153–54
Stark, Pete, 248
Starr, Gary, 53
State of Welfare, The (Steiner), 111
Steiner, George Y., 111
Steinert-Threlkeld, Tom, 198
Stephanoupoulos, George, 2–3
Stern, Andrew, 126–33, 134, 136–39, 144
Stern, Sol, 108–9, 212
Stimulus Bill (2009), 81, 214, 222, 229–30
Stokes, Jack, 78
Stopping War, Seeking Justice (Davidson
    and Katz), 158
STORM (Standing Together to Organize a
    Revolutionary Movement), 153–54
Street, Paul, 171
Strickland, Eliza, 234–35
Strom, Stephanie, 115
Student Afro-American Society (SAAS),
    31
Student Committee Against Apartheid
    (SCAA), 22–23, 25
Student Organization of Black Unity
    (SOBU), 32

Students for a Democratic Society (SDS), 4–5, 6, 26, 208
Students for a Democratic Society Days of Rage riots, 157, 214–15, 259
Students for Economic Democracy (SED), 20–21, 25–26, 278n26
"Subject of Palestine, The" (art exhibit), 17
Sullivan, John, 138
Sunstein, Cass R., 156, 169, 176–82, 195–97
Sweeney, John, 227
Sweet, Lynn, 9, 44–45, 157
Syuflana, Tatan, 78

Talbott, Madeline, 117
Tampa Tribune, 5–6
Telecommunications Act (1996), 190
Terry, Jim, 120, 121
Terry, Phillip, 21
Thayler, Richard, 179–80
Themba-Nixon, Makani, 190
Thierer, Adam, 201–2
Thomas, Kate, 139
Tides Center and Tides Foundation, 224–25, 238
Tranquada, Jim, 30
Trinity United Church of Christ (TUCC), 40–41, 45–47, 92
Trotsky, Leon, 110
Trumpet magazine, 46–47, 92–93, 94–95
TUCC (Trinity United Church of Christ), 40–41, 45–47, 92

Under Siege (Khalidi), 48
Undue Influence website, 238, 252
United Neighborhoods Organization (UNO), 60
United Power for Action and Justice (UPAJ), 63–64
USAction, 240–41, 242–44, 254, 256–59
U.S. Constitution, 67, 187, 195, 197, 200–201
U.S. Supreme Court, 69

Vadum, Matthew, 144, 146, 201
de Vattel, Emmerich, 68
Velásquez, Nydia, 139

Vietnam and the Haunted Generation (MacPherson), 26
Villaraigosa, Antonio, 226, 227
Voting for America, Inc., 109. *See also* Project VOTE! campaign

WABC Radio, ix
Walden, Andrew, 6
Wallerstein, Immanuel, 211
Wallsten, Peter, 48–49
Wall Street Journal, 248
Washington, Harold, 10, 156
Washington Examiner, 167, 168
Washington Post, 260
Washington Times, 44
Weatherman, 5, 7–8, 87, 155, 214. *See also* Ayers, Bill
Weather Underground, 5, 8, 110, 259–60. *See also* Ayers, Bill
Weekly Standard, 169
Weiner, Jon, 29
Welch, Matt, 31
Wellstone, Paul, 242
Werbach, Kevin, 203
West, Cornel, 81, 87–88, 101, 211
White, Jerry, 131
"Why Organize?" (Obama), 59
Wiener, John, 278n30
Wiley, George Alvin, 106, 108–9, 123, 238
Wiley, Maya, 238
Williams, Rev. Reginald, Jr., 95
Williams, Sandra V., 34
Woodhouse, Brad, 243–44
Woods Fund, 16, 48, 118–20, 128
Working for Us (WFU), 132
Worrill, Conrad W., 98
Wright, Rev. Jeremiah, Jr., 40–41, 91–99
Writings for a Democratic Society (review by Flacks), 30
Wu, Timothy, 203–4

Young, Mike, 5–7
Young, Quentin D., 86, 245–46, 262–63
Yousef, Ahmed, 50

Zinn, Howard, 211
De Zutter, Frank, 117

They come from the fields, and towns, and cities.

Sophisticates and the common.

They come to the power centers, exactly like their ancestors two centuries ago.

When American intuition tells the citizens that government by the people
and for the people is being threatened... they come to make their voices heard!

In this tribute to that spirit of America, *Don't Tread on US!* offers a pictorial record
of the new tea parties and their participants: classic signs that communicate most effectively
with our brethren all across the land who oppose what's going on in Washington today.

With a radical health-care agenda being marched across open territory,
those citizens — tens of millions of them — are rallying, and will make their voices heard.

The colonial heart still beats today, and the people have spoken: ***Don't Tread on US!***

WND Books

WND Books • A WorldNetDaily Company • Washington, DC • www.DontTreadOnUS.com